MODERN SCOTTISH HISTORY
1707 TO THE PRESENT

MODERN SCOTTISH HISTORY
1707 *to the* PRESENT

VOLUME I : THE TRANSFORMATION
OF SCOTLAND, 1707 − 1850

Edited by
Anthony Cooke, Ian Donnachie,
Ann MacSween and Christopher A Whatley

TUCKWELL PRESS

In association with
THE OPEN UNIVERSITY IN SCOTLAND

and
THE UNIVERSITY OF DUNDEE

First published in 1998 by
Tuckwell Press Ltd
The Mill House
Phantassie
East Linton
East Lothian EH40 3DG
Scotland

ISBN 1 86232 068 3

British Library Cataloguing-in-Publication Data
A catalogue record for this book is available on request
from the British Library

Designed by James Hutcheson

Typeset by Hewertext Composition Services, Leith

Printed and bound by
Cromwell Press, Trowbridge, Wiltshire

Preface

This volume and the series of which it is part have as their central purpose the study of the history of Scotland from 1707 until the present. The series seeks to combine the products of more recent research and general findings by some of the most prominent scholars working in the subject with the enthusiasm of those who wish to study it either in a systematic way or simply by reading one or more of these volumes at leisure.

Now is a particularly appropriate moment to bring this scholarship and the wider audience together. There is enormous latent enthusiasm for Scottish history, particularly, but not exclusively, of the modern period. This springs from a variety of sources: the new political agenda in Scotland following the 1997 Referendum; the higher profile of Scottish history in school, college and university curricula; the enhanced interest in local and family history; the success of museums and heritage ventures devoted to the more recent past; and the continuous flow of books on so many aspects of Scottish history. However, explicitly academic publications, with a few honourable exceptions, have been little read by any but specialists, so new findings have frequently had little impact on general perceptions of Scotland's more recent past.

There are two main aims encapsulated in these volumes, which are overlapping and complementary. The first is to present an overview of recent scholarly work, drawing on the approaches and findings of political, economic, social, environmental and cultural historians. This should be illuminating not only for those seeking an up-to-date review of such work, but also for anyone interested in the functioning of Scotland today - the essential historical background of present-day issues and concerns. The second, equally important, aim is to help readers develop their own historical skills, using the volumes as a tool-kit containing a wide range of primary sources and more detailed readings on specific topics. This and the other volumes in the series differ from most conventional academic publications, in that the focus is on **doing** history, rather than just absorbing the facts. The volumes are full of ideas on sources and methods that can be followed up by the interested reader.

Given the vast scope of the subject, we have had to put some limits on the coverage. The timescale is the early eighteenth century to the late twentieth century, a period for which sources not only abound but can also be readily understood and critically assessed. There is no attempt to give a detailed historical narrative of the period from the Union of 1707, which can readily be found elsewhere. Rather we present a blend of topics and themes, selected with a view to providing readers with a reasonably comprehensive introduction to recent work and a context and stimulus for further reading or investigation. Although there is an organisational divide at 1850, many of the themes are explored continuously over the whole period. Hence the first volume begins with the Union of 1707 and Jacobitism, and covers topics including industrialisation, demography, politics, religion, education, class, the environment, and culture, as well as looking at the differences between Highland and Lowland society and economy. The second volume from 1850 to the present also covers a wide range of topics. Some of these, such as industrialisation, demography, urbanisation, religion, class, education, culture and Highland and Lowland society, are continued while new topics include the state, Scottish identity, leisure and recreation. The third and fourth volumes contain carefully selected readings to accompany the topic / theme volumes and are likely to prove an invaluable resource for any reader wishing to pursue a particular subject in greater depth or perhaps investigate it in a local or regional project. The fifth volume in the series is a collection of primary sources for the history of modern Scotland designed to accompany the other volumes. It makes accessible between the covers of one book many of the documents of national and local importance from the eighteenth century and beyond and provides a unique and detailed insight into the period.

This book forms one part of the University of Dundee-Open University collaborative course, Modern Scottish History: 1707 to the Present. This is an honours level undergraduate course for part-time adult learners studying at a distance, and it is designed to develop the skills, methods and understanding of history and historical analysis with modern Scotland as its focus. However, these volumes are designed to be used, either singly or as a series, by anyone interested in Scottish history. The introduction to recent research findings, together with practical exercises, advice on the critical exploitation of primary sources, and suggestions for further reading, should be of wide interest and application. We hope it will encourage users to carry their enthusiasm further by investigating, for example, some aspect of their own community history based on one or more themes covered in the series.

A series of this kind depends on the efforts of many people, and accordingly there are many debts to record. Our enthusiasm was shared by the Scottish Higher Education Funding Council which provided a generous grant to fund the development of the course. Within the University of Dundee, Professor

David Swinfen, Vice Principal, has played a valuable supporting role. The authors produced their contributions to agreed formats and deadlines. While they are responsible for what they have written, they have also been supported by other members of the writing team and our editorial and production specialists. The material was developed collaboratively, reflected too in the cooperation and support we have had from our publisher, Tuckwell Press. Particular thanks to Tracey Walker, the Project Secretary, for her administrative support. Thanks also to Karen Brough and Jen Petrie who transcribed some of the texts for the articles and documents volumes.

USING THIS BOOK

Activities

Volumes 1 and 2 are designed not just as a text to be read through but also as active workbooks. They are therefore punctuated by a series of activities, signalled by a different format. These include short questions, exercises, and prompts for the reader articles in Volumes 3 and 4 or documents in Volume 5. Conversely the readings and documents refer back to topics/themes discussed in detail in Volumes 1 and 2.

References

While this book is free-standing, there are cross-references to other volumes in the series. This is to aid readers using all the books. The list of books and articles that follows each chapter generally follows the scholarly convention of giving details of all works cited. They are not intended as obligatory further reading.

Series Editors

Contents

PREFACE   v

ILLUSTRATIONS   x

CONTRIBUTORS   xiii

1   The Union of 1707   1
     Christopher A Whatley

2   Jacobitism   23
     Bob Harris

3   Politics   43
     Michael Fry

4   Religion   63
     Callum G Brown

5   Rural Transformation and Lowland Society   86
     Ian Whyte

6   Demography   108
     Neil Tranter

7   Aspects of Industrialisation before 1850   130
     Anthony Cooke and Ian Donnachie

8   Urbanisation   155
     Irene Maver

9   Highland Society in the Era of 'Improvement'   177
     Allan I Macinnes

10   Social Class   203
     W Hamish Fraser

11   Environment   230
     T C Smout

12   Culture   253
     Gerard Carruthers

13   Education   275
     Donald J Withrington

INDEX   299

Illustrations

The Articles of Union, 22 July 1706	6
The pre-Union Parliament in Edinburgh	13
King James VIII and III	29
Prince Charles Edward Stewart in tartan	36
John Campbell, 2nd Duke of Argyll	49
Henry Dundas	56
'Christmas Eve', by Sir William Allan	70
Thomas Chalmers	78
Swanston, a pre-Improvement ferm toun	91
A 'horse-gang'	97
Farm buildings in East Lothian	103
Alexander Webster	115
Page from Portpatrick Census	123
Stanley Mills	136
New Lanark	143
Women carrying coal	150
Glasgow Green, c.1820	162
Dundee from the west, 1803	169
Poltalloch House	182
Pamphlet about the clan chieftains, 1773	188
'Tussle for the Keg', by John Pettie	194
The dining room at Newhailes, Musselburgh	210
Francis Jeffrey	217
Chartist election poster from Roxburgh	224
Highland countryside, Glen Affric	235
Leading peats, Barra	240
John Slezer's 'Prospect of Edinburgh', c.1695	246
Princes Street, Edinburgh, 1825	257
The only meeting of Burns and Scott	262
Robert Burns' chair and writing desk	267
Infant school, 1836	282
The High School of Edinburgh	290

Picture Acknowledgements

The following are thanked for permission to reproduce illustrations in their collections:

Abbotsford House: *illus 29*; City of Aberdeen Art Gallery and Museums Collections: *illus 7, 21*; The British Museum: *illus 6*; Glasgow University Library, Department of Special Collections: *illus 31*; Keeper of the Records of Scotland: *illus 1, 13*; Mitchell Library, Glasgow City Libraries and Archives: *illus 17*; National Gallery of Scotland: *illus 28*; National Library of Scotland: *illus 20*; Royal Commission on the Ancient and Historical Monuments of Scotland: *illus 14, 22*; The Royal High School, Edinburgh: *illus 32*; Scottish Borders Archive and Local History Centre, Selkirk: *illus 24*; Scottish National Portrait Gallery: *illus 3, 5, 8, 12, 23*; Mick Sharp: *illus 30*; St Andrews University Library: *illus 18, 19, 25, 26, 27*; The Trustees of the National Museums of Scotland: *illus 2, 4*; Ian Whyte: *illus 9, 10, 11*.

List of Contributors

Callum G Brown, Senior Lecturer, Department of History, University of Strathclyde. Has published extensively on religious, social and cultural history, including *Religion and Society in Scotland since 1707* (1997).

Gerard Carruthers, Lecturer, English Department, University of Strathclyde. Writes on eighteenth, nineteenth and twentieth century Scottish literature and culture, and is currently co-editing Walter Scott's *Reliquiae Trottcosienses* for publication in 1998.

Anthony Cooke, Senior Lecturer, Institute for Education and Lifelong Learning, University of Dundee. Has published widely on the history of adult education and on textile history including recent publications on the cotton mills at Spinningdale, Sutherland and on Stanley Mills, Perthshire for Historic Scotland.

Ian Donnachie, Senior Lecturer in History and Director of the Centre for Scottish Studies, The Open University in Scotland. Among his publications are *Historic New Lanark* (1993) and *The Companion to Scottish History* on CDRom (1996), both jointly with George Hewitt.

W Hamish Fraser, Professor of History, University of Strathclyde. Has written extensively on aspects of social and urban history. Recent works include *Alexander Campbell and the Search for Socialism* (1996) and *Glasgow, Volume II: 1830 to 1912*, edited with I Maver (1996).

Michael Fry, Fellow, Centre for Research in Scottish History, University of Strathclyde. Author of *Patronage and Principle, a Political History of Modern Scotland* (1987) and *The Dundas Despotism* (1992).

Bob Harris, Senior Lecturer, Department of Modern History, University of Dundee. Specialist in eighteenth-century Britain and author of *A Patriot Press* (1993) and *Politics and the Rise of the Press: Britain and France, 1620-1800* (1996).

Allan I Macinnes, Burnett-Fletcher Professor of History, University of Aberdeen. Has written extensively on covenants, clans and clearances, including *Charles I and the Emergence of the Covenanting Movement, 1625-41* (1991) and *Clanship, Commerce and the House of Stuart, 1603-1788* (1996).

Ann MacSween, Project Manager, Distance Learning: Modern Scottish History Project, University of Dundee. Author of a number of books and articles on the archaeology of Scotland, including *Prehistoric Scotland* (1990).

Irene Maver, Lecturer in Scottish History, Department of History, University of Glasgow. Research interests are Scottish social and political history, with particular focus on the urban and municipal dimension. Has recently co-edited, with W Hamish Fraser, *Glasgow, Volume II: 1830 to 1912* (1996), and is currently writing on Aberdeen and Glasgow.

TC Smout, Director, Institute for Environmental History, University of St Andrews, and Historiographer Royal in Scotland. Author of various books on Scottish history, including *A History of the Scottish People, 1560-1830* (1969) and *A Century of the Scottish People, 1830-1950* (1986).

Neil Tranter, Senior Lecturer, Department of History, University of Stirling. His numerous publications on the history of population and social structure include *British Population in the Twentieth Century* (1996).

Christopher A Whatley, Professor of Scottish History, Department of Modern History, University of Dundee. Author of numerous publications on eighteenth-century Scottish economic and social history including *The Industrial Revolution in Scotland* (1997).

Ian Whyte, Professor of Historical Geography, Lancaster University. Author of many books and articles on the economic and social development of early-modern Scotland, including *Scotland before the Industrial Revolution* (1995).

Donald J Withrington, formerly Reader in History, University of Aberdeen. Has written widely on the ecclesiastical and educational history of Scotland since the Reformation.

The Union of 1707

Christopher A Whatley

INTRODUCTION

This chapter deals with a number of issues, which together are designed to help you to understand what the Union was and why it came about (and why there is so much disagreement between historians about this). The impact of Union will also be touched upon, although this will be dealt with in greater detail later in this volume. The chapter is divided into the following sections:

- Background to the Union
- The debate about the causes of the Union
- Making sense of the debate

By the time that you have worked your way through the chapter and studied the documents and the Reader articles you should have begun to understand why the Union was important and have a sound grasp of its nature and causes, the historiography surrounding it and why it remains a topic of scholarly debate.

On 1 May 1707, following a triumphal journey south through England by the Duke of Queensberry, Queen Anne's Commissioner in Scotland, rejoicing in London marked the inauguration of the Treaty of Union which created 'one united kingdom' of Scotland, England and Wales. Whereas 'at no time Scotsmen were more acceptable to the English' on that day, in Scotland no such public demonstrations of joy appear to have manifested themselves. Indeed in February, on Queen Anne's birthday, the country's leading political figures had refused to turn out for the usual celebrations in Edinburgh for fear of the angry response of the mob. The Union proposals had been deeply unpopular, with as many as nine out of ten Scots (a 'hardened, refractory and terrible people', wrote the English unionist propagandist Daniel Defoe) opposing 'incorporating' union according to one contemporary estimate. What this meant was that Scotland ceased to have its own Parliament and legislative authority for Scottish affairs passed to Westminster. Prior to 1707 the single-chamber Scottish Parliament (the Scottish Estates) had a total of 247 members, drawn from the nobility, the barons (or shire representatives) and the burgesses. Thereafter Scotland (with one-fifth of England's population) was to be represented at Westminster by 16 elected peers and 45 MPs, 30 of whom were to represent the counties, 15 the burghs.

Some semblance of Scottish independence was to remain, however, and did (Murdoch 1980), although to a somewhat lesser extent than was envisaged in 1706 and 1707. The existence of the presbyterian Church of Scotland was 'effectually and unalterably secured' under a separate Act passed in November 1706, but in 1711–12 a series of measures was passed at Westminster which limited the authority of the Scottish kirk. The distinctive Scottish legal system was secured, along with the 'heritable jurisdictions', the distinctive feudal system of estate justice which was prized by Scotland's powerful landed class. The Scottish Privy Council, however, was abolished in 1708 despite the guarantee for its future which was written into the Union agreement, while in 1747, in the aftermath of Culloden, the heritable jurisdictions were largely abolished. Such moves were not altogether unwelcome in Scotland, whence came demands, from some quarters, for the completion of the Union through further anglicisation.

Important as these issues were, the Acts of Union were concerned with more than political representation, the legal system and the church. The 25 Articles (reproduced in full, as **Document 1**) also specified regulations concerning the design of the new British flag, weights and measures, levels of taxation, and above all (although there are some historians who would challenge this), trade.

EXERCISE 1
Read the Articles (**Document 1**) and try to obtain an impression of their scope and nature. Too few commentators do read them in full. Why do you think the proposals met with such hostility in Scotland?

Loss of sovereignty was a major concern, as was the threatened imposition of higher taxes on a wider range of commodities, although pro-Unionists suspected that the 'mob' and others outside Parliament were being deliberately misled about the impact they would have. Although the effects (positive as well as negative) of the Union were and can be exaggerated and are sometimes misunderstood, there is no doubt that it was a 'defining moment' in Scottish history. 'In many respects the whole history of Scotland since the end of the seventeenth century appears to have been overshadowed by . . . the Union of Parliaments' (Smout 1969, 215).

EXERCISE 2
Do you agree with Smout? Can you think of reasons why the Union has had such an effect on Scottish history?

Smout's point of view is one which in varying degrees is shared by numerous writers whether their interest be economic history, political and constitutional history or Scottish literary and cultural studies. This will be seen in subsequent chapters in this volume. Like many events in Scottish history, the Union has also taken on a mythical quality: thus surveying and trying to account for Scotland's 'miserable' economic condition in 1716, one Jacobite pamphleteer argued that the '*Origo Mali*, the bitter Fountain from which all our calamities have flowed' was the Union of 1707. While the economic impact of the Union is a matter of dispute, there is no doubt that Scotland's economic difficulties pre-dated 1707.

One response which would find little favour nowadays is the idea that the Union was a necessity if Scotland was to cease to be the poverty-stricken, backward and Calvinist-blighted society as it was portrayed by an older generation of Anglophile historians. Although struggling to overcome short-term economic setbacks, later seventeenth-century Scotland is now perceived in fairly dynamic terms with the Union of 1707 being seen as a challenge and an opportunity for Scots to exploit, rather than as a necessary precondition of eighteenth-century economic and social advancement (Devine 1995). Contrary to older interpretations which tended to see the Union as a 'watershed' in Scottish history, some historians have suggested that the roots of the Enlightenment in eighteenth-century Scotland were to be found in the European-influenced intellectual flowering, the first signs of which were particularly evident in Edinburgh in the pre-Union period (Whyte 1995, Chapter 17).

In reality and in its mythical form, however, the Union had a considerable impact on Scotland in the eighteenth century and beyond. Regarding its causes, which are the main concern of this chapter, there is a wide range of interpretations but the fundamental historiographical divide has been between those who argue that the Union was advantageous for the Scots largely because the Union with England created and provided access to 'an Anglo-Scottish common market that was the biggest customs-free zone in Europe', and others who are inclined to see the Union as a shabby political deal, with Scotland's centuries-old independence being – in a phrase which has become associated with Robert Burns – 'bought and sold for English gold' (see Smout 1969, 215–7). The debate was often (and still can be) conducted along parochial lines, viewed either from a narrowly Scottish or an exclusively English perspective. More recently the approach to Union has been widened as historians have tried to replace the older nation-centred history with that of a history of the formation of the British state, of 'state-building in the archipelago', including Ireland (Ellis and Barber 1995; Robertson 1995). Because of the partisan nature of much of the debate, the serious student of Scottish history has to pay scrupulous attention to the construction of the arguments of those involved, and to the nature of the evidence and the ways it is interpreted. As many contemporaries, no less than modern-day commentators, had their own passionately-held positions on the rights and wrongs and costs and benefits of closer association with England, much of the evidence from the period itself – particularly the voluminous pamphlet literature published during the so-called 'pamphlet war' of late 1705 and 1706 – is heavily biased. There is also a temptation to over-simplify what are usually complex arguments and even to caricature them. Because the topic is one which continues to fascinate historians, the results of new research and fresh interpretations continue to appear in print, and have to be woven into reasoned analyses of the causes of the Union.

1. BACKGROUND

1.1. *Precursors*

Union between Scotland and England was not unprecedented. Indeed, as far back as the 1290s Edward I had attempted to rule Scotland on a colonial basis. The so-called 'Rough Wooing' of 1544–50 represented another attempt on the part of England to control Scotland. Since the regal union of 1603 when King James VI of Scotland had succeeded with ease to the throne of England, the two nations had been ruled by a single monarch, although until 1707 the Scots continued to have their own Parliament. James was an ardent advocate of parliamentary union as, to varying degrees, were succeeding British monarchs, with Queen Anne (in whose reign – 1702–1714 – the Union of 1707 was enacted) playing an active part in getting the desired legislation through the English and Scottish parliaments. In 1650–51, Oliver Cromwell had even succeeded in invading and conquering Scotland and imposing a short-lived political union with a single British Parliament. Geographical proximity made some sort of accommodation between the two neighbours essential.

1.2. *Pressure points*

Pressure for union did not emanate solely or even consistently from south of the Border. Court enthusiasm for further union notwithstanding, English ministers showed relatively little interest in a closer constitutional relationship with Scotland for much of the seventeenth century and were concerned rather to ignore their northern neighbour with whom relations were frequently cold, sour and acrimonious, periodically exploding into open hostility and warfare. It was only during periods of crisis that England's position changed. Such a crisis was one of the main factors which provided the background to the Union. The ageing Queen Anne was heirless (her last child died in 1700), and while the English Parliament favoured a Protestant Hanoverian successor, Sophia, Electress of Hanover, there were fears that the Scots' preference might be for her half-brother James Edward Stuart, the 'Old' Pretender, Roman Catholic son of James VII (James II of England) who had abandoned his Scottish throne in 1689. 'Half the nation', according to Ferguson (1977, 174), was 'Jacobite at heart'.

Another important consideration from the English perspective was that from 1702 (until 1713) England was embroiled in the War of the Spanish Succession. This was an imperial struggle, with the English and Habsburg monarchies allied to counter the dynastic ambitions of King Louis XIV of France (Robertson 1994). For good reason there were concerns in England regarding the attachment of considerable numbers of leading Scots politicians to the Stuart Jacobite cause (for fuller discussion see Chapter 2). Although William of Orange had been warmly welcomed in some quarters in Scotland in 1689, support was far from universal and subsequent events – the Glencoe massacre of 1692 and the failure of the Darien venture, for which King William III was held partly responsible – made it more likely that they would seek an accommodation with the French monarch and thereby threaten England's security on her northern frontier.

Otherwise Scotland had little to offer the English. As has been indicated, historians are now persuaded that Scotland's underdeveloped economy was strengthening in the second half of the seventeenth century. In the decades following the Restoration of Charles II (1660) the Scottish Parliament and Privy Council passed a series of measures designed to improve agriculture and to stimulate industry and trade, indications of a new-found determination to turn the Scottish economy round (see Smout 1969, 116–8). Even before this, linen exports from Scotland had begun to expand dramatically. Grain exports too had grown substantially, to such an extent that in 1705 the 1st Earl of Seafield, Scotland's Lord Chancellor and one of the most influential pro-unionists, but also a large landowner, was warned that 'unless we alter our methods, or fall on some nieu ways of export, our corne will become such a drug on our handes, that we will neither be able to live or pay publick dues' (Grant 1912, 415). Nevertheless Scotland was still relatively poor and English needs – such as black cattle and coarse linen cloth – could be secured through normal trading arrangements without sacrificing anything to the Scots. There were considerable fears that closer union would impose a financial burden on England, a perspective which is vividly conveyed in the sentiment attributed to a leading English Tory, Sir Edward Seymour, that union with Scotland would be like marrying a beggar and that 'whoever married a beggar could only expect a louse for a portion'. Notwithstanding the economic progress that had been made in the 1660s and 1670s from the end of the following decade, Scotland began to enter a period of economic difficulty which was to last until at least the 1720s (Smout 1969, 240–3).

The Scottish state was effectively bankrupt. In both military and naval terms and despite the undoubted military prowess of Scotland's army officers and soldiers, many of whom were engaged in the service of the Duke of Marlborough's army on the Continent and fought in key battles such as Ramilles, Scotland was unable to match the resources of England. Ominously, at a time of aggressive state-building, the costs and scale of warfare in early-modern Europe were rising beyond levels which the Scots could attain. Scotland's pre-1707 navy comprised two frigates.

1.3. Degrees of convergence

It is often suggested that in the long run there was a certain inevitability about the Union of 1707 and that in a number of respects the two countries had been moving more closely together from around 1560 when Scotland's traditional alliance with Catholic France was severed and the Scots, much influenced by the Calvinist John Knox, gravitated instead towards protestant England. In this sense some form of closer union between the two countries would appear to have had a more powerful internal logic than unions which were forged between some other states in early-modern Europe.

With the removal of the royal court from Edinburgh to London in 1603, it is assumed that a rapid process of anglicisation occurred, certainly on the part of the Stuart monarchs, and it has been argued that 'the greater nobility was not far behind' (Szechi 1991, 120). The Covenanting period (1637–52) apart, Scottish politicians were increasingly playing to an English audience and offering their services to a London-based monarch. By the turn of the eighteenth century several Scottish politicians had become, in effect, British politicians. Some, albeit very few at

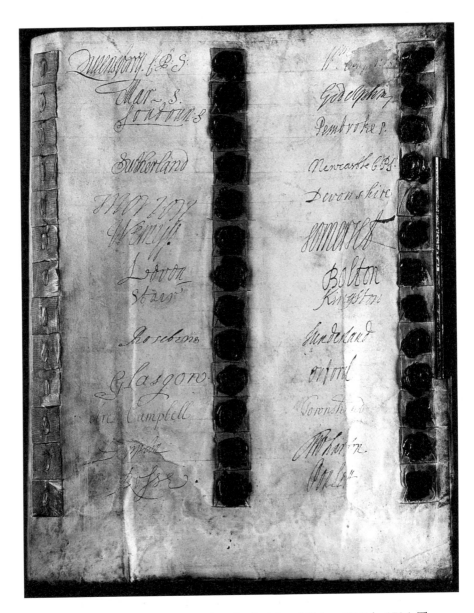

No. 1. Signatures and seals appended to the Articles of Union, 22 July 1706. The Scots are on the left, headed by the Duke of Queensberry, the Queen's Commissioner in Scotland. The English signatories are on the right. *Reproduced by kind permission of the Keeper of the Records of Scotland.*

this stage, saw themselves as North Britons rather than Scots. Thus George Mackenzie, Earl of Cromartie, who had 'lost faith in the viability of Scottish nationhood' (Kidd 1996, 368), wished to see the disappearance of the 'ignomious names of Scotland, of England' and their replacement by 'Brittains', 'our true, our honorable denomination' (quoted in Scott 1979, 25–6).

In cultural terms too convergence was apparently in evidence. As has been noted, both countries had rejected Roman Catholicism and in their distinctive ways were ardent espousers of a protestant culture which had united them in a common cause from the reign of Queen Elizabeth (Dawson 1995). The 'Glorious Revolution' in England in 1688 and the flight into exile of James VII and the subsequent arrival of King William of Orange as monarch of the two nations, were confirmation of their commitment to the 'true religion' and of a shared hostility (if less ardent in Scotland) to France and French expansionist ambitions under Louis XIV. Anti-Catholicism was widespread in both England and Scotland where almanacs (50,000 of which were sold annually in Aberdeen in the 1680s) 'seem to have been just as militantly Protestant . . . as their English equivalents' (Colley 1992, 20–2). Recent detailed research into where Scots attended university, what they were taught and the reading matter of the Scottish élite, has revealed how much they shared with their English counterparts an interest in European learning and ideas, with the numbers of Scots attending universities such as Leyden soaring from around 1630 (Emerson 1995). English was a commonly understood language outside the Gaelic-speaking parts of Scotland, although increasingly during the seventeenth century Highland chiefs were assimilating politically, socially and commercially with the south.

Yet the extent to which integration had occurred prior to 1707 can be exaggerated. According to Brown (1995, 240–1), surprisingly few Scots were members of the royal households of either Charles II or William III. '[Queen] Anne's court', he argues, 'was dominated by English Tory families and the Scottish presence was reduced to two doctors.' In the English House of Commons between 1660 and 1690 there were only 13 Scots peers or their sons (there were more Irishmen) and most of these were Englishmen or anglicised Scots. Scotland and England continued to have separate Privy Councils and, by and large, separate honours systems. No Scots were made Knights of the Bath, while the restoration of the Order of the Thistle in 1687 enabled the monarch to reward Scots, but outside the English system of honours.

The Scottish nobility rented rather than purchased London property and, owing to the high expense and sheer difficulties of travelling there, they spent less time in the capital than is sometimes assumed. Although it would be foolish to deny the impact of 'anglophile, aristocratic and courtly' energies in Restoration Scotland (Ouston 1988, 11), Scots 'played a minimal role as either patrons of or contributors to court culture'. There was a strong attachment to Scottish cultural forms and productions, and imported European ideas, fashions and architectural styles (Brown 1995, 238–9). If interracial marriage can be used as a measure of élite integration, then the fact that only around 96 marriages of Scots peers to English wives occurred

between 1603 and 1707 is hardly suggestive of a powerful movement. It is certainly
the case that the major territorial interests in Scotland – the Murray, Campbell,
Gordon, Douglas and Hamilton families – all formed English marriage alliances
after 1660, but an English marriage did not necessarily lead to anglicisation in that
the offspring of such arrangements were frequently to be found back in Scotland,
marrying fellow Scots. Many Anglo-Scottish marriages were second or third unions
and childless.

The case for pre-1707 linguistic conformity looks less convincing 'on the
ground' with Scots remaining the common currency of speech. It was after 1707
that the passion for linguistic anglicisation became intense (see Chapter 13). In the
religious sphere too the situation was more complicated than it appears at first sight.
Anglo-Scottish union would certainly bolster Protestantism against Louis XIV's
threatened Catholic Counter-Reformation empire in western Europe. Yet there was
a major problem for the far from united Scottish Presbyterians, the significance of
which should not be overlooked in the search to understand the moves which led
towards incorporating union.

EXERCISE 3
Examine the following extract and consider the consequences if the model
described for the rest of Europe had been applied in the Anglo-Scottish case.

Scotland's ecclesiastical politics were central to the debates which preceded the
Anglo-Scottish Union of 1707. In terms of contemporary political thought . . .
incorporating union of civil governments unaccompanied by a union of religious
establishments was a solecism. Uniconfessional states predominated in early
modern Christendom, not only in unitary kingdoms but also in composite
dynastic states. Although there were looser confederal unions, such as the Swiss
cantons and the Holy Roman Empire, in which different confessions were
established, and there existed successful experiments in toleration, in England
and in the confederal United Provinces of the Netherlands, there were
nevertheless no states with plural church establishments.

(Kidd 1995, 145)

Clearly the European norm was a single state church. In the new British state,
therefore, the most likely outcome, according to Kidd, was 'that the Presbyterian
Kirk would be absorbed within a pan-Britannic Episcopalian Church', subject to the
authority of the Archbishop of Canterbury and as a result threatened with the
imposition of bishops and the loss of its distinct religious forms. Such a prospect was
anathema to most Scots Presbyterians, particularly in the parishes and presbyteries:
in October 1706 the Earl of Mar, Secretary of State in Scotland, reported to Sidney
Godolphin, Lord Treasurer in England and Queen Anne's first minister, that 'the
humour in the country against the treatie or union is much increased of late . . . the
ministers preaching up the danger of the Kirk is a principal cause of it' (Hume Brown
1915, 176–7). Moderate Presbyterians were reassured only at a late stage in the

union negotiations, in November 1706, by the passing of the separate Act of Security for the Church of Scotland referred to earlier. Thereafter they took steps to curb anti-union zeal on the part of churchmen.

On the other hand, the Covenanting wing of the Kirk (and outside it, the Cameronians), which was especially strong in the South-West, remained virulently and even violently opposed to the proposed union, seeing it as a betrayal of the Solemn League and Covenant of 1643 which had taken upon itself the task of reforming the wayward English church, as well as a sinful conjoining with 'Satan's kingdom'. In short, in looking at the religious background to the Union of 1707 it seems reasonable to conclude with the judgement which Dawson (1995, 114) made of the sixteenth century, that 'Anglo-Scottish protestant culture could help to integrate the English and the Scots but it could not forge a new multinational British state'.

1.4. European dimension

Kidd's placing of the discussion about the religious background to the Union in the European context is in historiographical terms a relatively new approach. The wider dimension, however, can be enormously illuminating and does much to counteract what have often been somewhat parochial and blinkered analyses of Anglo-Scottish relations. Seen within this framework, the Union of 1707 looks far from anomalous. Between the fourteenth century and the end of the eighteenth century, the number of independent polities in Europe fell from around 1,000 to less than 350. Dynastic unions or 'composite monarchies' were particularly common in the early modern period, a time when the optimum size of the viable state changed. Reference has already been made to the rising scale and costs of war. The age was one of 'muscular mercantilism', of expanding states which jostled with each other to carve out great economic empires and to defend jealously guarded trading routes. As French power grew under Louis XIV in the seventeenth century, so pressures for closer unification grew in the Spanish and Austrian monarchies and the United Provinces, as well as in Britain. Significantly, between 1707 and 1716, albeit in different ways, the Austrians, the Spanish and the British reordered themselves (Elliot 1992).

The potential benefits of becoming part of a larger political-military entity were recognised early on by reflective Scotsmen, several of whom – the patriot Andrew Fletcher of Saltoun was one, William Seton of Pitmedden, younger, another – were well aware of the European context of Scottish-English relations. As early as 1605 Sir David Craig was anticipating a Britain which could match the Spanish monarchy, while on several occasions thereafter, the 1640s, 1670 and in 1689–90, 'unenthusiastic, but realistic' Scots sought to give to the regal union what has been described as 'institutional coherence' (Morrill 1995, 20). How that coherence was to be achieved, however, was a matter of what was sometimes passionate debate.

EXERCISE 4
Read Seton of Pitmedden's *Speech*, **Document 2**, and note those parts of his
argument which adopt a European perspective, and his solution.

Looking at the experience of federal unions elsewhere – between Spain and Portugal,
for example – Seton of Pitmedden was convinced that such arrangements were
unstable and in the Scottish case would lead to domination by England, as would a
continuation of the regal union. The federalist Andrew Fletcher of Saltoun, on the
other hand, favoured 'nearer Union with our Neighbours of England', but feared
that in a single British parliament Scottish interests could not be defended and that
the '45 Scots Members may dance round to all Eternity, in this Trap of their own
making' (Scott 1979, 23).

1.5. *Summary and the issues*

While providing the backcloth to the Union of 1707, regal union, convergence and
shared interests, anglicisation and international trends do not by themselves, or in
combination, explain either why the Scots entered into an incorporating union or
why this happened in 1707. Indeed, closer union had begun to look less likely after
1689 when the Scottish Convention of the Estates had issued its Claim of Right which
not only condemned James VII's abuses of power, but also established the right of the
moribund Scottish Parliament to be called regularly. Episcopalianism was replaced
by Presbyterianism. With the abolition of the Lords of Articles in 1690 – formerly a
major arm of royal influence in Scotland – and the transference of substantial powers
to a Parliament which acted with a new-found vigour and independence, the
mechanisms for conflict with the monarch were now in place. As Ferguson (1977,
166) has remarked, 'Scotland's role was changed from a relatively passive to a more
active one. And from the friction caused by this more abrasive relationship came the
crisis that ultimately led to the Treaty and the Acts of Union of 1707'.

1.6. *Precipitating factors*

Resolution, however, did not proceed smoothly or in a predetermined fashion. A
joint commission established by Queen Anne and backed by her supporters in
Scotland, led by the Duke of Queensberry, to discuss a treaty of union sat between
November 1702 and February 1703. Nothing came of this, though, largely owing to
the unwillingness of English representatives, who were grudging throughout the
negotiations, to compensate Scotland for the tax burden which would be imposed by
union. Circumstances would have to change dramatically if the deepening conflict
between the two countries was to be resolved.

Change came in 1703, with the election of a new Scottish parliament, but at first
sight it hardly seemed destined to lead to incorporating union. Riding on a rising tide
of national and sometimes anti-English fervour, and recognising that the regal union
was no longer working, this parliament was considerably less compliant than its

predecessor, and against the wishes of the pro-Hanoverian Court passed an Act of Security, the essence of which was that Scotland would not be bound to support England's nomination for a successor to Queen Anne. This was followed by a second declaration of Scottish freedom from the dictates of the Court, the Act Anent Peace and War, which reserved to the Scottish parliament the right after Anne's demise to declare war and conclude peace. Economic warfare was opened with the Wine Act, followed in 1704 with the passage of an act which forbade the import but allowed the export of wool, steps which were judged by English woollen interests to be hostile.

Reaction in England, in the country and in the Houses of Commons and Lords, was angry and decisive. With English forces now locked into the War of Spanish Succession and unable to risk the withdrawal of Scottish regiments from the north European theatre of war, and subsequent rumours (in July) that arms from France were *en route* for Scotland, the unruly Scots had to be brought to heel and accept the Hanoverian succession as well as to discuss, on English terms, a parliamentary union (although the succession question was the more important of the two). This was the thrust of the so-called Aliens Bill of March 1705, which demanded that unless agreement on the succession had been reached by Christmas Day 1705 and progress made on the question of union, there would be an embargo on the main components of Scotland's trade with England and all Scots (other than those already domiciled in England) would be declared aliens. This was a 'formidable economic bludgeon' (Lenman 1980, 81) which, with the fear in some minds that England might resort to the use of military force, had the desired effect. Paradoxically, although Anglo-Scottish relations were probably at their lowest ebb in the spring and summer of 1705, with the Edinburgh mob having lynched members of the crew of an English ship, the *Worcester*, in April, by September Parliament had with some reluctance agreed to authorise Queen Anne to nominate Commissioners who were to 'treat' for union. They and their English counterparts began their work in April 1706.

EXERCISE 5

This has necessarily been a brief narrative account of the political processes which resulted in the discussions leading to the Union of 1707. You may wish to deepen your understanding by reading one of the standard texts on the subject, listed at the end of this chapter. Before proceeding any further you should read Ferguson's narrative (**Article 1**) of what happened in the final critical session of the Scottish Parliament in 1706. This provides you with more detail than we have space for here.

2. THE DEBATE ABOUT THE CAUSES OF THE UNION OF 1707

2.1. *Statesmanship*

For many decades, from the Victorian era until the 1960s, the view of most professional historians who wrote about the Union of 1707 was that it was a 'good thing', an act of considerable foresight and political statesmanship on the part of those men who led the Scots into the 1706 negotiations. Thus, in 1962, Pryde could confidently declare that the Union, 'grounded on common sense and reached through fair and open bargaining, was one of the most statesmenlike transactions recorded in our history' (Pryde 1962, 55). Historians of this persuasion were impressed by the political skills, and in some cases by what they were convinced was the genuine commitment, of leading pro-Union politicians. Thus the Duke of Queensberry, the Queen's Commissioner in Scotland during the last crucial months of 1706, was praised for the 'masterly manner' in which he steered the Articles of Union 'through the stormy seas of parliamentary debate'; James Ogilvy, 1st Earl of Seafield and Lord Chancellor from 1705, was similarly applauded. Despite his unpopularity, which largely resulted from his involvement in the massacre of Glencoe in 1692, Sir John Dalrymple, Earl of Stair, was judged to be a tireless and public-spirited supporter of Union, even though 'no office or pension was ever bestowed upon him' (Mathieson 1905, 148, 153). The contributions to the parliamentary debates of William Seton of Pitmedden, the pro-Union pamphleteer, were 'at once full of matter and inspired by a grave sense of the national issues at stake' (Hume Brown 1914, 117–8).

2.2. *Economic arguments*

The 'bargain' to which Pryde referred was one which has a long historiographical pedigree. Put simply, it is the proposition that the Union of 1707 can be explained in terms of an exchange of parliamentary sovereignty for free trade with England and her colonies, primarily those in North America and the West Indies. For MacKinnon (1896), author of the most comprehensive Victorian account of the period, this was the 'secret' of Union. In recent times the historian who has been most closely associated with an economic explanation of the Union of 1707 is Smout, who first published work on the topic in 1963 (Smout 1963).

The essence of Smout's argument about the relationship between the economy and the Union, which has subsequently been added to, and refined by, a number of scholars, is that Scotland's economy, which had been growing during the seventeenth century, had become increasingly dependent upon England. By the later 1600s, he estimated, as much as half of Scotland's exports, mainly linen and black cattle, was being sent to England. Scotland's dependence became even greater from the end of the 1670s, however, owing to a series of external blows which wreaked havoc on the economy and exposed its underlying weaknesses. War with France had disrupted trade, while prohibition and tariffs, along with the rise of foreign competition, had had an adverse effect on important export commodities such as woollen cloth, fish, grain and coal. English commercial policy too was harmful to Scottish aspirations, with tariffs restricting several Scottish exports, while Glasgow's embryonic trade in tobacco with the Plantations was hit by the imposition of tighter regulation.

Worse was to come. Four severe grain harvest failures in the 1690s led to a significant loss of population (around 13% overall), and by the spring of 1700 the

Darien scheme, Scotland's ambitious attempt to found a trading colony on the Isthmus of Panama, had foundered. Scotland, this argument runs, needed English home markets, while what 'the disastrous experience of Darien had shown was the brutal fact that if the Scots were to trade overseas successfully they needed English acquiescence, and access to her colonies' (Whatley 1994, 34).

Without these outlets the Scottish economy would be in dire straits, as was recognised by the English proponents of the Alien Act. Scotland's need to maintain and exploit further the English connection, Smout was convinced, was recognised by the 'stanchest supporters of Union' in the Scottish Parliament, the Scottish nobility, the extent of whose direct involvement in trade had not been appreciated. (Previously historians had interpreted the opposition to Union by a majority in the Convention of Royal Burghs as an indication that the country's trading interest had not been persuaded of its economic benefits.) Perceiving that their interests lay in England therefore, and with few exceptions, men such as the Earl of Wemyss, a coal and salt proprietor in Fife, and the Earl of Cromartie and others with grain-growing estates in the North-East, voted in favour of incorporating union.

The core of this argument is the proposition that the Scots were primarily interested in free trade. It is certainly the case that this was a long-standing Scottish

No. 2. The 'Downsitting' of the Scottish Parliament showing the Scottish Estates as they assembled in the pre-Union Parliament in Edinburgh. © *The Trustees of the National Museums of Scotland.*

aspiration and it is striking that the IVth Article of Union (see **Document 1**) was carried with only 19 votes against, with 26 members who were generally opponents of Union voting for it. More recent research, however, has qualified this interpretation and moved away from the idea that the Scots saw Union *only* as an opportunity to enter a 'common market' with England, 'the final working out of forces which had been drawing the two countries closer together for over a century' (Whatley 1994, 33). There is evidence to suggest that from 1703 contemporaries were less certain than they had been beforehand about the benefits that unrestricted free trade would bring. There were fears that wealth would be drawn from Scotland to London and that Scottish manufactures would be unable to withstand competition from England, particularly if Scots goods – which were often of a low quality – were subject to the same taxes (see **Document 3**). As has been noted already, whatever its undoubted potential, the Scottish economy at the turn of the eighteenth century was in a fragile condition.

EXERCISE 6

Read Articles VI–VIII, X–XIV again and note their contents (**Document 1**). The italicised clauses are those which were inserted into the Articles by the Scottish parliament during the so-called 'Explanations', when the Articles presented by the Commissioners were examined and debated and voted upon one by one in November and December 1706. What were the intended effects of the Articles and amendments?

Built into the Articles of Union were a series of concessions, following Scottish proposals which, in the case of the Union Commissioners, were made 'in more detail and with far greater precision than in the previous [1702] negotiations' (Riley 1978, 184). These had the effect of protecting Scottish interests through the imposition of lower taxes (coal and salt, for example), and in some cases of making special provision for certain Scottish products in the form of 'drawbacks' and bounties (for example, the allowances payable on exports of herring, beef, pork and grain). A number of the tax concessions, which were in direct conflict with the principles of free trade and equal taxation, brought considerable benefits to the sectoral groups concerned, such as the landed coal proprietors of the Forth estuary who managed to hold onto their tax (and therefore price) advantage and thus exclude Newcastle coal from their main markets until 1794. Grain exports from Scotland reached an all-time high in the ten to fifteen years after 1707.

Evidence of this sort highlights the pragmatic nature of much support for the Union. It has been argued that at a time of rampant mercantilism throughout Europe, where trade, in the words of Andrew Fletcher, was the 'golden ball' to which all nations aspired, in their economic thinking the Scots were 'severely practical'.

EXERCISE 7

Read Seton of Pitmedden's speech on the First Article of Union (**Document 2**) and the petition of the burgh of Montrose to their parliamentary representative,

James Scott (**Document 4**). What, if any, support do these sources provide for this proposition?

Seton of Pitmedden and the provost and town councillors of Montrose were not alone in being acutely aware of the realities of the situation. Adopting a wider perspective than the burgh representatives, Pitmedden was convinced that 'This Nation being Poor and without Force to protect its Commerce' could not survive, let alone become richer, 'till it partake of the Trade and Protection of some powerful Neighbour Nation'. England was the only viable partner. Montrose was a trading burgh which sent large quantities of coarse linen cloth into England and without this 'only valuable branch of our trade' would be ruined. Judging from this there would seem to be substance in Mitchison's judgement that the Scots 'did not go into the union simply because they were poor and saw no other way of riches, but because they were poor and getting poorer' (Mitchison 1982, 311).

2.3. *Party, political management and bribery*

The two main arguments which have been outlined above have been subjected to a barrage of criticism. The concept of 'statesmenship' has been rejected by a number of historians who, from the 1960s, influenced by Sir Lewis Namier's debunking approach to eighteenth-century politicians and political history, have tended to see the Scottish parliamentarians who led and supported the moves to Union in a much less favourable light than did most of their predecessors. Much greater emphasis has been placed on the role of political parties, management and various forms of bribery in getting the Articles through the Scottish parliament, as well as the weaknesses inherent in the divided opposition.

The part played by economic considerations in persuading Scots to opt for Union has been judged as either small or of no importance whatsoever, an 'old theory' and a Victorian 'invention' according to the nationalist PH Scott (1979). For Riley (1978, 8), trade was 'hardly more than a propaganda argument for embracing or opposing a union designed for quite other reasons'.

The suggestion that Scotland's political élite bore little resemblance to the 'accomplished body of men' which so impressed Hume Brown in 1915 is not a new one. It was in 1714 that George Lockhart of Carnwath's *Memoirs Concerning the Affairs of Scotland* was first published. In it he produced scathing but persuasive descriptions of his contemporaries, the veracity of which has been underlined by Ferguson (1977, 175–6) who has referred to the pro-Union crown's 'need for . . . calculating and unpatriotic heads', men such as Seafield, an 'able and unscrupulous manipulator of opinions and consciences', or Queensberry and the Duke of Hamilton, and others, who shifted their political allegiance in accordance with their perception of what was in their personal or family interest. Judgements about the motives of the major players on the Scottish political stage should be based not on what they wrote (several penned eloquent letters and memoranda on the subject of union), but rather on their actions.

That men such as Queensberry, Seafield, the Duke of Argyll and John Erskine, 11th Earl of Mar, and others who worked in the cause of Union, were able to manipulate the political system in the interest of the Court is undeniable, and in this sense Ferguson's depiction of the Union as a 'political job' seems entirely reasonable. Nor are accusations of self-interest without strong foundation. For example, Argyll ('capable of the worst things to promote his interest', according to Lockhart) demanded a commission as a Major General before agreeing to return to Scotland in July 1706 to serve the Queen, as well as other favours for members of his family (see **Document 5**). In November 1704 Seton of Pitmedden was reported to have asked for a pension of £100 per annum in return for his services, a fact which has led one modern nationalist writer to question the depth of Seton's conviction (Scott 1992, 119). The Duke of Hamilton, nominal leader of the opposition Country Party, has long been condemned by nationalist historians in particular for failing, at crucial moments, to act patriotically. Thus, unexpectedly, it was Hamilton who proposed in September 1705 that Queen Anne should nominate the Scottish Commissioners who were to negotiate a union, while in January 1707, 'pretending to be seized of the toothache', he refused to attend Parliament to support a belated attempt to reject incorporation. Hamilton was heavily in debt, 'so unlucky in his privat circumstances' according to one contemporary, 'that he wou'd have complied with anything on a suitable encouragement'.

Ever since the publication of Lockhart's *Memoirs*, which provided persuasive proof of secret payments made to over 30 Scots, historians have debated the part played by bribery in persuading Scottish parliamentarians to support the Union proposals.

EXERCISE 8

Read Lockhart's 'Appendix' to the *Memoirs* (**Document 6**). What conclusions do you draw from it?

The evidence presented by Lockhart is certainly revealing, and even though much of the £20,500 which had been secretly distributed on behalf of Queen Anne by the Scottish Treasurer, the Earl of Glasgow, represented salary arrears and expenses (£12,325 alone went to Queensberry) and for most individuals the sums involved were relatively small (but less so if the figures are multiplied by twelve to convert them into pounds Scots), historians have identified some individuals who appear to have supported the Court against their usual political inclinations as a result of receiving favours. These transactions were conducted out of sight. Other forms of financial persuasion were much more public: the XVth Article, for example (see **Document 1**), which dealt with the Equivalent, a payment to the Scots of some £400,000 for undertaking to repay part of England's national debt but which also compensated shareholders of the Company of Scotland for losses incurred by the failure of Darien, with an additional 5% interest. Around £153,000, perhaps as much as one-quarter of Scotland's liquid capital, had been invested in the venture. Similarly, the favourable economic conditions created by several of the Articles, along with the amendments, can be interpreted as a means of 'sugaring the pill of incorporating union' for certain sectional interests as well as individuals such as Sir Peter Halkett of Pitfirrane, whose right to export coal free of duty was preserved in a general measure to retain such private privileges in the amended VIth Article (Whatley 1994, 42).

Riley was another historian who was unimpressed by the calibre of either English or Scottish proponents of the Union, which he concluded 'was made by men of limited vision for very short-term and comparatively petty, if not squalid, aims' (Riley 1978, xvi, 2–3). Rejecting the idea that the Union was inevitable or the result of forward-looking endeavour, Riley's emphasis was on the part played by growing party rivalry at Westminster after the passing of the Triennial Act of 1694. One effect of this was to increase the number of elections, with English interest in Scotland waxing and waning with the rise and fall of rival Whig and Tory administrations, Tories for instance having little wish to ally with the presbyterian Scots. The final thrust towards the Union of 1707 came from Godolphin and prominent Whig politicians (the 'Junto') who saw in an incorporating union the possibility of bolstering their numbers through the arrival in a united British parliament of Scottish Whig MPs. The leading Scottish politicians, busily 'scavenging what they could of the fringes' of this English rivalry, offered themselves to the highest bidder.

Although admirably detailed, and the work of a scrupulous scholar, it can be objected that Riley's approach was overly cynical. By looking too closely at the day-to-day machinations of the politicians he may have failed to discern the greater benefits to both countries which were observed by at least some contemporaries. Sir John Clerk, for example, was one of the greatest Scotsmen of his day, cultured, well-informed about Scottish finances, a polymath and Scottish patriot, a member of parliament and, initially at least, a reluctant Scottish Commissioner. Yet he supported the British union and over a period of some thirty years composed (in Latin) a *History* of it (which was not published in English until 1993), partly in order to counter what he called Lockhart's 'silly' memoir, within which was evidence 'that he did not understand what he was doing & that he was influenced only by the principles of the party he espoused' (Clerk 1993, 175). Lockhart was an ardent Jacobite. Clerk, however, was not blindly pro-Union, and recognised that incorporating union was a compromise – but nevertheless necessary for both England and Scotland – and in the circumstances in Scotland's best interests. Scottish independence was an illusion, while he could 'never conceive' what was meant by Scottish sovereignty; England could claim sovereignty of the seas, in Scotland's case this was solely 'within her own confines' (Clerk 1993, 199–200).

Clerk's case is not unique. Analysis by Macinnes of voting patterns within the Scottish parliament has revealed 'a level of principled commitment to Union hitherto underplayed . . . by historians'. Hitherto such qualities have usually been ascribed to opponents of Union such as Fletcher of Saltoun. However, thirteen members consistently supported the measure 'without benefit of office, financial inducement, committee service or ties of kinship', although eleven were ultimately rewarded one way or another (Macinnes 1990, 19). What this and other evidence suggests is that the more inflated claims which have been made about the extent and depth of Scottish venality – based in part on English caricature (and the demand of Scots post-1707 for scapegoats) – might be scaled down, although clearly the relatively small number of untarnished individuals lends support to Macinnes's conclusion that 'principled commitment' was a 'minority activity'. (This was so even amongst the opponents of Union, where instances of consistently principled voting are fewer than are commonly assumed.) It should be noted, however, that payments for political services were in Pryde's words part of 'the routine political methods of the day', the oil which kept the machinery of government moving but not its driving force (Pryde 1950, 34). It is unreasonable and anachronistic to apply modern expectations of political morality to the early 1700s when virtually the only route to political power was through patronage. Except for a handful of cases it is almost impossible to judge how far parliamentarians supported Union as a result of receiving bribes. What seems more likely is that disbursements from the £20,500 were used not to buy off opponents but rather to shore up Court party support and persuade waverers to vote in favour.

Although 'without the formal structure, organisation and discipline of British political parties as they emerged in the nineteenth century' (Whatley 1994, 21), political affiliations were 'measurably the most cohesive, comprehensive, and cogent influences on voting in the last session of the Scottish Estates' (Macinnes 1990, 15). There were three main party groupings in the pre-1707 Parliament: the largest, the Court Party, which included the officers of state; the opposition Country Party; and the smaller Cavalier Party, which was largely Jacobite. Vital, however (as the combined total of members from the last two was greater than the Court), was the so-called 'New' Party, otherwise known as the Squadrone Volante (see **Document 5**). Formed in 1704, led by the Marquess of Tweeddale and comprising some two dozen members, the New Party had from the outset been committed to the Hanoverian succession. Without Squadrone support, or had its adherents voted with the confederated opposition, several of the Articles would have been defeated. Squadrone votes were solid throughout and the Earl of Roxburghe was an eloquent advocate of Union. The question which is difficult to resolve, and which produces a divided response amongst historians, is how far Squadrone commitment to incorporating union was due to its members' concern for Scotland's future, or whether personal gain – Squadrone Volante members were generously rewarded – and political opportunism governed their actions, not least those of Roxburghe, who was 'working hard for a dukedom' (Riley 1978, 260–8; Ferguson 1977, 233).

3. MAKING SENSE OF THE DEBATE

3.1. *Economic considerations revisited*

Reference was made earlier to the rejection by some historians of an economic interpretation of the Union. The arguments and evidence surveyed in the preceding section leave little doubt that management and bribery eased the passage of the

Articles of Union through the Scottish parliament in the final months of 1706. Yet the implication that matters of substance were altogether absent from the minds of all but a very few Scottish politicians when they cast their votes on the Articles rests rather uneasily with the frequently-quoted words of the Earl of Roxburghe who explained why he thought there would be a majority in Parliament for incorporating union:

> The motives will be, Trade with most, Hanover with some, ease and security with others, together with a generall aversion at civill discords, intollerable poverty, and the constant oppression of a bad ministry . . . without the least regard to the good of the country . . .

EXERCISE 9
Look again at the Articles of Union (**Document 1**). How many of them are concerned with economic matters?

The prominent place Roxburghe gave to trade seems to be justified in that 15 out of the 25 Articles are related to trade, taxation and industry. That management had its limits and that principles were at issue is indicated by the many examples there were of cross-voting on the Articles, notably on the IVth, referred to above. Significantly, this dealt with trade, and indeed it was economic issues which often generated the most heated debates and produced the closest votes. Thus Daniel Defoe, witnessing the scene in Edinburgh in December 1706, described the debate over the salt tax (Article VIII) as the 'Grand Affair', while the Earl of Mar (an outstanding parliamentary manager) was convinced that without concessions the Court would be defeated. If the Union was simply a 'political job', why were these and other concessions (the separate Act protecting the Church of Scotland, for example) necessary? Why, indeed, was Daniel Defoe sent to Scotland to engage in a vigorous propaganda campaign?

It could be, as Riley argued, that the controversy over trade was 'a fashionable and convenient camouflage for less respectable motives', and close votes on the economic Articles were last-gasp gestures of independence by opponents of Union. The evidence, however, is ambiguous. On 21 December 1706 Defoe reported to Robert Harley in London that 'the present Design was to load the Treaty with Such amendments As they think will Ruine it in its Consequences' (Healey 1955, 179).

EXERCISE 10
Read the Earl of Seafield's letter of 7 November 1706 to Godolphin (**Document** 7), asking whether or not it supports this interpretation.

That Seafield reports that the 'Jacobite Pairtie' continued to oppose the Union 'with violence' is in keeping with Defoe's information. However, Seafield also expresses the hope that 'if the alterations be aloued, wee will carie it [the Union] in Parlament' (Hume Brown 1915, 101), while another contemporary, Viscount

Dupplin, talked about a 'considerable partie' which was not directly against the Union, 'yet goe in very naruly to inquire into the articles of it, and insist . . . for tyme . . . to consider them' (*ibid*, 173). The two propositions may be perfectly compatible.

By the time the Articles agreed by the joint Commissioners were presented in Edinburgh, it had become clear that the proposed union was to be an incorporating union rather than a federal arrangement. As control over economic policy would be lost, those Scots within Parliament who had something to lose, and those outside it who could make themselves heard, fought tenaciously to defend their interest, whether it be coal, or bread and butter issues such as the post-1707 price of malt or salt, or the future of the vulnerable woollen industry.

Although some historians have tended to dismiss the amendments which resulted as of little consequence, they may have underestimated their contemporary significance. There are historians who have been impressed by the 'remarkable' concessions in the form of preferential rates of taxation and subsidies for certain commodities which were wrested from Godolphin and the English union negotiators as a result of Scottish representations. Indeed it had by no means been a foregone conclusion that when the Commissioners from the two nations met in April 1706 the Scots would be granted access to England's West Indian and American colonies.

3.2. *Drawing conclusions*

It will have become clear that my own conviction is that economic opportunity as well as a concern to shield private and sectional interests from the colder winds of free competition within a 'common market' were, respectively, a powerful impetus towards Union and a factor which determined whether or not the Articles would obtain the approval of the Scottish Estates. The late concession of a separate Act for the Church of Scotland was also crucial. It is not intended, however, that readers should necessarily follow this line of argument and the evidence presented here can support alternative explanations. Few historians would now consider the Union of 1707 to have been a triumph of political vision. It is clear that the skilful management of the Estates and party affiliation, along with the judicious use of bribery and more open forms of inducement, played important parts in obtaining an incorporating union. How to weigh the various elements which led to the Union of 1707 is a problem which has perplexed historians in the past and will continue to do so in future.

REFERENCES TO BOOKS AND ARTICLES MENTIONED IN THE TEXT

Brown, K 1995 'The origins of a British aristocracy: integration and its limitations before the treaty of Union', *in* Ellis, SG and Barber, S (eds), *Conquest & Union: Fashioning a British State, 1485–1725*. London, 222–49.
Clerk, Sir J 1993 (ed D Duncan) *History of the Union of Scotland and England*. Edinburgh.

Colley, L 1992 *Britons: Forging the Nation, 1707–1837*. New Haven and London.

Dawson, J 1995 'Anglo-Scottish protestant culture and integration in sixteenth-century Britain', *in* Ellis, SG and Barber, S (eds), *Conquest & Union: Fashioning a British State, 1485–1725*. London, 87–114.

Devine, TM 1995 'The Union of 1707 and Scottish Development', *in* Devine, TM, *Exploring the Scottish Past*, East Linton, 37–53.

Elliot, JH 1992 'A Europe of Composite Monarchies', *Past and Present* 137, 48–71.

*Ellis, SG and Barber, S (eds) 1995 *Conquest & Union: Fashioning a British State, 1485–1725*. London.

Emerson, RL 1995 'Scottish cultural change 1660–1710 and the Union of 1707', *in* Robertson, J (ed), *A Union for Empire*, London, 121–44.

*Ferguson, W 1977 (1994 ed) *Scotland's Relations With England: A Survey to 1707*. Edinburgh.

Healey, G (ed) 1955 *The Letters of Daniel Defoe*. Oxford.

**Hume Brown P (ed) 1915 *Letters Relating to Scotland in the Reign of Queen Anne by James Ogilvy, First Earl of Seafield and Others*. Edinburgh.

Grant, J 1912 *Seafield Correspondence from 1685–1708*. Edinburgh.

Kidd, C 1995 'Religious realignment between the Restoration and the Union of 1707', *in* Robertson, J (ed), 145–68.

Kidd, C 1996 'North Britishness and the Nature of Eighteenth-Century British Patriotisms', *The Historical Journal*, 39, 361–82.

Lenman, B 1980 *The Jacobite Risings in Britain 1689–1746*. London.

Macinnes, A 1990 'Studying the Scottish Estates and the Treaty of Union', *History Microcomputer Review*, 6, 2 (Fall), 11–25.

MacKinnon, J 1896 *The Union of England and Scotland*. London.

Mathieson, WL 1905 *Scotland and the Union*. Glasgow.

Mitchison, R 1983 *Lordship to Patronage: Scotland 1603–1745*. London.

Morrill, J 1995 'The fashioning of Britain', *in* Ellis, SG and Barber, S (eds), *Conquest & Union: Fashioning a British State, 1485–1725*. London, 8–39.

Murdoch, A 1980 *'The People Above': Politics and Administration in Mid-Eighteenth Century Scotland*. Edinburgh.

Ouston, H 1988 'Cultural Life from the Restoration to the Union', *in* Hook, A (ed), *The History of Scottish Literature, Volume 2, 1660–1800*, Aberdeen, 11–31.

Pryde, GS 1950 *The Treaty of Union of Scotland and England*. London.

Pryde, GS 1962 *Scotland from 1603 to the present day*. London.

*Riley, PWJ 1978 *The Union of Scotland and England: A study in Anglo-Scottish politics of the eighteenth-century*. Manchester.

Robertson, J 1994 'Union, State and Empire: The Britain of 1707 in its European setting', *in* Stone, L (ed), *An Imperial State at War: Britain from 1689 to 1815*, London, 224–57.

*Robertson, J 1995 *A Union for Empire: Political Thought and the Union of 1707*. Cambridge.

Scott, PH 1979 *1707: The Union of Scotland and England*. Edinburgh.

*Scott, PH 1992 *Andrew Fletcher and the Treaty of Union*. Edinburgh.

Smout, TC 1963 *Scottish Trade on the Eve of Union*. Edinburgh.

Smout, TC 1969 *A History of the Scottish People, 1560–1830*. London.

Szechi, D 1991 'The Hanoverians and Scotland', *in* Greengrass, M (ed), *Conquest and Coalescence: The Shaping of the State in Early Modern Europe*, London, 116–33.

*Whatley, CA 1994 'Bought and Sold for English Gold?' Explaining the Union of 1707. Glasgow.

Whyte, I 1995 Scotland Before the Industrial Revolution: An Economic and Social History c.1050–1750. London.

FURTHER READING

Those references marked * in the above list are recommended further reading, along with the following:

Whatley, CA 1989 'Economic causes and consequences of the Union of 1707: a survey', Scottish Historical Review 68, 150–81.

SOME PUBLISHED PRIMARY SOURCES

Those references marked ** in the list of references referred to in the text are published primary sources which may be of interest, as are the following:

Daiches, D (ed) 1979 Fletcher of Saltoun: Selected Political Writings and Speeches. Edinburgh.

Lockhart, George, of Carnwath 1714 Memoirs Concerning the Affairs of Scotland from Queen Anne's Accession to the Throne to the Commencement of the Union of the Two Kingdoms of Scotland and England in May 1707, London; new edition, 1995, ed Szechi, D, entitled 'Scotland's Ruine': Lockhart of Carnwath's Memoirs of the Union. Aberdeen.

Mar and Kellie Papers 1904 Royal Commission on Historical Manuscripts. London.

Jacobitism

Bob Harris

INTRODUCTION

Jacobitism, or support for the claims of the exiled Stuarts, was born as a military and political force in Scotland in 1689, when John Graham of Claverhouse, Viscount Dundee ('Bonnie Dundee'), raised the Jacobite standard on the Law outside Dundee. Fought mainly in the eastern Highlands, the first Jacobite rising in Scotland (and Britain) was weakly supported, and the spectacular victory gained by Bonnie Dundee's forces at Killiecrankie on 26 July 1689 was a Pyrrhic one. It was the incorporating union with England (1707) which gave renewed impetus to Jacobitism and turned it into a major *national* threat to the Protestant and Hanoverian Succession established by the Glorious Revolution of 1689. When combined with the influence of Episcopalian political theology and the indifference or ineptitude of successive English ministries, this, or the slow, uneven acceptance of, or acquiescence in, the Union, ensured that substantial uncertainty hung over the political future of Scotland, and Scotland's place in Britain's expanding empire, until at least the bloody dénouement of nearly half a century of plotting and conspiracy at Culloden in April 1746.

This chapter is divided into a number of sections. Each section is designed to help you see Jacobitism from a different perspective. The sections are:

- Myths
- Definitions
- Who were the Jacobites?
- Invasion attempts and risings
- The failure of Jacobitism

In some sections, issues are raised without being answered. This is appropriate for a topic in which the evidence is often extremely problematic. It also reflects the current state of historiography on the topic.

I. MYTHS

A major problem confronting those who wish to study Jacobitism is getting beneath the many layers of myth that have built up around the Stuart cause, from its inception, whilst at the same time retaining a proper sense of its historical importance (see Pittock 1995). A good number of these myths derive from representations of Jacobitism that were constructed after its death as a practical

military and political force. Jacobitism had a second coming in the eighteenth
century (see Lenman 1980) which was associated with the growth of the romantic
movement from the 1770s. The Scotland memorialised in romantic image and myth
– a Scotland of brave but doomed Highlanders – was a dead one, however, and the
long (and unending) flirtation with Jacobitism, English as much as Scottish, could
henceforth proceed safely. This was also part of re-reading Scotland's past to create
a new Scottish identity compatible with continued commitment to participation in
the British state and empire.

    Jacobitism is also a subject notoriously susceptible to the temptation to ask
questions of the type 'What if?'. What if Bonnie Prince Charlie had marched south
from Derby in the early days of December 1745? What if the Earl of Mar had led the
1715 rising with greater strategic and military competence? Yet, as Youngson
(1985) has so rightly reminded us, these are hardly questions that the historian can,
or ought to, tackle. It is enough for us to recover, as fully as we can, the factors which
influenced, say, the decision to turn back from Derby in 1745. There is also, dare I
say it (as a British historian from England working in a Scottish university), an
unhelpful parochialism about much of the speculation. In 1745, Bonnie Prince
Charlie was set on the recovery of the thrones of England and Wales, as well as
Scotland. In this at least, his strategic and political sense was sound (see Black 1995).
The balance of political and military forces and calculations was broadly the same
that Scotland faced in 1706, and the balance was against independence, unless
England would have supported a restoration (for which, see below).

> EXERCISE I
> What reasons can you come up with to explain why Jacobitism is such a
> controversial topic in Scottish (and British) history?

You will get further ideas on this from the sections below. One issue, however, that is
worth considering at this stage is how often current preoccupations and concerns are
imported into debates on this topic.

2. DEFINITIONS

Jacobitism was a diverse and slippery force. The penalty for treason was death and
loss of one's estates and consequent ruin of one's family. Because of this, Jacobite
activity has left a trail of gaps and silences. Equivocation was also an important
feature of Jacobitism; people often said one thing and did another. It is impossible,
moreover, to say what proportion of Jacobites or potential Jacobites ever took up
arms against the Hanoverians. Many confined themselves to less threatening
displays of allegiance, such as drinking 'loyal' toasts. This raises the problem of
how to interpret the disloyalty of those who never went so far as to join military
action to restore the Stuarts. Lenman argues for restricting our definition of
Jacobitism to those who did actually rise in support of the Jacobites (Lenman
1982, 36). Pittock (1995, 3), by contrast, has recently chided those who appear to

think 'that only those prepared to risk all they owned and a gruesome death can be counted as interested in supporting the Stuarts'.

EXERCISE 2

How would you define Jacobitism? It is worth asking yourself in this context whether the protean realities of Jacobitism can (or should) be limited to a single definition.

It is also important not to overlook those attracted to the Jacobite cause by personal factors – roguery, the desire for advancement, adventure or excitement, or a combination of all of these. Some of the leading Jacobites fall within this group; perhaps the most famous is John Erskine, seventh Earl of Mar (see Gregg 1982), whose military incompetence played such a major role in the failure of the 'Fifteen. Szechi (1994, 23–4) has argued that without the involvement of such individuals, the history of Jacobitism might have been altogether less dramatic. It was often individuals motivated by personal dissatisfaction who were prepared to take the risks involved in plotting and rebellion where more ideologically committed Jacobites remained paralysed by indecision.

3. WHO WERE THE JACOBITES?

If a significant proportion of Jacobite activity must remain tied up with the politics of individual motivation, and if in talking of Jacobitism we must be always aware that we are talking of a diverse reality, there are nevertheless groups in Scottish society from which the Stuart cause could consistently expect or at least hope to pick up support. Examination of these groups tells us much about the conditions in which Jacobitism was able to survive into the reign of George II.

3.1. Socio-economic factors

Whatever earlier historians of Jacobitism have suggested, or as its romantic celebrators continue to imply, Jacobitism in Scotland was never principally a question of a clash of cultures, a struggle between a traditional Highland culture and a modernising, increasingly secular Lowland culture (see Lenman 1980, Chapter 6). This is not to say that Jacobitism's failure did not accelerate the subordination of the Highlands to the growing forces of commercialisation in Scottish society. The socio-economic differences between the Lowland and High-land gentry were in reality slight, and narrowing, although impoverishment was afflicting many of the Highland gentry by the 1730s and 1740s. This last fact was both a strength and a weakness to Jacobitism. The impoverished head of a clan might be pacified by government patronage; equally he might be alienated by its absence or withdrawal, as happened in the case of Simon Fraser, Lord Lovat, in the later 1730s (Lenman 1984, especially Chapters 6 and 7). Jacobite clan leaders turn out to have been agricultural improvers and not guardians of a traditional, threatened Gaelic culture. An attempt to explain support for Jacobitism in socio-economic terms also confronts the difficulty of the depth of Jacobite support in the north-east of Scotland. As the Taylers emphasised as long ago as the 1920s, Lowland Banffshire and Aberdeenshire were, throughout this period, notable strongholds of Jacobite sentiment (Tayler and Tayler 1928).

3.2. *Episcopalians, Catholics and Presbyterians*

Religious differences were, for most people, much more important than socio-economic ones in determining support for Jacobitism. Two confessional groups consistently tended to support the Jacobites – the Roman Catholics and the Episcopalians. Of the two groups, the Roman Catholics were the less important, not least because they were far fewer in number. Roman Catholicism in Scotland existed in small inaccessible pockets in parts of the Hebridean Islands such as Barra and in mainland areas to the west of Inverness. In 1745, it was the protection of the latter that provided the Young Pretender with the few crucial days he required to persuade his few supporters that his invasion of Scotland was not a massive blunder, or 'madness', as MacLeod of MacLeod put it from the comparative safety of Skye.

The Episcopalians, those ministers and laymen who could not reconcile themselves to the presbyterian settlement in the Church of Scotland imposed by a small, aggressive minority in 1690, were, by contrast, vastly more important, far greater in number, and far more diffused geographically. It was also from the flocks of the episcopalian clergy that most of the Scots who were out in the 'Fifteen, the 'Nineteen and the 'Forty-Five came. To understand why Episcopalianism was such fertile ground for the Stuart cause, it is necessary to grasp a number of comparatively simple facts. Firstly, the episcopalian church was the crucible of a deeply conserva-tive world view. Elements of this view are articulated very powerfully in **Document 8**. This is a sermon composed by James Garden, a Professor of Divinity at King's College, Old Aberdeen, and one of a delegation which presented a loyal address from the Episcopal clergy of Aberdeen to the Pretender in 1716.

> EXERCISE 3
> Read **Document 8** and describe the main tenets of political belief expressed in it. Explain also why you think they led to support for the Stuart cause. Pay particular attention in this context to the attitudes towards monarchy which are disclosed in the document and the explanations offered for the ills that Scotland had suffered after 1689.

A keystone of episcopalian political belief was that the monarch ruled by divine right. Because of this, monarchs were accountable only to God for their actions. Allegiance to them was, therefore, a religious duty. The Revolution of 1688 was also, according to such principles, an illegitimate act (or series of acts).

Episcopalian ministers maintained a tenacious influence on national life and culture, especially north of the Tay, despite official hostility after 1690. This was partly due to the dominance which the Episcopalians had achieved in the universities – the training ground of the ministry – during the Restoration; partly owing to distance (Highland parishes tended to be very large); and partly owing to the protection afforded episcopalian ministers by a sympathetic gentry and nobility. In parish after parish, especially north of the Tay, the removal of episcopalian ministers proved a remarkably protracted affair. A Toleration Act for the Episcopalians was passed in 1712. Under this act, episcopalian ministers were able to minister publicly to their flocks, but only if they took an oath of allegiance to the ruling monarch. They were also expected to pray in their meeting houses for Queen Anne and, later, the Hanoverian monarchs. Many episcopalian ministers survived the attacks of Presbyterians in their parishes because of a willingness to swear oaths abjuring the Stuarts while not meaning it, much to the irritation of many Presbyterians. They also ignored or circumvented the requirement that they pray for the ruling dynasty (see **Document 9**). Attempts to impose a presbyterian minister led to rioting in Fraserburgh in 1707. In a number of parishes in the North-East there was no presbyterian minister as late as the later 1710s (Lenman 1984, 130). Even when they were eventually removed, they might find shelter and employment as chaplains and tutors to the Scottish Jacobite landed élite, positions from which they could continue to exercise great influence.

In the aftermath of the 'Fifteen, the Episcopalians were singled out for retribution by the government. In the later stages and aftermath of the 'Forty-Five, much harsher repression took place; for example, on his arrival in Aberdeen in 1746, the Duke of Cumberland ordered that all episcopalian ministers be deprived of their livings and that all meeting houses and chapels should be destroyed. This was an order that was carried out both in the city and, later on, throughout the northern counties. In 1746, an act was passed suppressing episcopalian meeting houses.

To reduce Jacobitism simply to the political expression of Episcopalianism would be to distort the complexity of Jacobite motivations. As we shall see below, it was the mixture of episcopalian political theology with other grievances that was so potentially menacing to the political status quo. In the Highlands, amongst a small minority of clans, Jacobitism grew from clan rivalry, in particular opposition to the great Campbell empire in the South-West, rather than principle or religion. (Smout (1969, 224) exaggerates the importance of this as a source of threat to the Hanoverian regime and of Jacobite allegiance.) As Macinnes (1996) has recently argued, support for Jacobitism amongst episcopalian clansmen could also be undermined by growing tensions between them and their clan chiefs created by the latters' attempts to commercialise the running of their estates. Moreover, Jacobite ideology was more diverse and fluid than an emphasis only on episcopalian divine right principles would suggest. It tended to absorb other criticisms of Hanoverian rule, ones that focused on political corruption and threats of political virtue. The politics and personnel of the Hanoverian regime were seen by many, and not just by Jacobites, as a threat to British liberties. In early September 1745, Lord George Murray went so far as to argue: 'Upon the whole I am satisfied there is much greater need of a Revolution now to secure our liberties and save Britain from utter destruction than there was at the last [ie 1689] – even if the King's right [ie James VIII's right to the throne] were not in question' (quoted in Tomasson 1958, 39–40).

The importance of religion in explaining Jacobitism is further indicated by the role of Presbyterianism as a wellspring of opposition to it. In the immediate aftermath of the Union, there is some evidence that the Cameronians, extreme Presbyterians in the South-West, were prepared to support a rising in favour of the Jacobites (Gibson 1988). But Presbyterianism, and the Church of Scotland, fairly quickly became a bulwark of the Protestant succession in Scotland, certainly by the later 1710s and outside the Highlands. After 1714, anti-Catholicism, commitment to the religious status quo, and the control of patronage exerted by the remarkable political manager, Archibald Campbell, 1st Earl of Ilay, cemented their allegiance to the Lutheran Hanoverian dynasty. This is a role that has not been fully investigated, but the records of the General Assembly, presbyteries and, at the level of the parishes, kirk sessions, contain part of the story. Church of Scotland ministers also compiled an impressive record of defiance towards the Jacobites in 1745–6.

> EXERCISE 4
> Read **Document 10** which comprises extracts from a copy of a Jacobite pamphlet published during the 'Fifteen in Perth. What light does it shed on the importance of religion in determining both support for, and opposition to, Jacobitism in Scotland in the first half of the eighteenth century? What does it suggest about the difficulties for the Jacobites posed by the Catholicism of the Pretender?

3.3. National grievances

Lenman suggests that the militant Jacobite ideology espoused by the Episcopalians was probably fully shared by only a minority of the Highland and Lowland gentry. Yet he also suggests that a majority, at least in 1714–15, may have been vulnerable to the ideological force of divine right Jacobitism (see Lenman 1980, Chapter 6). However, it was only the fact that this disposition was overlaid with a formidable complex of political and national grievances that transformed such individuals into conspirators. These grievances were shared by many elements of Scottish society, particularly in the early 1710s, and it was their intensity and diffusion which made the 'Fifteen so potentially menacing. Many of the grievances stemmed from the same source – the Act of Union. Others stemmed from the singular insensitivity and clumsiness with which the English political establishment treated Scotland after 1707.

It is worth emphasising just how many groups and individuals were alienated, including those, a small minority, who were initially favourable to the Union. In 1711, Scots peers were aggrieved by the decision of the House of Lords to refuse the Duke of Hamilton admission to a seat in the Lords by virtue of his holding a British peerage, decreeing that Scots peers were already fully represented by the 16 elected peers provided for under the terms of the Act of Union. The 1709 Treason Act,

No. 3. Print: King James VIII and III (1688–1766) (Prince James Francis Edward
Stewart), by François Chereau after Alexis Simon Belle. *Scottish National Portrait
Gallery.*

bringing Scottish treason law into line with that of England on the matter of the number of witnesses to treason required (one not two), provoked widespread outrage, not least because it seemed to threaten the independence of the Scots legal system, supposedly protected by the Union. Economic interests were stung by clumsy economic regulations and legislation, while in 1711–12 the Kirk saw its religious monopoly broken in Scotland, again in spite of the terms of the Union. Meanwhile, the economic benefits of Union, so much touted in 1706–7 by propagandists like Defoe, were slow in emerging; the short-term effects were often harsh, particularly for those sectors of the economy which were oriented towards trade with the Continent. It is a telling indication of the depth of disillusionment with the Union that in 1713, when an attempt was made to extend the Malt Tax to Scotland in contravention of the terms of the Union, the Earl of Seafield moved in the Lords for an act to dissolve the Union. This was defeated by only four votes. As the Earl of Findlater, Seafield had been one of the architects and most active supporters of the Union in 1705–7.

With the benefit of hindsight, it is clear that part of the problem was government from a London in which Scottish politicians, few in number compared to their English counterparts, made only a weak impression. Yet it was also a product of a failure of sympathy and imagination on the part of English ministers. Even ardent supporters of the Protestant Succession in Scotland, such as the Duke of Atholl, could find themselves harassed by the English establishment who could not be bothered to separate out legitimate grievances about Scottish government from support for a Jacobite alternative. The effect of the resulting mixture of resentment and grievance was to generate a groundswell of support for the Stuarts and, as importantly, to denude the Hanoverian regime of active support when it most needed it. In 1715, had Mar shown more strategic expertise, there is no doubt that the essential fragility of the incumbent regime in Scotland would have been fully exposed.

It was partly by accident and partly by design that Jacobitism in Scotland came to be identified closely with opposition to the Union. Not all opponents of the Union were Jacobites, but it was only Jacobites who were committed to sundering the Union, by force if necessary. At the same time, legal means of expressing nationalist feelings were denied to Scots; bodies that might have provided this, such as the Convention of Royal Burghs, tended towards institutional sclerosis under the deadening touch of Whig patronage politics. Leading Jacobites, and the exiled Stuart court, were fully aware of the importance of making explicit the link between opposition to the Union and the Stuart cause. Towards the end of December 1725, George Lockhart, a leading member of a group of trustees organising the Stuart cause in Scotland, tendered the following advice to the Old Pretender:

> As the aversion to the Union dayly encreases, that is the handle by which
> Scotsmen will be roused to make a general and zealous appearance. This your
> enemies are so sensible of that on former occasions all pains were taken to buzz
> in the people's ears that they'd be disappointed in what they expected from the

King, for that to please your subjects of England, you was to uphold the Union. Now as I am fully perswaded the better part of the English are far from thinking the Union beneficial to either Countrey, I cannot see but it is expedient for the King to gratify his friends in Scotland, and thereby advance your own intrest, and in order thereto that so soon as your army lands a manifesto should be published (as designed formerly) with respect to religion and containing an ample assurance of your design to maintain the two kingdoms in their ancient independent state by dissolving the Union pernicious to both.

(quoted in Szechi 1989, 252)

On 9 October 1745, in Edinburgh, the Young Pretender declared the 'pretended union of the Kingdoms . . . at an end'. This was the politics of dramatic gestures, perhaps understandable in the heady atmosphere of optimism and sycophancy that prevailed in Edinburgh in the six weeks of Jacobite occupation in 1745.

EXERCISE 5

Read the above extract from Lockhart's letter and comment on his advice to the exiled James VIII. Why do you think such a powerful connection was forged between Jacobitism and opposition to the Union?

3.4. Popular Jacobitism

What of popular Jacobitism? South of the Border, historians have detected a remarkably vital and persistent Jacobite strand in popular politics. This manifested itself in print, crowd demonstrations and protest (Monod 1989, 161–232).

The depth of popular support for Jacobitism in Scotland is much more difficult to comment on, not least because the necessary research has yet to be done. Lenman, the principal recent historian of Scottish Jacobitism, tends to take the view that anything other than the politics of the élite in this period is unimportant (Lenman 1982, 40). The study of popular disturbance in Scotland is also much less advanced than in England, although Whatley (1990) is beginning to reveal the potential richness of the subject. As Whatley and others have shown, there were major popular disturbances in Scotland over such things as the imposition of customs and excises, food or its excessive price and scarcity, the Malt Tax, and the Porteous affair. But, as referred to earlier, these were never primarily motivated by Jacobitism; they were as likely to take place in areas of presbyterian strength, such as Glasgow and the West, as in areas of strong Jacobite support such as the North-East. Nor were they exploited by the Jacobites to any real degree.

None of this is to say that there was no popular support for Jacobitism in Scotland. Scattered traces can be found in the extant sources, particularly from around 1714–15, and again in the 1740s, but these need more systematic investigation. In Aberdeen in 1714, this took the form of a disturbance which broke out on 10 August. In the early hours of the morning, between 10 and 11 August, some young men marched through the streets, headed by two fiddlers playing tunes, one of which was 'Let the King enjoy his own again'. The crowd assembled round the well which stands in the Green, took water in their hands, and 'drank the Pretender King James his health'. In 1715, a Whig loyalist estimated that a large majority of the town's population was disaffected (SRO, Montrose MS, GD 220/5/455/5). Jacobite sentiment was also expressed in both Gaelic and English poetry and song (Pittock 1994; Donaldson 1988). This was circulated or sung or read out in the Highlands and Lowlands. It also gave full expression to the gamut of emotions that attended the Jacobite cause – a sense of loss and regret, on the one hand, and outrage and expectation, on the other.

4. INVASION ATTEMPTS AND RISINGS

There were risings in Scotland in favour of the Jacobites in 1715, 1719, and 1745–6. There was also an attempted invasion in 1708. With the exception of the 'Fifteen, a crucial component was support from a major foreign power. In 1708 and 1745–6, albeit too late, it was the French who lent their military power to the cause; in 1719 it was the Spanish. The fate of the Stuart cause was, therefore, intimately linked to European power politics. It was also the case that a precondition of most Jacobites coming out in open support of the Stuart cause was the presence on British soil of a foreign professional army, or its imminent arrival. (Mar led Scottish Jacobites to believe this would be forthcoming in September 1715.) This represented a victory for realism. Without this, as the aftermath of the 'Forty-Five bloodily and painfully illustrated, the consequences could be dire and tragic.

Dependency on foreign support was arguably one important factor that reduced the chances of a successful Stuart restoration. This was because, while Jacobitism was always able to find supporters at major foreign courts, notably but not exclusively Paris, it was always likely to be used or encouraged by foreign powers for reasons which had everything to do with European power politics and little to do with the wish to see a Stuart back on the English and Scottish thrones (see Black 1985; 1988). In 1708, France gave some support to an invasion of Scotland because of the military conditions in the War of the Spanish Succession and in particular in the Low Countries, where her military position was weak and deteriorating. Support for this strategy was, moreover, limited and lukewarm. It was partly for this reason that the French admiral leading the invasion attempt, the Comte de Forbin, showed such a lack of enthusiasm for the venture when his fleet reached the north-east coast of Scotland (Gibson 1988). In the later 1710s, the Spanish court only supported an invasion attempt in the context of war against both Britain and France, a war precipitated by Spanish territorial ambitions in Italy. Spanish ministers had also expected commercial pressures to deter Britain; it was only when these were seen to fail that they turned to using the Jacobites (Smith 1982). In both examples, foreign powers were using the Jacobites as a last resort, to apply pressure to Britain in the context of war.

The pattern at other stages in our period is essentially similar. Jacobite hopes revived in the later 1730s and early 1740s, because after a protracted period when she had remained isolated from European conflicts, Britain entered a war with Spain in 1739 and then saw herself become entangled in a major European war in 1741, the War of the Austrian Succession. France offered the best hope of foreign support for a restoration attempt. But it is significant that it was not until 1743 that this ever looked like occurring, whatever hints Cardinal Fleury, the French first minister, threw out in his final years. The crucial context was the changing military and diplomatic balance in the War of the Austrian Succession. Having swept all before them in 1741, France and her major ally, Bavaria, saw the military and diplomatic balance shift away from them. In 1743, moreover, French forces were defeated by Britain and her allies at the battle of Dettingen. At the end of that summer's campaign, France briefly looked open to invasion. It was to counteract this that the French ministers gave their support to an invasion attempt against England in support of the Jacobites in late 1743. This was postponed because of prevarication on the part of English Tory Jacobites. The postponement was crucial to the eventual outcome of the attempt, which ended in disaster (for the Jacobites) when much of the invasion fleet was destroyed or dispersed by a storm in the spring of 1744. By the time of the 'Forty-Five, military circumstances had swung round again in favour of the French. France had launched a series of devastating campaigns in the Low Countries, an area of major strategic importance. (French control of the area rendered Britain much more vulnerable to invasion.) She was therefore much less committed to pursuing an invasion in support of the Jacobites. Bonnie Prince Charlie's flight to Scotland in the summer of 1745 was in part a desperate bid to precipitate French support for the Stuart cause.

EXERCISE 6
Read the above section, and comment on why, and under what conditions, foreign powers were prepared to offer support to a Jacobite restoration attempt.

One further point to note in this context is the importance of Sir Robert Walpole's pacific foreign policy, a policy which was most clearly delineated in the 1730s, and the extent to which this denied the Jacobites significant opportunities for winning foreign backing. The existence of an Anglo-French alliance between 1716 and 1731 also arguably had a crucial impact on Jacobite fortunes.

If foreign support was one precondition of a successful Jacobite rising in Scotland, another was almost certainly support for a rising south of the Border. No English government could have tolerated an independent Scotland ruled by a Catholic Stuart monarch. Monod (1989) provides a good summary of recent debates about the likelihood of an English rising emerging. It is noteworthy that in neither 1715 nor 1745–6 was this forthcoming, despite plotting amongst major English politicians and despite the promises of support made in 1745–6 by the Young Pretender to the Jacobite chiefs and commanders in Scotland. It is also interesting to note that George Lockhart assumed in 1725, when plans were being discussed for another rising, that Scotland's role was basically to divert British forces from the main theatre of conflict, England and London (see **Documents 11, 12 and**

13). The plan in 1715 was essentially similar. The only problem was that the anticipated foreign invasion did not take place: neither did a major English rising.

> EXERCISE 7
> **Documents 11, 12 and 13** are further extracts from the letters of George Lockhart. Read these and comment on Lockhart's views about the conditions under which a Jacobite restoration attempt might be successful.

One issue these documents raises very clearly is that of coordination and communication between Jacobite conspirators in different parts of Britain. It was the weakness of these that was, in part, responsible for the failure of English Jacobites to rise in any significant number in 1745.

4.1. The 'Fifteen

The 'Fifteen was incompetently conducted and even more weakly conceived. It was largely organised by a group of ex-Tory ministers. Apart from the Earl of Mar, other leading conspirators included the former Commander-in-Chief of the Army, the Duke of Ormonde, and the former Chancellor of the Exchequor, William Wyndham. Faced with the threat of prosecution and worse (loss of their heads) by a vengeful Whig ministry, Mar and his associates started to scheme to restore a Stuart to the throne. Their plans involved assembling numbers of Tories and Jacobites in different parts of Britain – the West Country, the Borders and the Highlands. The West Country rising would join up with a French invasion force and march on London. The flaw in the plan was a major one: the elderly Louis XIV was neither willing nor in a position to back an invasion. The death of Louis XIV in the late summer of 1715 and the succession of a minor, his great-grandson Louis XV, represented the extinction of any lingering hopes of this emerging. The French Regent, the Duke of Orléans, was his ward's next heir. He had no interest in seeing a major war in Europe break out again. Rather, like George I, he had an interest in stability and maintaining the status quo. It was this basic convergence of interests that resulted in the conclusion of the Anglo-French alliance in 1716.

By the time Mar raised the Jacobite standard at Braemar in September, moreover, the remaining prospects of success had diminished even further. Ormonde, a leading figure in the English conspiracy, had fled to France in early August. The government in London was aware of the conspiracy and took measures to thwart the plans of the Jacobites. These involved arresting large numbers of suspected Jacobites in England and Scotland. In England, the effect was to break the back of the conspiracy. Many a Tory-Jacobite who, under the influence of wine, had toasted the Pretender in the summer of 1715, failed to rise in the autumn. Historians of English politics of this period debate whether they ever intended to take their treason further than their cups (or glasses). Whatever the truth of the matter, the fact is that no leading member of the Anglican Tory gentry was out in the 'Fifteen.

In Scotland, as already referred to, the mass of support for a rising was arguably much greater. The government also had few forces at its disposal to counter the threat – the Duke of Argyll was massively outnumbered by Mar and the Jacobite army. It was Britain's luck, and Jacobitism's misfortune, that Mar was an incompetent military leader. Had he engaged government forces which were massed at the strategic stronghold of Stirling, the way was open for the Jacobites to forge a path south and to join up with lesser Jacobite forces in the Borders and in the north-west of England. In the event, Mar did not march on Edinburgh until November, and on 13 November fought an indecisive battle against Argyll's forces at Sherrifmuir. This was in practice a victory for the government. In England, the rising was petering out and officers in an outnumbered army, made up of largely Catholic Englishmen from the North-West, Lowlanders from the south-west of Scotland and a detachment from Mar's army under Mackintosh of Borlum, were negotiating its surrender. For the Jacobites, the final stages of the rising in Scotland were dismal. The Pretender arrived at Peterhead on 22 December. Argyll, now provided with a much larger army, marched on Perth in the third week of January. The Jacobite army, already demoralised, simply melted away and James threw his artillery into the Tay. The army retreated to Montrose, but were abandoned by James and Mar, who sailed to France on 4 February. The 'Fifteen had reached its inglorious end.

4.2. The 'Forty-Five

Black (1993a) has described the 'Forty-Five as the most serious crisis which faced the Hanoverians in the eighteenth century, and the nature of this crisis has excited endless debate in recent years. Much of this debate concerns responses in England and the opportunities which confronted the Jacobite army as it marched south through England to Derby. As far as Scotland is concerned, the 'Forty-Five exposed yet again the weakness and unpreparedness of government and government forces when faced with a significant military threat. To the astonishment of contemporaries, what was a tiny Jacobite army, around 1,500 before arrival at Edinburgh, was able to march unmolested down the spine of Scotland, force the country's capital to surrender to it, and then inflict defeat on harassed government forces under General John Cope at Prestonpans on 21 September 1745. That Britain was then engaged in a major European war, and most of her forces were committed on the Continent, makes the early stages of the 'Forty-Five only marginally less remarkable.

But the 'Forty-Five also demonstrated the fact that active support for Jacobitism had shrunk since 1715. Only a minority of Highland clans came out in support of the rising, and support from Lowland areas was much weaker than in 1715 (see Lenman 1984, 231–59). Many Jacobite chiefs and lairds, moreover, acted with marked equivocation faced with the dilemma of whether to commit themselves to the Young Pretender's cause. As we have already seen, Cameron of Lochiel rose only after extracting a promise from the Young Pretender that he would receive money for his troubles, something which reflected in part his desperate financial straits in this period, but also his recognition that without French support a restoration attempt was likely to fail. It may also have reflected a recognition that the penalties of failure were going to be much worse than in 1715.

After a six-week stay in Edinburgh, and after prolonged argument, the Jacobite army, now around 5,000 strong, began to march south into England. By this stage, the government was fully aware of the threat posed by the rebellion, and was mobilising major forces to meet it, one army being led by the Duke of Cumberland. Under the skilful leadership of Lord George Murray, the Jacobite army not only eluded these forces, but at one stage got between them and London. The French were also preparing an invasion fleet to support the rebellion. Major towns fell to the Jacobites, including the castle at Carlisle (15 November), and on 4 December they arrived at Derby. This, however, was the beginning of the end of the rising, for it was at Derby that the fateful decision was taken to retreat. As Black (1993a, 115) has written, this and not Culloden 'signalled the end of the '45 and the failure of Jacobitism'.

Ironically perhaps, it was nationalism, which was so important to Scottish Jacobitism, that was to prove one factor in its undoing in 1745–6. This is because

No. 4. Bronze medal of Prince Charles Edward Stewart in tartan, 1745, possibly intended to be sewn on a garment. © *The Trustees of the National Museums of Scotland.*

frictions arose between the ambitions of the Young Pretender – to regain the English as well as Scottish crowns – and the Jacobite chiefs and commanders from Scotland. What made these frictions all the more destructive was the fact that Bonnie Prince Charlie had promised his Scots allies that French and English support for the rising would be forthcoming. The Prince's relationship with a number of Irish Jacobites in his contingent was a further source of tension. It was these pressures and tensions that came to a head at Derby on 4 and 5 December. The discussions at the crucial council of war, on 5 December, were later described by Lord Elcho, who had been present at them. Following are some extracts from Elcho's account:

> The 5 in the morning Lord George Murray and all the Commanders of Batallions and Squadrons waited upon the Prince, and Lord George told him that it was the opinion of Every body present that the Scots had now done all that could be Expected of them. That they had marched into the heart of England ready to join any party that would declare for him, that none had, and that the Counties through which the Army had pass'd Seemed much more Enemies than friends to his Cause, that their was no French landed in England, and that if their was any party in England for him, it was very odd that they had never so much as Either sent him money or intelligence or the least advice what to do, but if he Could produce any letter from any person of distinction in which their was an invitation for the army to go to London, or to any other part of England, that they were ready to go. But if nobody had either invited them or meddled in the least in their affairs, it was to be Supposed that their was either no party at all, or if their was they did not chuse to act with them, or else they would ere now have lett them know it. Suppose even the Army march'd on and beat the Duke of Cumberland yett in the Battle they must Lose some men, and they had after that the Kings own army consisting of 7000 men near London to deal with. One the contrary, if either of these armies beat them, their would not be a man Escape . . . And so the people that were in arms in Scotland would fall an Easy Sacrifice to the fury of the Government . . .

> So he [Lord George Murray] Said his Opinion was they Should go back and join their friends in Scotland, and live and die with them, and the French (who at Derby the Army Learned had landed in Scotland with Lord John Drummond but did not know the numbers but believed 4000 men) . . .

> It was urged too that Wades Army, who was following, must likewise be fought with as the other two armies would certainly Stop the Princes by fighting or other Methods, which would give Wade time enough to come up. The Prince heard all these arguments with the greatest impatience, fell into a passion and gave most of the Gentlemen that had Spoke very Abusive Language and said that they had a mind to betray him . . .

His Irish favourites to pay court to him had always represented the whole nation
as his friends, had diminished much all the force that was Against him & he
himself believed firmly That the Soldiers of the Regulars would never dare fight
against him, as he was Their true prince . . .

The Scots were all against it [marching on to London]; so at Night the Prince
Sent for them and told them he consented to go to Scotland, And at the same
time he told them that for the future he would have no more Councills, for he
would neither ask nor take their Advice, that he was Accountable to nobody for
his Actions but to his Father . . .

(quoted in Charteris 1907, 336–41)

The view of Lord George Murray and the Scots which prevailed – to return to
Scotland and secure the Stuart cause there – was a brave one, but wrongheaded.
Jacobitism in one country could not work, a fact that was to be discovered in a
brutally short space of time.

EXERCISE 8
Read the extracts from Elcho's account of the council of war at Derby on 5
December 1745, and comment on the attitudes revealed in them.

It is perhaps worth noting the petulant authoritarianism of the Young Pretender. His
determination not to listen to his most skilled commanders, particularly Lord
George Murray, was a major factor in the military disaster which overtook the
Jacobite cause at Culloden in April of the following year.

Many people in England assumed after the retreat from Derby that the rising
was all but over. The final stages of the rebellion involved, however, a series of
admittedly minor Jacobite victories – Clifton, Falkirk, Inverurie, the fall of Fort
Augustus – before the rebellion was finally crushed on Drumossie Moor on 16 April
1746. There was also a fascinating minor end game, which illustrates perhaps the
desperation of Jacobite chiefs and also the surges of (false) optimism that could still
course through Jacobite veins. This involved plans for continuing the campaign in
the Highlands with French support (see Gibson 1994). It is the existence of plans
such as these that makes some of the savage incidents of repression that followed the
battle in the Highlands understandable, if appalling, in their often indiscriminate
nature and brutality.

EXERCISE 9
Using material from the present chapter, identify the major points of similarity
and difference between the 'Fifteen and the 'Forty-Five. Try to assess which came
closer to succeeding. Remember to consider in this context the wider British and
European perspectives. See also the discussion of Jacobite failures and weakening
support below.

> Read **Article 2** by Hill and comment on the role of military technology and tactics in the failure of Jacobitism. Faced with far superior force, firepower and logistical organisation, was it merely a question of time before the Jacobites were defeated in 1745-6?

It is worth emphasising in this context that the Jacobite army in 1745–6 was not the Highland rabble of popular myth. It contained officers with considerable military experience and expertise. It was also organised along conventional military lines. It was, however, heavily reliant on surprise, on the capacity of its attacking infantry to disrupt and inflict terror on its opponents. Such tactics could only work under certain conditions.

5. THE FAILURE OF JACOBITISM

Why did Jacobitism fail? In recent years, it has become fashionable to stress the role of contingency in this, the role of chance. Attempts to suggest deeper-rooted causes are likely to be greeted with cries of writing history from the standpoint of the victors. There is something in this; we should not write the Jacobites out of history, nor should we downplay the magnitude of the threat that the Jacobites posed to the Hanoverian regime as late as the 1740s. It is also necessary to acknowledge that much depended on international affairs, which were in this period notably unpredictable and susceptible to rapid changes. But equally, history should be about explaining movement and change, and it is possible to suggest reasons why Jacobitism was a weakening force in Scottish society, certainly by the 1730s.

5.1. A record of failure and misadventure

To succeed, and to nurture active or potentially active support, Jacobitism could not afford too many demoralising failures. Yet it suffered these repeatedly, most obviously the 'Fifteen, but also the 'Nineteen. The effects of this were simply compounded by time. The longer the Stuarts were across the water, the more difficult it became to imagine their return, the easier it became to acquiesce in the status quo. In 1727, on George I's death, there was talk of another rebellion. James actually moved himself to the duchy of Lorraine in preparation for this. George Lockhart was, by this time, so disillusioned that he firmly urged James to abandon the notion and return to Italy.

5.2. Improving economic conditions

As Colley (1992) has recently emphasised, the appeal of the status quo may also have grown in the 1720s and certainly by the 1730s. This was because the Scottish merchants and businessmen had by then responded to the economic challenges opened up by the Union and were beginning to prosper. There were also efforts made, through institutions like the Royal Bank of Scotland and the Board of

Manufactures and Fisheries, to make the Union work more effectively. This changing economic outlook may not have produced enthusiasm for Hanoverian rule and the Union, but it is likely to have made open opposition to it much weaker. Rebellion, bringing with it civil war and armies, threatened the livelihood of many people. In Stirling during the 'Forty-Five, local fishermen found their trade totally disrupted, as did colliers in Fife.

5.3. Growing anti-Jacobite sentiment

Inertia may also have become its own justification. A pragmatic attachment to the status quo may have taken a steadily intensifying hold on important elements of Scottish society. In this context, it is striking not how little support Bonnie Prince Charlie gained in 1745, but how much active anti-Jacobite activity and demonstration in Scotland there was. The extent of this has almost certainly been underestimated by historians. But if the evidence of the Scottish press and much contemporary correspondence is to be believed, it was very widespread, not just in obvious Presbyterian strongholds such as Glasgow, but also in less likely locations such as the burghs of Fife or even in Aberdeen in the episcopalian North-East. In some sections of society, hostility or indifference had replaced enthusiasm and active support.

5.4. Consequences of failure

Jacobitism's failure had far-reaching effects on Scotland, although disentangling these from other forces and factors can be difficult (see the comments in Smout 1969, 224–5). Most importantly, it accelerated the integration of Scotland into Britain, forcibly and bloodily in the case of the Highlands. This integration is one of the most important strands in Scotland's history in the eighteenth century. It is a development that had many roots. From the perspective of Jacobitism, however, what perhaps stands out is the role of armed force. It was armed force that, ultimately, held the Union together before the mid-century. If we are looking for surviving symbols of this fact, we would do well to look no further than the massive fortress of Fort George at Ardersier Point near Inverness, built after the 'Forty-Five, which cost over £100,000 to build. As Black (1993b, 50) has noted, this fortress symbolised the power on which the political system rested; it also symbolised the determination of successive ministries to enforce the policies and politics of Westminster politicians throughout the British Isles. How far this was accompanied by the growth of a genuine sense of Britishness, in England and Scotland, is something that is worth considering.

REFERENCES TO BOOKS AND ARTICLES MENTIONED IN THE TEXT

Black, J 1985 *British Foreign Policy in the Age of Walpole*. Edinburgh.
Black, J 1988 'Jacobitism and British Foreign Policy, 1731–5', *in* Cruickshanks, E and Black, J (eds), *The Jacobite Challenge*, Edinburgh, 142–60.

*Black, J 1993a *Culloden and the '45*. Stroud.

Black, J 1993b *The Politics of Britain: 1688–1800*. Manchester.

Charteris, E (ed) 1907 *Lord David Elcho: A short Account of the Affairs of Scotland in the Year 1744, 1745, 1746*. Edinburgh.

*Colley, L 1992 *Britons: Forging the Nation, 1707–1837*. New Haven and London.

Donaldson, W 1988 *The Jacobite Song: Political Myth and National Identity*. Aberdeen.

*Gibson, JS 1988 *Playing the Jacobite Card: the Franco-Jacobite Invasion of 1708*. Edinburgh.

*Gibson, JS 1994 *Lochiel of the '45: The Jacobite Chief and the Prince*. Edinburgh.

Gregg, E 1982 'The Jacobite Career of John, Earl of Mar', *in* Cruickshanks, E (ed), *Ideology and Conspiracy: Aspects of Jacobitism, 1689–1759*, Edinburgh, 179–200.

Hill, JM 1986 *Celtic Warfare 1595–1763*. Edinburgh.

*Lenman, BP 1980 *The Jacobite Risings in Britain, 1689–1746*. London (reprinted in 1995, Aberdeen).

Lenman, BP 1982 'The Scottish Episcopal Clergy and the Ideology of Jacobitism', *in* Cruickshanks, E (ed), *Ideology and Conspiracy*, Edinburgh, 36–48.

*Lenman, BP 1984 *The Jacobite Clans of the Great Glen, 1650–1784*. London (reprinted in 1995, Aberdeen).

Macinnes, AI 1996 *Clanship, Commerce and the House of Stuart, 1603–1788*. East Linton.

Monod, PK 1989 *Jacobitism and the English People, 1688–1788*. Cambridge.

*Pittock, M 1994 *Poetry and Jacobite Politics in Eighteenth-Century Britain and Ireland*. Cambridge.

Pittock, M 1995 *The Myth of the Jacobite Clans*. Edinburgh.

Smith, LB 1987 'Spain and the Jacobites, 1715–16', *in* Cruickshanks, E (ed), *Ideology and Conspiracy*, Edinburgh, 159–78.

*Smout, T C 1969 *A History of the Scottish People, 1560–1830*. Glasgow.

**Szechi, D (ed) 1989 *Letters of George Lockhart of Carnwath*. Scottish History Society.

*Szechi, D 1994 *The Jacobites: Britain and Europe, 1688–1788*. Manchester.

*Tayler A and Tayler, H 1928 *Jacobites of Aberdeen and Banffshire in the Forty-Five*. Aberdeen.

Tomasson, K 1958 *The Jacobite General*. Edinburgh.

Whatley, CA 1990 'How tame were the Scottish Lowlanders during the Eighteenth Century?', *in* Devine, TM (ed), *Conflict and Stability in Scottish Society 1700–1850*, Edinburgh, 1–30.

Youngson, AJ 1985 *The Prince and the Pretender: A Study in the Writing of History*. London.

FURTHER READING

Those references marked * in the above list are recommended further reading, along with the following:

Black, J 1995 'Military Aspects of the '45', *in* Lynch, M (ed), *Jacobitism and the '45*, 49–57.

Cruickshanks E (ed) 1982 *Ideology and Conspiracy: Aspects of Jacobitism, 1689–1759*. Edinburgh.

Cruickshanks, E and Black, J (eds) 1988 *The Jacobite Challenge*. Edinburgh.

Insh, GP 1952 *The Scottish Jacobite Movement*. Edinburgh.

Lynch, M (ed) 1995 *Jacobitism and the '45*. London.

McLynn, FJ 1981 *France and the Jacobite Rising of 1745*. Edinburgh.
Tayler A and Tayler H 1934 *Jacobites of Aberdeen and Banffshire in the Rising of 1715*. Aberdeen.

SOME PUBLISHED PRIMARY SOURCES

Those references marked ** in the list of references referred to in the text are published primary sources which may be of interest, as are the following:

Blaikie, WB (ed) 1975 *Origins of the 'Forty-Five*. Edinburgh.
Lenman, BP and Gibson JS (eds) 1990 *The Jacobite Threat: a Source Book*. Edinburgh.
Seton, Sir BG and Arnot, JG (eds) 1928–9 *The Prisoners of the '45*. Scottish History Society.
Warrand, D (ed) 1923–30 *More Culloden Papers*. Inverness (5 volumes).

Politics

Michael Fry

INTRODUCTION

In this chapter we shall examine Scottish politics from the Union till the mid-nineteenth century, a period spanning events both of British national importance, such as the Irish Union of 1801 or the Reform Act of 1832, and of international importance, including revolutions in America, France and other European countries. Scotland was much quieter, perhaps inevitably after the traumatic experience of the Union of 1707 and the two main Jacobite rebellions. You have already studied these and their effects. But history does not consist simply of crises, and the normal political processes may well reveal more about what was really going on: certainly the crises are better understood against that background. So here our concerns are more directly with how Scotland was governed and how Scottish politics worked.

We shall approach the subject under the following headings:

- Changing perceptions and historiography
- The shape of Scottish politics
- The course of Scottish politics
- The meaning of Scottish politics

By the time you have completed this chapter and the associated reading, you should have a good understanding of the mechanics of Scottish government and of the influence of politics on the social, economic and cultural developments of the period.

I. CHANGING PERCEPTIONS AND HISTORIOGRAPHY

According to Smout, the politics of Scotland after the Union became 'so moribund as to be scarcely relevant any longer to a general history of Scottish society' (Smout 1969, 218). Thirty years on, a good many historians still seem to agree with his verdict, to judge from the rather meagre amount of political history written in the meantime, compared to social or economic history. The idea that Scottish politics do not matter very much, and are provincial and boring when set beside British or even purely English politics, has a long pedigree. It is also an idea we owe to Scots rather than to English scholars, one which goes back to the mid-nineteenth century. In passing the Reform Act of 1832, the Whigs defeated the Tories and swept away the political system which had evolved under the Union. This was a prelude to rapid, radical and destructive changes in the national institutions which the Treaty intended to preserve. The most obvious example was the Disruption of the Church of Scotland in 1843 which brought bitter sectarianism into every area of public life. In particular, it forced wholesale reorganisation of the schools and universities, often under anglicising pressures. The existing apparatus of Scots law seemed powerless to prevent any of this. There followed, according to contemporaries and to most later observers, a widespread erosion of native values and customs. It was by no means uncommon to regard the history of Scotland as over and done with: the future seemed beyond any question to lie in a Greater Britain and in the Empire. William Law Mathieson, writing in the early twentieth century, completed his work as follows: 'The ecclesiastical history of Scotland, in so far as it concerns the national historian, may thus be said to end in 1843, as the political history had ended with the abolition of the Scottish representative system in 1832' (Mathieson 1916, 373).

From the early twentieth century until the upsurge of Nationalism in recent times, next to no modern Scottish political history was written: to all intents and purposes, the subject did not exist. With the head removed, as it were, from the body politic, historians attended mainly to the body, to the life of the people. In a sense this reinforced Scotland's provincial status, since the dominant school of English history was still obsessed with high politics, with the Mother of Parliaments, with the processes by which British institutions had been perfected and with the activities of the few hundred people in London who had charge of the processes at any given time. But it was not as if Scots scholars led the way in social history either: their mentality and their methods remained old-fashioned, unsystematic and anecdotal, till Smout transformed the scene. When the originator of the older Scottish school, Henry Grey Graham, first went into print in 1895, he actually apologised for not being able to accept, as any English historian would, the primacy of politics in his chosen period, the eighteenth century. It was because Scottish politics consisted in:

> . . . obscure intrigues and factions, Whig and Tory, Presbyterian and Jacobite, who were servile followers of English ministries, manoeuvres of Scots nobles and placemen who travel southwards on horseback or in coach to win favour with great statesmen at Westminster or courtiers at St James – figures not very real to us today as they flit across the stage, 'transient and embarrassed phantoms'. To the end of the century . . . political life in North Britain was virtually non-existent.
>
> (Graham 1937, vi)

Graham's judgement is now impossible to sustain, for several reasons. The first is that historians have entirely revised their view of the nature of English politics in the eighteenth century. What used to be received wisdom is now laughed at as ludicrous caricature: the myth that philosopher kings gathered at Westminster and were constantly engaged in serene contemplation of how to reconcile the imperial destiny of England with her ancient constitution of liberty. The revisionist historian, Sir Lewis Namier, showed that, on the contrary, while men of vision were doubtless present, large numbers of English politicians were certainly no better and possibly rather worse than those we see today, mediocre men in the game for personal advancement whose lives were consumed in petty manoeuvres, intrigues and squabbles with constituents below them or statesmen above them. In other words, English MPs of the eighteenth century were certainly no better and possibly rather worse than Scots MPs of the eighteenth century. So it is, to say the least, perverse to ascribe high importance to such activity when it is carried on by one set of MPs, but absolute insignificance when it is carried on by another.

The second reason is the discovery that Scotland had what could reasonably be called a political system, a fact denied during the middle of this century when the academic literature was fixated on a theory of British homogeneity. An apparatus of government in Edinburgh and a range of institutions round it, partly inherited and partly created in recognition of Scottish distinctiveness, were closely linked to wider circles of civil society. The whole moved and acted in ways impossible to understand as just a regional variant of the English system, perhaps most clearly in the electoral results. The present governmental apparatus dates from the end of the nineteenth century, but it had antecedents going back at least to the Union. If much of our public life is still shaped by the Church, by Scots law and by the proud traditions of Scottish education, it is because the deal struck in 1707 ensured that this would be the case. So strong was the influence of the national institutions in the first century of the Union that historians have even called that a period of semi-independence: Scotland retained a high degree of internal autonomy and waived only a say in foreign affairs which she had lost anyway. Clearly the influence has meanwhile weakened. Yet in some form or other it has just as clearly been continuous. We can therefore be justified in saying that the Scottish political system did not spring up in the recent past, but is the outcome of a process of development stretching back over three centuries and more.

The third reason is the evidence of contemporaries. It was especially hard for an older school of historians to see Scottish politics in action when they would not look. Now that a younger school has started to examine the national records with that in mind, an enormous wealth of material stands revealed, much of it still to be explored thoroughly. The papers of Henry Dundas (1742–1811), political boss of Scotland, amounted to one of the half-dozen largest extant British archives of his era. It is obvious from his papers that Dundas corresponded on a wide range of major and minor political matters with everyone of importance all over Scotland, and with many of no importance. On a popular level we find also that Robert Burns composed political poems, often with Scottish subjects, and that Walter Scott included political material in his works, while another writer, John Galt, might almost be regarded as primarily a political novelist. They each dealt with Scottish issues patently familiar to the thousands who read their books. The origins of the modern higher journalism can be traced back to the *Edinburgh Review*, first published in 1802, and to the rivals which followed it. They devoted column after column to Scottish politics. It is undeniable from all this that contemporaries saw the semi-independent political system in Scotland as important, wanted to know about it and affect it so far as its rules allowed. It would be an act of breathtaking arrogance on our part to conclude that they were wasting their time.

> EXERCISE 1
> Reflecting on this discussion, why do you think perceptions of Scottish politics in the eighteenth century have changed?

Earlier historians dismissed Scottish political activity as parochial, but modern scholarship has revealed that British political activity was, in general, parochial in much the same way. Only a little of all the parliamentary effort at Westminster went on the great issues of the time. Perhaps, then, Scottish political activity was not so much inferior as different, even semi-independent. Inquiry into the workings of the national institutions, as into contemporary publications and manuscripts, gives some support to this view.

2. THE SHAPE OF SCOTTISH POLITICS

Before 1707, Scotland was governed by the monarch, by his or her officers of state, most in Edinburgh but some in practice resident in London, and by a Parliament of three estates – nobility, shires and burghs – all sitting in one chamber. Though a Scottish political system survived after 1707, it is not so easy to describe. The Treaty of Union, while going into exhaustive detail on certain technical subjects, and setting out solemn guarantees on the matters of most importance to the Scots, said little about how the United Kingdom would work. Scotland's presence in the Parliament at Westminster was specified (45 MPs and 16 representative peers), but nothing else was said on the purely political arrangements. The likeliest explanation is that the commissioners who drew up the Treaty simply did not know how, or perhaps if, it would work.

At one extreme was the possibility that the country would be turned into 'Scotlandshire' and would simply be taken over by the English. In the early years of the Union, some unwelcome changes were made which might indicate that was the real intention. The Scottish Privy Council, which most had expected to take charge of day-to-day administration, was abolished. Parliament brought back lay patronage into the Church of Scotland in 1712, in defiance of the presbyterian settlement of 1690 and of the Act of Security (1706) safeguarding it, under which congregations were to elect their ministers. Then the Government levied taxes which the Treaty had expressly prohibited. These moves struck the Scots as so obnoxious that in 1713 a group of peers moved for dissolution of the Union, and were only narrowly defeated in the House of Lords. The Jacobite rebellion of 1715, which won unexpectedly wide support, revealed how discontented the Scots really were. The Government seemed to realise that casual abuse of the terms of the Union had gone too far, and was afterwards more respectful of Scottish opinion (Phillipson 1970, 140).

These disputes ironically revealed the robustness of a Treaty which did not say too much. Scotland would never become Scotlandshire because, in the end, that was impossible. The preserved national institutions were so distinctive that they could only be manned by Scots: it would be no use trying to put Anglican vicars into the Kirk, or English barristers into the courts, or dons from Oxford and Cambridge into the universities. Altogether, the option of, in effect, repudiating the Treaty and treating Scotland as a conquered province had little to recommend it. While the Hanoverian regime in England was engaged in European wars and imperial expansion, that option would only ask for trouble from a neighbour nation willing to co-operate if its promised rights were honoured in practice, and which showed it was ready to cause a great deal of trouble if they were not. Obviously the more sensible course was to leave well alone. At the same time, the Government had a legitimate interest in seeing that Scotland remained loyal and tranquil: the removal of a threat to England's security by the back door was her main motive for the Union. The solution lay in compromise, in devising arrangements acceptable to both sides.

If we posit a continuing political system, we would expect it not just to reflect Anglo-Scottish relations but also to show a domestic face. Assuming the notion of semi-independence has some substance, Scots ought to have been able to treat with the English, but then also to decide some things for themselves. A compromise on these lines could hardly be straightforward, though, when the Union brought such upheaval in the political system. A chief Minister, now Secretary of State for Scotland, was still in post, but as a member of the British Cabinet (and usually treated as a junior one). Other offices of state vanished, with the major exceptions of the Lord Advocate and Solicitor General, in charge of the legal system. As already stated, the Privy Council was abolished. The MPs and peers sat at Westminster, so there was no longer any debate in the chamber of the Scots Parliament in Edinburgh, now turned into law courts. All down the line, the apparatus by which Scotland had governed herself was pruned, and many lost their jobs. Some compensation came as the British state extended its own structure. For example, Adam Smith senior, father of the founder of economic science, had been clerk to the Scottish military court. After 1707, when the armies of Scotland and England merged, he was unemployed. He suffered some years of hardship before being appointed to Kirkcaldy, in charge of a branch of the new customs service introduced in all Scottish ports; there his son was born. Not everyone had such luck, and the Union brought rising demands from the middle ranks of Scottish society for jobs in England and the colonies. The provision of them through a machinery of patronage would become a central political concern (Murdoch 1980, 11).

As in all representative systems, one way of channelling and managing such demands was through political parties. Here too, Scotland remained distinct: indeed in the whole period since 1707, Scottish political behaviour has mirrored or conformed to English political behaviour only for relatively short stretches of time. The Scots Parliament had contained discernible parties, though they were much looser than anything today, with the personal bonds among their members counting for more than their commitments on policy, or even ideology. Still, one clear ideological contrast lay between Whigs and Jacobites. Whigs on the whole (though not unanimously) supported the Union, the Hanoverian succession and the presbyterian settlement in the Kirk, all of which they identified with liberty. Jacobites opposed all three: they wanted an independent Scotland under the ancient royal House of Stewart, with the Crown appointing bishops to rule over the Church of Scotland, and they generally stressed the advantages for society of obedience to God-given authority. In the first Parliaments after the Union, Jacobites maintained a fair presence. But the rising of 1715 put them beyond the pale politically. The outspoken George Lockhart of Carnwath, the Stewarts' principal agent in Scotland, held his seat of Midlothian till the General Election of 1722. After he went out, it was rare for Jacobites to be elected, and as a parliamentary force they dissolved.

Politics for the rest of the eighteenth century was conducted within a broad, diffuse coalition of Whigs, more or less agreed on a few principles but nearly always split on policies and personalities. Another division which preceded and survived the Union was between Court and Country or, in homelier terms, between the 'ins' and the 'outs': literally a division between men holding office, with their supporters and dependants, and men who for one reason or another had been passed over but hoped to topple those in power. Parties did not go to the polls as united bodies with a recognised leader who, if he won, assumed office by virtue of that. Instead they were collections of factions grouped round a range of prominent figures, from whom the King was free to choose his Ministers as he liked. Once he had done so, the Cabinet set about gathering a parliamentary majority – as a rule after the election, not before. Broadly speaking, the factions which came together in the majority then formed the Court party, and those left out formed the Country party. Since Governments could change within a single Parliament, which from 1715 sat for seven years at a time, it was quite possible for an MP to find himself sometimes in the one and sometimes in the other. In Scotland, however, there survived a core of Country Whigs normally though not always acting together. They were known for their opportunism as the Squadrone Volante (Italian: the flying squadron), and it was by their votes that the Treaty of Union had been passed in the teeth of hostile public opinion. They claimed they were truer to their principles than the Court party, which merely did whatever the Government wanted. But in standards of political behaviour there was in reality little to choose between the two (Fry 1992, 18).

Amid such individualistic politics, the ability and conduct of each MP was of the first importance to his constituents. To some extent, this compensated for the fact that so few Scots had the vote. The Union did not affect the existing qualifications. In the counties, they limited the franchise in effect to large landowners. In the burghs, the MPs were chosen by the town councils, but since councillors elected their own successors at the end of their terms (and often re-elected themselves), the arrangements here were even less democratic. Voters in the counties numbered about 2,500, and in the burghs about 1,500, in a population which passed one million some time early in the eighteenth century. It was a narrow, oligarchical system and it became open to corruption as time went on. Still, the extent of the franchise is not perhaps the sole criterion on which a political system should be judged, especially in the

No. 5. Portrait of John Campbell, 2nd Duke of Argyll, by William Aikman.
© *Scottish National Portrait Gallery.*

eighteenth century when in most European countries nobody had the vote, and when even in the freer societies stiff qualifications had to be met to acquire it (Sher 1982, 202).

In the Scottish counties, all electors were men of wealth and standing. They expected their MP, usually one of their own neighbours, to represent them in such a way as to reflect credit on himself and the county, to express their views at the centre of power in London and to be efficient in pursuit of their interests. Once a year they met to regulate the affairs of the constituency, and on these occasions they often discussed what he had done, or called him to account if he had displeased them. There were several instances of what we would call deselection. Some scholars have seen in this a distinctive Scottish political convention which made the MP a delegate of his constituents, sent to Westminster to carry out their instructions, rather than a man with the representative status set out in English constitutional doctrine, always ready to listen to his constituents but in the end exercising his judgement independently (Whetstone 1981).

In the burghs, public spirit was less obvious. In fact most fell under the control of landed interests in the surrounding counties, and their politics was a mere extension of what went on there. The larger burghs, especially Edinburgh, were more independent. In a period of rapid urban expansion, when public financial resources were small, the councils tended to attract men, or their agents, interested in speculative developments of various kinds. They stood ready to put private capital into their burghs and they expected, through control of the council, to gain back profit or influence. It can be said in favour of this system that it did indeed bring successful urban expansion. Edinburgh, Glasgow and Aberdeen grew into some of the finest cities in Europe during the era before industrialisation, and if we look round the many historic small burghs of Scotland we can see that these people were not just jerry-building. Equally, however, the system had obvious drawbacks.

EXERCISE 2

Look back over the discussion in this section, and think about the following questions:
1. Why did the Scottish national institutions survive?
2. How did political parties work in the Scotland of the eighteenth century?
3. What were the effects of the electoral system?

These are key questions, so if you are in any doubt, re-read the section. The national institutions survived because they had vital social functions, because they enjoyed legal status under the Treaty of Union and because, despite contrary temptations, no better means were on hand to keep Scotland loyal and orderly. One prime task for political parties was to distribute patronage and ensure that their own supporters manned the national institutions, tasks sometimes carried out in competition and sometimes in co-operation with other parties. In general, these were looser formations than their modern equivalents, though their rivalry could be real enough. All business was conducted on a much more personal basis than we are used to nowadays, not least because of the very small electorate, with power kept firmly in the hands of the landed class.

3. THE COURSE OF SCOTTISH POLITICS

Amid the upheaval of the Union, Scotland went first through a period of disorientation, not helped by the cavalier English attitude towards the terms of the Treaty in the years immediately after 1707. At Westminster it was a time of fierce partisanship. Before 1715, the parliamentary term was only three years. General Elections produced huge swings and Whig or Tory Governments rapidly followed each other in and out. It was sneeringly noted that the Scots MPs seemed to follow whichever held power, but as a form of insurance that proved not always successful. Your volume of documents contains a sharp exchange between Lockhart of Carnwath and the Chancellor of the Exchequer, Robert Harley, which gives something of the flavour of the period (**Document 14**).

In 1714 Queen Anne, last of the Stewarts, died. She was succeeded by the Elector of Hanover, George I. The Jacobites made their bid to restore the Old Pretender the following year, and failed. After that, the overwhelming need of the new regime, completely dominated by Whigs, was stability. The man who provided it in England was Sir Robert Walpole, Prime Minister from 1721 to 1742, who still holds the record for the longest time in the job. He was an unscrupulous but shrewd politician, and he realised that the problem of ruling Scotland had not yet been solved. He decided that the best course would be to rely on a Scot, who could be left to do much as he liked so long as he kept his own country quiet, and would normally be free of erratic interference by ignorant Englishmen.

The man he chose to manage Scotland in this way was John Campbell, 2nd Duke of Argyll. The Campbells had a traditional role as the instrument of central government in the Highlands, and stood high in the regard of all patriotic, presbyterian Scotsmen for their sacrifices in the national causes of the seventeenth century. Argyll himself had had a distinguished military career, and supported the Union in 1707 but also the dissolution of the Union in 1713. As commander-in-chief of the army in Scotland, he suppressed the Jacobite rising. Not a person of profound principles, he was all the same an able and eloquent politician. On behalf of Walpole, he set out to unify, satisfy and pacify Scotland. By and large he succeeded. You can see that Sir Walter Scott, writing about him a century later, still held his personal qualities in high esteem.

EXERCISE 3
Read **Document 15**. What was Scott's opinion of 'John, Duke of Argyle and Greenwich'?

Note that the chapter is headed with a quotation from a ballad implying that the duke was not a consistent or even a reliable man. The rest of the passage is concerned to refute that allegation. Scott stresses that Argyll was rather apolitical and circumspect, which made him no great favourite in London. But the air of detachment about him gave his opinions great weight at a crucial moment.

The reversals of fortune accompanying the Hanoverian succession had thrown the Court party into confusion, so from 1715 the Scottish administration was entrusted to the Squadrone, with the Duke of Roxburghe as Secretary of State. He and his lieutenants were slow to co-operate with Walpole, and in due course found themselves eased out. Instead the Court party reformed round Argyll, and for that reason was from now on also often known as the Argathelian party (from the Latin for Argyll). At the General Election of 1722, the Duke triumphed in Scotland. But he moved cautiously to extend his control. For three years, he kept Roxburghe and the other Ministers from the Squadrone in office. He chose his moment to get rid of them, and did so without trouble in 1725 when they opposed the Government's proposal to impose a malt tax on Scotland. Argyll did not take office as Secretary of State himself but allowed the job to go into abeyance, as too much of a focus for disaffection. He was now free, though, to build a system of management.

One element which Argyll tackled was control of the parliamentary representation. He lobbied the constituencies to elect his own followers. If he failed, he would often try to reverse the result at the polls by alleging technical irregularity. On those grounds, Argyll could usually rely on Walpole's majority in the Commons to unseat the offending MP. At his height, he controlled all but half-a-dozen Scottish seats. For the elections of representative peers, he developed the convention of the King's list, by which the Government named in advance those it wished chosen. Beyond that, Argyll paid close attention to the Church of Scotland and the universities, since clergymen did so much to form public opinion, and the universities educated them. The ministry still had an evangelical or even a covenanting character, a tendency to hurl fire and brimstone from the pulpit and to excite the people, mostly over their own sins, but sometimes over the sins of their rulers. The Duke preferred a more docile Kirk. With the help of lay patronage, much of it in the hands of the Crown, he followed a policy of appointing ministers more sedate in opinion and expression, who gradually gained control of the General Assembly. In the universities, Argyll looked for men of intellectual distinction rather than of religious orthodoxy. Glasgow, where the college was run by Campbells, became an early centre of the Enlightenment, notably with the philosopher Francis Hutcheson. Later, David Hume and Adam Smith both benefited from Argathelian patronage.

Altogether, Argyll made patronage the central activity of Scottish politics, more important than policies or ideologies. It was not abnormal for the age, and he tried to work it wisely. It fitted the character of a hierarchical society, where most people felt a dependency on those above them, who in turn acknowledged that dependency and sought to reward it. So it was easy for one man or a few of his supporters at the top to manage a small country. A break in his network of personal connections brought Argyll's career to an end. Walpole was always very strong on law and order. He felt outraged in 1736 when Edinburgh suffered the Porteous Riot, famously described in the opening chapter of Scott's *Heart of Midlothian*. The Prime Minister determined to exact retribution for the defiance of authority, with humiliating penalties on the capital of Scotland. This was too much for Argyll who, whatever his principles, had a high sense of honour (Fry 1992, 9–11). He opposed the measures, in the terms reported by Scott (**Document 15**).

EXERCISE 4
Look again at **Document 15** for confirmation of Scott's views on Argyll in the aftermath of the Porteous Riot of 1736.

There is no need to comment on this further, but note the unionism, rather than nationalism, that Scott chooses to bring out: the idea that the Union rightly interpreted is good for both parties to it.

With the Duke of Argyll out of favour – and dead a few months later – the Argathelian party suffered heavy losses at the General Election of 1742. The Squadrone now came back, with the Marquis of Tweeddale as Secretary of State. He made some attempt to dismantle the Argathelian apparatus, but his weakness and idleness were cruelly exposed by the incompetence of the Scottish administration during the Jacobite rising of 1745. He was sacked in January 1746, once the Highland army had turned back from Derby. For good measure, his job was abolished. That may have given satisfaction to the more hawkishly anti-Scottish Ministers in London, but still left the problem of how to rule Scotland. Some argued that the Scots had shown themselves so unreliable that the rest of their national institutions should be abolished if at all likely to cause more trouble. Once again, however, the practicalities of creating a Scotlandshire proved too daunting.

The mere suggestion panicked the Scottish factions into burying the hatchet. The Squadrone and the Argathelians moved into coalition, co-operating on policy, sharing the parliamentary representation and the major offices. The 3rd Duke of Argyll spent most of his time in London, and was content to have his affairs organised at home by a loyal lieutenant, the judge Lord Milton. The head of the Squadrone, Robert Dundas of Arniston, had been Lord Advocate under Tweeddale, then in 1748 became Lord President of the Court of Session. The public business of the country was, then, conducted by officials, usually with some legal experience. It never made for lively politics but at least, amid a crisis and without a Secretary of State, the Scots managed to retrieve an arrangement they could run themselves.

It did not work too badly. A united front was consciously presented to the English, because quarrels within Scotland had proved ruinous. Reforms constitutional in the sense of entailing amendment to the Treaty of Union were introduced. That was the practical effect of abolishing heritable jurisdictions, under which, in about a third of Scotland, justice had been wielded by local noblemen, not by the central courts in Edinburgh. The system, while guaranteed in the Treaty, seemed to the English to have preserved the social conditions which made rebellion possible, through keeping clansmen in subjection to their chiefs. With different emphasis, most Scots now agreed: the jurisdictions were a relic of the feudal past and the time had come for a modern Scotland to cast them away. The matter was clinched by the willingness of the Government in London to offer financial compensation for them.

So here was a change in the terms of the Union negotiated and paid for, a very different situation from the one straight after 1707.

As part of the package, Robert Dundas gave Scotland a new system of local government, under the office of sheriff. In every county the sheriff would be the representative of the state, administering justice, organising elections, collecting taxes and dealing with disturbances. He would also be a man acceptable to the county, because his appointment was always made in consultation with its leading figures. The reform endowed Scotland with a more efficient system than England or, for that matter, most other countries enjoyed at the local level. At this level the Kirk was also prominent, educating the young in the parochial schools, administering the Poor Law for the destitute and seeing to the morals of the people by use of the notorious stool of repentance. Its place in a more rationally governed country was secured by a rising generation of ministers who wished to conduct its affairs in a seemly fashion, but without heavy-handed political control. They found means to do so through the disciplinary powers of the General Assembly. This Moderate party, led by Rev William Robertson, future principal of the University of Edinburgh, reclaimed a degree of autonomy, as the leaders of the Church of Scotland themselves undertook to keep its ministers and members in order (Paterson 1994, 35–6).

> EXERCISE 5
> What were the major instruments of local government after Robert Dundas's reforms? To what extent do you think they allowed the Scots to govern themselves?

Robert Dundas gave the office of sheriff a central role in representing the state at the local level, in charge of justice, elections, taxation and the maintenance of order. This rounded out the local functions of the Kirk, which included education, welfare and public morals. Both institutions were wholly Scottish, having no close English equivalent. Since they made Scotland a well-ordered country, there was usually no reason for the Government in London to interfere.

The 3rd Duke of Argyll died in 1761. His successors to the title were uninterested in public affairs, and the Argathelian party dissolved. The situation was further complicated by events in London. George III, the first Hanoverian king to be born in Britain, took a more personal interest in politics than his German-speaking predecessors had been willing or able to do. The earliest sign of it was his promotion of his old tutor, the Earl of Bute, to Prime Minister. The appointment caused uproar in England, where Scots were still unpopular, and Bute was forced to resign within a couple of years. He had placed his own men in charge of Scotland, but they did not outlast him. For the next few years, Scottish politics were leaderless.

The vacuum allowed Henry Dundas, son of the Lord President, to take over and establish a political dynasty known as 'the Dundas Despotism' that lasted more than half a century. Till this point his family, though active in politics, had remained in contemporary terms of lesser importance, since Scottish society still looked to the nobility for leadership. The Dundases were plain lairds from Midlothian, their prominence due to their ability, not to the size of their estates. That they, representatives of a different class, now rose to political control of Scotland was in itself significant. If their convictions were conservative, they represented a new Scotland of achievers.

Henry Dundas was already Solicitor General when he entered Parliament in 1774. The following year he became Lord Advocate, and set about a busy programme of useful measures which soon put his stamp on Scottish politics. Followers gathered round him, and in the turmoil at the end of the War of American Independence he played a key role as a power-broker. It was largely through him that William Pitt the younger became Prime Minister and put an end to the crisis in 1783. In the reforming efforts of the next decade, Dundas was always his leader's right-hand man. He himself concentrated on India, giving the British territories there a new and effective administration. In 1792 he became Home Secretary, and suppressed radicals sympathetic to the French Revolution. Hostilities with France broke out in 1793, and Dundas was appointed Secretary of State for War the next year, conducting the struggle till his resignation along with Pitt in 1801. He was then created Viscount Melville, and returned as First Lord of the Admiralty in 1804. Within a few months, however, Parliament impeached him for irregularities in administration of the navy, the last British Minister to be subjected to this procedure. Though he was acquitted, a second comeback proved beyond him. He died in 1811.

In Scotland, Dundas had set out to restore the political unity lost with the passing of the Argathelian regime. His own background lay in the Squadrone but he used Argathelian methods, indeed perfected them. This was most obvious in his assiduous attention to the constituencies. Argyll had often been accused of arrogance and heedlessness, but for Dundas no detail was too trivial, no person too unimportant, to fit into his vast bank of information and machinery of patronage. Once, in his friendship with Pitt, he had secured his position at the centre of power in London, he became supreme in Scotland. In his turn he established control of most parliamentary seats, and of the elections for the peerage. With the outbreak of war against France, almost the whole country rallied patriotically behind him. After the General Election of 1796, the Government was supported by 43 of the 45 Scots MPs (Fry 1992, Chapters 4 and 5).

EXERCISE 6
Read **Document 16**. What does this reveal about Dundas's methods as he starts to consolidate his power?

The manoeuvres dealt with in this letter, against an opponent of Dundas's, required a detailed grasp of a local situation, especially of what jobs or other favours the electors wanted. On a more general level, Dundas was mobilising local landowners to seize control of the burghs: note especially David Scott who had made a lot of money in India. The only overt appeal to a principle was that Scots ought to support the Government.

Dundas applied similar methods to the other national institutions. The Squa-

No. 6. Contemporary cartoon of Dundas, by James Gillray, combining the figure of kilted Scot and turbaned oriental despot, with one foot in London, the other in Bengal. © *The British Museum.*

drone had traditionally been aligned with the Evangelicals in the Kirk, but he valued the orderly habits of the Moderates. His solution to their rivalry was to keep the Moderates in overall control, but to give a fair share of patronage to the Evangelicals as well. Similarly in the universities, he made clear that the combination of talent and loyalty would always be rewarded. He himself had been brought up in enlightened Edinburgh, and loved the cut and thrust of the city's intellectual life. A clubman full of bonhomie, he was a firm friend to the *literati*, and not just in a social sense. He found official positions for Adam Smith, Adam Ferguson and others, and he gave them influence. Economic reforms adopted by the British Government were owed directly to Smith, while Ferguson guided efforts to repair the shattered social fabric of the Highlands. In the law, too, Dundas wanted, and largely managed, to give Scotland a system which was at least as efficient as and rather more liberal than the English one (Fry 1987, 79).

With untiring energy and care for detail, Dundas carried his methods far beyond Scotland. In the Empire and in the armed forces, he always made sure Scots got their cut of jobs, money and privileges. The wheeler-dealing has not struck observers, then or since, as very noble. But it worked: it benefited and pleased the Scots, and brought them into partnership with the English, rather than into subordination on the Irish model. Dundas saw himself above all as an imperial statesman. In war he disliked direct engagement of the British army in Europe and preferred a maritime strategy, where the navy took the lead in seizing the enemy's colonies. That extended Britain's network of international trade, with exotic commodities from distant outposts feeding the commerce and manufactures of the mother country. He told the Parliament at Westminster not to let itself be obsessed by narrow English concerns, because it was now a legislature with worldwide responsibilities. He set an example himself, taking personal charge of Scottish, English, Irish, Indian, West Indian and American legislation. If the imperial enterprise was to succeed, the peoples of the British Isles had to be willing partners in it: Englishmen should not imagine that they could give the law to the rest. In Scotland, Dundas succeeded – though not in Ireland, despite her Union with Great Britain in 1801. You can gauge how far he had the same aims for both countries from his speech in support of that measure (**Document 17**).

EXERCISE 7
Read **Document 17**. How far were Henry Dundas's aims reflected in his management of Scottish affairs?

Dundas's main argument is perhaps essentially an imperialist one. He claims that, through the Union of Parliaments, Scotland held on to what she most valued but had her horizons widened, because Scots could also exploit the opportunities of the British Empire and their MPs could take part in ruling it. The same chance is now held out to Ireland. Dundas concedes that there are costs as well as benefits, but asserts that the costs to Scotland were actually greater than those in prospect for Ireland: the overall balance-sheet had turned out positive all the same. Yet a different view from Dundas's would be possible, and you might like to come back again to this exercise once you have reached the end of the chapter.

While Dundas's grip on Scotland loosened towards the end of his life, his system was sturdy enough to survive him. For another twenty years, it would be run by his son, Robert, 2nd Viscount Melville. At the end of the French wars in 1815 came a deep economic depression which exposed not only acute social tensions but also the inadequacy of existing means for dealing with them. The industrial revolution was creating a very different Scotland, with a downtrodden proletariat in the big cities and a new élite, separate from the old landed one, of merchants and manufacturers. These people had vast wealth yet only indirect access to power. They demanded constitutional reform. Since the 1780s there had been protests at political abuses in Scotland, with calls for a wider franchise and the suppression of corrupt practices. At first the protests arose within the ruling class, though the impact of the French Revolution spread them wider. Nothing could be done while the wars went on, and after 1815 it at once became clear that the whole scale and intensity of the country's problems had altered. Workers turned radical while bourgeois reformers, gathered in a new opposition calling itself Whig, warned that refusal to respond was likely only to lead to revolution.

For the first time since 1745, there was opposition not just in the Scottish political system but to the Scottish political system. It could therefore not be bought off by the usual method of offering patronage to the dissidents. Even so, if they sought to overthrow the system, this did not mean repudiating the Treaty of Union that underlay it. On the contrary both Whigs and radicals, whose alliance formed the basis of Victorian Liberalism, wanted to bring Scotland into line with the supposedly superior liberties of England. When the Dundases refused to make concessions, it only reinforced the claim that their system was past saving: the best thing would be to sweep it away and give Scotland a fresh start on English lines. That is the burden of Henry Cockburn's remarks in his letter of 1827 (**Document 18**). He no longer wanted Scotland run by 'a horrid jobbing Scot', a reference to the system of management. He preferred her affairs to be directly overseen by the Home Secretary. Unfortunately that office had always been, as it is again today, a purely English one. The Whigs' idea was to appoint a couple of advisers who would keep the Minister in touch with Scotland and offer recommendations on policy there. But Cockburn, even after becoming Solicitor General in 1830, found it impossible to make the idea work: Home Secretaries were just not interested. In the end the post of Secretary of State for Scotland would have to be restored, though not till 1885 (Fry 1992, Chapters 9 and 10).

The destruction of Scottish management formed only the prelude to the Whigs' Reform Act of 1832. The project of extending the franchise was, of course, a British one, but Scotland had to have her own measure to take account of the inherited system. It turned out cautious: Whig words were always stronger than Whig deeds. Scotland would now get 53 seats in the House of Commons (still less than her population merited) and keep 16 representative peers. The electorate grew to about 64,000 voters, in a population of two million, so the franchise remained restricted to the well-off. In its technical aspects the measure was bungled, out of the Whigs' ill-advised contempt for Scots law, which they dismissed as authoritarian. They left so many loopholes that the elections often went on in much the same way as before, except for being more expensive. Reform did make a real difference to the burghs, by creating a popular parliamentary suffrage for the first time and then, by a second Act in 1833, abolishing self-election in the councils. Most burghs turned into radical strongholds, and some chose only Liberal MPs right till that party collapsed a century later. But in the counties, as can be seen from the memorandum drawn up for the gentlemen of Midlothian (**Document 19**), there was nothing in the reformed system that Tories could not deal with. They soon won back much of the ground lost in the Liberal landslide at the first General Election under the new franchise.

EXERCISE 8

Reflecting on the discussion here, what impact do you think the Reform Act had on Scottish politics?

The main effect was an extension of the franchise, from the small circles of landowners and town councillors under the old system to a new system which embraced many prosperous tenants in the countryside and most of the urban middle class. It sufficed to ensure the hegemony of the Liberal party in Scotland for the rest of the nineteenth century. Yet the reform was still relatively cautious and continued to deny the right to vote to the great mass of working men, as well as to all women. The universal adult suffrage of modern democracy lay a long way off yet. A final result was the extensive dismantling of the special Scottish political arrangements that had rather casually evolved since 1707, so that the government of Scotland became much more like the government of England.

The most far-reaching consequence of reform would come paradoxically not in the state but in the Church. Established religion was still a part of everyday life. Scots expected reform here to be the next step. In particular they wanted to choose their ministers exactly as they now elected their MPs. For that, they had to get rid of the lay patronage imposed back in 1712. That put clerical appointments in the hands of the same landed class that had now been drummed out of its political dominance. The Kirk's own efforts at internal reform were pulled up short because lay patronage was a matter of statute which the General Assembly could not simply set aside. But it proved impossible to construct the parliamentary majority for an acceptable change. Other efforts to resolve a mounting crisis by negotiation or litigation failed. It all came to a head in 1843, when a third of the ministers and probably a greater proportion of members seceded to form the Free Church of Scotland. This was the greatest Scottish domestic event of the nineteenth century, with far-reaching effects on the whole of society. They cannot be followed here, but the implications for what had in many ways remained an autonomous constitutional and political system are brought out in my survey, 'The Disruption and the Union' (**Article 3**). The system came to an end but one result of that, a greater formal integration into the United

Kingdom, was balanced by another, the reawakening of patriotic sentiment as a prelude to the modern Nationalist movement.

EXERCISE 9

Read **Article 3**, 'The Disruption and the Union'. What are the central arguments of this essay?

The essay posits not just a national tradition in Scottish politics but a whole different set of constitutional principles: the idea of a balance between Church and state rather than the English doctrine of absolute parliamentary sovereignty. Over the particular point at issue in 1843, these proved utterly incompatible. Forced to choose, the ruling élite in Scotland opted for the English doctrine, now upgraded to a British one, rather than for the Scottish tradition. Large numbers of their fellow Scots did not agree, but the only course for them was then to set up voluntary institutions, separate from the state. The choice was therefore not straightforward, and had unexpected side-effects. You might like to go back over some of the previous narrative in this chapter and see how it might fit into the thesis set out in the essay.

4. THE MEANING OF SCOTTISH POLITICS

The run of British historiography regards the constitutional relationship between Scotland and England as an abstract question, if a question at all. The train of thought goes like this: two countries gave up their separate existence in 1707 to form one country, so in what sense can it be useful to think of a constitutional relationship between them, any more than it is useful to think of a constitutional relationship between, say, Yorkshire and Lancashire? One or two theoretical works have given the matter serious attention, but most ignore it.

Still, British intellectual tradition is pragmatic, concerned with outcomes rather than principles. The outcome of three hundred years of Union is that, though vastly changed, Scotland remains Scotland, identifiable and distinct from all other countries. Clearly, there has been a long-term trend towards assimilation of various kinds: with England, with the British Empire, now with Europe. But the trend is not linear: it twists and turns under different influences in different directions in different periods. On one type of political evidence – say, the volume, content and effect of legislation – it could be argued that Scotland has become much more like the rest of the United Kingdom in the past few decades. Yet on another type of such evidence – say, the tenor of public opinion and the electoral choices made – Scotland has diverged sharply from England. In summing up three centuries, it would be a plausible starting hypothesis that some internal dynamic may exist which modifies as it interacts with those external forces, so that even a stateless Scotland does not simply succumb to them (Fry 1992, 14).

While politics can only be one part of the dynamic, Scottish historians are today less liable to overlook it. Perhaps the really important forces in any given historic

society are the ones at work deep within it, barely conceived or understood by those
they affect, but leaving the historian the useful task of unearthing and defining them,
which he does by burrowing in evidence never properly valued or evaluated. In other
countries, this has usually meant stressing social and economic history at the expense
of traditional political history. In Scotland, though, we may have to do the opposite.
Here social history and economic history have flourished, if seldom on agendas set in
Scotland, while political history has languished, as something subordinate to the
course of an integrative British political history.

But, on the subject of why Scotland remains Scotland, Scottish political history
may after all have something to say. Many transformations have come over the
country in the course of three hundred years, as its membership of the United
Kingdom and of the British Empire has worked on it. But other things have remained
recognisably themselves and changed more gradually. Tensions have often arisen
from the conflict between a desire to press forward in a social or economic sense,
which may tend to make Scotland more like other countries, and a desire to hold on
to the past, which tends to keep Scotland Scottish. The political system is one
mechanism through which the brakes can be applied. So the history of it may, for
example, be especially useful in telling us about the continuities in the life of the
country.

Management and semi-independence have been two concepts often mentioned
in this chapter, and we might sum up by drawing a contrast between them. It is
possible to say that Scotland is a victim of historical forces. She was too small and
weak to have stayed independent. Since 1707 she has been subject to the will of a
bigger and stronger neighbour which, if seldom overtly hostile, in the end brooks no
opposition to its own wishes. The English might offer a few sops to the Scots, but
they make sure the people who rule Scotland are at their beck and call. Evidence for
that view might be sought in the system of management in the eighteenth century
where, it could be said, a ruthless and corrupt Scottish political establishment
suppressed all opposition and ruined native culture into the bargain.

Comforting though the view just set out may be when Scots are feeling sorry for
themselves, a closer look at the evidence must cast some doubt on it. Once teething
troubles were over after 1707, the English only interfered in Scotland when they felt
a threat from Scotland, as in the case of the Jacobites. They let the Scots otherwise
look after themselves, as the Treaty of Union said Scots should do. It is hard to see a
crushed and colonised country behind the glorious intellectual achievements of the
Enlightenment. Nor do we get the impression from the enterprising, successful Scots
of the nineteenth century that they were sons or daughters of a nation robbed of its
character and vitality. Semi-independence is a less straightforward concept than
management. But perhaps it gives, among other things, a better explanation of the
Enlightenment, as the flowering of an essentially native culture in a liberating
environment. It also offers one, though not the only, reason why Scotland inside the
Union did not follow the road of Ireland, but remained a country proud of itself and
capable of excellence across a vast range of activities (Keating 1988, 56).

So we come finally to a question as pointed in our own day as it was in the

eighteenth century, when Scotland was no bigger than she is now: is she doomed to
fall under the control of others and depend on them for sustenance, or can she by use
of her talents and energies still decide some important things for herself? Since
politics bears on that question, it is surely relevant to the general history of Scottish
society in the period 1707–1850, and beyond.

REFERENCES TO BOOKS AND ARTICLES MENTIONED IN THE TEXT

*Brown, SJ and Fry, MRG 1993 *Scotland in the Age of the Disruption*. Edinburgh.
*Dwyer, J, Mason, RA and Murdoch, A (eds) 1992 *New Perspectives on the Politics and
    Culture of Early Modern Scotland*. Edinburgh.
*Fry, MRG 1987 *Patronage and Principle, a political history of modern Scotland*. Aberdeen.
*Fry, MRG 1992 *The Dundas Despotism*. Edinburgh.
Graham, HG 1937 *The social life of Scotland in the eighteenth century*. London.
Keating, M 1988 *State and Regional Nationalism*. Brighton.
*Mathieson, WL 1916 *Church and reform in Scotland: A History from 1797 to 1843*.
    Glasgow.
*Murdoch, A 1980 *'The People Above': Politics and Administration in Mid-Eighteenth
    Century Scotland*. Edinburgh.
*Paterson, L 1994 *The Autonomy of Modern Scotland*. Edinburgh.
*Phillipson, NT 1970 'Scottish Public Opinion and the Union in the Age of the Association', *in*
    Phillipson, NT and Mitchison, R (eds), *Scotland in the Age of Improvement*, Edinburgh,
    125–47.
Sher, RB 1982 'Moderates, managers and popular politics in mid-eighteenth century
    Edinburgh: The Drysdale 'Bustle' of the 1760s', *in* Dwyer, J, Mason, RA and Mur-
    doch, A (eds), *New Perspectives on the Politics and Culture of Early Modern Scotland*,
    Edinburgh, 179–209.
Smout, TC 1969 *A History of the Scottish People, 1560–1830*. London.
*Whetstone, AE 1981 *Scottish County Government in the Eighteenth and Nineteenth
    Centuries*. Edinburgh.

FURTHER READING

Those references marked * in the above list are recommended further reading.

Religion

Callum G Brown

INTRODUCTION

Religion was a very important aspect of social, cultural and political life in the eighteenth and early nineteenth centuries. This applied in Scotland as it did across most of Europe. The role of religion was, nonetheless, subjected to enormous forces for change during this period. Indeed, it may be said that it was during these hundred and fifty years that religion was transformed from a pattern first set during the Middle Ages into one that was essentially modern. Various factors contributed to these forces for change. Firstly, there was the impact of economic change through agricultural improvement, commercial expansion and industrialisation. Secondly, there were the social forces of the 'birth of social class' and population expansion. And thirdly, there were the physical and structural forces brought on by urban growth, creating a new scale to 'community' and an alien physical environment for religion to work in.

Within this context, this chapter will focus on the reshaping of religion in Scottish society between 1700 and 1850. It looks especially at how the structure of the churches in Scotland was recast by emerging social divisions and by immigration. The impact of urban growth will be tackled more extensively in Volume 2 (1850 to the present). The present chapter is divided into six sections, each designed to explore the role of religion from a different perspective:

- The Church of Scotland 'by law established': the parish state
- Evangelicalism, Moderatism and the Enlightenment
- Patronage and protest
- The Dissenters
- Thomas Chalmers, the Disruption and the Free Church of Scotland
- Roman Catholicism and sectarianism

By the time you have completed this chapter you should have a good understanding of the role of religion in Scottish society and of the main developments which took place before 1850. This will be vital to your study of the later period.

I. THE CHURCH OF SCOTLAND 'BY LAW ESTABLISHED': THE PARISH STATE

The Church of Scotland had emerged from the Revolution Settlement of 1690 as both presbyterian in structure and doctrine, and the only lawful church in the country. This section explores what the 'established' status of the Kirk meant in both ecclesiastical and everyday life in the eighteenth century.

There were two main ecclesiastical traditions within post-Reformation Scottish church life: Presbyterianism and Episcopalianism. Whilst the minority episcopalian clergy and laity were permitted, by the freedom of worship granted by the Westminister Parliament in the early eighteenth century, to found a separate denomination, most Presbyterians continued to regard the Church of Scotland as the monopolistic state church. Presbyterianism was founded upon a literal inter-pretation of the Bible as the Word of God, and used the Westminster Confession of Faith of 1643 as what was called its 'principal subordinate standard' (ie subordinate to the Bible). In doctrine, Presbyterianism held that the head of the church was Christ, that the Kirk was independent from interference by the state though dependent on it for protection, and that the government of the church should rest on a hierarchy of courts – stretching from the kirk session at parish level, to the presbytery at district level, to the synod at provincial level, and finally to the general assembly at national (Scottish) level. In each of these courts, members were supposed to be selected in what we would describe today as a 'democratic' way: the minister and elders were to be selected by the congregation, elected representatives from kirk sessions were to sit on the presbytery, and so on. In practice, this supposedly 'democratic' system was modified in a number of ways, leading – as we shall see – to controversy and protest.

The way in which the Church of Scotland acted as the state church was most apparent and effective not at national level but at local level. The parish church was in most places in the eighteenth century the principal – and often the only – community venue. Parishioners met there for Sunday worship. This included psalms (not 'human' hymns which were unworthy of praising the Lord), sung with no accompaniment from musical instruments (as only the human voice singing the Word of God could praise Him); each line of a psalm was read or sung by a precentor, who might stand in a special booth underneath the minister's pulpit, whilst the worshippers sat to sing. There would be prayer, and there was a long sermon which could last over an hour in which the minister would often use Scriptural example to exhort improved moral and social behaviour amongst the hearers. In the seventeenth century, the people in most rural parishes had been accustomed to sit on stools or small seats, but increasingly in the eighteenth century the urban practice of having fixed pews, allocated to individuals or families, became more common. Where there was one large landowner in the parish, he (rarely she) and his family sat in a 'laird's loft' constructed inside the churches, whilst in royal burghs the provost and town council often had their own loft or reserved pews. In this way the parish church on a Sunday increasingly mirrored the sharpening social gradations in the parish at large. Sunday worship was affirming the social order, and, as we shall see shortly, this became a cause for controversy as the social order changed between 1700 and 1850.

In each parish, the Church also assumed vital functions in relation to social welfare, community spirit, social order, morality, education and the rites of passage (birth, death and marriage). The minister supervised the schoolmaster (the 'dominie') who conducted the parish school, whilst the beadle had a variety of functions – including renting out a mortcloth for covering the dead at funerals in the kirkyard. The kirk session, composed of the minister and upwards of four lay elders, was the instrument of 'regular discipline' upon the people – a heritage of the early-modern period in which it was 'an affirmation by the community of its membership of the elect' (Mitchison and Leneman 1989, 17). The kirk session was the local court for the trying of cases against parishioners accused of ecclesiastical offences, but many of these were also civil offences (such as profaning the Sabbath). The staple offence was that of fornication (sexual intercourse outwith marriage), with adultery as the next most common offence. Discovery of a pregnant spinster was usually the starting point for such cases, with the result that women were, by modern standards, rather harshly treated. One concern of church authorities was that the father of an illegitimate child should be identified to ensure its financial support, preventing a single mother making claims on the poor fund. The Kirk above all sought acknowledgement of guilt and submission to its authority: failure to do so could cause a variety of problems to an accused person, including the refusal of the minister to provide a 'testificate' (or testimonial) to a parishioner wishing to move to another parish. Punishment usually came in two forms: a fine, and the 'purging of the scandal' by standing or sitting in a prominent place in church (in some places on a 'punishment stool') for up to three successive Sundays whilst the minister 'ranted' at the offender.

> EXERCISE I
> Read the fornication case (**Document 20**). What observations would you make about the conduct of kirk-session justice, the attitudes and concerns of the two accused and three witnesses, and the reasons why the local church put such emphasis on discovering and punishing fornicators?

Your answer could include comment on the formalism of the proceedings, the Kirk's strenuous pursuit of the case, and possible reasons why the session failed to reach a decision. Additionally, you should ask questions of the document, such as: Why did Christian McGregor not 'compear' before the kirk session until the eighth month of her pregnancy? Do you think she came 'voluntarily' as stated? Why might Robert have finally accepted his guilt two years later? And how might opposing pressures from Christian and from Robert have influenced the witnesses' evidence? Not all of these questions may be answered with certainty, but they are worth considering.

In some cases, voyeuristic evidence of sexual encounters was heard, and in some places kirk sessions became excessive in their scrutiny of sexual behaviour – even when fornication seemed remote. For example, the session book of Thurso records in March 1722:

> Donald Manson Sailor & Christian Nicol formerly delated [charged] of
> scandalous behaviour viz of walking together at unseasonable hours and

particularly their sitting together one night a little above the Chappel of pennyland betwixt the hours of ten & eleven at night and he the said Manson sitting hard by her with his arms about her neck, both of them being cited . . . acknowledged what was delated against them to be truth . . . but at the same time they declare that the design of their meeting upon that night was to concert matters with respect to their contract & marriage and that they would not frequent one anothers company so much if they had not intended to marry very soon. The Session finding . . . that the foresaid Donald Manson sailor is in suit [promised to marry] of her and that they actually Intend to marry and likewise consider that nothing can be proved against them but what may be allowable to persons that intend to marry do give up with this process.

(quoted in Mitchison and Leneman 1989, 179–80)

But whilst sexual matters tended to dominate the business of many kirk sessions, there could be a much a wider remit for this key local institution. At Dunnichen parish in Angus in the 1790s, the minister publicly recommended from the pulpit that parents get their children inoculated against smallpox, whilst it was common for kirk sessions to investigate offences as varied as wife-beating, suspicious death and even bakers selling under-weight loaves.

The parish state was not confined to the organisation of religious worship and moral discipline. It also had a prominence in the economy of the parish as each minister was paid by having a glebe of land to farm, and a stipend paid out of the 'teinds' – a tax collected usually at harvest time in the form of oats, barley, fish or other produce. Parishioners were also expected to undertake labour services in support of the church, such as roofing the kirk or manse, or collecting the minister's harvest. In some parishes, notably in royal burghs, ministers' stipends were paid in cash. Not all of these aspects of the parish were organised by the kirk session, but by a body called the Board of Heritors. 'Heritors' were the landowners, and the Board was a civil court composed of the landowners of the parish and supervised by the Court of Session in Edinburgh. The Board of each parish had statutory responsibilities for the provision of a parish church capable of holding two-thirds of the population aged over twelve years, a manse and glebe of set proportions, a stipend collected from the teinds and, from the middle of the eighteenth century, a shared responsibility with the kirk session for the provision of poor relief.

In these ways, the parish church represented the fulcrum of much of the life of the parish. The minister, the 'dominie', the precentor (who was invariably the dominie and also the clerk to both the kirk session and the Board of Heritors), the church beadle (who had responsibilities for burials and church maintenance), and the lay elders (who reported to the kirk session on misdeeds amongst parishioners) were the key authority figures in virtually all parishes. Only in royal burghs did slightly different arrangements prevail: town councils usually constituted the Board of Heritors, and no parish schools were required by law. Otherwise, circumstances in town and country were little different during the first three-quarters of the eighteenth century.

EXERCISE 2
Describe the variety of ways in which the Church of Scotland exerted control over the lives of ordinary people, especially in the eighteenth century.

Briefly, it did so by reinforcing the social hierarchy, maintaining social order and morals, and through the provision of social welfare and education.

You should use the preceding section and **Document 21** to compile an impression of the Church of Scotland's role, and challenges to that role, in local society. Note the varying attitudes of the ministers towards the common people in their parishes.

2. EVANGELICALISM, MODERATISM AND THE ENLIGHTENMENT

As the eighteenth century proceeded, the unity of the presbyterian church both at national and at local level increasingly disintegrated. Divisions emerged within the church – some over church law, some over church doctrine and liturgy, but underscoring all the divisions was the issue of whose Kirk it was. A large divide emerged between, on the one hand, those clergy – predominantly of rural parishes – who in matters of social ambience and taste became aligned with the rising class of large landowners, and on the other hand those – including most urban clergy – who remained ardently committed to what they perceived as the 'true reformed' tradition. These groups became known respectively as the Moderate Party and the Evangelical or Popular Party.

The Moderates were perceived as the establishment or government party, a group backed by the wealthy landowners and well-organised by Edinburgh lawyers, who ensured through strict discipline a Moderate majority in crucial votes in the annual general assembly. In worship the Moderates favoured a lightening of the puritan yoke, giving in pulpit sermons a stress on elegance and refinement rather than on exhortation to acknowledgement of sin. Some Moderates were noted for their tendency to games and drinking, and they were likely to be less confrontational with parishioners over morality and behaviour. Indeed, they were seen by their opponents as 'lukewarm' in religion. The following comment by Rev Andrew Murray, parish minister at Auchterderran in Fife in the 1790s, gives some impression of Moderate sensibilities. It symbolises the divide between the liberal and the puritan in eighteenth-century presbyterianism. Murray decried the absence of sport amongst adults in his parish, and the fact that Handsel-Monday was the only 'merry-making holiday' of the year:

Among the infinite advantages of the Reformation, this seems to have been one disadvantage attending it, that, owing to the gloomy rigour of some of the leading actors, mirth, sport, and chearfulness, were decried among a people already by nature rather phlegmatic. Since that, mirth and vice have, in their apprehension, been confounded together. Some of the sectaries [ie presbyterian dissenters – see section 4] punish attendance on penny weddings, and public

dancing, with a reproof from the pulpit, in the presence of the congregation: so
that the people must either dance by themselves, or let it alone.

(Statistical Account vol 1, 458)

The Evangelicals were seen as contrasting clergy, more strict in their adherence to
doctrine, but capable of radical revision of it. They were also much divided among
themselves. The Evangelicals agonised over doctrine, notably the relative merits of
the doctrine of predestination (the backbone of conventional Calvinism, which
prescribed that only the Elect are saved, distinguishable by their 'assurance' or
confidence of salvation) and the doctrine of universal atonement (which prescribed
that Christ died for all those who committed themselves to being saved). The birth of
the Evangelical Party can be dated from 1718 when a book by an Englishman named
Edward Fisher called *The Marrow of Modern Divinity*, first published in 1646, was
re-published with a Scottish preface. This book was doubly significant: it argued for
the doctrine of universal atonement, and it acted as the manifesto of a discontented
group in the Church that was to become in time the Evangelical Party (Drummond
and Bulloch 1973, 35–37). But Evangelicals were not united on doctrinal matters, as
there were divisions over the degree to which a person's 'assurance' of salvation was
permanent or secure (thus raising doubts about the certainty of predestination for
the Elect), and division over the power of the conversion as a sign of assurance gifted
by God to all who might genuinely seek and accept it. 'Calvinists', as Bebbington
(1989, 43) comments, 'faced a problem', one not confined to Scotland, but one
which had acute consequences there. Evangelicals – as well as many Moderates –
could agonise over this fundamental issue of how individuals were 'saved'. Two
traditions could almost merge in one preacher. John Willison, minister of South
Church in Dundee, urged intending communicants in 1716:

> I pity those poor trembling, and doubting souls, who cannot attain to any light
> or clearness about their [spiritual] condition. To such I would say, that you
> ought to wait on God, and hold on in the way of duty to your lives' end, and
> whatever disadvantages you may meet therein, God in his own time will let you
> know that your labour is not in vain.
>
> (quoted in Bebbington 1989, 44–5)

'A persistent phase of gloom', Bebbington notes of some evangelicals, 'was a sign of
true religion' (*ibid*, 45).

But during the course of the eighteenth and nineteenth centuries, the evangelical
conversion was becoming noted for its suddenness, violence and its subsequent
joyousness. Equally, and more contentiously, it was becoming noted for taking place
in mass events, or 'revivals'. The most noted event was at Cambuslang and Kilsyth in
1742, when at a summer communion held on the 'preaching braes' a revival
occurred (known locally as the 'Cambuslang Wark') with local and visiting people
succumbing to the preaching of many visiting clergy, including the English
Methodist George Whitefield. The revival at Cambuslang followed a pattern that

was to become common in the following century and a half, with mass conversions of people in distress through crying, sobbing and sometimes alarming manifestations. The minister of Kilsyth sought to 'play down' such features:

> There was a great variety in the expressions uttered by those who cried out in public. Their different outcries were such as these: I am undone. What shall I do? "What shall I do to be saved?" "Lord, have mercy upon me." Oh, alas, O this unbelieving heart of mine. Some cried out bitterly, without uttering any words. Others restrained crying out while they were in public, who did it bitterly after they retired to their homes, and sometimes in their way homeward, and thereby gave no disturbance to the public preaching of the word . . .
>
> (Robe 1989, 90)

Thousands of people were present at one time. On such occasions, usually only a portion were 'saved'; amongst those classified as converts at Cambuslang, 68% were women – of whom 75% were unmarried and the vast majority were in their teens and twenties (see Smout 1982, 116 – **Article 4**). Revivalism was extremely controversial within Presbyterianism, both because of doctrinal doubts over the validity of encouraging people to believe that they could be agents in their own salvation, and because a revival overturned social and ecclesiastical good order: people neglected their work and sometimes undermined the authority of a local parish minister. Campaigns against revivalist clergy could result, including charges of heresy levelled in church courts.

The causes of increasing revivals in Scotland during this period are explained differently. Ecclesiastical historians such as Fawcett (1971) will acknowledge the impact of famine and rural social change, but will also emphasise the power of Christian preaching; some may explain it as 'the Will of God'. Landsman (1989) has pointed to important ways in which revivalist preaching resonated with the interests of urbanising artisans in the west of Scotland, whilst a sociologist like Bruce (1983) explains the revival in late eighteenth-century Ross-shire in terms of the very rapid and traumatic community change taking place there.

EXERCISE 3

Read **Article 4** by Smout, and discuss the impact of religious revival in a local community. You might include in your response the reasons for opposition to revivalism amongst the landed gentry and aristocracy.

In summary, the revival at Cambuslang attracted people – mostly young single women – from families in which the main breadwinners were predominantly small tenants or low-status craftsmen. The level of social impact included a heightened spiritual awareness and neglect of work, and the hostile reaction of the landowners revealed a profound dislike of popular religion.

The emergence of the Enlightenment had a strong bearing on the division between Moderates and Evangelicals. The Enlightenment's emphasis on reason seemed intrinsically hostile to the evangelicals' resort on occasion to emotion. Moderate clergy were certainly prominent amongst the Edinburgh *literati* who were so important to the Scottish Enlightenment (Sher 1985), and the tolerance of escapist entertainment that characterised Moderatism was certainly in tune with the liberal tendencies of the Enlightenment. But as Landsman (1993, 195) has argued, 'the evangelical movement of the eighteenth century, in spite of its visionary manifestations and its outburst of enthusiasm, had a much more complicated and complementary relationship with social change and enlighten- ment', especially in Glasgow and the west of Scotland where it emerged as a popular alternative to what he calls 'the more polite but élitist enlightenment of the Moderates'.

3. PATRONAGE AND PROTEST

The division between Moderates and Evangelicals was not merely a product of different doctrines, personal styles or philosophical inclinations. The key issue to shape the divide in Presbyterianism throughout the period from 1733 to 1850 was patronage. This was the system whereby hereditary owners (or 'patrons') had the right to select (or 'present') the minister in a parish church. This right had been bypassed at the 1690 settlement, with these rights passing to elders and heritors, but it was reinstated by the Patronage Act of 1714. This Act was passed as a measure to

No. 7. 'Christmas Eve' (formerly titled 'The Penny Wedding') by Sir William Allan. © *City of Aberdeen Art Gallery and Museums Collections.*

mollify Scottish landowners in the midst of the looming Jacobite crisis. The results were slow to materialise, but they were to become decisive in Scottish church and civil life. Patrons were generally wealthy large landowners (often the nobility), town councils, universities, or – as in a third of parishes – the Crown, and from the late 1710s until the 1730s they started to invoke their right to select a new minister on the death, retiral or removal of the previous minister. The ministers being selected by the Crown and nobility were ones they felt to be sympathetic to their own social pretensions; invariably, these were the clergy who by the 1750s were dubbed the Moderates. Large numbers of parishioners objected in such cases – both because they perceived their right to a say in the running of their church was being lost, and because they disapproved of the type of minister being chosen.

In a parish where the congregation opposed the selection of the minister, lengthy legal moves generally followed. Objections would be laid before the local presbytery which had to confirm and induct (or formally install) the minister in a service in his new church. Such legal moves would involve nit-picking over the formalities of presentation, and could last some years. At the end of the day, the presbyteries generally upheld the patron's choice, and a Sunday would be selected for the presbytery to induct the clergyman into his new pulpit. On that day, objecting parishioners would seek to physically prevent the clergyman from entering his church. Human barricades would be formed, the church would be locked and the key conveniently 'lost', and many inductions were postponed for a week or more. Often, the presbytery would seek civil assistance, and it became common for a detachment of troops or cavalry to attend the next attempt. These occasions became standard in Scottish parishes after 1740, elevated to a defining event in popular culture of the eighteenth and early nineteenth centuries. They entered literary folklore, the best fictionalised account being contained at the start of John Galt's novel *Annals of the Parish*. Galt invites the reader to sympathise with the luckless narrator, Rev Micah Balwhidder, on being selected by the patron of Dalmailing parish and being opposed by the congregation.

EXERCISE 4
Refer to **Document 22**, and from what has been said about patronage disputes, assess the value of a contemporary novel as a source for the historian.

I would regard a work of literature as potentially a useful source, though with qualifications. As fiction, it might well crystallise a wider social reality, and reflect the novelist's own acquaintance with incidents and characters involved – who, through the change of names, could be revealingly portrayed without fear of legal action. Most accounts of patronage disputes emphasise the severity of the rift that was created between parishioners and the 'intruded' minister. Galt's account is more sympathetic than many towards the minister, and suggests that the divide was not as stark as is often supposed.

Given its significance in Scottish social history of this period, historians have paid scant attention to the patronage dispute. Ironically, we know more about the less frequent disputes in towns than in country parishes. Sher (1985, 202–3), in his study of a dispute in Edinburgh in the 1760s, shows how tradesmen opposed the choice of a minister, and in the process the protest 'constituted a critical step in the development of a "modern" democratic consciousness among the "people" of Scotland'.

The patronage dispute was the defining event in Scottish local history between 1714 and 1850. But it was not the only cause of disgruntlement in congregations. The actions of patrons joined the actions of the heritors (the landowners) in raising congregational protest. Landowners were criticised for a number of things. Firstly, they were neglecting the fabric of church buildings (and manses) that they were legally required to maintain. All over Scotland churches fell into severe disrepair, and by the 1790s clergy were complaining openly about dampness, falling roofs, lack of ventilation or heating, and unsurfaced floors where the rubbing of worshippers' feet was unearthing skeletons. Secondly, heritors were introduced to more refined forms of worship in England, and they were the instigators of unwelcome reform of worship at home – notably the abolition of precentors 'reading the line' of psalms for those without a Bible or reading skills. Thirdly, heritors failed to build new churches or extend existing ones to accommodate the increase in population during the eighteenth century. And fourthly, with so many heritors living only part of the year in their home parish (and sometimes none of the year there), they sought to pass over costs of maintaining the growing burden of the poor to the worshippers; this they did through the device of using the poor fund to install fixed pews which, after the allocation of a portion to their family, friends and tenants, were rented out to parishioners at 'economic' rates. As a consequence of these four developments, the poor in rural and village society tended to feel excluded from the parish church, many of the rising commercial classes took umbrage at being forced to pay proportionately more than the wealthy for the upkeep of the poor, and all felt cheated at having to pay more to worship in their parish church whilst having no say in who their minister should be. 'When the distribution of power between élite groups like the Crown, landowners and urban merchants, middle-rank groups like most tradesmen and small and medium landowners, and the rest of the people shifted out of balance, the parish church became the principal venue for social contest' (Brown, C 1990).

In this way, an acrimonious climate developed in very many parishes between the landed élites and the common people, and the parish church became the venue for battling it out. The church became increasingly the class battleground for the wider divisions introduced by agricultural improvement and, in the Highlands and Hebrides, for the Clearances. The parish church became the symbol of a lost proprietorship not only of organised religion but of the parish itself.

4. THE DISSENTERS

Once a patron's choice of minister had been 'settled' upon a congregation that contained protesters, worshippers were invariably so divided that they could not amalgamate again. Opponents of a selection usually refused to enter the parish church for worship, and instead met on a hillside, in a barn or a house to worship and plan the creation of a dissenting presbyterian church and congregation. Though there were already small groups of hardline Presbyterians in some Lowland areas by the eighteenth century (often referred to collectively as the Covenanters), real and effective dissent only emerged in 1733 when four Church of Scotland ministers denounced patronage and began to organise a separate 'presbytery' which developed – after their expulsion from the Kirk in 1756 – into what became known as the Secession Church. The Seceders developed a reputation as strict Calvinists, recruiting well in rural areas where patronage disputes left parishioners in need of 'sermon and superintendance', and they created a strong central control of their denominations. They became subject to enormous internal rancour, and they split into different churches repeatedly between the 1740s and the 1800s. Moreover, a large number of denominations and sects emerged as a result of opposition to patronage in the Church of Scotland, including the Relief Church (formed 1756), the Glasites and the Old Scots Independents (Brown, C 1987, 22–54; for schematic diagrams of the divisions in Scottish Presbyterianism, see MacLaren (1974) and Burleigh (1960)).

If patronage has been under-researched, the Dissenters of the eighteenth and early nineteenth centuries have been almost neglected in recent scholarship. They were enormously important, reflecting the changing economic and social structure of Scottish Lowland society. They recruited from different places and social groups at different times, mirroring the different stages of economic modernisation. Between the 1730s and 1780s they recruited strongly from agricultural tenants, farm servants, weavers and craftsmen who were each feeling the impact of agricultural improvement, commercialisation of society and alienation from both parish church and the landowners (heritors) that resulted. But from the 1790s, Dissenters started to recruit more strongly in urbanising and industrialising districts like Glasgow, Greenock, Monklands and Edinburgh. By 1800 anything from 20% to 70% of the people in Lowland parishes were Dissenters, whilst by 1826 one calculation is that 38% of the Scottish people as a whole were Dissenters (Brown, C 1988, 148–52).

Presbyterian dissent shifted its social composition during this growth. Between the 1750s and 1790s, the Dissenters were often characterised as poorly educated rustics, channelling their grievances against landowners into a surly Sabbath walk to a dissenting meeting house. Around 1800 John Ramsay, a Perthshire landowner, made the following comment about the Antiburghers, the largest group of Seceders:

Not many years ago, in walking upon the highroad, every bonnet and hat was lifted to the gentry whom the people met. It was an unmeaning expression of respect. The first who would not bow the knee to Baal were the Antiburghers when going to church on Sunday. No such thing now takes place, Sunday or Saturday, among our rustics, even when they are acquainted with gentlemen. It is connected with the spirit of the times.

(Ramsay 1888, 557)

Indeed, the Sabbath and its proper observance became, during agricultural improvement and early industrialisation, an important aspect of evangelical and especially dissenting culture. A Borders shoemaker wrote in 1849:

> There is no walk that a working man can take on the surface of his native earth
> like a walk to his place of worship. Here the harassments – the toils and
> anxieties of his every day life, appear as if cleared away before his footfall. Here
> he feels more certainly than at other times the true dignity of his own existence
> and ultimate destination!
>
> (Younger 1849, 26)

A stern plebeian puritanism thus lay at the origins of dissent. 'As class consciousness developed, the Sabbath was incorporated into proletarian culture. Keeping its sanctity became not a test of civil conformism but a statement of class unity and independence' (Brown, C 1987, 106).

Yet, Dissenters were not in any overall sense the poor, dispossessed and deprived. On the contrary, membership of a dissenting congregation usually signalled a strong social and economic aspiration to 'get on' – to succeed in the new economic climate. This was especially so in the towns and cities where dissenting strength lay by the first half of the nineteenth century. Between 1790 and 1850, there was a very noticeable social elevation of dissenting congregations as each generation did better in manufacturing, business and commerce than the previous generation. By the 1840s, the Secession and Relief Churches were dominated by lower-middle-class and upper-working-class groups, and their number included many town councillors and provosts. In 1847, these two churches amalgamated to form the United Presbyterian Church, an evangelical denomination accounting for a fifth of Scottish churchgoers and even more of those who lived in cities. From being in 1750 small in number and lowly in rural society, the Dissenters had, by 1850, become the upwardly mobile and 'new rich' of industrial Scotland.

5. THOMAS CHALMERS, THE DISRUPTION AND THE FREE CHURCH OF SCOTLAND

Evangelicalism was not merely represented by those who left the Church of Scotland in the eighteenth and early nineteenth centuries. Many more grew up within the state church, forming a growing Evangelical Party that eventually won control of the general assembly in 1834. The Assembly immediately gave congregations the power to veto a patron's choice of minister, and sought over the next ten years (in the so-called 'Ten Years' Conflict') to get Parliament to abolish patronage. This struggle was of immense political and social significance, giving rise in many localities to much agitation and legal battles in civil as well as ecclesiastical courts. The leading light of the Evangelical Party – Rev Dr Thomas Chalmers – became a household name in Scotland, and one of the most prominent Protestant clergy anywhere in the nineteenth-century English-speaking world.

Thomas Chalmers (1780–1847) had been raised in Fife, attended St Andrews University, and first became a minister for the rural parish of Kilmany. Developing an evangelical, though somewhat paternalistic, outlook on society, he was translated in 1814 to the Tron Parish in Glasgow where he started to develop strong ideas about the collapse of religious belief and self-reliance amongst the urban working classes, and about the disintegration of the bonds – centred on the parish church – between élites and the common people. He proposed to his heritors, the town council of Glasgow, that a new parish, called St John's, be erected in the working-class east end of the city where a rural-style parish church should be created and developed. In the 'territorial system' he developed at St John's after 1819, he organised committed elders to visit the people in their designated streets, he attracted committed evangelical laity who set up day schools, infant schools and Sunday schools, and he created an entirely independent poor-relief system that relied on voluntary contributions only and encouraged family self-reliance rather than dependence on 'handouts' from the church-organised poor relief. Though St John's is generally seen as a failure as a welfare system, Chalmers nonetheless became famous, attracting middle-class support for his alertness to urban problems of crime, to confrontational politics and industrial relations, and to the lack of religious piety amongst the 'masses'. It was he who popularised, in his published sermons and his books, the great nineteenth-century discourse on 'the lapsed masses' – a discourse which dominated ecclesiastical and élite attitudes to the working classes and the poor during the Victorian and Edwardian periods. Chalmers observed in 1821:

> . . . the religious spirit, once so characteristic of our nation, has been rapidly subsiding . . . more particularly in our great towns, the population have so outgrown the old ecclesiastical system, as to have accumulated there into so many masses of practical heathenism.
>
> (Chalmers 1821)

Chalmers offered solutions: a coherent programme for urban evangelisation (the outcome of which will be examined in Volume 2); an independent religious identity for the emerging large class of urban bourgeoisie and upper working classes; and, by opposing patronage, he appealed to many sections in Scottish society who had, for generations, been seeking a church free from rule by heritors and patrons. As well as the cities, the reinvigorated evangelicalism, of which Chalmers was a leading light within the Church of Scotland, appealed to the emergent crofting communities of the Highlands and Hebrides. When, in 1842, the government refused to abolish patronage and to accede to Chalmers' demands that the Church of Scotland should be permitted sovereignty within the state, church schism loomed immediately. Chalmers orchestrated the spectacular walk-out of the Evangelicals from the general assembly in St Andrew's Church in Edinburgh's George Street on 18th May 1843, and led them to the shouts of thousands of jubilant onlookers to a hall in Canonmills where the Free Protesting Church of Scotland was inaugurated. (The word 'Protesting' was soon dropped.) On that and the following days, the state church lost 37% of its clergy and somewhere in the region of 40 to 50% of its adherents.

EXERCISE 5
Look at **Document 23**. What were Thomas Chalmers' ideas on religion in cities and why might they appeal to the emerging urban middle classes?

Chalmers regarded cities as creating working-class 'masses' devoid of religiosity, partly due to the breakdown of the urban church. His solution rested on his principle of 'locality' – of creating small church parishes in cities in which the population were closely supervised, educated and encouraged by a revised poor-relief system towards self-reliance. This appealed to the middle classes because it seemed to offer a solution to growing urban problems of social breakdown and the rising costs of poor relief.

The Disruption, as it is known, has been the subject of renewed interest amongst historians in recent years. The principal biographer of Chalmers, Stewart J Brown, has argued (1982, 373–4) that the Disruption was a 'failure' for Chalmers, ending the unity and established status of the state church for which he had fought and in which he still believed, and was 'also a tragedy for organized religion in Scotland'. According to Brown, Chalmers' vision of creating in the cities a 'godly commonwealth', akin to that designed by the Scottish reformers for pre-industrial society, was destroyed by the Disruption. However, this negative judgement on the role of the Disruption in Scottish ecclesiastical idealism is challenged by other historians. Whilst the long-term heritage of the Disruption will be looked at in Volume 2, it is worth observing here that Chalmers' scheme for cities has recently been criticised by the present author as being out-of-date and unworkable, but that his dream of a 'godly commonwealth' was modernised, updated and widely implemented as the basis of municipal government in Scotland after 1850 (Brown, C 1996).

A more controversial debate has arisen as to the significance of the Disruption in Scottish national identity. Many historians and political commentators of the late 1980s and 1990s have asserted that the Disruption was a disaster for Scottish presbyterian nationalism, but that it nonetheless represented an outburst of patriotic frustration with the Westminster parliament. Stewart Brown (1993, 2) has written:

> The Disruption of the Church of Scotland was the most important event in the history of nineteenth-century Scotland. The events of 1843 shattered one of the major institutional foundations of Scottish identity, divided the Scottish nation, and contributed significantly to the process of assimilation into a larger British parliamentary state that was increasingly secular in orientation. The Disruption was not only the break-up of the national religious Establishment; it was also a disruption in Scottish identity, a radical break from its Reformation and Covenanting past, and a turning-away from the vision of the unified godly commonwealth. The Disruption undermined the Presbyterian nationalism that had shaped early modern Scotland, with the ideal of the democratic intellect preserved in parish schools, kirk sessions and presbyteries.

This interpretation has become quite widespread since 1975 when two ecclesiastical historians first wrote: 'Before the Disruption Scotland had a national identity; afterwards she had not' (Drummond and Bulloch 1975, 4). Late twentieth-century constitutional concerns in Scotland have led to rash statements from some historians; Clough (quoted in Storrar 1990, 36) asserted that: 'what might have developed into a declaration of independence . . . merely turned into the Disruption of the Kirk, and not the rupture of the state'. This fashionable tendency to see the Disruption as ending presbyterian national identity, or as anti-English protest, needs to be treated with extreme caution. Firstly, it is not an interpretation shared by the bulk of research scholars whose work on the event – as we shall see next – has tended to focus on its class dimensions in the context of social change. Secondly, a late twentieth-century 'nationalist' gloss on the events of 1843, though much asserted, lacks substantive contemporary evidence to support it, as most commentary at the time focused on the divisions *within* Scotland which instigated it (Brown, C 1996b). And thirdly, even some nationalist writers admit that the English did not cause the Disruption and were not the objects of the Free Church protesters' wrath (Paterson 1994, 57).

The third, and by far the most research-active, area of contention regarding the Disruption has been its significance to class identity, class consciousness and class struggle. A consensus has long been held that in the Highlands and Hebrides the Disruption gave final ecclesiastical definition to the stark division between lairds and crofters-fishers. Whilst the landowning classes almost universally supported the Church of Scotland of which they were legally heritors, and whilst many of them either worshipped there or in Episcopal chapels, between 80 and 97% of the people defected to the Free Church. Hunter (1976, 104; 1974) has commented: 'In the Highlands the Disruption was not an ecclesiastical dispute. It was class conflict'. This view has been widely held by historians who see the Free Church as the end-product of the eighteenth-century puritanisation and presbyterianisation of the Gaelic-speaking peasantry during the break-up of the clan system (Durkacz 1983; Withers 1984). However, Ansdell (1991) has recently questioned how widely applicable the class-conflict interpretation is in the Highland Disruption, arguing that in the Isle of Lewis much less antagonism was aroused. Nonetheless, from Lowland rural areas there is strong evidence of the interaction between the Disruption and economic and social change – as in Aberdeenshire where the church schism coincided with the formation of large farms, resulting in identification of dispossessed small tenants with the Free Church (Carter 1979).

The social implications of the Disruption in cities and towns have been debated somewhat differently. MacLaren (1974) argued that in Aberdeen the Disruption marked the emergence of a new rising middle class of commission agents, travellers and people of similar occupations, who used the Disruption as the cue to challenge an older middle class whose wealth was founded in part on agricultural connections. Part of this challenge was to leave the old city centre of Aberdeen and to create new suburbs to the west; another part was to leave the Church of Scotland and build their new Free Churches in those suburbs. MacLaren provides an image of the urban

No. 8. Portrait of Thomas Chalmers by David Octavius Hill and Robert Adamson. © *Scottish National Portrait Gallery.*

presbyterian church as the fiefdom of infighting 'fractions' of the middle classes, with elders almost wholly bourgeois in occupation and status, and the Free Church as little short of the private club of the upwardly mobile. The working classes of Aberdeen, MacLaren (1967) argued in contrast, were alienated from the presbyterian churches – by a kirk-session discipline over drink, sexual morality and even unacceptable occupations which was hostile to proletarian culture, by financial demands (for pew rents for instance) which the working classes could not afford, and by a general unwelcoming air at Sunday worship.

This approach has been vigorously challenged, notably in research by Hillis (1981) which shows that in Glasgow the *eldership* of presbyterian churches was – as in Aberdeen – dominated by the middle classes, but that the *membership* was dominated by the working classes, and especially the upper working classes. Hillis showed that the Free Church in Glasgow had a high degree of upper-working-class exclusivity, but that neither the Free Church nor the Church of Scotland was governed in a way which generally alienated the working classes as a whole. In wider research he has demonstrated that the sociology of the Disruption was very varied across Scotland, with the Free Church recruiting a surprisingly wide cross-section of social classes in Lowland rural areas, overwhelmingly crofters in the Highlands, and predominantly upper-working class and lower-middle class in towns (Hillis 1993).

By this stage you should have some idea of the way in which different groups of historians have different agendas when looking at the Disruption: the 'national identity' agenda, and the 'social class' agenda. This does not mean that there is agreement within each group of historians. Indeed, there are major disagreements between MacLaren and Hillis in relation to class identity in Presbyterianism. However, you should note how those like MacLaren and Hillis, who employ detailed local and regional analysis, focus on the *social* dimension of the Disruption and say little or nothing regarding *national* identity.

EXERCISE 6
Read **Article 5** by MacLaren and **Article 6** by Hillis. Discuss the key issues over which they disagree concerning Presbyterianism and social class in mid-nineteenth-century Scotland.

The long-term consequences of the Disruption will be examined in Volume 2. In the short term, it was a disaster for the Established Church. By 1851 the Free Church was attracting virtually the same number of worshippers as the Church of Scotland – each with 32% of churchgoers (Brown 1987, 61). The Church of Scotland was left with many kirks less than half filled at Sunday worship: some were all but empty. The Free Church took away from the 'Auld Kirk' most of the remaining energetic evangelicals – those who promoted schemes of evangelisation and religious innovation. The 'Frees' were socially complex, marking different class restructurings in different places, yet being held together by offering an ecclesiastical dimension to different class identities, common puritanical ideals, and a common hostility to the power of large landlords. Backed by urban middle-class wealth, it quickly became a rich church with kirks and manses planted in nearly every parish in Scotland, frequently sited opposite the doors of the Church of Scotland to make a point. The Free Kirk was the symbol of an energetic, evangelical and puritan crusade that was to be unleashed in Scotland in the second half of the nineteenth century.

6. ROMAN CATHOLICISM AND SECTARIANISM

Though Roman Catholicism had survived the Scottish Reformation in certain rural areas (mostly in the western Highlands and the North-East), the Catholic Church had no official hierarchy in Scotland between the sixteenth century and 1878. Its regeneration occurred as a result of growing immigration from Ireland between the late eighteenth and mid-nineteenth centuries. (A good introductory account is Handley 1943.) Between 1810 and 1850 as many as 25,000 Irish harvesters came annually to Scotland, but the availability of cheap steamboat travel during that time also facilitated more permanent migration. Between the 1810s and 1840s, west-coast ports and towns, such as Greenock, Port Glasgow, Glasgow and Coatbridge, became the home of first-generation Irish Catholic migrants. Generally poor, they invariably formed a major element of the lower working classes of Scotland's industrial areas, becoming labourers, carters, dockers, weavers, miners and iron-workers. The city of Glasgow became the focus of the Catholic community in Scotland; from reputedly only 30 Catholics in the city in 1778, the numbers rose to 2,300 in 1808 and 27,000 in 1831, to be followed by a significant surge in the late 1840s after the Irish potato famine.

The Catholic Church and practice of the Catholic faith were subject to extensive legal impediments. Eighteenth-century Scotland inherited a battery of measures from the previous century: Catholic mass was illegal, Catholics could not inherit or sell property or become teachers, and even *being* a Catholic was illegal, with kirk presbyteries having the power to declare them rebels (see **Document 24**). Though such measures were rarely enforced in the eighteenth century, the Protestant host society was extremely hostile to Catholicism. This hostility was institutionalised within all echelons of the presbyterian establishment. When, in the late 1770s, an attempt was made in Parliament to provide 'relief' (or freedom) for British Catholics, the urban élites of Edinburgh and Glasgow helped organise the artisanal mob to sack property owned by Catholics (Donovan 1979). A newspaper recounted one disturbance in Glasgow in October 1778:

> . . . during the time of morning service, a mob gathered round a house just by the College Church, where they understood that a few Catholics assembled for worship. The mob not only insulted, but terrified the poor people to the highest degree. The only person like a gentleman among the Papists escaped in a [sedan] chair, amidst the curses and imprecations of the multitude. Some poor Highland women had their caps and cloaks torn off them, and were pelted with dirt and stones. In short, the rabble continued their outrages till night, when they broke all the windows of the house, breathing blood and slaughter to all Papists, and in

every respect profaning the Lord's day in a grosser manner than ever was known to be done in Britain.

(Scots Magazine 1778, 684–5)

This account mirrored the treatment of other Scottish newspapers. Despite their evident prejudice against Catholics, they opposed such anti-Catholic disturbances because of their uncivilised tenor and because they desecrated the Sabbath. However, in Edinburgh the following January a flysheet was 'industriously dropt in several places' urging destruction of a Catholic chapel:

Men and Brethren
Whoever shall find this letter will take as a warning to meet at Leith wynd on Wednesday next in the evening to pull down that pillar of Popery lately erected there.
Edinburgh Jan 29, 1779

A PROTESTANT

P.S. Please to read this carefully, keep it clean, and drop it somewhere else.
For King and Country
Unity.

(quoted in Scots Magazine 1779, 107)

Even if hostility to 'papistry' continued in the middle and upper ranks of society, the desire for good order was becoming greater. As a result, the presbyterian establishment became divided; by the 1820s Thomas Chalmers and others – especially in the east of Scotland – supported Catholic Emancipation (Muirhead 1973a and 1973b), but popular anti-Catholicism hardened in Glasgow and the west of Scotland where the bulk of the immigrants were located.

EXERCISE 7
Read **Documents 21c, 24 and 25**, and describe the presbyterian discourse on the nature of the typical Catholic and the supposed dangers to Scottish society from Catholic faith and practice.

Presbyterians viewed Catholics as ill-educated and superstitious peasants, whether from the western Highlands or from Ireland. Catholicism threatened Scotland by undermining the presbyterian Church of Scotland (including ministers' income), by promoting 'delusion', and 'perverting' the people.

The issue of religious sectarianism between Catholic and Protestant is one to which we shall return in Volume 2. It is worth taking time now to include in your exercise your own observations on the longevity of this anti-Catholic discourse in modern Scotland. Are there elements of it which are familiar in late twentieth-century Scotland?

In the eighteenth century the Catholic Church to all intents and purposes did not exist in those places like Glasgow to which Irish Catholics were to come in such large

numbers after 1810. The construction of churches and the provision of clergy were
major problems. The Catholic Church had significant funding difficulties in Scotland between 1700 and 1830, not least because of the loss of money invested in
France at the time of the Revolution there (Johnson 1983). In recent work, Sloan
(1991) has demonstrated that shortage of resources was a factor restraining Catholic
mass attendance in Glasgow between c1830 and 1850; however, he points to how
the poverty of most Catholics kept church seats less than full: 'the most materially
impoverished were far less likely to regularly practise their faith' (ibid, 84).

Poverty mixed with ethnicity in hindering the growth of mass attendance. Most
priests before 1850 were Scots-born, and there was a certain degree of antagonism
between them and their new Irish-born flocks in west-central Scotland. The practice
of seat renting caused particular problems of payment amongst poor Irish Catholics
in Scotland, but this only marked a wider cultural and ethnic divide. Referring to
problems at the Catholic chapel in Paisley, the Glasgow-based Catholic Bishop
Andrew Scott wrote in 1812:

> As to the threat I mentioned of placing in the passes [ie Church aisles] after a
> few Sundays to prevent those who do not take [pay for] seats from occupying
> them, I should think it essentially necessary (from the experience I have of the
> Irish character and of the fertility of their genius in framing plausible excuses for
> not doing what is disagreeable to their passions) I should think it, I repeat,
> essentially necessary to put it in execution . . . The Irish must be treated in a
> different manner from our Scots people, or they never can be helped on the way
> to salvation.
>
> (quoted in Johnson 1983, 145)

Bishop Scott was in turn the object of criticism from an anonymous writer in 1820 to
a neighbouring bishop. Scott's own chapel in Glasgow was reportedly not in a happy
state:

> I request you to be so good as to write and admonish our Pastor, the Revd.
> Andrew Scott as he has of late used several Expressions tending to hurt the
> Feelings of the Irish, a people naturally proud and rather easily offended when
> their relative Poverty has been made the subject of their Reproach also it
> would be well if seats that has been appointed for the Poor that was unable to
> pay for their seats was Returned to them and Not to keep them standing up as
> a gazing stock during the sermon that Every Person present may know their
> Poverty . . .
>
> (quoted in Johnson 1983, 145)

A process of assimilation to the ways of both the host society and to the Catholic
Church in Scotland was underway, inducing changing perceptions of the social
meaning of churchgoing. An Ayrshire priest noted in the 1830s:

The Irish will not come out on Sunday and go to chapel unless they can be clothed and appear like natives. They will not go in ragged clothes as they went in Ireland.

(quoted in Ross 1978, 33)

There is no doubting that the success of the Church in forging a Catholic community in Lowland Scotland centred on the provision of both churches and priests. The major task of undertaking this took place in the 1840s. In 1800 there were no officially-formed Catholic parishes in west-central and south-west Scotland; by 1830 there were ten, but only one in Glasgow; by 1850, there were forty-one, with nine in Glasgow alone (calculated from data in Fitzpatrick 1986, 156–68). From these early beginnings, the Catholic Church was, after 1850, to establish its institutional presence in Scotland, and the Catholic community was to grow in size and importance in Scottish society.

REFERENCES TO BOOKS AND ARTICLES MENTIONED IN THE TEXT

Ansdell, DBA 1991 'The 1843 Disruption of the Church of Scotland in the Isle of Lewis', *Records of the Scottish Church History Society* 24.

Bebbington, DW 1989 *Evangelism in Modern Britain: A History from the 1730s to the 1980s.* London.

Bruce, S 1983 'Social change and collective behaviour: the revival in eighteenth-century Ross-shire', *British Journal of Sociology* 34 (1983), 554–72.

*Brown, C 1987 *The Social History of Religion in Scotland since 1987.* London and New York.

*Brown, C 1988 'Religion and social change', *in* Devine, TM and Mitchison, R (eds), *People and Society in Scotland. Volume I 1760–1830,* Edinburgh, 143–62.

*Brown, C 1990 'Protest in the pews: interpreting presbyterianism and society in fracture during the Scottish economic revolution', *in* Devine, TM (ed), *Conflict and Stability in Scottish Society 1700– 1850,* Edinburgh, 83–107.

Brown, C 1996a ' "To be aglow with civic ardours": the "Godly Commonwealth" in Glasgow 1843–1914', *Records of the Scottish Church History Society* 26, 169–95.

Brown, C 1996b 'Religion and national identity in Scotland since the Union of 1707', *in* McLeod, H (ed), *Church and People in Britain and Scandinavia.* Lund.

Brown, S 1982 *Thomas Chalmers and the Godly Commonwealth.* Oxford.

*Brown, S 1993 'The Ten Years' Conflict and the Disruption of 1843', *in* Brown, SJ and Fry, M, *Scotland in the Age of the Disruption,* Edinburgh, 1–27.

Burleigh, JHS 1960 *A Church History of Scotland.* London.

Carter, I 1979 *Farmlife in Northeast Scotland 1840–1914: The Poor Man's Country.* Edinburgh.

Chalmers, T 1821 *The Civic and Religious Economy of Large Towns.* Glasgow.

Donovan, RK 1979 'Voices of distrust: the expression of anti-Catholic feeling in Scotland, 1778–1781', *Innes Review* 30, 62–76.

*Drummond, AL and Bulloch, J 1973 *The Scottish Church 1688–1843: The Age of the Moderates.* Edinburgh.

*Drummond, AL and Bulloch, J 1975 *The Church in Victorian Scotland 1843–1874.* Edinburgh.

Durkacz, VE 1983 *The Decline of the Celtic Languages*. Edinburgh.

Fawcett, A 1971 *The Cambuslang Revival: The Scottish Evangelical Revival of the Eighteenth Century*. London.

Fitzpatrick, TA 1986 *Catholic Secondary Education in South-west Scotland before 1972*. Aberdeen.

*Handley, JE *The Irish in Scotland 1798–1945*. Cork.

*Hillis, P 1981 'Presbyterianism and social class in mid-nineteenth century Glasgow: a study of nine churches', *Journal of Ecclesiastical History* 32, 47–64.

*Hillis, P 1993 'The sociology of the Disruption' *in* Brown, S and Fry, M (eds), *Scotland in the Age of the Disruption*, Edinburgh, 44–62.

*Hunter, J 1974 'The emergence of the crofting community: the religious contribution 1798–1843', *Scottish Studies* 18, 95–116.

Hunter, J 1976 *The Making of the Crofting Community*. Edinburgh.

Johnson, C 1983 *Developments in the Roman Catholic Church in Scotland 1789–1829*. Edinburgh.

Landsman, N 1989 'Evangelists and their hearers: popular interpretation of revivalist preaching in eighteenth-century Scotland', *Journal of British Studies* 28, 120–49.

Landsman, N 1993 'Presbyterians and provincial society: The Evangelical Enlightenment in the West of Scotland, 1740–1775', *in* Dwyer, J and Sher, RB (eds), *Sociability and Society in Eighteenth-century Scotland*, Edinburgh, 194–209.

*MacLaren, AA 1967 'Presbyterianism and the working classes in a mid-nineteenth century city', *Scottish Historical Review* 46, 115–39.

*MacLaren, AA 1974 *Religion and Social Class: The Disruption Years in Aberdeen*. London.

Mitchison, R and Leneman, L 1989 *Sexuality and Social Control: Scotland 1660–1780*. Oxford.

Muirhead, IA 1973a 'Catholic emancipation: Scottish reactions in 1829', *Innes Review* 24, 26–42.

Muirhead, IA 1973b 'Catholic emancipation in Scotland: the debate and the aftermath', *Innes Review* 24, 103–20.

Paterson, L 1994 *The Autonomy of Scotland*. Edinburgh.

Ramsay, J 1888 *Scotland and Scotsmen in the Eighteenth Century, volume II*. Edinburgh and London.

Robe, Rev James 1989 *When the Wind Blows* (reprint of *A Faithful Narrative of the Extraordinary Work of the Spirit of God at Kilsyth, & c.* Belfast.

Ross, A 1978 'The development of the Scottish Catholic community 1878–1978', *Innes Review* 24, 30–55.

Scots Magazine 1778 and 1779.

*Sher, RB 1982 'Moderates, managers and popular politics in mid-eighteenth century Edinburgh: the Drysdale "Bustle" of the 1760s', *in* Dwyer, J *et al* (eds), *New Perspectives on the Politics and Culture of Early Modern Scotland*, Edinburgh, 179–209.

Sher, RB 1985 *Church and University in the Scottish Enlightenment: The Moderate Literati of Edinburgh*. Edinburgh.

*Sloan, W 1991 'Religious affiliation and the immigrant experience: Catholic Irish and Protestant Highlanders in Glasgow, 1830–1850, *in* Devine, TM (ed), *Irish Immigrants and Scottish Society in the Nineteenth and Twentieth Centuries*, Edinburgh, 67–90.

*Smout, TC 1982 'Born again at Cambuslang: New evidence on popular religion and literacy in eighteenth-century Scotland', *Past and Present* 97, 114–27.

Statistical Account of Scotland 1791–99. 21 volumes. Edinburgh.

Storrar, W 1990 *Scottish Identity: A Christian Vision*. Edinburgh.
Withers, CWJ 1984 *Gaelic in Scotland 1698–1981*. Edinburgh.
Younger, J 1849 *The Light of the Week: or the Temporal Advantages of the Sabbath Considered in Relation to the Working Classes*. London.

FURTHER READING

Those references marked * in the above list are recommended further reading.

Rural Transformation and Lowland Society

Ian Whyte

INTRODUCTION

During the later eighteenth and early nineteenth centuries Lowland rural society underwent profound changes. Many of these were related to the development of agriculture from largely subsistence-oriented production to a highly efficient commercial system. This transformation has been conventionally labelled the 'Agricultural Revolution'. As in England, there has been considerable debate over the chronology, nature and even the existence of this 'revolution'; see the debate in Whittington (1975), Adams (1978) and Whyte (1978) and also Whittington (1983). As we shall see, there is still general agreement about the speed of economic and social change in the Lowland countryside at this period. Our knowledge of agriculture and rural society has increased considerably since Smout's *History of the Scottish People* was first published. Although he provides a good account of many aspects of social change in the later eighteenth century, his picture of pre-improvement conditions is rather pessimistic and underestimates the amount of change which occurred before the 1760s. Space does not permit detailed discussion of pre-Improvement farming; but you can find a short introduction to this in Gray (1988a). Whyte (1979), Dodgshon (1981) or Devine (1994) all provide further background.

We approach this topic under the following headings:

- Rural society in the early eighteenth century
- The impact of agricultural improvement: the later eighteenth and early nineteenth centuries
- Rural society in the mid-nineteenth century

When you have completed this chapter you should understand the main developments in agriculture and the historical controversy which surrounds the changes that occurred in the Lowland countryside before 1850.

1. RURAL SOCIETY IN THE EARLY EIGHTEENTH CENTURY

By the early eighteenth century the old feudal ethos of Scottish society had almost disappeared. Country houses had replaced castles and feudal tenures were in decay. Land was seen increasingly as an economic asset rather than the basis of social prestige and political power. The link between tenant and proprietor was largely a commercial one tempered by vestiges of paternalism. Nevertheless, the continued payment of rents in kind and services still effectively insulated many farmers from the market. Rural society in many areas was dominated by subsistence production and family labour: a classic peasant system. The structure of rural society at this time is revealed in the poll tax lists from the mid 1690s (Table 1). The proportion of the rural population made up of tenants was as low as 15% of heads of household in some parishes in the Lothians and the Merse, around 20–25% in lowland Aberdeenshire, 30–40% in Renfrewshire and as high as 80% in parts of upland Aberdeenshire. This reflects regional and local differences in social structure resulting, among other things, from variations in farming systems, holding sizes and farm structures.

TABLE I: EXTRACT FROM THE 1695 POLL BOOK FOR TWO FARMS IN BELHELVIE PARISH, ABERDEENSHIRE.

Cranboge

Thomas Gibson, tennent ther, his proportione of his maisters valowed rent 13s. 10d, with 6s. of generall poll for himself and wife is	£1	5	10
Item Marjorie and Margrat Gibsones, his daughters in familia, generall poll is		12	0
Item Patrick Gibson, his son in familia, his poll is	0	6	0
Item, James Pirrie, his servant, fee £13 4s., fortieth part and generall poll	0	12	7
Andrew Thomson, herd, fee £8, fortieth part and generall poll is	0	10	0
Item, Issobell Poter, servant, Fee £12, fortieth part and generall poll is	0	12	0
Item, John Dick, cottar ther, and his wife, poll is	0	12	0
Item, Robert Wishert, cottar ther, his own, his wife, his daughter, and Jean Milne, their servant	1	4	0
Item, Janet Wallace, grasswoman, her poll is	0	6	0
Item, Jane Bisset, grasswoman, her poll and daughters is	0	12	0

Balmade

William Cowper, tennent ther, his proportion of valouatione is £1 7s. 8d., and for his mother-in-law, and Janet Mor in familia, their generall poll is	2	11	8
Item, William Mill and William Muirson, servants, fee £20 each, fortieth pairt and generall poll is	1	2	0
Item, Margrat Talzor and Elizbeath Beufort, fee £20 each, fortieth pairt and generall poll is	1	2	0

Item, Alexander Archbald and Alexander Mitchell, herds, fee £8 each, fortieth pairt and generall poll is	1	0	0
Item, Jane Forrest, a widdow, of poll	0	6	0
Alexander Sim, John Talzor, and Thomas Simson, cottars, and their wyves	1	16	0
Item, Issobell Nicoll, ane widow women, her poll is	0	6	0
Item, Alexander Talzor, cottar and wyver, his poll is	0	18	0
Item, John Salmond, cottar and cobler, and his wyfe, their generall poll is	0	18	0

EXERCISE 1

Try tabulating the above data into different social groups. What problems do you find? What is the percentage of tenants and cottars on the two farms? What does this suggest about the social structure in this area?

Apart from the poll tax returns, what other kinds of sources might provide information about rural society at this time? You will find references to some of them below. How many of them represent the interests and viewpoints of the landowning élite?

You would be right in thinking that this raises as many questions as it answers. For a start, the status of some people is not clear – were the widows formerly married to cottars or tenants? What is the distinction between widows and grasswomen? The children listed must be over sixteen to qualify for paying the poll tax – what roles did they perform? We do not know how many children under sixteen were included in the various families. The social structure can be analysed in various ways. There are only two tenants but seven cottars and six male servants; so tenants make up only 13% of adult males. If these farms are typical, this suggests that rural society in Belhelvie was quite sharply polarised with a small, relatively well-to-do group of tenants on fairly large holdings. If you classify all listed adults, male and female, 22% are in tenant families, 39% in cottar families, plus 28% male and female servants, mainly in tenant households, and 11% grasswomen and widows.

Other sources which can provide information about rural society in the early eighteenth century include parish registers, testaments, rentals, leases, estate accounts and surveys: the last four were produced for the purposes of estate management and reflect the interests of the landowners, as is clear in our subsequent discussion.

Tenant farmers formed the most important social group in terms of wealth and status. Their formal position is recorded in estate rentals, accounts and collections of leases but we still know little about their lifestyles. Later eighteenth-century writers on agricultural improvement saw them as reactionary, ignorant and conservative, but a study evaluating them more objectively is badly needed. At the bottom of tenant society were smallholders: crofters and pendiclers who often had trades and by-employments and who were only distinguished from cottars by virtue of leasing their land direct from a proprietor rather than sub-letting from a tenant. At the other extreme were the occupiers of large arable farms in the Lothians or extensive sheep runs in the Borders.

Tenant structure on any estate depended upon landlord policy. A substantial proportion of Lowland farms was still worked by groups of farmers, though farms of this type were gradually becoming less numerous. Holdings on such farms were often small, their arable lands intermixed, and there must have been a good deal of co-operation between tenants, pooling equipment and labour for the main tasks in the agrarian year. On estates where multiple-tenant farms were still common, rural society was probably not markedly differentiated, distinctions between tenants and cottars being blurred. In areas where larger single-tenant farms were more common, society must have been more sharply polarised into masters and workers.

TABLE 2: RANGE OF RENTS AND HOLDING SIZES ON THE PANMURE ESTATES IN FORFARSHIRE IN THE EARLY EIGHTEENTH CENTURY

| RENT | | APPROX ACREAGE | |
BOLLS OF GRAIN	MONEY £ SCOTS	UNDER CULTIVATION (SCOTS ACRES)	% OF ALL HOLDINGS
1–5	5–20	0.5–4	34
6–10	21–40	5–8	14
11–20	41–75	9–16	9
21–40	76–100	17–35	15
41–60	101–200	36–48	15
61–100	200+	49–75	10
	100+	76+	3

Source: Whyte and Whyte 1984a, 162.

EXERCISE 2
What does the table tell us about the social structure of the Panmure tenantry?

You could reasonably conclude that the tenantry on the Panmure estates were a very varied group; there was a considerable proportion of crofters – smallholders leasing direct from the proprietor – but also a solid block of middling-sized farmers and a significant minority of large farmers.

Tenants held their land by written leases, verbal agreements or tenancies at will which simply continued from year to year. The prevalence of short leases has convinced some historians that insecurity of tenure was widespread, giving farmers no incentive to invest labour or capital in improvement, and encouraging high rates of turnover. In fact, continuing paternalism helped to keep families in possession of particular holdings for generations, son succeeding father, sometimes 'beyond memory of man'. The majority of leases surviving in estate collections are renewals to sitting tenants. On the Panmure estates a long run of annual rentals in the late seventeenth and early eighteenth centuries allows mobility and rates of turnover of farmers to be studied in detail. The amount of land needed by a tenant family might change over the years with different life-cycle phases but it was often possible to increase or reduce the size of a holding without moving by taking on or relinquishing fractions of the farm. The geographical mobility of tenants into or within the estates operated over very short distances (Whyte and Whyte 1984a and 1984b).

Holding size was crucial to the ability of tenants to survive a crisis or accumulate capital. In the early eighteenth century it was possible for a prosperous farmer to occupy a farm of perhaps 300 acres in the south-eastern Lowlands or a pastoral one of 1,000 acres in the Border hills. The tenants of many large Lothian farms chose to style themselves as 'gentlemen' in the 1690s poll tax returns, incurring an extra payment for the privilege (Devine 1994, 7). They were forerunners of the more commercially minded farmers who emerged in the late eighteenth and nineteenth centuries. Most tenants worked much smaller holdings, though. The occupiers of many multiple-tenant touns must have held only 30–40 acres or less in many parts of the Lowlands. In the North-East, where holdings seem to have been smaller, 20–30 acres may have been more normal. On the basis of calculations from the poll tax, Devine has estimated that the proportion of tenants farming over 100 acres of arable was only 2% in Aberdeenshire, 5% in Renfrewshire but as high as 36% in Midlothian. On the other hand, in lowland Aberdeenshire 45% of tenants held less than 20 acres. The proportion in the upland areas of the county was higher still. Even in Midlothian 37% of holdings were under 30 acres (*ibid*, 8).When it is realised that portions of these already small holdings were sublet to cottars, it is easy to see why so many tenants lived on the margins of poverty.

Historians have portrayed Lowland rural society as impoverished, with tenants hardly differentiated from their cottars, and a marked lack of social stratification. This picture is exaggerated. In most areas there were wide variations in wealth and status within the farming community. On the Panmure estates there was a certain amount of mobility up and down the farming ladder. Most farmers, however, ended their careers on similar-sized holdings to the one they started with. The wealthier tenant farmers, occupying larger holdings, were a self-perpetuating group; few men succeeded in working their way up from the position of cottar or small tenant to the tenancy of a large farm. On the other hand extreme downward mobility was not too common either (Whyte and Whyte 1984a). The evidence of their testaments suggests that most tenants operated with slim reserves. The picture of an impoverished tenantry should not be overdrawn, though, for wealthier farmers did exist and some had money to lend to their landlords. Debt and credit may have been related to life-cycle phases, many families probably being net recipients of credit at some stages and net providers at others. Evidence for the Panmure estates suggests that while the ability of smaller tenants to accumulate capital was not changing, in the early eighteenth century the position of larger tenants was improving (Whyte and Whyte 1988).

A high proportion of the rural population in the Lowlands was below the tenant class but little is known about them. Unlike England there was no sharp divide in Lowland Scotland between those who had some land and those who depended on selling their labour to others. Access to land was much more widespread in Scotland where there were few landless labourers and almost everyone, at some time or other, had at least a fragment of land to call his own. The most numerous group were cottars who sublet small portions of arable land from the tenants with some grazing rights and a kailyard in return for providing labour. Some male cottars were full-time agricultural workers but many were part-time tradesmen, shoemakers, tailors, weavers and wrights providing the basic services which rural communities required. The poll tax returns from the 1690s also list many female cottars including, in the North-East, 'grasswomen' who merely had a cottage and some grazing rights. The maintenance of such a significant smallholding element on the land was one of the most distinctive features of Lowland rural society and a barrier to improving agricultural productivity. Cottars supplied labour for the peak periods of the agricultural year such as ploughing, harvesting and peat cutting. Many tenants also had to render labour services to their landlords including cultivating the mains, cutting and carrying peat, and transporting grain rents to market. Much of this labour was performed by cottars. By paying them in land, tenants were saved any

No. 9. Swanston, near Edinburgh; a rare example of a surviving pre-Improvement ferm toun or hamlet cluster. © *Ian Whyte*.

cash outlay at a time when a money economy was far from fully developed in many districts. In addition, some cottars paid rent for their holdings, providing tenants with additional income. Day labour on estate mains and policies was usually done by cottars as an extra source of income; there was not enough work to support full-time labourers (Gibson 1990). Cottars paid heavily for their small plots, and chances of upward mobility were limited. Gibson and Smout's (1995) calculations of model household budgets demonstrates the hand-to-mouth nature of existence for cottar families. Most of them lived close to the margins of poverty. In order to make ends meet their wives would have had to earn as much as possible from by-employments. Table 3 shows a document for the farm of Plowlands in Fife, dated 1714, which gives details of the cottars there.

TABLE 3: THE COTHOUSES BELONGING TO THE WITHIN FARM CALLED THE PLOWLANDS -

1. *Archd Myles in Craigburn possesses a hous yeard and one acre of Land laboured be the Tennent.*

2. *Alxdr Miller in Knowhead 2 acres and a half Laboured and payes 3 bolls and 21 lib of money.*

3. *James Leslie and hous yeard and ane acre Labourer*

4. *John Robison sheepherd a hous yeard and ane acre in 2 divisions.*

5. *David Reekie 2 acres with hous and yeard and land Laboured payes 5 bolls bear 1 shearer and – of money.*

6. *David Patie ane acre with hous and two yeards and land Laboured pays 2 shearers and seven lib. of money.*

7. *William Lanceman ane acre without hous or yeard to it 12 lib.*

8 & 9. *The Whythons and yeard with 4 acres to it possest by Will: Patrick and Christian Tollow in 2 Divisions.*

10. *Thom: Shipherds relict a hous yeard and 2 acres of Land.*

11. *Wm. Greig a hous and yeard without Land payes 7 lib.*

12. *Janet Shipherd ane hous yeard and acre.*

13. *Andrew Baxter a hous yeard and payes 5 lib it has ane acre of land belonging to it but not possest by him.*

14. *Alexdr Mackie in hillhead about ane – acre*

15. *Alexdr Paterson 3 acres whereof two are on the Westermost march above the highway.*

Source: Devine (1994, 12).

EXERCISE 3
How much variation in landholding, and possibly wealth, among the cottars of Plowlands does this document reveal?

Again, this list shows that the cottars were far from a uniform and amorphous group. Some had no land at all apart from a house and a vegetable plot (yard); others had as much as four acres of arable land. This suggests a good deal of variation in possible wealth, but note that the list does not mention grazing rights or tell you how many of the cottars possessed a trade in addition to agriculture.

Living-in farm servants formed, in Gray's phrase, 'a seamless group' with the cottars (Gray 1988a, 54). They were a life-cycle phase rather than a separate social class, being generally young and unmarried. It must have been the normal experience of most cottar children and many from tenant families to go into service in their early to mid teens. In the South-East, though, many male servants were married, with some land and grazing but, unlike cottars, they worked full-time for their masters. In areas where holdings were small and could be worked mainly by family members, servants were fewer. Male farm servants accounted for only 8–9% of the recorded adult males in parts of upland Aberdeenshire. In the Lothians and Berwickshire, where larger holdings required more hired labour, the figure was as high as 40% in some parishes. Male and female servants received bed, board and some money wages. Their contracts were normally for six months or a year and, as in England, they moved frequently in search of new masters (Houston 1985).

The role of women in Lowland society was very much a subordinate one. Tenancies of large farms were sometimes held by women but this was often a temporary arrangement between the death of a spouse and the succession of a son. Wages paid to women were about half those for men. Women's income, whether from agricultural work or domestic industry, was designed to supplement a male income. Widows and spinsters often led a precarious existence on or below the poverty line, their modest incomes sometimes supplemented by meagre handouts from the parish poor box.

Farming at this time has received a bad press from improving writers whose adverse, but strongly biased, comments have often been accepted uncritically; see Handley (1953) for some good examples. Agriculture and rural society were not immutable but the pace of change was slow – in Chapter 11 of this volume Professor Smout shows that the ethos of improvement predated the Union of 1707. The Union was not a significant watershed in Scottish agriculture in the short term. All the trends in Scottish agriculture which are evident in the first half of the eighteenth century had their origins before 1707. Yet in the longer term the Union made Scottish landowners more familiar with English farming practices and opened up wider markets for Scottish livestock and grain. The powerful control exercised by landowners over the inhabitants of their estates meant that when conditions were ripe they could institute sweeping changes without hindrance. The later 1690s brought a series of harvest failures and famines. In the worst-hit areas, such as upland Aberdeenshire, there was heavy mortality among tenants as well as cottars, and widespread abandonment of farms (Tyson 1985). Even in less severely hit Lowland areas tenants built up massive arrears which hung over them for years (Whyte and Whyte 1984a). This disaster focused the minds of many landowners on the need to improve agriculture (Whyte 1979). These famines were, however, atypical and did not occur again. During the first half of the eighteenth century there were a few years of shortage, especially in 1740–41, but none of widespread dearth. This may have been due in part to a gradual improvement in the organisation of parish poor relief, which failed so dismally in some parishes in the 1690s, and to increased earnings from domestic industry such as spinning linen and woollen yarn.

Until Devine's study (1994), remarkably little was known about agricultural and social change in the first half of the eighteenth century. It was not clear whether change occurred gradually or only accelerated rapidly in the 1760s. Devine has shown that there was a continuation of trends already evident in the later seventeenth century. Written leases became almost universal and long leases for nineteen years became common. There was a widespread trend towards the commutation of rents in kind to money payments. The removal of multiple-tenant farms continued and by the 1760s single-tenant farms were almost universal. These structural changes indicate that agriculture was shifting slowly towards production for the market. By removing multiple tenancies with their constraints of communal working and land fragmentation and by increasing average holding size, the enclosure of farms later in the century was made far simpler. Moreover, these slow changes gradually created a class of wealthier market-oriented farmers ready to work with landowners in the process of improvement, while operating sufficiently slowly to avoid dramatic displacement of population and consequent social tensions.

Changes in farming systems were, however, much slower. In the first half of the eighteenth century developments were largely confined to estate mains and policies, hobby farming rather than a serious commercial undertaking. The plantation of trees and the laying out of enclosures was linked with experiments in livestock breeding and the trial of new crops and rotations, but on few estates did landowners attempt enclosure on a large scale (Whyte 1979). Evidence from the Mains of Yester in East Lothian indicates a gradual rise in crop yields but such improvements did not spread among the tenantry (Whyte 1993). Forty years were to pass in most areas between these first experiments and the onset of full-scale improvement. For both landowners and tenants there was insufficient incentive, in terms of rising prices, to encourage major investment (Gibson and Smout 1995). A few enthusiastic innovators, like John Cockburn of Ormiston, introduced change from social as much as economic motives. From 1716, Cockburn tried to transform his East Lothian estate by introducing improved English farming methods, including enclosure, new crops and rotations. He encouraged his tenants by giving them long leases and sending their sons to England to learn better husbandry. In 1736 he founded a local society for agricultural improvement, the first of its kind in Scotland. He overreached himself, however, and went bankrupt (Smout 1969, 292–4). More common were men like George Dundas of Dundas, who succeeded to a small estate near South Queensferry in 1706. His diary records, over a fifty-year period, his gradual improvement of the estate with modest resources of capital and labour. He proceeded cautiously, initiating changes year by year which were small in scale but significant cumulatively (Whyte 1981).

One area where large-scale enclosure affected tenanted farms was Galloway. Large cattle parks, under the personal management of proprietors, rearing better-quality animals for the droving trade, were established in the later seventeenth century on some estates in this region. Their extension in the early eighteenth century led to dispossession and the 'Levellers' Revolt' of 1724–25, an uncharacteristic instance of large-scale agrarian protest during which bands of tenants and cottars went round the countryside throwing down the new enclosure walls. The Government sent in troops to pacify the area but the relatively lenient treatment of those offenders who were caught suggests a recognition that local landowners had overstepped the mark in their enthusiasm.

2. THE IMPACT OF AGRICULTURAL IMPROVEMENT: THE LATER EIGHTEENTH AND EARLY NINETEENTH CENTURIES

From the 1760s market conditions for Scottish farming changed dramatically. One influence was population increase. The average rate of growth of 0.6% per annum between the 1750s and 1801 greatly increased demand for agricultural products, as urbanisation and industrialisation created huge new markets for food and raw materials. Standards of living rose for both ordinary workers and the middle classes, stimulating demand for meat and dairy produce as well as cereals. The result was rising prices which encouraged rapid economic and social change in the Lowland countryside with the onset of full-scale improvement. The model of a late eighteenth-century Agricultural Revolution has long been abandoned for England. For Lowland Scotland, while it is now clear that developments in the early eighteenth century, discussed above, laid the foundations, this does not undermine the idea that from the 1760s there was a sharp acceleration in the pace of change bringing equally dramatic social transformation. The speed with which the Lowland countryside was altered was unprecedented in Scottish history and unique in Europe. This period is much better recorded than the first half of the eighteenth century, with treatises and surveys by agricultural improvers, two sets of county reports produced for the Board of Agriculture, and the detailed parish descriptions of the *Statistical Account of Scotland*. Such material should, however, be treated with caution and cannot always be taken at face value.

Many landowners now began to invest heavily in improving their estates because they could see the likelihood of considerable returns on their capital within only a few years. The chronology of improvement is clear from the parish reports of the *Statistical Account*, written in the 1790s. In only a few parishes was the start of change dated to the 1740s or 1750s. The 1760s and 1770s were the crucial decades with widespread enclosure and the adoption of improving leases specifying new rotations and new crops including sown grasses, though these sometimes proved unduly restrictive (Devine 1994; Whittington 1983). Holdings and farms were consolidated into compact blocks, amalgamated and enclosed to make them more commercially efficient. Balanced rotations were adopted including sown grasses and root crops as well as cereals. Improved ploughs, especially the one designed by James

Small, became general: drawn by two horses rather than a team of oxen, they allowed much more efficient cultivation. Full commutation of rents in kind to money payments was widespread with the removal of most services. Lingering paternalism was eliminated under the pressure of the commercial ethos. The pace of innovation varied from one region to another and, within particular districts, between estates. The Lothians were in the vanguard of improvement, as were many counties in the Central Belt, but significant change did not affect the North-East until the end of the century (Gray 1988b). Progress was not uninterrupted, though; there were difficult years in the 1770s and particularly the 1780s before further acceleration occurred in the 1790s. Bad weather, some poor harvests and the failure of the Ayr Bank in 1772 were among the causes, but although there was a good deal of hardship, the difficulties were short-lived (Devine 1994). The view that the first burst of enclosure in the late eighteenth century was merely a progressive fashion and often a failure seems unduly pessimistic (Whittington 1983).

EXERCISE 4

Read **Document 26**. What restrictions did the lease impose on the tenant and how much flexibility did he have?

There is a lot to this but you might note in particular that the cropping clauses are quite tight and restrictive including the use of manure and fertiliser but there is little leeway for variation. On the other hand the tenant is encouraged to make his own improvements, including enclosure, with reimbursement from the proprietor.

As this example illustrates, some landowners played a major role in instituting improvements, not only in providing the finances but in dictating what should be done (Adams 1980; Campbell 1977). They had to provide a lead by replanning the structure and boundaries of farms and fields before the tenants could respond. The ethos of improvement had an important social as well as economic dimension. Many proprietors were concerned to remodel rural society as well as agriculture on rational and efficient lines. The efforts of tenants were also considerable, though, and have received less attention. It was they who had to translate the fashionable ideas of their landlords into economic reality, investing their own money as well as labour.

Such a transformation inevitably had a major impact on rural society. Larger farms were seen as essential to commercial efficiency. This has led some writers to claim that substantial dispossession of smaller tenants occurred in the later eighteenth century. Devine's analysis of rentals and processes for removal in sheriff courts has shown, however, that on several Lowland estates the rate of tenant reduction was relatively moderate, between 10% and 20% being common over periods of forty to fifty years or more (Devine 1994, 115). The process of consolidation was gradual, giving the farming community time to adjust. There was no mass clearance of tenants; the reduction in multiple tenancies and increases in holding size in the late seventeenth and early eighteenth centuries had already achieved much of this. There was a difference between the ideals advocated by improving writers and actual practice. They argued that a minimum farm size of 100 acres was necessary for commercial viability but farms below this threshold remained common throughout the Lowlands in the early nineteenth century. In west-central Scotland particularly dairying and market gardening were well suited to smaller holdings. These trends, however, related to arable, mixed farming and dairying areas. In upland pastoral areas there was a greater shake-out of tenants as commercial livestock rearing with a subsistence arable element was replaced by full commercialisation of the livestock sector and the abandonment of cultivation (Dodgshon 1983). In parts of the Borders, south Lanarkshire, south Ayrshire and the Angus glens the scale of change and social dislocation was greater. In parishes like Lamington and Roberton in upper Clydesdale, population was halved between the 1750s and the 1790s. In these areas the scale of tenant displacement may have been comparable with the Highland Clearances (Devine 1994, 126).

More profound changes occurred at a lower level of rural society with the widespread removal of cottars. The new farming systems required a different labour structure. The improved systems of husbandry required work to be spread more widely through the farming year due to more intensive ploughing and the use of new labour-intensive crops like turnips and potatoes. The cottar system had been well

No. 10. A polygonal 'horse-gang' for a horse-powered threshing machine, one of the few mechanical innovations to have a significant effect on the use of labour in Scottish agriculture in the late eighteenth and early nineteenth centuries. © *Ian Whyte.*

suited to conditions in which demand for labour was concentrated in a few brief periods. Instead of having one or two servants working full-time supplemented by cottar labour at busy periods, farmers now needed more full-time workers: married servants or, more commonly outside the South-East, single ones, fully under the farmers' control. In arable areas the work routine centred around maximising the efficiency of the horse teams with full-time ploughmen being responsible for a particular pair of horses. With rents rising rapidly, farmers had to evaluate their costs much more carefully. It made economic sense to remove cottars, absorb their holdings and rely on full-time wage labour supplemented, at harvest time, by seasonal workers drawn from nearby villages and towns or further afield from the Highlands. Minister after minister in the *Statistical Account* referred to the numbers of ruined cottages in their parishes and the widespread removal of their occupants. The pace of change and the scale of dispossession varied from one estate to another. Nevertheless, the removal of cottars was a more fundamental change than the dispossession of small tenants. The transformation was easily accomplished because cottars had no leases, no legal rights, and could be removed at the will of the proprietor or farmer. Their position was being undermined in any case by the division of commonties and the improvement of waste which deprived them of grazing and sources of building materials and fuel (Devine 1994, 142).

The removal of cottars must have created considerable mobility within the Lowland countryside in the late eighteenth century, but levels and patterns of migration are difficult to determine.

EXERCISE 5

What kinds of source material might provide information on migration within the countryside or movement to the towns?

Within the countryside you might note that testimonials of good conduct issued by kirk sessions have been used to chart local-scale mobility, as have estate rentals and leases, the feu charters for plots of land in planned villages, and parish register entries – particularly marriages. Kirk session records also contain information on vagrancy. For the towns, apprenticeship records provide information on one particular category of migrant but court depositions, marriage registers and kirk sessions also contain useful data.

Such sources provide evidence of net out-migration from many purely agricultural parishes and an inflow to parishes with an urban and industrial base or a large estate village. The removal of cottars did not automatically lead to widespread rural depopulation, though. The new farming systems required more rather than less labour though in a different form. While some displaced cottars probably migrated to the towns, many remained as farm servants, labourers or tradesmen. The creation of the improved landscape generated more demand for labour building new farmsteads, enclosures and roads, digging drains, planting hedges and carting materials. Unlike the early eighteenth century, there was now enough work to keep day-labourers in year-round employment.

Many cottars moved short distances to the new planned villages which were being established throughout the Lowlands, especially between the 1770s and 1820s (Lockhart 1980). Some 300 were laid out with concentrations in the North-East, Angus, lowland Perthshire, and the South-West. These allowed landowners to increase their income by attracting tradesmen who would pay rent, service the local farms and absorb local produce. Some villages also attracted larger-scale manufacturing, Gatehouse-of-Fleet in Galloway with its cotton-spinning mills being a prime example. As well as new villages, many existing rural kirktons with small populations had grown into settlements with several hundred inhabitants by the end of the eighteenth century. The ability of these settlements to absorb dispossessed cottars and re-orient their labour to suit the new improved farming systems may go a long way towards explaining the lack of social unrest or serious labour supply problems in the Lowland countryside (Devine 1994, 157–62). The removal of cottars should not be viewed simply as a process of coercion and dispossession. The new farming systems and the activities needed to service them offered many positive opportunities for men to switch to being full-time specialist workers at a time when real wages were rising substantially. In many parishes the countryside emptied as scattered ferm touns and cot touns were replaced by large farms housing their own full-time labour force, with labourers and tradesmen concentrated in the villages.

Improvement sharpened the differences within rural society. For those families who remained tenants, rising prices brought increasing prosperity manifested by greatly improved housing conditions, better-quality furniture, clothes bought in towns rather than made locally, more material possessions and a much more varied diet including wheaten bread, coffee, tea, sugar, wine and butcher's meat. Such a lifestyle, a couple of generations earlier, would have been envied by many small lairds. George Robertson (1829, 71–2) described the older style of farmhouse which was still found in the Lothians in the 1760s:

> These biggins were commonly arranged in one row. The dwelling-house in the middle, with the barns at one end, and the cattle-houses at the other. They were all low in the walls, and were all covered with straw, in some cases interlaid with thin sods or turfs, to keep it together. The sit-house or dwelling . . . consisted of two main divisions, distinguished by the names of the but and the ben. The first was used as the kitchen and servants' apartment, where all the household assembled at meal times, and where the female part of the family slept – that is, the daughters and the maid-servants; the second, or ben-the-house, was the master's (or the gudeman's) peculiar quarters, where he and his wife and younger children lay, and where friends or other strangers were at times entertained. The walls of this part of the steading, both but and ben, were generally raised a foot or two higher than those of the other coterminous houses. This gave room for a low storey above, which served for various purposes; as a lumber room or store-place . . . and also where was a bed or two for the young lads of the family.

EXERCISE 6

In what ways do you think such living conditions would have affected day-to-day life?

Well, one major effect would have been an almost total lack of privacy – this might have made for sociability in some senses but would have made courtship rather difficult. It would also have worked against the farmer maintaining much social distance from his servants – they would have eaten at the same table.

The widespread rebuilding of farmsteads from the 1840s further improved their accommodation. Improved housing conditions came first for farmers, then for their livestock and only belatedly for their workers. Cottar houses in the 1760s were described by Robertson (1829, 78–9):

> They were very mean hovels. The walls, not exceeding five feet in height, were usually composed of round land-stones and divets, in alternating layers. As this frail fabric was deemed to be insufficient to support the roof, the wooden work of it was constructed . . . of upright kebbers of rough timber, inserted into the heart of the walls . . . A cottage of this kind was constructed in all its parts by the gudeman and his servants in a single day, they having previously collected all the materials.
>
> The size of these cottar huts might be about twelve feet square inside, sufficient to contain all the plenishing which in those times was wont to be required. When they had a chimney . . . it was constructed in the same fashion as the kitchen lum of the master, but of less size. In many cases there were none. The fire was kindled on the hearth while the smoke escaped by a hole in the roof, or as often by the door or window; which last was not always furnished with glass, but consisted of a single shutter . . . There were many cottages of this description to be seen, even in the Lothians, at the time alluded to, (1765), and in remoter parts of the country I have seen some such, fifty years after that time.

There was a revolution in housing standards for farmers in the last forty years of the century with two-storey Georgian-style houses of mortared stone with slate roofs becoming widespread. The next generation of houses, rebuilt in the early to mid-nineteenth century, was often built away from the steading, as if physically to distance the farmer and his family from their servants and from the dunghill. Steadings were increasingly redesigned on more rational, efficient and spacious lines. In arable areas the outbuildings were arranged around a courtyard for feeding cattle, with barns and cart sheds on one side and byres on the other, often still thatched but gradually being replaced by tile and slate.

3. RURAL SOCIETY IN THE MID-NINETEENTH CENTURY

By the 1830s rural society was starting to settle down after the dramatic changes of the previous seventy years. The first three decades of the nineteenth century had seen changes penetrate to every part of the Lowlands. As in the later eighteenth century, progress was not uninterrupted. Depression in the 1820s bankrupted many farmers. Conditions were not static, though. The work of improvement had not been completed, even in the South-East. As the parish reports of the *New Statistical Account* well document, agriculture reached a peak of prosperity in the 1840s which continued until depression set in during the 1870s. Investment in improvements, such as undersoil drainage and new farmsteads, remained considerable. This was the era of 'high farming': high capital inputs and high output. The work patterns which were established by the 1830s, and the society which was built around farm labour, remained in place with only relatively minor changes for the next century (Gray 1984). Many aspects of rural society were very different from conditions a century earlier but there were also important underlying continuities: for instance, the continuation of systems of long-hire labour, the use of married farm workers in the South-East, the survival of payments in kind and the marked differential in wages for men and women. The allowances in kind for a Lothian hind in the 1850s had changed very little from the 1650s (Levitt and Smout 1984).

Improvements in standards of accommodation for farm workers lagged behind those for farmers and their livestock. While more solid walls and watertight roofs provided more effective shelter, conditions inside were often still spartan. As early as the 1790s cottar houses in parts of Fife were described as being better built than farm houses thirty to forty years before but primitive hovels with walls of turf, fieldstones or clay remained normal in many areas, as did one-roomed cottages occupied by large families and sometimes additional female outworkers. When moving to another farm cottage, married workers had to take their own locks, window frames, ovens, grates and shelves. Chaumers and bothies for single men were often damp, cold, draughty and cheerless places where it was difficult to get soaked clothes to dry and where the only furniture was wooden built-in beds and the men's kists (chests). The 1840s saw a flood of writing on farm workers' housing which led to real improvements on many estates with two- and three-room cottages being constructed. Most of the rows of cottages which are still attached to farmsteads in the South-East date from the mid-nineteenth century or later (Fenton 1976).

Different farming systems had different labour requirements producing marked variations in the structure of the rural workforce. In south-east Scotland the emphasis was on large-scale arable farming combined with livestock husbandry based on turnips and rotation grasses. Here the employment of married male farm servants, or hinds, continued. Hinds were in farm service all their working lives, with little chance of advancement. They received 80–95% of their wages in kind, including an allowance of grain, land for growing potatoes and grazing a cow, as well as a rent-free cottage and free carriage of coals. A hind was required to provide a female outworker or bondager. Usually this was a family member but sometimes hinds had to hire and board female outworkers (Orr 1984). A hind's wife would provide free labour for perhaps twenty days in harvest to pay for the rent of their cottage and up to four days a week paid labour as required. This ensured that female labour was available but only when needed. The emphasis on green crops, especially turnips, increased the need for full-time female workers. The labour force on the large arable farms of the eastern Lowlands was huge. East Barns, near Haddington, had a full-time population of 150 workers supplemented by 100 seasonal workers to lift potatoes. Before the advent of the reaper and reaper-binder large numbers of women were needed for harvest. In the Lothians seasonal women workers from the Highlands and increasingly from Ireland were accommodated in barrack-like bothies (*ibid*).

In the North-East improvement came late but fast, from the 1790s. Cattle rearing was the mainstay of the economy away from the environs of the larger towns. Farms were smaller than in the South-East and unmarried male and female servants more common. Their wages were largely in cash but they also received food and accommodation. In Aberdeen, Banff and Moray men ate in the farm kitchen and slept in a chaumer, usually above or adjoining the stables. On small farms, where the farmer ate in the kitchen with his workers, there was less social distance between master and man, but on the larger farms the tenants and their families increasingly ate in the parlour, distancing themselves socially from their servants (Carter 1979; Gray 1988a).

A peasant farming element remained alongside capitalist agriculture as a result of the creation of crofts in marginal areas. These provided reservoirs of seasonal labour for the big touns. A farm worker might move on from bothy or chaumer by breaking out a new croft. Many men dreamed of working their own land and of being independent, even possibly of moving up the farming ladder and taking on a larger tenancy. Their independence was often illusory, though, as they depended on the large farms for seasonal work and sometimes also for the hire of labour and equipment. Independence was often bought at the price of the servitude of their families. By the mid-nineteenth century reclamation was ceasing and it became harder to move up the farming ladder. With rising rents and lower prices crofters had to get even more work from their families in order to make ends meet, and the class began to decline as fewer sons and daughters were prepared to stay at home as unpaid labour (Carter 1979).

In Angus, the Mearns and parts of Fife, the normal system of accommodating male farm workers was in bothies where they cooked for themselves. They were often able to sell part of their meal allowance to buy a few luxuries. Bothy life was sometimes condemned by outsiders for its hard living conditions and lack of civilising influences but the independence it gave was often valued by the men. Married farm servants in this region often lived in bothies and chaumers rather than their own cottages. They often had to leave their families in a village some distance away and might only see them once every two weeks.

In the West and South-West, with a concentration on dairying, and long periods under sown grass, small family farms remained normal. Cottages for married farm workers were few and much of the work was done by the farmers' families, a system which some contemporaries likened to slavery. Dairying near towns often meant a 2am or 3am start to a sixteen-hour working day. Dairying was skilled work and experienced dairymaids were relatively well paid (Campbell 1984). On larger farms a ploughman, an 'odd' man for byre work and some female workers supplemented family labour. In this region of smaller farms it was still possible for a farm worker to save hard, marry and move up to a holding of his own in a way that had become impossible in the eastern Lowlands.

On large farms the work discipline became increasingly impersonal. The farmer became a manager rather than someone who worked alongside his servants. There was a sharper definition and greater specialisation in farm work. By the 1820s the change to horses for ploughing, especially Clydesdales, had become general, even in the North. Ploughing was virtually a full-time job: in the Carse of Gowrie two hundred days' ploughing a year was required from each team. Around half the male workers were ploughmen. Farm workers developed an elaborate hierarchy based on the nature of the work they did, their age and experience. The labour force on a large farm was headed by the grieve, then the horsemen in strict order of seniority. Orramen were general workers while baillies looked after the cattle (Carter 1979). In the Borders shepherds were well paid, having an equal status to grieves (Robson 1984). A substantial part of their wages was a grazing allowance for 40 to 50 sheep of their own. Young boys started at between age twelve and fourteen as herds before becoming halflins or apprentice horsemen. Female labour included kitchen maids, dairymaids and out-workers. Women continued to be important as family labour on

No. 11. Mock-castellated early nineteenth-century outbuildings on an East Lothian farm. © *Ian Whyte.*

small farms, as seasonal workers and also as full-time employees doing almost every job on the farm, inside and out, apart from working with horses. Despite long hours of work and a wide range of tasks, they were still only paid at about half the rate of men. In the North-East farm service was often a life-cycle stage for men and women who were the sons and daughters of crofters and who would go back to a croft when they married. Elsewhere it was almost impossible to rise beyond the level of a grieve. Hard physical labour and cold, damp living conditions encouraged arthritis so that many ploughmen had to give up before they were fifty. Older ploughmen who could no longer manage such hard work might serve as orramen or cattlemen, or they might move to the towns, broken by toil and ill health.

For most agricultural workers and their families there was little social life beyond the farm. Hours of work were long and holidays few. For a ploughman the normal working day consisted of two five-hour yokings, separated by a break to rest the horses rather than the men. Feeding and grooming the horses, cleaning the stable and other work like threshing further lengthened the working day so that in summer they might have to rise at 4 am. Regular flitting at the end of a six– or twelve–month fee gave little opportunity for putting down roots. It was the tradesmen along with the farmers who provided the stable element in rural society and who were more active in local organisations (Sprott 1984). Many rural businesses stayed in the same families for generations. Agricultural improvement, along with rising housing standards, provided an increasing amount of regular work for smiths, saddlers, joiners and builders though rural shoemakers, tailors and weavers, and eventually millers, disappeared as production became concentrated in the towns.

As in earlier times much socialising centred on the farm kitchen. Social venues away from the farm were the smithy and the inn. Breaks from the hard routine of farm work included the end of harvest supper, the meal-and-ale, perhaps the last vestige of the former closer relationship between farmer and servant, and fairs and ploughing matches (Cameron 1978). One of the best-known aspects of nineteenth-century farm workers' culture are the 'bothy ballads' recorded mainly in the North-East but probably sung more widely (Buchan 1984). They celebrated the skills of farm workers, their camaraderie and the events of the farming year as well as the harsh conditions of employment. Many songs concern seasonal events: hiring fairs, ploughing matches or harvest. Others criticise conditions at particular farms, a subtle way of blacklisting particularly hard or mean employers. Fear of getting a bad reputation might keep a farmer from being too harsh, as might the sanction of a 'clean toun', when the grieve and all his workers left together at the end of a term (Carter 1979). Unremitting hard work had been the lot of the Scottish farm worker from the early eighteenth century and before but not in such a highly organised fashion: in the process labour relations had become more impersonal.

CONCLUSION

In a single chapter generalisation is inevitable and it is impossible to convey the tremendous range of variation which occurred in rural society, not just regionally, but locally. While the broad outlines of social change in the rural Lowlands during the eighteenth and early nineteenth centuries are now established, there is a need for many more detailed case studies to show how individual districts and communities were affected and how they responded. Having read this chapter, I hope that you may be encouraged to carry out some research of your own in your own area.

EXERCISE 7

Having read this chapter, now read **Articles 7, 8 and 9** from *Area*, by Whittington, Adams and Whyte. Evaluate the standpoints of each of the three authors and suggest where their interpretations may be incorrect.

This is by no means a model response but you should have picked out the following. Whittington emphasises the possibility of a good deal of enclosure having occurred before the period of the classic 'Agricultural Revolution' and that there was more evolutionary change. Subsequent work by Whyte (1979) and Devine (1994) has shown that this is correct up to a point. The point about infield-outfield farming being more flexible has also been shown to be true. However, as Devine makes clear, there was still a marked acceleration of progress in improvement from the 1760s. Adams goes to the opposite extreme in writing off seventeenth-century acts for improvement as 'dead letter legislation' – again this is overstating the case. However, his anchoring of the chronology of the main phases of agricultural change has been supported by later research. Whyte argues the case for organisational change having underpinned later technical changes but his evidence is drawn from the seventeenth century – until Devine's (1994) study there was very little information on the extent and significance of such developments in the early eighteenth century.

Many of the issues we have discussed here impinge on other topics covered in this volume. You should now be in a better position to understand the differences between the Highlands and the Lowlands, and the relationship between agrarian change, industrialisation, demography and urbanisation, as well as the rural dimension in other themes you will be studying in subsequent chapters.

REFERENCES TO BOOKS AND ARTICLES MENTIONED IN THE TEXT

Adams, IH 1978 'The Agricultural Revolution in Scotland: Contributions to the Debate', *Area* 9, 198–205.

Adams, IH 1980 'The Agents of Agricultural Change', *in* Parry, ML and Slater, TR (eds), *The Making of the Scottish Countryside*, London, 155–76.

Buchan, D 1984 'The Expressive Culture of Nineteenth Century Scottish Farm Servants', *in* Devine, TM (ed), *Farm Servants and Labour in Lowland Scotland, 1770–1840*, Edinburgh, 226–42.

Cameron D 1978 *The Ballad and the Plough*. London.

Campbell, RH 1977 'The Scottish Improvers and the Course of Agrarian Change in the Eighteenth Century', *in* Cullen, LM and Smout, TC (eds), *Comparative Aspects of Scottish and Irish Economic and Social History 1660–1900*, Edinburgh, 63–89.

Campbell, RH 1984 'Agricultural Labourers in the South West', in Devine, TM (ed), *Farm Servants and Labour in Lowland Scotland, 1770–1840*, Edinburgh, 55–70.

*Carter, I 1979 *Farmlife in Northeast Scotland 1840–1914*. Edinburgh.

*Devine, TM (ed), 1984 *Farm Servants and Labour in Lowland Scotland, 1770–1840*. Edinburgh.

*Devine, TM 1994 *The Transformation of Rural Scotland. Social Change and the Agrarian Economy 1660–1815*. Edinburgh.

Dodgshon, RA 1975 'Farming in Roxburghshire and Berwickshire on the Eve of Improvement', *Scottish Historical Review* 54, 140–54.

*Dodgshon, RA 1981 *Land and Society in Early Scotland*. Oxford.

Dodgshon, RA 1983 'Agricultural Change and its Social Consequences in the Southern Uplands of Scotland, 1660–1780', in Devine, TM and Dickson, D (eds), *Ireland and Scotland, 1600–1850*, Edinburgh, 49–59.

*Fenton, A 1976 *Scottish Country Life*. Edinburgh.

Gibson, A 1990 'Proletarianisation? The Transition to Full Time Labour on a Scottish estate, 1723–1787', *Continuity and Change* 5, 357–89.

Gibson A and Smout, TC 1995 *Prices, Food and Wages in Scotland, 1550–1780*. Cambridge.

Gray, M 1984 'Farm Workers in North-East Scotland', in Devine, TM (ed), *Farm Servants and Labour in Lowland Scotland, 1770–1840*, Edinburgh, 10–28.

Gray, M 1988a 'The Processes of Agricultural Change in the North East, 1790–1870', in Leneman, L (ed), *Perspectives in Scottish Social History*, Aberdeen, 125–40.

Gray, M 1988b 'The Social Impact of Agrarian Change in the Rural Lowlands', in Devine, TM and Mitchison, R (eds), *People and Society in Scotland. Volume I, 1760–1830*, Edinburgh, 53–69.

Handley, JE 1953 *Scottish Farming in the Eighteenth Century*. Edinburgh.

Houston, RA 1985 'Geographical Mobility in Scotland, 1652–1811', *Journal of Historical Geography* 11, 379–94.

Levitt, I and Smout, TC 1984 'Farm Workers' Incomes in 1843', in Devine, TM (ed), *Farm Servants and Labour in Lowland Scotland, 1770–1840*, Edinburgh, 156–87.

Lockhart, DG 1980 'The Planned Villages', in Parry, ML and Slater, TR (eds), *The Making of the Scottish Countryside*, London, 249–70.

New Statistical Account of Scotland 1845. 15 volumes. Edinburgh.

Orr, A 1984 'Farm Servants and Farm Labour in the Forth Valley and South East Lowlands', in Devine TM (ed), *Farm Servants and Labour in Lowland Scotland, 1770–1840*, Edinburgh, 29–54.

Robertson, G 1829 *Rural Recollections: or the Progress of Improvement in Agriculture and Rural Affairs*. Edinburgh.

Robson, M 1984 'The Border Farm Worker', in Devine, TM (ed), *Farm Servants and Labour in Lowland Scotland, 1770–1840*, Edinburgh, 71–96.

Smout, TC 1969 *A History of the Scottish People, 1560–1830*. Glasgow.

Sprott, G 1984 'The Country Tradesman', in Devine, TM (ed), *Farm Servants and Labour in Lowland Scotland, 1770–1840*, Edinburgh, 143–54.

Statistical Account of Scotland 1791–99. 21 volumes. Edinburgh.

Tyson, RE 1985 'The Population of Aberdeenshire, 1695–1755. A New Approach', *Northern Scotland* 6, 113–31.

Whyte, ID 1978 'The Agricultural Revolution in Scotland: Contributions to the Debate', *Area* 10, 203–5.

*Whyte, ID 1979 *Agriculture and Society in Seventeenth Century Scotland*. Edinburgh.

Whyte, ID 1981 'George Dundas of Dundas: the Context of an Early Eighteenth Century Scottish Improving Landowner', *Scottish Historical Review* 60, 1–13.

Whyte, ID 1993 'Crop Yields on the Mains of Yester, 1698–1753', *Transactions of the East Lothian Antiquarian Society* 22, 23–30.

Whyte, ID and Whyte, KA 1984a 'Continuity and Change in a Seventeenth Century Scottish Farming Community', *Agricultural History Review* 32, 159–69.

Whyte, ID and Whyte, KA 1984b 'Geographical Mobility in a Seventeenth Century Scottish Rural Community', *Local Population Studies* 32, 45–53.

Whyte, ID and Whyte, KA 1988 'Debt and Credit, Poverty and Prosperity in a Seventeenth Century Scottish Farming Community', *in* Mitchison, R and Roebuck, P (eds), *Economy and Society in Scotland and Ireland, 1500–1939*, Edinburgh, 70–80.

Whittington, G 1975 'Was there a Scottish Agricultural Revolution?', *Area* 7, 204–6.

Whittington G 1983 'Agriculture and Society in Lowland Scotland 1750–1870', *in* Whittington, G and Whyte, ID (eds), *An Historical Geography of Scotland*, London, 141–64.

FURTHER READING

Those references marked * in the above list are recommended further reading.

Demography

Neil Tranter

INTRODUCTION

Underpinning the major social, economic and political developments of the period were significant changes and shifts in population. This chapter reviews Scotland's demographic history before 1850, the topic being approached under the following headings:

- Sources
- Population growth and location
- The mechanisms of population growth with particular emphasis on migration, illegitimacy and mortality
- The causes of population growth

When you have worked your way through this chapter, the associated documents and readings, you should have a good understanding of the sources the historian can draw upon for the study of Scottish demography, the main mechanisms at work during the period, and the problems of interpretation arising.

I. SOURCES

Until around the middle of the nineteenth century, when improved methods of census-taking and the civil registration of births, marriages and deaths were introduced, the ability of historical demographers to provide a comprehensive and reliable range of data on the size and rate of growth of Scotland's population, its age, sex and marital structures, and on the mechanisms of fertility, mortality and migration which shaped variations in growth and structure, is severely limited by deficiencies in the sources on which they are forced to rely. As in England and Wales, regular, decennial counts of the number of inhabitants of each sex, compiled by the state, were not begun until 1801 and, at least initially, even these cannot be regarded as entirely accurate. Data on age structure were not included in the civil census until 1821, and then only in a crude form. Not until 1841, following the adoption of separate enumeration schedules for each household, did the censuses begin to include data on age to the nearest year, marital status and place of birth. Only from 1841 and 1851, therefore, do the published census returns, and the manuscript enumerators' books on which these are based, provide material of a sufficient quantity and quality to satisfy most of the requirements of demographic analysis.

For the period before the introduction of the civil census, material of this kind is a good deal sparser and less reliable. For Scotland, as for England and Wales, private listings of inhabitants, in the Scottish case usually drawn up for ecclesiastical purposes or as the basis for returns made to the *Statistical Accounts* of the 1790s, are extant for only a handful of communities. Few contain more than an estimate of total numbers, often either incomplete or of questionable, at best untestable, veracity. Most refer merely to single parishes and are therefore of little value for the study of national or regional population trends.

Before 1801 the only nationwide survey of population undertaken anywhere in mainland Britain was that carried out by Rev Alexander Webster for Scotland in 1755. The Webster census, reproduced in full by the Scottish History Society (Kyd 1952), gives the total population of each parish and county and, for the country as a whole, an estimate of the number of people at each year of age. In the absence of a detailed understanding of how they were derived, these data must be approached with caution. Most commentators, however, accept that the Webster census provides at least a reasonably accurate guide to the size and age structure of the Scottish population in the mid-eighteenth century. Certainly, nothing remotely comparable in range and quality is available for other dates. Useful though they may be for particular areas, neither the hearth tax returns of 1691 nor the poll tax books of 1693 and 1695 are sufficiently extensive, uniform in content and accurate to form the basis of even crude estimates of the national population at the beginning of the century. Compiled by Sir John Sinclair from returns submitted by parish ministers in the early 1790s, the *Statistical Accounts*, which provide figures on the numbers of males and females for parishes covering about 40% of the country's population, and rough age distributions for around a quarter of all parishes, are on the face of it a more promising source, examples being provided in **Documents 27 to 32**. But here too, the reliability of most of the data is uncertain and impossible to verify, and the geographic coverage too scattered, to permit studies on a national or broad regional scale.

Satisfactory data on numbers of births, marriages and deaths, and thus on trends in the vital rates of fertility, nuptiality and mortality, are even more difficult to produce. In Scotland, where opposition to civil registration from the established church and the burghs was particularly strong, state responsibility for the registration of births, marriages and deaths was delayed until 1855, almost twenty years later than in England and Wales. For estimates of birth, marriage and death totals before this date, students of Scottish historical demography have to rely principally on baptism, marriage and burial entries in the parish registers of the Church of Scotland. The problem is that, compared with their English equivalents, these are notoriously deficient. Firstly, particularly in the case of burial registers, the proportion of parishes for which registers are extant is relatively small and those which do survive are heavily biased towards eastern parts of the country. Secondly, even more so than in England, the surviving registers substantially under-record the number of vital events that occurred. In the course of the late eighteenth and early nineteenth centuries, as a result of higher rates of population growth, urbanisation and secession from the Church of Scotland, the extent of under-registration increased. By the mid-nineteenth century the baptism registers were recording no more than a quarter to a third of all births in their catchment areas. Marriage registers, themselves usually records of proclamations of intent to marry rather than of the marriage itself, included only those marriages to be conducted by a minister of the established church and excluded a large and growing number of other forms of legally-binding union. In the case of burial registers, which were often simply records of those who paid to use the parish mortcloth and therefore normally excluded the burials of infants and young children, the degree of under-registration, though impossible to quantify, was probably greater still. Because of the scale of omission and the difficulties involved in trying to assess regional and chronological variations in its extent, it is unlikely that the Church of Scotland registers can ever be made to yield the kind of information on trends in fertility, nuptiality and mortality that Wrigley and Schofield (1981) have compiled for England. This is all the more unfortunate since, except for occasional and dubiously reliable data on ages at and causes of death in urban 'bills of mortality', and estimates of levels of illegitimacy based on cases of pre-marital fornication in kirk session records (for the period down to the 1770s), the parish registers are the only reasonably extensive source for the study of trends in Scotland's vital rates of birth, marriage and death before 1855.

Students of early Scottish demographic history are only marginally better served by their sources of information on migration. Estimates of the gross volume and net balance of movement between the different regions and counties of Scotland (and between Scotland and the outside world) cannot be devised until the 1860s when census and civil registration data first become jointly available. At a more localised level, however, evidence on geographic mobility is more abundant, especially from 1841 when the censuses begin to record place of birth. Before the 1840s, rough indications of the *extent* of migration within Scotland can be derived from analyses of the survival rate of names in successive nominative listings such as tax returns, parish registers and gild and corporation rolls. For evidence on the *direction* and *range* of internal migration, historians can turn to the data on place of birth or last residence contained in a variety of sources – burgh apprenticeship records, kirk session testimonials of good moral conduct, tenancy agreements, parochial marriage registers, chartulary books (Lockhart 1978), and private listings of inhabitants. Although usually provided in a non-quantified form, there is also much useful comment on patterns of migration, into and out of as well as within Scotland, in the *Statistical Account* and *New Statistical Account*, again seen in **Documents 27 to 32**.

Direct information on the movement of people into and out of Scotland is less plentiful. Apart from James Cleland's census for Glasgow in 1820, which records country of origin (whether Scotland, England, Ireland or Foreign), extensive data on the numbers of non-native residents of Scotland are available only from 1841 when they are first recorded in the civil censuses. In practice, the only extensive source of information on migration into and out of the United Kingdom is the lists of passengers travelling to and from destinations outside Europe. Before the second half of the nineteenth century, when steamships came to dominate the carriage of passengers on ocean-going routes, it is reasonable to assume that most of those travelling between Europe and the New World were genuine emigrants rather than simply temporary travellers. Only from 1855, however, were returns requested for incoming passengers, and only from 1870 were they required by law. As a result, estimates of the volume of inwards passenger movement and of the net balance of inwards and outwards passenger flows cannot be compiled for earlier dates.

Lists of passengers leaving Scotland for non-European destinations were first collected in the early 1770s but survive in large numbers only for the period December 1773 to April 1776, and even then are far from complete. Not until 1820 does a regular series of statistics on the number of steerage passengers leaving Britain and Ireland for countries outside Europe become available. Not until 1825 do these distinguish between passengers departing from Scottish, English, Irish or Welsh ports, and only from 1853, when ship masters were asked to state passengers' nationalities, is it possible to estimate the number of Scots (and Irish) who left from English ports. Given that many vessels failed to submit their passenger manifestos to the customs authorities, the published totals must be assumed to understate the numbers leaving. The lack of data on other than steerage passengers, before 1863, and on passengers to Europe, before 1890, to some extent further diminishes the value of the passenger statistics as guides to the volume of movement from the United Kingdom.

For more detailed information on emigrants to overseas destinations we must turn to the manuscript lists of passengers which ship masters were required to supply to customs officers in the USA, from 1820, and Canada, from 1828. Similar returns are available for various British colonies, though in this case only for passengers assisted by colonial government funds. Although these too understate the true extent of the exodus, they are particularly valuable for the detailed information they contain on the individual migrant, including age, occupation, country of origin and, in some instances, place of last residence (Erickson 1972; Brayshay 1979).

Overall, the sources available for the study of eighteenth- and early nineteenth-century demography are less satisfactory for Scotland than England. While the quality of the data on the size of the Scottish population, its age, sex and marital structures and patterns of *internal* migration compares favourably with that for England, Scottish data on rates of fertility, nuptiality and mortality and on the extent of mobility into and out of the country are decidedly inferior (Flinn 1977, 45–97, 250–60; Tranter 1985a, 3–33; Houston 1988, 10–12; Harper 1988, 20–30; Mitchison and Leneman 1989, 16–43, 134–40). The relative deficiency of the sources goes far towards explaining why our understanding of Scotland's early demographic evolution is less advanced than that of England.

EXERCISE I

Reviewing the foregoing discussion, what are the major sources available for studying Scottish demography and how do they compare to those in England during this period?

Briefly, the major sources include:

- hearth and poll tax books
- private censuses (Webster, Cleland)
- Statistical Accounts
- Kirk records
- shipping records
- official censuses from 1801

While there are some strengths, the records are very patchy compared to England.

2. POPULATION GROWTH AND LOCATION

In the absence of reliable sources it is not easy to estimate the size of the Scottish population at the beginning of the eighteenth century. Calculations based on the admittedly fragile evidence of hearth and poll tax returns suggest a total population of just over one million on the eve of the famine of the late 1690s, similar to that indicated by the Webster census for 1755. This implies that in Scotland, as in England, the first half of the eighteenth century was an era of demographic stagnation during which periods of population growth alternated with periods of population decline (Flinn 1977, 13, 200, 209–29).

TABLE I: POPULATION OF SCOTLAND, 1755–1851

	TOTAL (IN MILLIONS)	RATE OF GROWTH (% PER ANNUM)
1755	1.25	
1801	1.61	0.6
1811	1.81	1.23
1821	2.09	1.58
1831	2.36	1.31
1841	2.62	1.08
1851	2.89	1.03

As Table 1 shows, the 1750s saw the start of what was ultimately to prove a revolutionary transformation in rates of population growth, a transformation which, with some variation in timing and extent, was common to most European countries. Between 1755 and 1851, the number of inhabitants more than doubled. Throughout the second half of the eighteenth century, rates of population increase averaged a relatively modest 0.6% a year, rising above this figure only between the mid-1760s and the late 1780s. By the first half of the nineteenth century they had soared to well over 1% a year and at their peak in the period 1801–31 were between two and two and a half times greater than in the preceding half-century. A similar pattern of moderate, and then more pronounced, acceleration in rates of population increase occurred in England and Wales, though in both cases growth rates were higher than in Scotland.

EXERCISE 2

Examine Table 2 and comment on the changes in population distribution it highlights.

TABLE 2: POPULATION OF SCOTLAND BY REGIONS (% OF TOTAL)

	1755	1801	1811	1821	1831	1841	1851
Far North	4.8	4.3	3.8	3.9	3.9	3.7	3.5
Highland Counties	15.9	15.2	14.4	14.0	13.1	12.0	10.8
North-East	17.3	13.7	13.1	12.8	12.7	12.2	12.1
Western Lowlands	14.3	20.6	22.8	24.4	26.6	30.2	32.1
Eastern Lowlands	36.1	34.6	34.3	33.6	33.2	32.3	32.1
Borders	11.7	11.5	11.5	11.2	10.4	9.6	9.4

Sources: 1755 based on Kyd (1952, 82, Appendix 1); 1801–51 based on Flinn (1977, 306, Table 5.1.3).
Far North: Caithness, Orkney, Shetland
Highland Counties: Argyll, Bute, Inverness, Ross and Cromarty, Sutherland
North-East: Aberdeen, Banff, Kincardine, Moray, Nairn
Western Lowlands: Ayr, Dumbarton, Lanark, Renfrew
Eastern Lowlands: Angus, Clackmannan, East Lothian, Fife, Kinross, Mid Lothian, Perth, Stirling, West Lothian
Borders: Berwick, Dumfries, Kirkcudbright, Peebles, Roxburgh, Selkirk, Wigtown

Population growth was accompanied by a dramatic change in the geographic distribution of the country's inhabitants. Despite a modest drift of population away from the counties of Fife and the Lothians towards the Western Lowland counties of Ayr, Dumbarton, Lanark and Renfrew, the distribution of residence in 1755 was much the same as it had been fifty years earlier (Flinn 1977, 197, 200). Beginning in the 1750s, the shift of population towards the Western Lowlands intensified. Between 1755 and 1851 the share of Scotland's population living in Western Lowland counties more than doubled while that in all other major regions of the country steadily declined. The decline was especially marked in the Far North, Highland and North-East regions (Table 2).

3. THE MECHANISMS OF POPULATION GROWTH: FERTILITY, MORTALITY AND MIGRATION

Variations in rates of population growth over time and space are a combined result of changes in levels of fertility (both legitimate and illegitimate), mortality and net migration. It is a particularly frustrating feature of Scottish demographic history that prior to the second half of the nineteenth century the available sources yield little reliable data on the behaviour of these mechanisms. In spite of this, there is general agreement that variations in national and regional rates of population increase owed far more to the influence of net migration and mortality than to that of fertility.

TABLE 3: ILLEGITIMACY RATIOS IN SCOTLAND 1760S AND 1858–60

	1760S	1858–60
Lothians	1.0	7.3
Fife	1.8	5.4
Central Lowlands	2.5	8.2
Eastern Highlands	4.0	7.5
Western Highlands	3.9	8.2
Aberdeenshire	3.5	13.7
North-East	4.9	12.1
Caithness	7.6	7.3
Ayrshire	4.8	8.8
South-West	6.1	14.6
Whole country from selected parishes	3.6	9.5

Source: Leneman and Mitchison (1987, 59, Table 2).

As Table 3 shows, illegitimacy ratios (the number of illegitimate births per hundred live births) were lowest in the Lothians, Fife and the Central Lowlands, higher in the Eastern and Western Highlands and highest in North-Eastern and South-Western counties. Between the 1660s and 1720s, although higher than in England, Scottish illegitimacy ratios declined. In England, bastardy rates began to rise from the 1720s, to a peak in the 1840s (Laslett and Oosterveen 1973, 260), and by the 1750s exceeded those in Scotland where they remained roughly constant through the second and third quarters of the eighteenth century. By the mid-nineteenth century, however, levels of bastardy in Scotland were again higher than in England and markedly higher than they had ever been before. Without adequate parish register and kirk session evidence for the late eighteenth and early nineteenth centuries, it is impossible to say precisely when the rise in Scottish illegitimacy ratios began. In

No. 12. Portrait of Rev Alexander Webster by David Martin. © *Scottish National Portrait Gallery.*

Ayrshire and the South-West (Dumfries and Galloway) it seems to have begun in the 1750s. Elsewhere there is no sign of any increase until at least the 1770s and even this may have been a temporary upswing rather than the onset of a sustained rise (Leneman and Mitchison 1987, 49, 53–4, 58; 1989, 134, 140–2, 146–7, 155; Houston 1988, 17–18). Evidence for the Banffshire parish of Rothiemay, where bastardy levels only began to increase after about 1820, and the Wigtownshire parish of Portpatrick, suggests that it was not until well into the nineteenth century that Scottish illegitimacy rates generally began their rise to the heights which so disturbed contemporary observers in the 1850s (Blaikie 1994, 43; Tranter 1985b, 36–8).

Because the great majority of children were born to married couples, variations in levels of illegitimacy in any case played only a minor role in determining variations in national and regional levels of total fertility. In England, where mortality gave way to fertility as the principal causal mechanism of population growth after 1750, gross reproduction rates (the number of female births per woman), having remained relatively constant throughout the first half of the eighteenth century, rose from 2.37 around 1761 to a peak of 3.06 around 1816, before falling to 2.4 around 1851 (Wrigley and Schofield 1981, 229–30, 244–5). In the case of Scotland, by contrast, scattered evidence on ages at marriage, the proportions marrying and age structures suggests that in the period 1750–1850 rates of total fertility at best rose only slightly and at worst may even have fallen (Flinn 1977, 14, 249, 259; Houston 1988, 13–14, 18–20, 24). In the absence of reliable, direct data on fertility it is, of course, impossible to be sure. But it does seem that in Scotland the increase in rates of population growth which began in the second half of the eighteenth century owed far less to rising fertility than it did in England.

Until very late in the eighteenth century the volume of immigration into Scotland was negligible. From around 1780 its scale increased, chiefly as the result of a growing influx from Ireland. By 1841 there were 126,326 Irish-born residents. In the course of the following decade the number of Irish immigrants rose to over 110,000 and by 1851 the proportion of Irish-born had increased to 7.2% (Flinn 1977, 17, 303, 455, 457).

Throughout the eighteenth century and first half of the nineteenth century, however, the volume of immigration was dwarfed by that of emigration. Though modest by subsequent standards, a substantial, if fluctuating, exodus of Scots long pre-dated the era of mass emigration to the New World which became so marked a feature of European demographic history in the decades after 1850. Between 1688 and 1715 an estimated 200,000 people left Scotland to settle in Ireland. After 1715 emigration to Ireland gave way to a small, but growing, movement of Scots to the American colonies. By the mid-1770s at least 10,000 Scots, the majority from the Highlands and Islands, had emigrated to the New World. Beginning in the 1760s and 1770s the volume of emigration increased. Between 1763 and 1815 a minimum of 27,000 people left Scotland for American and West Indian destinations, an average of over 2,000 a year during peak periods. Between 1825 and 1850, excluding those who left from English ports, the number of Scots leaving for overseas countries soared to 130,274, an average of roughly 5,000 a year. In addition, an unknown number was lost on the net balance of migration between Scotland and England which always heavily favoured the latter (Flinn 1977, 8, 14, 23, 303, 443, 446; Bumsted 1982, 228–9; Harper 1988, 1, 6–7; Houston 1988, 23; Gray 1990, 7, 11–12).

Estimates compiled by Wrigley and Schofield (1981, 227–8) indicate that an excess of emigrants over immigrants reduced rates of English population growth between 1701 and 1841 by no more than about 10%. In the case of Scotland, the impact of unfavourable migrational balances on rates of population growth was somewhat greater. But even at times of greatest loss, between 1775 and 1801, when it removed from 12.5% to 15.6% of the country's natural increase, and during the 1830s when it accounted for as much as 22%, net emigration had only a modest effect on the size of the Scottish population. Only in the period 1861–1939, when it removed over half the excess of births over deaths, did net emigration become the dominant influence on rates of population growth (Flinn 1977, 8, 14, 20, 303, 441–2). Throughout the eighteenth century and first half of the nineteenth century, variations in rates of population growth were determined primarily by changes in the relationship between the numbers of births and deaths.

Of the relative effect of net migration and natural increase on variations in rates of population growth between the main regions of Scotland, it is more difficult to be sure. Despite rising levels of permanent and seasonal migration from Highland to Lowland areas (Withers 1985, 395, 399, 412; Houston 1988, 21–2; Whyte 1989, 39, 57; Whyte 1991, 88), the extent of inter-regional mobility in the late eighteenth century and early nineteenth century remained surprisingly limited. As late as 1851, for example, just 12.8% of the resident population of Scotland's most popular internal destination, the Western Lowlands, had been born in another region of the country (Flinn 1977, 461). At least down to the 1830s, in Scotland as in England it seems, inter-regional variations in rates of population growth owed more to variations in levels of natural increase than to variations in the balance between in- and out-migration (Tranter 1985a, 40).

In Lowland areas especially, the extent of migration *within* regions was much greater and more akin to the high levels of short-distance mobility found in England than the lower levels typical of peasant communities in Europe (Lockhart 1980; Houston 1985; Whyte 1989, 37, 48–9, 53, 58; 1991, 87–8, 101). The probable corollary of this is that net migration contributed more to variations in rates of population growth within regions than to those between regions. But whether even here its influence exceeded that of variations in levels of natural increase requires further investigation (Flinn 1977, 28; Whyte 1989, 44; Gray 1990, 17).

In Scotland and all other northern and western European countries apart from England, and possibly Ireland, the mechanism primarily responsible for the rise in rates of population growth in the second half of the eighteenth century and early nineteenth century was falling mortality. Between the mid-1750s and the 1790s crude death rates (deaths per thousand total population) fell from 37–38 to 24 and infant death rates (deaths in the age-group 0–1 per thousand live births) fell from 236–238 to 164, while the average expectation of life at birth rose from around twenty-seven years, well below that for England (thirty-seven), to about thirty-nine years, above that for England (thirty-six to thirty-seven years). Significantly, when urban death rates rose in the second quarter of the nineteenth century, the pace of Scottish population growth slowed (Flinn 1977a, 16–17, 249, 259, 269–70, 377; Wrigley and Schofield 1981, 529; Tranter 1985a, 46; Houston 1988, 13–14, 17, 22). Whether or not mortality exerted a similarly dominant influence on variations in rates of population growth between and within the different regions of Scotland has still to be determined.

EXERCISE 3
Which had the greatest influence on patterns of Scottish population growth – variations in fertility, migration or mortality?

Any answer to this complex question should emphasise mortality and migration rather then fertility. The main explanation is falling levels of mortality and 'push-pull' factors affecting migration, for example poverty, employment opportunities, desire to own land, or the need to preserve religious and cultural cohesion.

4. THE CAUSES OF POPULATION GROWTH

In recent years much effort and ingenuity has been expended on trying to explain the patterns of illegitimacy, migration and mortality which, in the absence of significant differentials in legitimate fertility, determined the pace of population growth. Only in the case of migration, however, is it safe to conclude that this has provided a satisfactory understanding of the forces at work. On the causes of spatial and temporal variations in illegitimacy and mortality, current knowledge is far less complete.

4.1. Migration

Changes in the volume and direction of migration are the product of a complex and intricately intertwined mix of factors: the push of poor conditions and prospects in the areas from which migrants come; the pull of more attractive opportunities in the areas to which migrants go; the magnitude of the differential between the opportunities in sending and receiving areas; and the extent to which transport facilities, levels of income and a knowledge of conditions elsewhere permit potential migrants to respond to the influence of push and pull forces.

In the period between the 1760s and the end of the Napoleonic Wars in 1815, conditions in many parts of rural Scotland became increasingly conducive to permanent or at least temporary migration. In rural Lowland districts the potential for emigration was fuelled by a combination of higher rates of natural increase, rising rents and the dispossession of many smaller tenants, sub-tenants and cottars by 'improving' landlords keen to consolidate and extend farms in the interests of greater efficiency and profit. In the Highlands and Islands, where supplies of unused, productive land were more limited and where there were fewer alternatives to employment in agriculture, the impact of rising rates of population growth on standards of living was even more severe and the pressures for emigration even greater. Here the concern of landowners to maximise incomes by dispensing with the services of tacksmen, raising rents and consolidating farms for sheep merely aggravated the underlying problems (Flinn 1977, 29–30, 444; Bumsted 1982, 27–59; Harper 1988, 1–3; Gray 1990, 6, 9). Had it not been for the earnings sent back by the growing stream of seasonal emigrants to the Lowlands, itself partly a reflection of intensifying pressures on employment and resources at home (Houston 1988, 21; Whyte 1989, 57), the income generated by the continued prosperity of the cattle and kelp trades and the addition to the food stock made possible by the spread of potato cultivation, the volume of permanent emigration from Highland and Island districts before 1815 would undoubtedly have been a good deal higher (Flinn 1977a, 47–64; Bumsted 1982, 229; Gray 1990, 9, 25).

After 1815 the impetus for emigration which came from push forces greatly increased. Higher rates of natural increase and ever-more determined attempts on the part of landowners to protect their incomes by means of rent increases, restrictions on the number of workers they employed and the further enlargement of farm holdings swelled the potential pool of emigrants from rural Lowland areas. In urban Lowland communities, employment opportunities more seriously and more frequently failed to keep pace with the supply of labour. In the Highlands and Islands the effects of population growth and the clearance of land for sheep were compounded by a sharp decline in cattle and fish prices and the collapse of the kelp industry in the face of renewed imports of barilla and potash. By the second quarter of the nineteenth century Highland lairds were as firmly in favour of the wholesale emigration of their tenants as their predecessors had been opposed to it, and forced evictions, hitherto rare, became more and more common. For those who remained there was little choice but to depend increasingly on the cultivation of the potato to eke out a livelihood. With the arrival of the potato blight in 1836–7 and, more dramatically, in 1846, even this precarious support was removed (see Chapters 9 and 10). Mass emigration was now the sole option (Flinn 1977, 21, 34–6; Devine 1979, 344–59; 1988, 39, 95–9; Gray 1983, 108–9; 1990, 14–15, 25–8, 31; Harper 1988, 7–8).

Important though push forces were, their role should not be exaggerated. The growing frequency of migration in late eighteenth and early nineteenth-century Scotland also required the operation of two other conditions. The first was the existence of places where opportunities were not only greater than those available at home but also sufficiently attractive to outweigh the considerable material and emotional costs involved in moving. The second was an ability on the part of would-be migrants to respond to the lure of better prospects elsewhere.

Migration within Scotland, from Highlands to Lowlands and from rural to urban, was as much a consequence of the pull of higher wages and greater employment opportunities in Lowland and urban areas as the push of low incomes and poor employment prospects in Highland and rural areas. Emigration to the USA and British North America in particular would likewise not have occurred on the scale it did but for the opportunities afforded by an abundance of free or cheap land and the growing demand for labour in the agricultural, fishing and timber industries (Flinn 1977, 39, 444; Bailyn 1986, 190–1; Harper 1988, 21; Whyte 1989, 57–8; Gray 1990, 6, 15–17, 19).

To suggest that push forces were solely, or even mainly, responsible for the burgeoning exodus of Scots to overseas destinations fails to take adequate account of the characteristics of the typical emigrant. Analysis of the data contained in the passenger lists of 1773–6, the USA ship lists of 1831, 1841 and 1851, and the assisted passenger lists compiled by Australian immigration agents for the period 1831–60 shows that, with the probable exception of emigrants from the Highlands in the 1840s, most of those who left Scotland (and other parts of mainland Britain) between the late eighteenth century and mid-nineteenth century were not drawn from the ranks of the very poorest and least skilled. In the main they were small farmers, craftsmen, mechanics and tradesmen with sufficient resources to meet the costs of moving and more often than not accompanied by their wives and children (Donaldson 1966, 114–20; Erickson 1981, 188; Van Vugt 1988, 417; Erickson 1989, 362, 365–7; Gray 1990, 13, 21, 26–7, 31; Schurer 1991, 107; Haines 1994, 231–5, 237–42, 246–7). The implication of these findings would seem to be that emigration to the New World was impelled more by a desire to *improve* prospects or to avoid the *possibility* of subsequent destitution than by the actuality of unemployment and poverty. Typically, the decision to emigrate was taken before, not after, destitution struck (Van Vugt 1988, 418–9, 426; Harper 1988, 4, 7–8, 345; Gray 1990, 7, 10, 17). All too often those who would have benefited most from emigration were too poor or too limited in ambition and knowledge to take advantage of the opportunities overseas. Generally, the push of material deprivation at home worked to promote emigration only among those for whom the extent of hardship was not too severe.

To the influence of push and pull forces we must add the contributions made by earlier migrations, improvements in methods of transport, and the increased availability of information on conditions and opportunities in other areas. The greater the distances involved, the more important each of these factors became. Thus, rising levels of emigration to the New World in the late eighteenth century and early nineteenth century were, in part, an almost inevitable consequence of previous emigrant flows which had created familiar economic, social and cultural environments in distant lands and which, through the advice, encouragement and financial assistance they provided, reduced the traumas of emigration for later generations. In part, they stemmed from reductions in the cost of trans-oceanic travel made possible by the development of the North American cotton, tobacco and timber trades which provided ships that would otherwise have had to return to the New World largely unladen. But they also owed much to the part played by newspaper reports and advertisements, periodicals and guidebooks, emigrants' letters and the promotional work of the local agents of colonial governments, land and shipping companies in disseminating information on the kind of conditions and prospects which were available in other countries. The result was that many more people than ever before were able to make a reasonably well-informed comparison between opportunities at home and overseas. Without this capacity for informed comparison the number who chose to go would certainly have been smaller (Bumsted 1982, 238–55; Bailyn 1986, 142; Harper 1988, 3–4, 8, 48–79, 343–4; Gray 1990, 12, 19).

Fundamentally, the growing frequency of human mobility in late eighteenth and early nineteenth-century Scotland was a combined consequence of higher rates of population growth and a process of economic development distinguished by increasingly wide differentials in income and employment opportunities between nations and between regions within nations. Where levels of income and knowledge and facilities for transportation allowed, the wider was the divergence in these opportunities, and the greater the volume of the emigrant flow. It was for this reason that within mainland Britain migrational balances favoured England and Lowland Scotland, where resources and employment prospects were relatively plentiful, at the expense of Scotland and the Scottish Highlands and Islands, where they were more meagre. That the percentage of natural increase lost to emigration overseas was greater for Scotland than England likewise largely reflects the fact that the divergence between domestic and overseas prospects was noticeably wider in the case of the former than the latter. Quite simply, coming from a more backward economy, the Scots had more to gain from moving. Only Ireland, where the differential between internal and external opportunities was wider still, lost a larger proportion of its population to emigration.

EXERCISE 4
Reviewing the foregoing discussion, how would you characterise the typical migrant of this period and how does this help us understand the underlying causes of migration?

You would have to consider both internal and external migration and the influence of push and pull conditions, the role of earlier migration and the contribution made by improvements in transport and communication. The typical migrant was a small farmer or artisan accompanied by his family, motivated by the desire for self-improvement and equipped with adequate resources to make the move, usually to North America.

4.2. Illegitimacy

Why rates of Scottish illegitimacy were higher by the mid-nineteenth century than at any time since the mid-seventeenth century, and why they were higher in the rural North-East and South-West than in other rural, and most urban, areas of the country, are questions that have puzzled historians as much as they did contemporaries.

In their attempts to explain the unusual prevalence of bastardy in north-eastern and south-western regions, historians have found it easier to determine what did not cause it rather than what did. Laslett and Oosterveen's suggestion (1973, 257, 282–4) that regional variations in rates of illegitimacy in England may have owed something to variations in the size of what they describe as a 'bastard prone sub-society' (defined as unmarried women who bore more than one child out of wedlock and families with an especially strong tradition of bearing illegitimate children) does not appear to apply to Scotland where at no stage between the mid-seventeenth and mid-nineteenth centuries is there any indication of regional concentrations in either the extent of kin-related bastard-bearing or, except in the North-East, in the percentage of women who had more than one illegitimate child. Nor, to judge from the evidence for Rothiemay on differences between the ages of women who bore illegitimates and the ages of women who bore their first child within marriage, and from the absence in areas like the North-East of frequent references to unfulfilled promises of marriage, can regional variations in bastardy readily be related to variations in the extent to which courtship failed to result in a legally recognised union (Leneman and Mitchison 1987, 50, 52; 1989, 149; Blaikie, 1993, 99, 109, 112, 118).

TABLE 4: PRE-MARITAL BIRTHS AS A PERCENTAGE OF ALL CHILDBEARING
MARRIAGES, ROTHIEMAY, BANFFSHIRE, 1751/60–1891/1900

1751–60	7.3	1831–40	9.7
1761–70	6.6	1841–50	19.3
1771–80	–	1851–60	21.8
1781–90	8.2	1861–70	31.6
1791–1800	4.6	1871–80	28.1
1801–11	–	1881–90	34.8
1811–20	15.9	1891–1900	44.8
1821–30	9.3		

Source: Blaikie (1993, 103, Table 4.9).

Other potential explanations are less easily dismissed. High levels of illegitimacy in the North-East, it has been argued, were the consequence of a capitalist farming economy in which hired labour was relatively mobile and unsupervised and male and female workers lived in close proximity to each other. In the South-West it is more likely to have stemmed from the bias of the economy towards dairy farming which provided an abundance of employment for females and thus minimised the financial burdens imposed by having an illegitimate child. Perhaps, too, high rates of bastardy in the South-West owed at least something to the persistence of a particularly strong culture of resistance to all forms of authority, including that which the Church of Scotland tried to exercise over sexual behaviour. In this context it may be significant that in areas like the Lothians, Fife and the Central Lowlands, where the populations were more willing to accept the discipline of the Church, rates of illegitimacy were relatively low (Leneman and Mitchison 1987, 52, 58; 1989, 142, 145–7, 241, 243; Houston 1988, 17; Blaikie 1993, 27). It should be stressed, however, that more research is needed to test the validity of these claims.

The search for an acceptable explanation of the rise in Scottish illegitimacy to the high levels prevalent by the mid-nineteenth century is not helped by the fact that we do not know precisely when the rise began. As noted above, the probability is that in most parts of Scotland it did not begin until well into the nineteenth century. Only in the South-West can we be certain that it dates back to as early as the 1750s.

Why the South-West pioneered the trend to higher levels of bastardy is far from clear. According to Leneman and Mitchison (1987, 52, 56–7, 59; 1989, 145, 149–50, 154–5, 159), it cannot be explained by increases in either the extent of resistance to ecclesiastical authority, the production of illegitimate children by a sub-stratum of bastard-prone females, or the percentage of courtships which failed to result in marriage. Nor can it be related in any obvious way to the process of economic growth. Most of the more important developments in the Scottish economy during the second half of the eighteenth century – the expansion of linen manufacturing, the emergence of the tobacco trade and the spread of new techniques and structures in agriculture – were located not in the South-West, where rates of illegitimacy rose, but elsewhere in Lowland Scotland, where they failed to rise. Whatever may be true

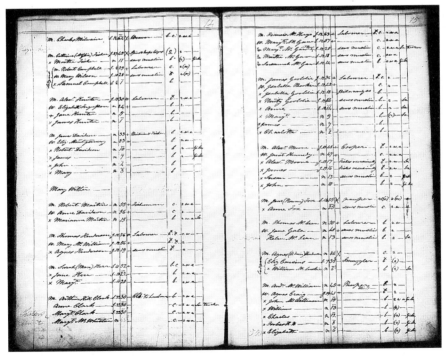

No. 13. Page from the Urquhart Census of Portpatrick, 1832–53. *Reproduced by kind permission of the Keeper of the Records of Scotland.*

for England, rising levels of illegitimacy in south-west Scotland in the third quarter of the eighteenth century owed nothing to the stimulus of rising incomes and employment opportunities to either the extent of courtship or the willingness of unmarried females to indulge in more liberated sexual practices. Rather, Mitchison and Leneman conclude, the explanation is more likely to involve the forces of cultural change. But what these forces were remains a mystery.

Of the causes of the more general rise in Scottish illegitimacy which began some time in the first half of the nineteenth century it is no easier to be precise. Mitchison and Leneman (1989, 239–40) see it as a response to a combination of the spread of capitalist structures in agriculture, the lessening attractions of strict Calvinist values and the decline of the disciplinary powers of the established church as the institutions of religion became increasingly fragmented. Blaikie (1993, 106, 119–20, 155–6; 1994, 50–5) argues that in the North-East its origins lay in a complex mix of factors, among them the demise of peasant farming and the rise of wage labour, the decline of kirk session control over sexual conduct and the emergence of a sufficiently large population of grandparents willing to act as childminders for the illegitimate offspring of their daughters. But on this aspect of Scottish illegitimacy, too, there is as yet no consensus.

> EXERCISE 5
> Referring to Tables 3 and 4 and to **Article 10**, what are the most convincing explanations for regional and chronological variations in levels of illegitimacy?

You would need to stress the differences between peasant and capitalist farming economies, the extent of female employment opportunities (farm or mill work, domestic service), resistance to authority, especially to that of the Kirk, and the role of grandparents.

4.3. Mortality

Because of its apparently predominant role in determining population trends, historians of early modern Scottish demography have paid particular attention to the causes of variations in mortality. None, however, would claim that their efforts have so far yielded definitive results.

In Scotland as in England and Wales the increase in the average expectation of life which occurred between the mid-eighteenth century and the start of the second quarter of the nineteenth century was largely due to a reduction in mortality from infectious disease, and primarily from air-borne rather than food-, water- or insect-borne infections (McKeown 1976, 66–72). There are two broad categories of possible explanation. The first comprises improvements made by man to personal or public health conditions – improvements which originated in either advances in the knowledge and practice of medicine, higher standards of sanitation, waste disposal and personal hygiene or higher levels of nutrition, which worked to curb mortality either by reducing the frequency of human contact with disease viruses or by raising levels of resistance to disease. The second comprises changes in the virulence of disease organisms or in the ability of the human host to resist them, over which man had no control.

In the case of Scotland, some of these potential explanations can be speedily dismissed. While improved quarantining practices undoubtedly contributed to the disappearance of bubonic plague, the disease had ceased to be a major cause of death in Scotland by the second half of the seventeenth century and was therefore of no relevance to the decline in mortality which occurred in the late eighteenth century and early nineteenth century (Flinn 1977, 8, 149). The contribution made by the growing numbers of hospitals, dispensaries and medical practitioners was severely restricted by the fact that surgical techniques and standards of care differed little from those of the past and were in any case available only for a relatively small proportion of the population. The only new, life-saving medicines introduced during the period were cinchona and mercury, for the treatment of malaria and syphilis respectively. But neither of these diseases ranked among the principal causes of death. Under the impact of rapid urbanisation, standards of public health in Scotland deteriorated rather than improved and, as demonstrated by the key role they played in the rise of Scottish death rates in the second quarter of the nineteenth century, hindered rather than assisted the decline in mortality which had been a feature of the preceding decades (*ibid*, 17–20, 248, 371, 396; Tranter 1985a, 72–80; Houston 1988, 16). For a more convincing explanation of Scotland's late eighteenth and early nineteenth-century mortality decline we need to look elsewhere.

According to Wrigley and Schofield (1981, 416), levels of mortality in pre-industrial England were governed principally by changes in the relationship between infective parasites and their human host which occurred more or less independently of human action. No such extravagant claim has ever been made for Scotland. None the less, the fact that the virulence of diseases like plague, smallpox, typhus, measles and whooping cough does fluctuate naturally has persuaded scholars to accept that in Scotland, too, an autonomous reduction in the severity of disease viruses played at least some part in the mortality decline (Flinn 1977, 8–9, 248; Houston 1988, 16).

Without detailed evidence on trends over time in the case-fatality rates of each of the main infectious diseases, of course, the thesis is impossible to verify. Equally, however, it is impossible to disprove. In view of this, the wisest course is to regard it as no more than a possible, partial explanation (Tranter 1985a, 65–8).

Of greater significance was the introduction of inoculation and vaccination against one of the most common causes of death, smallpox. Inoculation, which became increasingly widespread during the second half of the eighteenth century, probably had only a modest effect on Scottish death rates. The practice was always far more extensive in the Highlands than in the more heavily populated Lowlands where it met considerable opposition on religious, medical and financial grounds and received little support from the bulk of the population. As late as the 1790s smallpox still accounted for as much as one-fifth of all deaths in Glasgow, a ratio very similar to that in most of the more populous parts of the country throughout the second half of the century. The impact of vaccination, discovered by Edward Jenner in 1798, was more dramatic. As a result of the promotional efforts of the Edinburgh College of Surgeons and the General Assembly and ministers of the Church of Scotland, it is likely that vaccination was adopted more rapidly and extensively in Scotland than in any other country. Between 1801 and 1811 deaths from smallpox fell from 15% to 5% of all deaths, a saving of life that may have accounted for as much as a third to a half of the decline in overall rates of Scottish mortality during the decade (Razzell 1974; Flinn 1977, 15–16, 291–2, 392–5; Tranter 1985a, 76–7; Houston 1988, 15–16; Brunton 1992, 406, 425). Mercer (1985) has argued that in Britain and elsewhere much of the responsibility for the early nineteenth-century reduction in death rates stemmed directly from the decline in the number of smallpox deaths and indirectly from reduced levels of mortality from diseases like respiratory tuberculosis to which those who recovered from smallpox were subsequently especially prone. Had it not been for vaccination, the rise in Scottish mortality in the second quarter of the nineteenth century would have been even more pronounced.

It is, however, generally agreed that the single most important cause of the increase in life expectation in late eighteenth and early nineteenth-century Scotland was a rise in average standards of nutrition. Down to as late as the 1690s the growth of the country's population was persistently interrupted by surges in mortality provoked by famine and famine-related disease. By the second half of the eighteenth century, though food shortages continued to occur, they no longer had the same catastrophic effect on death rates. At first, this was a consequence of improvements in the methods of marketing and transporting food, coupled with rising levels of *per capita* income made possible by economic growth and the availability of more generous and efficient systems of famine relief supplied through the agencies of the poor law, central and local government, private landowners and philanthropic organisations. In the course of the first half of the nineteenth century the volume and regularity of the food supply were further augmented by the wider adoption of the improved methods of production associated with the Agricultural Revolution and the general acceptance of the potato as a food fit for human consumption. Until its effects were temporarily negated by the deterioration in environmental conditions brought about by urbanisation, the result, it is claimed, was a rising standard of diet and its corollary, increased resistance to disease and a steady advance in life expectancy (Flinn 1977, 4–13, 246–8, 423–4, 426, 428–9, 433–5).

Admittedly, the emphasis given to improved nutritional standards as the chief cause of mortality decline remains contentious. Firstly, the rise in food output may have been as much a consequence as a cause of population growth and the fall in death rates which largely accounted for it. Secondly, while there is no doubt that the *aggregate* supply of food increased, so too did the number of mouths available to consume it. Convincing proof of an increase in food output *per head*, on a scale sufficient to have had significant implications for mortality, has still to be provided. On the other hand, because of the problems involved in compiling reliable estimates of food output, the possibility cannot be ruled out. And, in any case, circumstances in Scotland were different from those in England where a similar inability to prove conclusively that *per capita* food output rose has persuaded most historians to look elsewhere for the causes of mortality decline. In England the association between food supplies and mortality had disappeared long before the upturn in rates of population growth which began in the second half of the eighteenth century. In Scotland, by contrast, the relationship between the two variables persisted to the eve of demographic 'take-off'. The implications of its disappearance, therefore, are likely to have been considerably more significant (McKeown, Brown and Record 1972; Razzell 1974; Tranter 1985a, 82–7).

EXERCISE 6

What is the most important factor which contributed to declining levels of mortality?

Rising standards of nutrition and resistance to disease brought about by improved agriculture, distribution of food supplies, and famine relief when appropriate should figure in your answer.

5. CONCLUSION

Hampered by the unusually severe limitations of their source-materials, historians of Scottish demography have so far been able to provide no more than a tenuous and incomplete account of the mechanisms and causes which shaped regional and chronological variations in rates of population growth in the eighteenth and first half of the nineteenth centuries. It is to be hoped that future research will remove at least some of the present uncertainties. In the meantime, it is already clear that Scotland's early modern demography was not merely a replica of that of England. In the predominance of falling mortality over rising fertility, in the acceleration of population growth rates during the late eighteenth and early nineteenth centuries, and in the disproportionate importance of improvements in nutrition to the decline in mortality, the Scottish experience differed substantially from the English. In both respects, Scotland's demographic evolution in the period 1700–1850 more closely resembled that of mainland Europe.

EXERCISE 7

Read the extracts from the Statistical Accounts, **Documents 27 to 32**. What do the writers identify as the main causes of population change in their localities?

REFERENCES TO BOOKS AND ARTICLES MENTIONED IN THE TEXT

Bailyn, B 1986 *Voyagers to the West*. London.
Baines, D 1991 *Emigration from Europe, 1815–1930*. London.
*Blaikie, A 1993 *Illegitimacy, Sex and Society, North-East Scotland, 1750–1900*. Oxford.
*Blaikie, A 1994 'A kind of loving. Illegitimacy, grandparents and the rural economy of North-East Scotland, 1750–1900', *Scottish Economic and Social History* 14, 41–57.

Brayshay, M 1979 'Using American records to study nineteenth century emigrants from Britain', *Area* 11, 156–60.

Brunton, D 1992 'Inoculation and demographic trends in eighteenth century Scotland', *Medical History* 36, 403–29.

Bumstead, JM 1982 *The People's Clearances: Highland emigration to British North America, 1770–1815*. Edinburgh.

*Devine, TM 1979 'Temporary migration and the Scottish Highlands in the nineteenth century', *Economic History Review* 32, 344–59.

Devine, TM 1988 *The Great Highland Famine: Hunger, Emigration and the Scottish Highlands in the Nineteenth Century*. Edinburgh.

Donaldson, G 1966 *The Scots Overseas*. London.

*Erickson, CJ 1972 'Who were the English and the Scots Emigrants to the United States in the late Nineteenth Century?', *in* Glass, DV and Revelle, R (eds), *Population and social change*, London, 347–81.

*Erickson, CJ 1981 'Emigration from the British Isles to the USA in 1831', *Population Studies* 35, 175–97.

Erickson, CJ 1989 'Emigration from the British Isles to the USA in 1841: Part I. Emigration from the British Isles', *Population Studies* 43, 347–67.

*Flinn, MW (ed) 1977 *Scottish population history from the 17th century to the 1930s*. Cambridge.

*Gray, M 1983 'Migration in the rural lowlands of Scotland, 1750–1850', *in* Devine, TM and Dickson, D (eds), *Ireland and Scotland, 1600–1850*, Edinburgh, 104–17.

*Gray, M 1990 *Scots on the move. Scots migrants 1750–1914*. Dundee.

Haines, R 1994 'Indigent misfits or shrewd operators? Government-assisted emigrants from the United Kingdom to Australia, 1831–60', *Population Studies* 48, 223–47.

*Harper, M 1988 *Emigration from North-East Scotland. Volume 1: Willing exiles*. Aberdeen.

Houston, RA 1985 'Geographical mobility in Scotland, 1652–1811', *Journal of Historical Geography* 11, 379–94.

Houston, RA 1988 'The demographic regime', *in* Devine, TM and Mitchison, R (eds), *People and Society in Scotland. Volume I, 1760–1830*, Edinburgh, 9–26.

Kyd, JG (ed) 1952 *Scottish population statistics including Webster's analysis of population 1755*. Edinburgh.

Laslett, P and Oosterveen, K 1973 'Long-term trends in bastardy in England', *Population Studies* 27, 255–86.

*Leneman, L and Mitchison, R 1987 'Scottish illegitimacy ratios in the early modern period', *Economic History Review* 40, 41–63.

Lockhart, DG 1978 'Chartulary books: a source for migration in Scotland, 1740–1850', *Local Population Studies* 21, 40–42.

Lockhart, DG 1980 'Sources for studies of migration to estate villages in North-East Scotland', *Local Historian* 14, 35–43.

McKeown, T, Brown, RG and Record, RG 1972 'An interpretation of the modern rise of population in Europe', *Population Studies* 26, 345–82.

McKeown, T 1976 *The modern rise of population*. London.

Mercer, AJ 1985 'Smallpox and epidemiological-demographic change in Europe: the role of vaccination', *Population Studies* 39, 287–307.

*Mitchison, R and Leneman, L 1989 *Sexuality and social control. Scotland, 1660–1780*. Oxford.

New Statistical Account of Scotland 1845. 15 volumes. Edinburgh.

Razzell, P 1974 'An interpretation of the modern rise of population in Europe – a critique', *Population Studies* 28, 5–17.

Schurer, K 1991 'The role of the family in the process of migration', *in* Pooley, CG and Whyte, ID (eds), *Migrants, emigrants and immigrants. A social history of migration*, London and New York, 106–42.

Statistical Account of Scotland 1791–99. 21 volumes. Edinburgh.

*Tranter, NL 1985a *Population and Society, 1750–1940. Contrasts in population growth*. London and New York.

Tranter, NL 1985b 'Illegitimacy in rural Scotland: a puzzle resolved?', *The International Journal of Sociology and Social Policy* 5, 33–46.

Van Vugt, WE 1988 'Running from ruin? The emigration of British farmers to the USA in the wake of the repeal of the Corn Laws', *Economic History Review* 41, 411–28.

Whyte, ID 1989 'Population mobility in Early Modern Scotland', *in* Houston, RA and Whyte, ID (eds), *Scottish Society, 1500–1800*, Cambridge, 37–58.

Whyte, ID 1991 'Migration in early modern Scotland and England. A comparative analysis', *in* Pooley, CG and Whyte, ID (eds), *Migrants, emigrants and immigrants. A social history of migration*, London and New York, 87–105.

Withers, CJW 1985 'Highland migration to Dundee, Perth and Stirling, 1753–1891', *Journal of Historical Geography* 11, 395–418.

Wrigley, EA and Schofield, RS 1981 *The population history of England, 1541–1871. A reconstruction*. London.

FURTHER READING

Those references marked * in the text are recommended further reading.

Aspects of Industrialisation before 1850
—— *Anthony Cooke and Ian Donnachie*

In this chapter we will look at industrialisation and the Industrial Revolution in Scotland before 1850. This needs to be seen in a comparative context, drawing on developments elsewhere in Britain and internationally. Scottish industrialisation certainly did not happen in a vacuum and external factors (such as expanding overseas trade and technical change) helped shape internal developments before and during the period. Industrialisation remains an important subject in the scholarly and critical debate about the growth of the British economy, to which Scotland contributed substantially before and after 1850.

We will examine the topic – highly selectively – under the following headings:

- Defining industrialisation
- Stages of growth, backwardness and revisionism
- Proto-industrialisation
- Causal factors
- Three key industries: textiles, coal and iron
- Employment structures

It would serve as a useful introduction to our discussion if you read Smout (1969, 240–57) before proceeding. We will also be referring to two articles in the Reader and a number of sources in the Documents volume. On completion of the present chapter you should be able to define the process of industrialisation, have some appreciation of the historical debate surrounding it, understand the main causes, and specify some of the fundamental features in Scotland, particularly the key industries most affected by the first phase and some of the characteristics of those in the 'second phase' from *c* 1830 onwards.

I. DEFINING INDUSTRIALISATION

Industrialisation brought about a fundamental discontinuity in the rate of economic change in the then developing world, the nucleus being western Europe but radiating through settlement and overseas trade (in which Scots played a prominent role) to many parts of the globe. This discontinuity has been graphically illustrated in the British context by findings (O'Brien 1993, 9) which suggest that if the economy had continued to grow after 1750 at the same rate as during the previous fifty years, it would have taken national income a hundred and twenty years and per capita income three hundred and forty-six years to double in size! By 1825 national income could be predicted to double every twenty-eight years and per capita income every sixty-three years.

Although England has often been described as the 'first industrial nation', other parts of the British Isles, Continental Europe and the United States, benefiting from the transfer of ideas and technology, were affected about the same time and in varying degrees by the same process. So, comparatively, Scotland shared much the same experience as, say, Ulster, Silesia or New England, and taking the global view it is worth thinking about what, if anything, was distinctive about Scottish industrialisation.

Explaining why industrial growth began where it did, in Britain rather than, say, France or Germany, would take us beyond the confines of this course. But we must not assume that pre-industrial economies, like England's, or Scotland's for that matter, were static and tradition-bound. Industrialisation could be seen as the culmination of institutional and technical improvements over the long term which allowed more systematic exploitation of natural resources, starting with agriculture, the processing of primary products and mineral exploitation. And, as we will see, there was an interesting halfway house, the 'proto-industrial' phase, affecting primary processing, textiles, mining and other activities, which Scotland shared with other areas. But first, we need to get to grips with some basic definitions which help to set the context for our discussion of the Scottish experience.

Broadly speaking, industrialisation can be defined in two distinct ways. The first is a general process of technological innovation involving the substitution of inanimate energy for human or animal power, the mechanisation of handicrafts, and the partial or total displacement of manual skills by machinery. Classic innovations related to specific inventions were Arkwright's water-frame and Watt's separate condenser which resulted in a viable steam engine. Indeed, the last example, dependent for its ultimate success on Watt's relationship with his business associate, Matthew Boulton, shows that invention is not a sufficient condition for innovation. Innovation also required entrepreneurs to finance technical improvements, and assumed rising and consistent demand (domestic or overseas) for the new manufactures. While there is a considerable amount of debate about the timing and impact of earlier developments, there is general agreement that a burst of technological innovation occurred in the later eighteenth century, which raised the annual growth of the economy to unprecedented levels. Economic growth based on this level of innovation proved to be 'self-sustaining', replacing some age-old craft-based modes of production with the 'factory system', hence the burst of activity which attracted the label of 'Industrial Revolution'.

The second definition relates to structural change, both within the labour force and different sectors of the economy. This involved a major redistribution of labour from primary to secondary production, which brought about a reduction in the proportion in agriculture and an increase in industry. As more capital was invested in industry and in infra-structural developments like improved transport (roads, canals, railways), the productivity gains in manufacturing outstripped those in agriculture. The continued growth of the manufacturing sector was sustained by enhanced demand in both domestic and overseas markets (though historians have debated which was more important). There was a corresponding rise in the proportion of Gross National Product or GNP (the value of the country's total output of goods and services produced annually plus income from abroad) generated by manufacturing and, as industrialisation proceeded, the gap between primary and secondary sectors widened further.

> EXERCISE I
> Industrialisation or Industrial Revolution? Historians tend to use the words interchangeably, but on the basis of the discussion so far what do you think is the difference between the two concepts?

Put succinctly, 'industrialisation' suggests a process, while 'Industrial Revolution' suggests an event. Industrialisation as a process could be long- or short-term in impact, but it is more likely to be the former. The term 'Industrial Revolution' certainly suggests revolutionary (if not dramatic and violent) change in the short term. But are the two mutually exclusive?

2. STAGES OF GROWTH, BACKWARDNESS AND REVISIONISM

In *The Stages of Economic Growth*, first published in 1960, the American economist, WW Rostow, claimed to have discovered the conditions needed for an economy to shed traditional constraints and enter a phase of rapid and continuous growth (Rostow 1960). Rostow identified five stages in the process, involving:

- the 'traditional' society
- the pre-conditions for take-off
- the take-off into self-sustained growth
- the drive to technological maturity
- the age of high mass-consumption

For an economy to take off into self-sustaining growth in the way Rostow suggested requires the following preconditions:

> (i) the existence or rapid emergence of a political, social and institutional framework which will promote industry, the mobility of labour and capital.
> (ii) the growth of one or more rapidly expanding manufacturing industries, which he called 'leading sectors', generating vertical and horizontal links to ancillary industries. This must be accompanied by changes in industrial structure, mass production and specialisation. Labour will need to be more mobile and

willing to accept factory discipline. Dynamic entrepreneurship is required, and this was to be seen at its most innovative in the cotton industry.

(iii) a rise in productive investment from 5% (or less) to over 10% of national income (but note that this assumes reliable data on which to base such a calculation).

With the pre-conditions fulfilled, the economy takes off and is launched on a drive to technological maturity and ultimately reaches the stage of high mass consumption. A time chart showed how this model applied to various countries. While Rostow first pinpointed Britain's take-off very precisely to 1783–1802, his later chart (Rostow 1978, 51) indicates a much longer timescale, say 1780–1830.

Revisionist historians, using fresh calculations, claim that the growth of the economy never reached the levels Rostow stated. The doubling of the rate of investment took much longer than the twenty years originally designated as the 'take-off' phase. Again, if we are to assume the data are credible, productive investment took seventy years to rise from 6% of GNP in 1760 to nearly 12% in 1830, which even discounting what was happening beforehand provides evidence of much more gradual change (Crafts 1985). Cotton, however, still stands out as a 'leading sector', important in itself but with valuable linkages to other sectors such as engineering, chemicals and overseas trade.

Rostow's model has had a diminishing influence on historical thinking about industrialisation but the original concept and the revisionism both have validity, especially in the Scottish context, where there was almost certainly a longer 'lead-in' time (to the mid- or even late 1780s or early 1790s) followed by a great burst of activity (1790s-1820s) and sustained, if halting, growth thereafter.

Another theory about the conditions for development and industrialisation which has some relevance for Scotland is Gershenkron's work on economic backwardness (Gershenkron 1966). Briefly, he argued that the speed of industrialisation in Continental Europe and the United States was affected by the extent to which individual countries lagged behind Britain and that Britain's phase of industrialisation was slow because it was first. The late starters, benefiting from imported advanced technology and know-how (and in some instances, like those of Germany and Russia, greater state intervention than occurred in Britain), industrialised faster and had a tendency to 'bigness' in terms of capital investment and size of business enterprises.

If we separate the Scottish experience from the British, or at least compare Scotland with England, we can certainly see a later start, relying to some considerable degree on imported technology, skills and capital, a period of rapid catching up, and in the longer term the emergence of comparatively large business units in key sectors like textiles, mining, metals, engineering and shipbuilding (Hudson 1992, 115). So the late starter idea has some relevance, if we assume the existence of relative backwardness compared to England.

Economic models provide a useful frame of reference but can be somewhat detached from historical events. The major socio-economic pre-determinants of industrialisation, as we will see, can help to explain the Scottish growth process, but before we return to the classic Industrial Revolution era in more detail you might like to think about what else was happening internationally and domestically. For example, what impact did the wars of the period have on developments? Are they likely to have encouraged or retarded growth? If so, how?

3. PROTO-INDUSTRIALISATION

Franklin Mendels' phrase 'proto-industrialisation' entered the terminology of economic and social historians in 1972, initially in relation to textile production in Flanders. It refers particularly to manufacturing located in the countryside where people combined cottage industry with farming. Textile production is the classic example of proto-industrialisation, which was less often found in mining or metal smelting where larger amounts of capital were required. Mendels saw it as 'a first phase which preceded and prepared modern industrialisation proper'. He cited four features as defining characteristics:

- goods were produced for the outside market
- they were produced by peasant manufacturers
- rural manufacturing stimulated a market for food
- towns became market centres rather than manufacturing centres

He also stressed the crucial nature of location, initially arguing the importance of areas of high ground and infertile soils where peasant smallholders were obliged to supplement their incomes by industrial activity (Clarkson 1990, 151; Hudson 1992, 112).

Mendels' theories have been criticised by other historians who have cited many exceptions but they have been influential nonetheless. How useful are they in understanding what was happening in Scotland in this period? Certainly, there were close connections between proto-industrialisation and Scottish agriculture in milling, brewing, distilling, tanning and textiles. Whyte (1989, 234), however, has argued that the late survival of monopoly privileges in royal burghs and burghs of barony in Scotland meant that the commercial production of textiles and other commodities was more urban in character in Scotland than in other European countries.

Certainly, Scotland does not fit neatly into the locational framework devised by Mendels. The dominant industry prior to 'take-off' was linen which accounted for two thirds of Scottish exports in 1700. By the 1750s, according to one estimate, 180,000 women (four-fifths of the adult female population) were employed from time to time in linen spinning (Durie 1979, 159; Whatley 1997). Linen production became increasingly concentrated, the main centres being Angus, Lowland Perthshire and Fife in the East and Lanarkshire and Renfrewshire in the West. These areas, particularly those in the East, were not the marginal, upland areas of the Mendels hypothesis but fertile arable areas where much of the labour for the flax industry seems to have come from cottar families who worked in cottage industry during the slack periods of the agricultural year (Whyte 1989, 232–240).

Some have seen proto-industry as a trigger for population expansion as alternative sources of income came into agricultural households and the demand for child and female labour increased. Scottish evidence for this is anecdotal and inconclusive. The minister of the Fife parish of Kettle wrote that:

> The looms find employment for women and children; and hence a family being advantageous, the men marry early; and hence one of the principal causes of the increased population.
>
> (*ibid*, 240)

However, population figures from rural textile parishes in this period show both increases and absolute decreases in population.

The spinning and weaving of linen, but not bleaching and finishing, were carried out as a cottage industry for most of the eighteenth century until the introduction of water-powered flax spinning from England in 1787 began the mechanisation of spinning. Weaving had to wait till the introduction of power looms in the 1830s. The industry was organised on a semi-capitalistic basis with master weavers and journeymen in the towns and 'putters out' or travelling merchants who put out raw flax and yarn to spinners and weavers in the countryside. The latter arrangement was probably encouraged by the fact that much of the raw material was imported from the Baltic although some flax was grown in Scotland. The 'putters out' included men who were very influential in the next stage of industrialisation in Scotland such as David Dale, the 'father' of the Scottish cotton industry, and the Cox and Baxter families who founded textile dynasties in flax and jute in Dundee. Most of the finished product was exported, initially to England, although markets widened later. Much of the effort of the government-sponsored Board of Trustees for Fisheries and Manufactures, founded in 1727 with money allocated at the time of the Union of 1707, went towards raising quality by giving premiums for inventions, and encouraging technology transfer by grants towards the cost of travel and settlement for skilled foreign workers (Whyte 1995, 301).

Although the spinning and weaving of linen were slow to mechanise, the preparation and finishing stages both saw significant advances in technology. Water-powered lint mills for scutching (beating and preparing flax) were introduced as early as 1729 from Holland and spread rapidly till there were around 250 in operation by 1770. Bleaching technology also borrowed heavily from the Low Countries and by 1745 some 25 bleachfields had been established in Scotland. The use of sulphuric acid for bleaching was introduced in the 1750s from Holland but by 1799 home-grown technology was leading the way with the invention of dry bleaching powder by Charles Tennant at the St Rollox Works in Glasgow (Whyte 1995, 301; Whatley 1997).

The picture of Scotland's dominant manufacturing industry is a mixed one with some elements of proto-industrialisation surviving in spinning until the 1780s and in weaving even after the 1830s. Bleaching required significant amounts of fixed capital in the form of land, buildings and machinery, and was making the change from natural to chemical bleaching agents. In other industries, specialisation emerged much earlier. Iron smelting, for example, was developed, by English capital and technology, first in the Highlands where the York Buildings Company set up a short-lived furnace at Abernethy on Speyside in 1730. This was followed by more successful attempts in the West Highlands where companies from the Lake District established charcoal smelting ironworks at lochside sites such as Furnace and Bonawe and brought in English labour to work them. Scotland's first 'modern' ironworks was founded in 1759 at Carron near Falkirk, by Dr John Roebuck, a Yorkshire Quaker, Samuel Garbutt, a Birmingham merchant, and William Cadell, a merchant from Cockenzie (Campbell 1961). Here again, workmen had to be brought from England to build the ironworks, as they had been brought twenty-five years earlier to build the Adam-designed Wade Bridge at Aberfeldy .

Similarly, coal production in Scotland required access to land and capital, and a specialised labour force. There seems to have been no equivalent in Scotland of the Free Miners of the Forest of Dean who combined agricultural work with coal mining. The same was true of lead and copper mining which had been developed by immigrants from Augsburg in Germany under aristocratic or merchant patronage at

No. 14. Stanley Mills: Bell Mill, west side. © *Royal Commission on the Ancient and Historical Monuments of Scotland.*

places like Leadhills and Wanlockhead in the Southern Uplands, Glen Esk in Angus, or Tyndrum in Perthshire. Salt manufacture and lime burning also required capital investment, specialised labour and the consent, if not the active involvement, of the local landowner.

Other industries, however, remained in a semi-domestic state for much of the century. In brewing, for example, there was the contrast between the large integrated brewery established in Leith in 1670 by Sir James Stansfield and the 522 separate brewers in Fife, including 70 in St Andrews alone, who signed a petition against excise duties in 1700 (Donnachie 1979). Whisky production remained in a proto-industrial (and semi-legal) state for most of the eighteenth century until the emergence of distilleries into the legal light of day after the halving of duties in 1823 when 'persons of respectability and capital' entered the industry (Barnard 1887).

Elements of proto-industry were to be found in most of the processes of linen manufacture, the Scottish 'staple'. It was important in promoting manufacturing skills that were to be vital in the next stage of industrialisation. When Arkwright visited Perth in the early 1780s to look at the viability of building cotton mills at Stanley, it was the quality of locally made cotton muslins that persuaded him to become involved. The merchants involved in 'putting out' became the entrepreneurs for the next stage of industrialisation as they had acquired not only capital but knowledge of managing a workforce, quality control, markets, credit systems etc. However, the proto-industrial model does not provide us with much help in explaining the 'second phase' of Scotland's industrial development – based on coal, iron and engineering.

EXERCISE 2

How far is the concept of proto-industrialisation a useful one when applied to Scotland in this period? How far was it an essential pre-condition for later industrial development?

With a few reservations, notably about the relevance of locational factors and the growth of specialisation, it seems reasonably appropriate. The second question is more difficult but the existence of proto-industry certainly aided subsequent development, even although new technology, amongst other factors, played an important role.

4. CAUSAL FACTORS

For many years, historians stressed the impact of the Union of 1707 on the Scottish economy, which gave access to the large English and colonial markets. Certainly, the Union had a strong economic focus – it has been pointed out that fifteen of the twenty-five articles of the Act of Union were economic in character (Whatley 1989). Many historians have seen an almost automatic connection between industrialisation in England and that in Scotland. Smout, for example, writes:

It was above all the response of the linen trade, the cattle trade and the tobacco
trade to stimuli that originated in England that carried the economy forward and
the close connection between the two countries allowed the immediate
transmission of technological advances from one to the other.

(Smout 1969, 244)

More recently, others have emphasised the regional dimension of industrialisation
and economic change. The examples of Ireland or the Scottish Highlands demonstrate that simply being tied politically and economically to a larger partner that is
industrialising is no guarantee of industrial development but can lead to depopulation and de-industrialisation. Certainly, there were few immediate economic benefits
to Scotland from the Union. Longer term, however, it does seem to have provided a
channel for economic growth in Scotland through access to wider markets, political
stability and through easing flows of capital, skills and technology. Another
argument has emphasised the way in which Scotland's landowners and lawyers,
with fewer opportunities for political advancement, channelled their energies into
economic development (Whyte 1995, 299).

What was it about the Scottish Lowlands that enabled them to benefit from the
common market with England after 1707 in a way that the Scottish Highlands or
Ireland were unable to? In an important article, Devine (1995, 47–9) has identified a
number of key factors including:

- resources of coal and iron close to water
- the commitment of the political and social élite to economic improvement
- Scottish scientific and technological ingenuity
- the entrepreneurial nature of the Scottish business class
- the nature of rural society in Scotland

We can look at each of these areas in turn.

4.1. Resources

Cipolla (1980, 11), who saw industrialisation as an essential 'discontinuity' with the
past, singled out a certain conservatism and the absence of coal as the reason why
Holland lost out to England in the race to be the first country to industrialise. The
presence of coal and blackband iron ore in close proximity in the West of Scotland
was clearly a prerequisite for the second stage of Scottish economic growth after
Neilson's discovery of the hot blast technique in 1828. Both Glasgow and Edinburgh
and other industrial towns such as Paisley were close to coal supplies, and more
distant industrial centres such as Aberdeen and Dundee could have coal brought in
by sea from the Fife and Lothian coalfields.

Coal and iron reserves were of particular importance for 'second phase'
industrialisation after 1830. They may be crucial in explaining why industrial
development carried on in the Scottish Lowlands after 1830 when it failed or

petered out in Ireland or the Highlands. Less remarked on perhaps is the importance of Scotland's resources of water power and timber from 1750 to 1830. These resources, along with cheap labour, were a prime reason why English industrialists were willing to relocate north. It was supplies of charcoal timber that tempted English companies to build blast furnaces in remote areas of the western Highlands where they had to import not only iron ore but also skilled labour. The richness of Scotland's water-power resources explains why the cotton industry in Scotland continued to have a higher proportion of plant powered by water into the nineteenth century than the English industry – 43.6% of total HP in Scotland in 1835 compared to 18.6% in the North of England (Chapman 1987, 19).

4.2. *The role of the political and social élite*

The dominance of the landowning élite in Scotland has been well described by Smout (1969). In 1814, Sir John Sinclair estimated that there were 7,654 landed proprietors in Scotland. This was more of an indigenous and resident élite than was the case in Ireland, although London connections and residences meant that it was a group with rising social and economic expectations. It was also an élite which was broadly in favour of 'improvement' whether it took the form of support for agricultural enclosure, laying out a planned village, encouraging mining development on an estate, planning a road, canal or harbour, or leasing land and water rights for a textile mill or bleachfield. Most landowners shared these views regardless of political affiliation – many Jacobite landowners planned agricultural or industrial improvement on their estates. There were also close links between the landowning and business classes in Scotland often brokered by an important intermediate class of lawyers. Devine's work on the Glasgow 'Tobacco Lords' shows that 'most successful tobacco merchants owned estates at some time during their life', mainly but not exclusively in the Glasgow region (Devine 1990, 18).

This was not an insular élite but one with strong economic and social connections with England and overseas. The west of Scotland had particular links with the West Indies and the American colonies but many Scottish families had economic links with the East. The East India Company had strong Scottish connections through landowners such as the agricultural improver Scott of Dunninald in Angus. Even a seemingly out-of-the-way place like Blairgowrie could be home to a mill-owning family like the Dicks who boasted not only members of the Edinburgh judiciary but a Governor-General of Bengal amongst their immediate family.

Scottish landowners controlled access to mining rights on their estates as in the case of the Duke of Hamilton in the Lanarkshire coalfields or the Earls of Elgin whose estates lay above the West Fife coalfields and who laid out a harbour, planned village, limekilns and tramway system at Charleston in Fife in the 1770s at a cost of £17,000. Their involvement in industrial development was far from passive – the Duke of Atholl went to the extent of advertising in the Manchester papers for a

developer for the cotton mills at Stanley outside Perth and sent an agent to Cromford
to persuade Arkwright to become involved.

The landowners' dominance of the political process meant that their support
was essential for parliamentary approval for enclosure and for infrastructure
improvements such as turnpike trusts, canals, harbours and later railways. In
Scotland, there was state backing for manufacturing industry through the Board
of Trustees for Improving Manufactures and Fisheries.

4.3. Technology

Although Devine cites 'Scottish scientific and technical ingenuity' as a causal factor,
the early stages of industrialisation in Scotland were heavily dependent on English or
overseas technology. Many inventions in linen, such as water-powered lint mills for
preparing flax or the use of sulphuric acid in bleaching, originated in Holland. The
cotton industry was almost totally dependent on English technology, and in the case
of Stanley, workers were sent to Derbyshire to be trained. The Carron ironworks
were modelled on Coalbrookdale in Shropshire, and Roebuck, who played a key
role at Carron, and in founding vitriol works at Prestonpans, was a Yorkshire
Quaker who had graduated from both Edinburgh and Leiden universities.

However, Scots soon embraced technical innovation, first by modifying
imported technology, then taking the lead themselves. At both New Lanark and
Deanston significant modifications were made to cotton machinery, notably
William Kelly's adaptation of Crompton's mule to power spinning. Soon, Scots
were taking the lead as in the development of dry bleaching powder by Charles
Tennant at his St Rollox Works in Glasgow in 1799. Thomas Telford, another
genius, emerged from humble origins in the Scottish Borders to dominate the new
discipline of civil engineering. Henry Bell's *Comet*, launched on the Clyde in 1812,
was the second steamship in the world following earlier experiments in Scotland by
Miller and Symington. Most significant of all was the work of James Watt, first with
Roebuck at Bo'ness then with Boulton in Birmingham, transforming the steam
engine by the development of the separate condenser and of the rotary engine.

Where did this burst of creative energy come from? Some historians have cited
the education system with its widespread system of parish schools and the more
open attitudes of the Scottish universities compared to their English counterparts.
Others have stressed the impact of Presbyterianism with its emphasis on conscience,
self-criticism and the need to do better. Combined with the Calvinist belief in predestination, these attitudes planted in the individual 'a high motivation towards
achievement' (Whatley 1997).

> EXERCISE 3
> What particular factors in Scottish society do you think favoured invention and
> innovation in this period? What limitations might there be on the introduction of
> new techniques and ideas?

Amongst favourable factors we can include the desire for improvement, the demand for new and better products and the ideas of the Enlightenment, particularly as they affected education and scientific research (the Scottish Enlightenment had a very practical bias). Limitations might include the continuance of more conservative ideas and the survival of old production techniques and attitudes.

4.4. The Scottish business class

The influence of Calvinism may also go some way towards explaining the success of the Scottish business class in this period (see Smout 1969, 361–90). Scots businessmen were active in shipping, insurance and banking. They certainly scared their English competitors – the English cotton manufacturer Samuel Oldknow complained in 1786 that 'Scots impudence and perseverance is above all'. The growth of foreign trade, particularly the Glasgow tobacco trade, had led to the creation of a group of 'men devoted to commerce: men concerned with fine calculations of profit and loss, men of wide horizons whose attitudes communicated themselves in various ways throughout their societies' (Rostow 1960, 31). It is no accident that Adam Smith's *Wealth of Nations*, published in 1776, was written against this background.

Unlike their Irish counterparts, Scots businessmen largely controlled Scottish shipping and also were more involved in marine insurance. Most striking, however, was the early development of banking in Scotland which challenges notions of 'backwardness' in this period. The Bank of Scotland was founded as early as 1695 by William Paterson, a London-based Scot, who had founded the Bank of England a year earlier. 1727 saw the foundation of the Royal Bank of Scotland. The British Linen Bank grew out of the British Linen Company, founded in 1746. Many smaller provincial banks were founded in the latter part of the eighteenth century, aided by the easier laws on joint stock companies compared to England, though the failure of the Ayr Bank in 1772 brought a check to this expansion. Through the banking system, surplus profits from agriculture or trade were made available for industrial development, transport improvements or foreign trade (Checkland 1975; Munn 1981). It has been calculated that the total assets of Scottish banks rose from around £600,000 in 1750 to around £3,700,000 in 1770 (Smout 1969, 245).

4.5. The nature of rural society in Scotland

The eighteenth century was a period of far-reaching change in rural society in Scotland. Population was growing, although probably not as fast as in Ireland or England, and improvements were being introduced both in the Highlands and the Lowlands. The emerging social structure was that of landlord, tenant and landless labourer rather than peasant proprietor (see Chapter 5 of this volume). In farming, a capitalistic structure was emerging based on a relatively small number of politically powerful landowners who favoured improvement.

The dominance of the landowning classes meant that agricultural change could be pushed through with little effective resistance. When Thomas Graham of Balgowan in Perthshire was considering enclosure on his estates in 1773, his factor reported, 'the lands around the Almond needed improvement and the people were docile' (Cooke 1984, 49). Surplus population was brutally cleared in extreme cases like Sutherland or moved into planned industrial or fishing villages. Many agricultural workers moved themselves – either into manufacturing villages or towns, into the army or navy or overseas. The absence of security of tenure ensured considerable mobility of labour. The presence of manufacturing industry, particularly linen, in the countryside, meant that many rural workers possessed more than simply agricultural skills, which must have eased the transition.

> EXERCISE 4
> Do you think any of the causal factors cited above was dominant in sparking industrialisation in Scotland? Are there any other causal factors not cited here which you think might have been important?

Whilst the social and institutional frameworks were very important, the resources and skills might well strike you as dominant (but you might think differently, for good reason). Another important factor is expanding markets both at home and overseas which we refer to in Section 1.

5. THREE KEY INDUSTRIES

While there were many important developments across a wide range of manufacturing, early industrialisation in Scotland, as south of the Border, was undoubtedly dominated by the rapid growth of textiles, especially cotton, and the rising output of both coal and iron.

5.1. *Textiles*

The changes in the textile industry at the end of the eighteenth century can be described as revolutionary since they introduced mechanisation and large-scale mass production for the first time. The industry provides an excellent case-study of how the various factors of production came together. Our earlier discussion is confirmed in **Article 12** by Donnachie and Hewitt (1993), which *inter alia* summarises key developments in linen and its close relationship with cotton in the late eighteenth century.

> EXERCISE 5
> What were the major factors favouring the development of the linen industry?

The various causal factors we have described contributed to a substantial degree of structural change and rapid growth in linen. Nevertheless technical change was beginning to impinge more overtly by 1770, at which date some mechanisation had crept in and the production of hybrid yarns using imported cotton as well as flax was already a modest but established feature of Scotland's most successful industry. Feeding into trends elsewhere, the Scottish textile industry could be seen to be following a similar course to that in Lancashire around the same time.

The remainder of the Donnachie and Hewitt article stresses how much the growth of mass-production cotton spinning was owed to imported technology and expertise allied to local entrepreneurship, capital, labour and water power. The key innovations came from England: the spinning jenny, developed by Hargreaves (1764–7); the water frame of Arkwright (1769); and the spinning mule of Crompton (1779). The earliest spinning mills based on Arkwright's water frame were established at Penicuik (1778) and Rothesay (1779) by partnerships in which English entrepreneurs, including one of Arkwright's former employees, played a significant role. By the early 1780s there were another six mills, but still on a fairly small scale.

Why should these Englishmen, and in particular Arkwright himself, be interested in Scotland, which, after all, was remote from the centres of the English cotton industry?

EXERCISE 6
Read **Article 11** by Donnachie and Hewitt and **Article 12** by Cooke and suggest why Arkwright extended his business interests to Scotland.

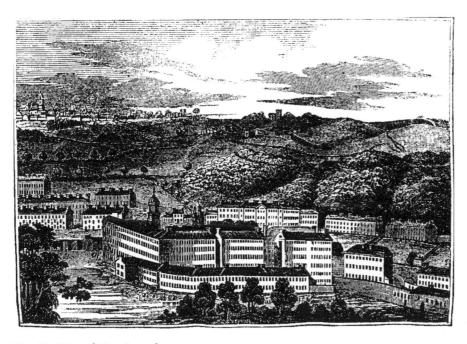

No. 15. Print of New Lanark.

While the quality of relatively cheap, skilled labour and water-power resources were both highly significant, another powerful factor seems to have been Arkwright's attempt to gain some return from his inventions even although the patent did not apply north of the Border. Having tolerated several years of what amounted to piracy of his invention, he fought back and judiciously sought partnerships with local entrepreneurs (able to access ready capital) and landowners (who held the water rights).

The timing was highly significant, for Arkwright's patent rights lasted for spinning from 1769 to 1783, and for preparatory systems from 1775 to 1785. Even if of short duration, his move north, as Cooke suggests, was partly to gain revenge on English pirates (especially in Manchester, which had rapidly become the main centre of the industry) by undermining their business, but more plausibly to exploit his inventions more fully in the last part of Britain where clear potential still existed. When the patents expired he could continue to capitalise on the partnerships he had already entered, and, given his expertise, he would be in a strong position to seek others. Hence Arkwright's interest in the major spinning mills established in the Scottish Lowlands, notably those at Stanley and New Lanark.

Admittedly it would only have been a matter of time before cotton spinning took off on the scale it already had in the North of England, but it seems probable that Arkwright's intervention was the catalyst. While Arkwright was briefly associated with Dale, the Glasgow linen merchant turned banker, in founding the mill at New Lanark, he soon dropped out, leaving Dale as sole proprietor. Dale was certainly a key figure in masterminding the Scottish cotton industry but in most of his other ventures he was merely a partner. So the arrangements into which Arkwright entered in the Stanley project were more typical.

EXERCISE 7
Read **Document 33**. What is it and what are the main provisions?

It is a legal contract binding the signatories to its various clauses. After a preamble which gives something of the background to the partnership, the provisions cover a ratification of previous obligations entered into, the share distribution and capital, the profit and loss arrangements and the spreading of the risk of the enterprise among the partners, the arrangements for management of the concern and the keeping of the books.

Both the preamble and Cooke's article show that plans to build a mill and village at Stanley had been formulated for some time and that the partners had not only secured a lease of property and water rights from the Duke of Atholl, but had also taken steps to ensure the training of key personnel at Cromford, where they would be 'taught the constructing and making of the Machinery' for cotton spinning. Similar arrangements were made by Dale at New Lanark, where some of the artisans recruited were either clockmakers or millwrights with appropriate mechanical backgrounds.

The Stanley partnership united interests from a variety of backgrounds including Atholl, the major local landowner, Dempster, the local MP and an active 'improver', who played a pivotal role, a clutch of local merchants, at least one of whom (like Dale) had connections with the linen trade, and of course Arkwright himself. Apart from entrepreneurship, capital and innovation, the remaining factor of production, labour, was perhaps more readily procured than at New Lanark, for Perth and Angus were among the most important linen-producing districts in the country, as well as being a magnet for migrant Highlanders (Withers 1986).

What impressed visitors to the new spinning mills was their sheer scale, for large factories were unusual and so was the number of workers required. While Stanley with its several hundred workers was large, New Lanark was bigger still, the workforce consisting of men, women and children, numbering upwards of 1,500 by the early 1800s. Some workers were migrants from the Highlands, enticed to the mills by Dale after the storm-damaged ship in which they were bound for North Carolina put into the Clyde for repair. Others were orphans drawn from institutions in Glasgow and Edinburgh, for New Lanark, like the other spinning mills, had a high proportion of children in the labour force.

Workers were found to be 'averse to indoor labour', partly because of the long hours and factory discipline, but Dale's regime did have some compensations, such as regular wages, housing and schooling. While we might question his motives, Dale also made sure that considerable attention was given to the child apprentices who were adequately housed in dormitories, fed and kitted out with specially designed uniforms. Education, with a strong element of religious instruction, was fitted in after working hours six days a week and on Sundays. Dale stuck to the letter of the law regarding the employment of children, but his son-in-law, Robert Owen, managing partner at New Lanark between 1800 and 1824, later sought further improvements. Owen explained his aims and achievements in 1816.

EXERCISE 8
Read **Document 34**. What kind of source is this? What major reforms did Owen claim, how successful had they been, and what do you think his objectives were?

This is an extract of evidence taken by a parliamentary select committee on children's employment, mainly in mills, since they were then the major 'manufactories'. Owen stopped employing children under ten, cut the working hours, and reformed the schools by introducing a new curriculum. He claimed the reforms had been very successful in raising educational and moral standards, which he regarded as the prime objectives. However, we might note that such provision ('in a pecuniary view', as Owen puts it) encouraged families to stay at New Lanark, working for lower wages, and that the schools were, in effect, self-financing from the profits of the company store. Owen aimed to produce a more efficient and docile workforce.

There can be little doubt that however unappealing factory work and its associated discipline might have been at places like Stanley and New Lanark, it was altogether more disagreeable elsewhere, especially in the smaller country mills and the urban mills of Glasgow and Paisley.

The cotton-spinning industry grew so rapidly that *c* 1795 there were no fewer than 91 mills, with half that number located in Lanarkshire and Renfrewshire, and the bulk of those in Glasgow. Gradually, as steam power began to dominate after the early 1800s, the industry concentrated increasingly in Glasgow, and by 1839 the city and neighbourhood had 98 out of a total of 192 mills. But small-scale domestic spinning survived longer than we might imagine and the power loom's elimination of the hand loom weaver was very gradual. Hand-weaving, as in the linen industry, was widespread throughout the Lowlands. After 1830 many plants integrated both spinning and weaving, so the handloom weaver ultimately became a casualty of technical change. An important finishing industry, bleaching, dyeing and printing, developed to service the cotton and other textile trades, concentrating in Renfrewshire and the Vale of Leven in the West and Angus and Perthshire in the East.

Compared to England, the Scottish cotton industry had a late start but caught up on both technology and growth very quickly. Comparative costs, particularly cheaper wages, as Owen observed, worked to the advantage of the Scottish industry. As in Lancashire, while the industry enjoyed a period of dramatic expansion (partly driven by the demands of the export market), substantial investment was made in then state-of-the-art technology represented by the water frame and mule. While specialisation in finer yarns helped to sustain Scottish spinners, the industry became less competitive and the earlier impetus was lost. Long before 1850 there was a failure to invest in new technology, a feature also present in Lancashire, the area which in competitive terms posed the biggest long-term threat to the Scottish cotton industry (see Knox 1995).

5.2. Coal and iron

Apart from textiles, two closely related activities, coal mining and iron manufacture, helped lay the basis of Scotland's industrial economy before 1850.

While the productive capacity of coal mining during the eighteenth and early nineteenth centuries remains a subject of debate, recent findings suggest that the performance of the industry in Scotland was much more impressive than was previously supposed. Scottish output appears to have risen by eight or ten times between *c* 1700 and 1800, almost double the rate for Britain as a whole, which made Scotland one of the fastest-growing-coal producing regions. In the longer time-frame output may have risen ten to 13 times from 1700, reaching around three million tons by 1830 (Whatley 1994, 7). The most rapid and sustained growth coincided with the classic industrialisation era. While this seems impressive enough, the growth of the industry in the succeeding two decades was dramatic: when the first official statistics were published for 1854, there were 368 collieries employing 33,000 miners and producing 7.5 million tons of coal, over 12% of the British total.

During the seventeenth century the shores of the Forth became studded with coal mines, expansion being partly based on shipping coastwise or for export, and partly related to increasing domestic and industrial demand generated by population growth. Coal was needed for salt production and on a more modest, but growing, scale for a variety of manufacturing processes including brewing, pottery, glass and soap. Coal was also being mined in the west of Scotland in Lanarkshire and in north Ayrshire, the latter having an important, if fluctuating, export trade to Ireland. In the eighteenth century prime movers in developments were the landowners, such as the Clerks of Penicuik, who saw mining as a logical extension of estate 'improvement', so successfully in Sir John Clerk's case that in 1755 the mines at Loanhead produced more revenue than the rentals of his entire estate.

Coal mining had particular problems meeting demand. Employee-labour relations were characterised by the 'fettering bonds' which apparently enslaved colliers (and salters) to their masters throughout much of the eighteenth century. Although wages were relatively high and hours of work shorter than those of other comparable groups of workers, coal masters found it difficult to recruit labour because of the taint of 'serfdom' and the arduous conditions. Hence as the industry grew more rapidly the masters campaigned energetically for emancipation, a move which it was hoped would encourage more workers to enter the industry and, just as importantly, weaken the workers' capacity to form 'combinations', to raise wages and restrict output.

Always labour-intensive, the industry was also constrained in its early growth by the prevailing level of technology, particularly as it affected drainage, haulage and transport. To solve the first two, resort was made to animal and water power, and, more exceptionally, Newcomen steam engines, the first models being installed at collieries between 1719 and 1734. More followed after 1760 and by the end of the century Scotland accounted for 17% of all steam pumping engines in Britain. Transport problems were eased by road improvements, the construction of wagon-ways linking to harbours, and, more limited geographically than in England, canals, such as the Monkland and Forth and Clyde. It was the increased efficiency of steam power, improved transport (especially the railways), and the growth of the iron industry which contributed most to the expansion of coal mining during the early nineteenth century.

Coal provided the fuel for a plethora of energy-using industries and the raw material for gas manufacture and chemicals, which via bleaching and dyeing brought important links to textiles. Its prime use was in the iron industry with which mining became more closely associated as industrialisation proceeded. Like textiles and coal mining, iron production had an interesting pre-industrial stage based not on coal but on charcoal. But as we noted, the major break with the past occurred in 1759 when the Carron Company established an ironworks near Falkirk to exploit local iron ores using imported coke-smelting techniques. With the Seven Years' War raging, the manufacture of munitions provided a profitable opportunity for the fledgling partnership. The first guns were cast in 1761, and munitions were quickly established as among Carron's most important products.

Carron was followed by a series of coke-smelting plants on the coalfields, notably in Lanarkshire and Ayrshire. In common with the practice at cotton mills, prying eyes were often discouraged, so any surviving descriptions are valuable, if impressionistic.

EXERCISE 9
Read **Document 35**. What kind of source is this and what clues does it give to the author's background? What were the main reasons for establishing these works, what were their products, and why the secrecy?

These are extracts from a travel diary and the author, Charles Hatchett, was clearly well-informed about technical and scientific matters. The prime locational factors were the accessibility of raw materials and good transport. Notice the high degree of integration between the mining and smelting operations at both works. Both Carron and Clyde produced a wide range of iron goods, cannon being the most strategically sensitive. Having failed to see the casting and boring of cannon at Carron, Hatchett does not actually confirm that he did so at Clyde.

As Hatchett suggests, an important manufacturing industry, producing every-thing from a spade to a steam engine, had already developed in response to the demand for iron products. While the industry was initially triggered by imported technology, Scottish inventors contributed substantially to its subsequent expansion. They included Mushet, who discovered the value of local blackband ironstone, and Neilson, who introduced the hot blast for smelting iron ore in 1828. The application of Neilson's hot blast and the use of blackband iron ores greatly reduced the costs of the Scottish iron industry at a time when both domestic and overseas demand for pig iron for railway metal and the engineering trades was increasing. After 1830 entrepreneurs like the Bairds of Gartsherrie, the Dixons of Govan and Houlds-worths of Coltness, established large enterprises controlling not only the ironworks, but also iron and coal mines. During the period 1830–43 the expansion of the iron industry was comparable only to that in the cotton industry in the 1780s and '90s.

By 1845 Scotland supplied 25% of Britain's output of pig iron. Although by 1850 a high proportion left Scotland without being processed further (a potential weakness in the longer term), up to a third was absorbed by the expanding railway, engineering and shipbuilding industries, which rapidly became the mainstays of Scotland's heavy industrial economy.

6. EMPLOYMENT STRUCTURES

What was the occupational pattern in Scotland as a result of the first stage of industrialisation? We have included two breakdowns of occupational structures in Scotland in Tables 1 and 2. One is Sir John Sinclair's estimates of numbers employed in manufacturing in Scotland published in 1825 but taken from earlier figures. The second is a summary of the 1851 census for Scotland broken down by rather large occupational groups.

TABLE I: MANUFACTURES OF SCOTLAND

1. *Manufactures, principally from domestic materials*

	MALES EMPLOYED ABOVE 20 YEARS OF AGE	WOMEN	MALE AND FEMALE YOUTHS AND CHILDREN	TOTALS
1. *Woollen*, (hats included).	7,500	12,560	4,740	24,800
2. *Linen and Hemp*	17,000	38,100	21,500	76,600
3. *Leather*	2,400			2,400
4. *Iron*	10,400	130	2,650	13,180
5. *Pottery*, including brick and tile and tobacco pipe-makers	360	40	150	580
6. *Paper*	2,330	225	845	3,400
7. *Cutlery*	110	0	70	180
8. *Liquors, fermented and distilled*	2,410	1,565	415	4,390
9. *Glass*	530	45	565	1,140
10. *Cooper Work*	1,860	0	750	2,610
11. *Salt*	188	5	12	205
12. *Ship & Small Craft*	1,200	0	200	1,400
13. *Combs and Spoons*	430	90	190	710
14. *Soap*	530	130	150	810
II. *Manufactures produced from foreign materials*				
1. *Cotton*	60,500	24,500	69,000	154,000
2. *Silk by itself, and mixed with other materials*	1,010	790	700	2,500
TOTAL	108,788	78,180	101,937	288,905

Bleachers are included in the cotton and linen branches above stated; dyers are included in the cotton, linen, woollen and silk branches.

Source: Sir John Sinclair 1825 *Analysis of the Statistical Account of Scotland*. Edinburgh.

No. 16. Women carrying loads to the surface of a stair-pit. From *A short history of the Scottish coal-mining industry,* published by the National Coal Board, Scottish Division (1958).

TABLE 2: OCCUPATIONAL GROUPS – SCOTLAND 1851 CENSUS

OCCUPATIONAL GROUP	MEN	WOMEN	TOTAL
Agriculture, forestry, fishing	255,614	60,643	316,257 (24%)
Mining, quarrying	53,146	485	53,631
Food, drink, tobacco	43,100	9,106	52,206
Chemical and allied products	4,142	830	4,972
Metal manufacture	36,107	103	36,210
Mechanical engineering	10,076	15	10,091
Instrument engineering	1,703	–	1,703
Shipbuilding and marine engineering	4,395	1	4,396
Vehicles	3,183	5	3,188
Metal goods	5,168	329	5,497
Textiles	120,436	136,691	257,127 (20%)
Leather, fur	4,879	333	5,212
Clothing and footwear	53,256	52,636	105,892
Bricks, pottery, glass, cement	5,089	811	5,900
Timber, furniture	19,150	1,268	20,418
Paper, printing, publishing	8,083	3,157	11,240
Other manufacturing	1,168	123	1,291
Construction	66,647	38	66,685
Gas, Electricity, Water	1,012	8	1,020
Transport and communication	48,396	1,353	49,749
Distributive trades	6,092	4,295	10,387
Insurance, banking, finance	637	–	637
Professional and scientific services	22,400	6,566	28,966
Miscellaneous services (includes domestic service)	17,537	133,734	151,271 (12%)
Public admin. and defence	11,607	359	11,966
Not classified	53,138	2,119	55,257
Total employed	856,161 (62%)	415,008 (27%)	1,271,169 (44%)
Total population	1,375,479	1,513,263	2,888,742

Source: CH Lee 1979 British Regional Employment Statistics 1841–1971. Cambridge.

EXERCISE 10

What were the dominant manufacturing industries in Scotland in the early nineteenth century according to Sinclair's tables? What do you notice about the balance between the number of men and women employed in different industries? Why should 'Male and Female Youths' (those under twenty) play such an important part in manufacturing industry in this period?

What were the major areas of employment in Scotland in 1851? Which categories of employment were dominated by males and which by females? Can you suggest reasons for this? Are there employment categories where you might have expected a larger or smaller workforce at this period?

We will not provide specimen answers in this instance but simply ask you to relate your findings closely to the general trends in our earlier discussions accounting for the changes that took place in this period.

7. CONCLUSION

We have suggested several models which provide a useful starting point for understanding Scottish industrialisation in a wider context. But as those who study developing countries at the present day know only too well, there are many problems in applying models to economic and social change. For historians interested in early industrialisation there are difficulties of interpretation arising from reliance on impressionistic accounts or unreliable data. Surviving statistics assume the existence of a national economy which, even by the 1800s, is highly dubious. Regional differences might have been much more significant than national trends and, in any case, disaggregating Scotland from Britain is no easy task. There were major regional differences within Scotland itself, and clearly significant movements within different sectors of the Scottish economy at different stages in industrialisation.

Industrialisation in Scotland was a complex process. On the one hand it derived some of its characteristics from longer-term development during the eighteenth century and maintained well into the following century modes of organisation and production more readily identifiable with pre- or proto-industrialised economies. On the other hand, it demonstrated, in certain key sectors, the successful coordination of the factors of production, partly driven by technical change, and leading to rapid and sustained growth, especially in textiles and a cluster of interrelated heavy industries.

Throughout much of this period industrialisation seems to have proceeded along two distinctive yet parallel paths, with the result that large-scale mass-production enterprise, typical of later starters in the process, was juxtaposed with smaller-scale production on more traditional lines. The geographical concentration of resources in the Lowlands meant that industrialisation was inevitably concentrated there and went hand-in-hand with urbanisation and longer-term migration from the rural Lowlands and the Highlands. But much early industrialisation (mainly but not exclusively based on primary processing, such as the linen and woollen industries) occurred in the countryside or focused on the smaller burghs. Even when improved transport, in particular the railways, brought greater integration, the prevailing pattern of dispersal in certain industries remained. Over the long term the story needs to be taken beyond 1850, which is an artificial boundary only in the context of this course, and can be followed up in the relevant sections of Volume 2.

The social implications of early industrialisation were altogether more important and far-reaching than the present discussion has suggested, but you will find that Smout (1969) and other chapters in this volume devote considerable space to issues of population growth, migration, urbanisation, and living and working conditions, which are vital to a deeper understanding of the process.

BOOKS AND ARTICLES MENTIONED IN THE TEXT

Barnard, A 1887 (reprinted 1969) *The Whisky Distilleries of the United Kingdom*. Newton Abbot.

Campbell, RH 1961 *The Carron Company*. Edinburgh and London.

Chapman, SD 1987 *The Cotton Industry in the Industrial Revolution*. London (2nd edition).

Checkland, SG 1975 *Scottish Banking: A History, 1695–1973*. Glasgow and London.

Cipolla, C 1980 'Introduction', *in* Cipolla, C (ed), *The Fontana Economic History of Europe. Vol 3: The Industrial Revolution*, Glasgow, 7–21.

Clarkson, LA 1990 'Proto-Industrialisation: The First Phase of Industrialisation?', *in* Clarkson, LA (ed), *The Industrial Revolution: A Compendium*, London, 149–209.

Cooke, AJ 1979 'Richard Arkwright and the Scottish Cotton Industry', *Textile History* 10, 196–202.

Cooke, AJ (ed) 1984 *A History of Redgorton Parish*. Dundee.

Crafts, NFR 1985 *British Economic Growth during the Industrial Revolution*. Oxford.

Devine, TM 1990 *The Tobacco Lords. A Study of the Tobacco Merchants of Glasgow and their Trading Activities, c. 1740–90*. Edinburgh.

Devine, TM 1995 *Exploring the Scottish Past*. East Linton.

Donnachie, I 1979 *A history of the brewing industry in Scotland*. Edinburgh.

Donnachie, I and Hewitt, G 1993 *Historic New Lanark. The Dale and Owen Industrial Community since 1785*. Edinburgh.

Durie, AJ 1979 *The Scottish Linen Industry in the Eighteenth Century*. Edinburgh.

Gershenkron, A 1966 *Economic Backwardness in Historical Perspective*. Cambridge.

*Hudson, P 1992 *The Industrial Revolution*. London.

Knox, WW 1995 *Hanging by a thread: The Scottish cotton industry, c. 1850–1914*. Preston.

Munn, CW 1981 *The Scottish Provincial Banking Companies, 1747–1864*. Edinburgh.

O'Brien, PK 1993 'Introduction: Modern conceptions of the Industrial Revolution', *in* O'Brien, PK and Quinault, R (eds), *The Industrial Revolution and British Society*, Cambridge, 1–30.

Rostow, WW 1960 *The Stages of Economic Growth*. Cambridge.

Rostow, WW 1978 *The World Economy: History and Prospect*. Austin, University of Texas.

*Smout, TC 1969 *A History of the Scottish People, 1560–1830*. London.

Whatley, CA 1989 'Economic causes and consequences of the Union of 1707: A survey', *Scottish Historical Review* 68, 150–81.

Whatley, C 1994 'New Light on Nef's Numbers: Coal Mining and the First Phase of Scottish Industrialisation, c 1700–1830', *in* Cummings, AJG and Devine, TM (eds), *Industry, Business and Society in Scotland since 1700*, Edinburgh, 2–23.

*Whatley, CA 1997 *The Industrial Revolution in Scotland*. Cambridge.

Whyte, I 1989 'Proto-industrialisation in Scotland', *in* Hudson, P (ed), *Regions and Industries. A Perspective on the Industrial Revolution in Britain*. Cambridge.

*Whyte, I 1995 *Scotland Before the Industrial Revolution, c. 1050 to c. 1750*. London.

Withers, CWJ 1986 *Highland Communities in Dundee and Perth, 1787–1891. A Study in the Social History of Migrant Highlanders*. Dundee.

FURTHER READING

Those references marked * in the above list are recommended further reading, along with the following:

Devine, TM and Mitchison, R (eds) 1988 *People and Society in Scotland. Volume I: 1760–1830*. Edinburgh.

Fraser, WH and Morris, RJ (eds) 1990 *People and Society in Scotland. Volume II: 1830–1914*. Edinburgh.

PUBLISHED PRIMARY SOURCE

Campbell, RH and Dow, JBA 1968 *Source Book of Scottish Economic and Social History*. Oxford.

Urbanisation

Irene Maver

INTRODUCTION

This chapter seeks to explain why and how Scotland's urban profile was transformed before 1850. Although Scotland was initially on the periphery of Europe's
urbanised regions, the process of expansion during the late eighteenth century was
so fast as to wholly reverse its lowly status in the league table of town development.
As the impact of industrialisation intensified, creating new employment and market
opportunities, patterns of settlement underwent often profound changes. During the
mid-eighteenth century, less than a tenth of Scots were urban dwellers, yet by 1850 –
using the specific criterion of 10,000 inhabitants or more – almost one third could be
identified as living in towns (Devine 1988, 29). Only England and Wales had
become more urbanised, with just over two-fifths of their combined populations
falling into this category. Moreover, the threshold of 10,000 people was too stark a
definition of what constituted 'urban' at this time. According to the 1851 Census,
the towns of Ayr, Elgin and Lanark, for example, all had populations that fell short
of this figure. Scotland was still characterised as having many small-town communities, indicating that the demographic balance had not yet shifted decisively in the
direction of large-scale concentration, despite the spectacular growth of the cities.

We will look at this theme by studying the following five topics:

- The burghal legacy
- The eighteenth century
- The changing urban environment
- Local government
- The nineteenth century

By the time you have worked your way through these topics and the associated
reading, I hope that you will have a good understanding of the urbanisation process
and its impact before the mid-nineteenth century.

An underlying theme here is the complex and sometimes contradictory nature of
Scottish urbanisation, which makes it difficult to generalise about towns and cities in
this period. The dominating images of Enlightenment Edinburgh and industrial
Glasgow have tended to cloud perceptions of the broader urban experience, creating
stereotypes that were by no means representative. Of course, 'urban' is a word that
too readily has connotations of metropolitan magnitude, which perhaps helps
explain this distorted focus. Yet, as far back as 1950, Saunders described the

diverse range of urban identities prevailing beyond the major cities, some with roots in the distant past, others much more recent.

EXERCISE 1
Read **Article 13** by Saunders. What different types of urban communities does he describe?

Saunders identifies four main types of towns, what he calls local capitals, or county towns, industrial centres (some old, some new), burghs (mainly ancient and of several types and sizes) and resort towns. Many had mixed functions, typical of some of the older burghs.

Given the obvious variety of Scotland's urban experience, and the unusually precocious rate of urban growth from the mid-eighteenth century, it is surprising that not more has been published about such an important aspect of the nation's development. There is a plethora of attractive and copiously-illustrated volumes currently available about individual localities, but these tend to be narrowly focused and journalistic in their approach. In terms of weightier studies, Edinburgh and Glasgow have attracted the lion's share of historical interest; understandably so, because of their size and status, but at the expense of research into other urban centres, especially the smaller communities. Even within the relatively familiar territory of Scotland's two largest cities, the picture is far from complete; for instance, much work still needs to be done on political power-structures and the position of women in urban society. The raw overall state of research has also afforded little opportunity to draw meaningful comparisons between towns and cities, including the ubiquitous Edinburgh and Glasgow, or place them in the wider European context. Scholarship is steadily advancing, and serious efforts have recently been made to rectify the balance (eg Devine and Jackson 1995; Houston 1994). However, for the meantime, Scottish urban history between 1707 and 1850 remains an area of rich, yet relatively unexploited, research potential.

The question as to precisely why historians have not made more use of the sources for Scottish towns and cities is an intriguing one. Adams (1978, 9) tried to unravel this conundrum in his study of urban Scotland, rather caustically attributing the deficit to 'the historical preoccupations with Mary Queen of Scots and Bonnie Prince Charlie, and the geographical preoccupation with the Highlands'. Compared with these icons of romanticised Scottish identity, town and city life can appear rather impersonal and unexciting, especially when dealing with the minutiae of administrative history. And it is perhaps the sheer abundance of such sources that has proved so daunting. Burgh records, for instance, provide copious detail about the day-to-day affairs of urban government, but are often labour-intensive. Scotland is particularly rich in this kind of primary material, but more general information about urban society – visual sources, contemporary newspapers and periodicals, gazetteers and statistical accounts – are also widely available. Moreover, because of its integrated focus, urban history covers a range of disciplines that can tend towards specialisation. It accommodates geographical and sociological analyses, legal and architectural history, as well as politics, economics and culture. In piecing together the overall picture of Scottish urbanisation between 1707 and 1850, a complex variety of sources must therefore be drawn on, including both the general and the particular.

EXERCISE 2

How would you describe your own place of abode? Is it urban or rural? What do you know about its history? How would you find out?

I will not provide a response here, for the obvious reason that only you know the answers! But I hope that you will have discovered them for yourself by the time you have completed the chapter.

1. THE BURGHAL LEGACY

Smout (1969, 157–83) devotes a substantial section to the intricacies of burgh organisation and society during the pre-Union period. This retrospective focus has considerable relevance for the progress of Scottish urbanisation between 1707 and 1850, given that the burghal legacy provided such an enduring framework for governing towns and cities. Indeed, the origins and functions of Scotland's burghs have long preoccupied historians, and are a subject that has been meticulously documented and much-debated (Whyte 1995, 54–60).

For our purposes, it is sufficient to recognise that the roots of the burgh system stretched back to the twelfth century, when the Crown sanctioned the creation of chartered, self-contained communities, with exclusive trading privileges. These were the royal burghs, the most prestigious group in the burghal hierarchy, which numbered 66 at the time of Union, including the four main Scottish cities. More numerous, though initially with lesser trading privileges, were the burghs of barony and regality; prior to 1707, over 300 had been established. Not all of these burghs were thriving communities; many failed to prosper commercially after receiving their charters, or declined after the focus of trade shifted elsewhere, indicating that burghal status did not necessarily equate with urban progress. The proliferation of burghs in a certain geographic location could thus reflect economic circumstances that had been already overtaken by the eighteenth century. For instance, Lanark, which eventually became Scotland's most urbanised county in population terms, had only three officially recognised royal burghs, as opposed to Fife's dozen.

As Morris (1990, 73) has commented, the burghal system gave Scotland a form of local authority, 'located in space and associated with distinctive powers', which was very different from elsewhere in the United Kingdom. The status of communities varied widely south of the Border, to the extent that 'system' would be a misnomer as far as the classification of urban institutions was concerned, at least until the reform of the municipal corporations in the 1830s. In Scotland, on the other hand, there was much more cohesion and uniformity, especially in the administration of the royal burghs. Their constitutions were regulated by the Convention of Royal

Burghs, a uniquely Scottish body and determinedly self-protective, which had its origins in the thirteenth century. The Convention's careful custodianship of the burghs had the effect of rendering them, if not identical, then with no significant differences in the limits of their authority (Smout 1969, 158–9). Not that this led to harmonious co-existence among the burghs. With the movement towards sustained urban growth, especially from the 1780s, there was mounting resentment in the cities over the influence of the smaller burghs in Convention affairs, whose strength in numbers could often override the interests of far more populous communities (see **Article 13**).

Because of their pivotal commercial role, the burgess institutions were the dominating influences in the royal burghs up to 1833, especially the merchant guilds, and their authority was exercised via the Town Councils. Historians have repeatedly stressed the unyieldingly oligarchic nature of pre-reform civic government, with the retiring members nominating their favoured successors as town councillors (e.g. Adams 1978, 127–9; Smout 1969, 161–2). Whatever controversy this aroused at the time over the issue of public accountability, it concentrated power in the royal burghs, and ensured continuity (if not necessarily efficiency) in urban administration. The system was undoubtedly open to nepotism and abuse, as John Galt depicts with considerable irony and humour in his 1822 novel, *The Provost*. In one of the smaller royal burghs, identifiable as Irvine, James Pawkie, the ambitious central character, manipulates his way through assorted civic offices, until he ·achieves the prime position of Provost. As the personification of the unreformed regime, Pawkie straightforwardly admits that throughout his career 'I have, to a certainty, reaped advantage both in my own person and that of my family', but adds with typical contrary logic, 'no man living can accuse me of having bent any single thing pertaining to the town and public, from the natural uprightness of its integrity' (Galt 1822, chapter III).

The burghs of barony and regality (collectively, the 'baronial' burghs) did not have the same organisational framework as the royal burghs, and their evolution was consequently much more piecemeal, with power dependent on their degree of autonomy from local landowners. However, all groups shared a range of responsibilities, most crucially for preserving the peace, punishing offenders, and ensuring a wholesome and safe environment. The legal definition of 'policing' was a broad one and included more than just crime prevention. It extended to areas like drainage, paving, street-lighting and cleansing, and ultimately to public health (Morris 1990, 86). Given the unprecedented pace of urbanisation in Scotland from the mid-eighteenth century, and the resulting social pressures, these were concerns that increasingly came to preoccupy the burgh authorities. In the rapidly burgeoning urban entity of Glasgow, where the population had risen from nearly 43,000 to over 77,000 during the last two decades of the eighteenth century, the professionalisation of policing services became a priority of the town council, largely because of vocal public complaints about the inadequacies of the existing system (Maver 1995, 249–51).

Despite the unrepresentative nature of pre-reform civic government, it was therefore far from unresponsive, and in the royal burghs there was often a paternalistic commitment to the welfare of the community. This was enshrined in the notion of the 'common good'; again, a uniquely Scottish institution, which was the collective designation for the assets of the burgh, including lands, rents and other revenues. The common good was important because of the degree of financial autonomy it afforded town councils north of the Border, at a time when the option of direct local taxation was not politically feasible. It allowed a certain amount of latitude for borrowing, especially to fund public works, and Edinburgh's city fathers were noted (and later notorious) for their liberal use of the common good to help finance New Town construction from the 1760s. But beyond its material practicality, the common good also represented a genuine focus for civic identity in Scotland; a theme that Provost Pawkie was to make much of in his efforts to demonstrate that at heart he was not wholly self-interested. It provided the rationale for measures that might otherwise have been regarded as too interventionist, and in this context, comment has been made on the 'authoritarian' tradition of local government that prevailed in Scotland, especially the need to maintain an ordered environment (Fraser and Maver 1996a, 433; Morris, 1990, 91). The common good was thus a very useful moral device for binding communities together, in an effort to offset any dangerous tendencies towards social fragmentation, especially under the strains of urbanisation during the early nineteenth century.

EXERCISE 3
Do you think that institutional structures made much of a difference to the process of urbanisation, and responses to the resulting problems?

Up to a point, institutional structures did make a difference. Town councils exercised considerable control over many aspects of urban life and in terms of responsiveness were particularly active in public works, embracing activities as diverse as civic building, drainage, lighting, cleansing, water supply, etc, some of which extended far beyond 'policing'.

2. THE EIGHTEENTH CENTURY

With some 35,000 inhabitants by the 1700s, Edinburgh was Scotland's most populous city, and remained so throughout the eighteenth century. However, unlike London or Dublin – the two largest cities in the British Isles prior to 1800 – Edinburgh did not dominate the urban hierarchy, despite its superiority in numbers. Glasgow, Aberdeen and Dundee remained important regional centres, whose status reflected the continuing emphasis on local identity in Scottish society (Whyte 1995, 178). Significantly, many of the newer urban growth areas in the eighteenth century were directly connected with these older royal burghs, notably Greenock and Port Glasgow, as the ports created to service Glasgow's trade.

The west of Scotland experienced the most marked demographic increase as the century progressed. While every other region remained static or declined in population between 1755 and 1801, the West's share increased from 14% to over 20% of the national total, with Glasgow's population more than tripling to over 77,000. This was a rate of growth that far outstripped Edinburgh, although it was not until 1831 that the second city overtook the capital in population numbers. Up to this time, there was no significant shift in the ranking of Scottish towns, notwithstanding the profound changes to the economic base. As Devine (1988, 16) has pointed out, the thirteen largest towns of the early eighteenth century were much the same as those a century later. There was thus considerable continuity in Scotland's urban structure, which retained its integrity to a much greater extent than England and Wales.

In 1707 Scotland's urban population was overwhelmingly concentrated in the Lowlands, especially in the communities clustered around Edinburgh and the Firth of Forth, which had densities among the highest in Europe. In contrast, relatively few burghs had been created in the Highlands, and those that were established prior to the Union owed their origins to Government anxiety about the need for stability in the region, rather than a primary concern for economic development. Campbeltown was one such community which had been nurtured by successive Earls and Dukes of Argyll during the seventeenth century and eventually became a royal burgh in 1700. From the mid-eighteenth century the Argyll dynasty was also instrumental in wholly restructuring the Campbell base at Inveraray, partly to bequeath a lasting monument in the imposing edifice of Inveraray Castle, partly to enhance the strategic importance of this long-established baronial burgh (Glendinning *et al* 1996, 137).

Inveraray was a prestigious example of the numerous planned settlements that were effectively 'planted' by landowners throughout Scotland during the eighteenth century. The north-east of Scotland was a particularly favoured location, with the success of New Keith in Banffshire influencing the construction of a number of emulative communities. Highland settlements included Bowmore, Tobermory and Ullapool. Their rationale was to provide employment and stimulate the economy, especially by creating marketing outlets for local produce. However, as Adams (1978, 64) suggests, there was also an ideological motivation in the desire to bind communities more closely to the Hanoverian regime by instilling a sense of order, progress and industry. Smout (1969, 292–4) has detailed the career of John Cockburn of Ormiston, the prototype planned settlement enthusiast, who set rigorous standards for the shape and design of his 'new town' of Ormiston, East Lothian, commenced in 1735. Cockburn's model community was strongly inspired by patriotic sentiments and the 'improving' impulse of the time; as Smout puts it, 'This was his bit for Scotland, his way of dragging her into the eighteenth century'.

Ormiston constituted part of the intricate network of towns and villages in close proximity to Edinburgh, which served the growing consumer needs of Scotland's capital. From the mid-seventeenth century, Edinburgh's economy had been moving towards specialisation in the professional and service sectors, with an unprecedented incursion of lawyers to administer the processes of criminal justice and civil jurisdiction (Smout 1969, 373–7). Although Edinburgh's population did not rise dramatically during the first half of the eighteenth century, the city boundaries remained confined to the narrow limits of the medieval burgh, thus creating congested and uncomfortable conditions for the accommodation of the ambitious new professional classes. Improved living standards and the desire to conspicuously display wealth further stimulated demand for more spacious dwellings. This connection between consumerism and Edinburgh's restricted room for expansion is crucially important, as it set the context for the development of the city's own 'new town', on a far grander scale than that envisaged by Cockburn for Ormiston.

It should be immediately stressed, however, that old Edinburgh was not quite the 'picturesque, odorous, inconvenient, old-fashioned town' that the nineteenth-century writer, Robert Chambers (1825, Chapter I), so vividly portrayed in his hugely popular chronicles of social life in the city. Tentative attempts had been made during the late seventeenth and early eighteenth centuries to break away from the burgh's medieval layout by demolishing and rebuilding properties in a more integrated and uniform style. These projects (such as James Court, in 1727) established the distinctive pattern of tenemental blocks and terraced dwellings that was thereafter to characterise the Scottish urban environment (Glendinning *et al* 1996, 135). Yet although they undoubtedly embellished the fabric of the Old Town, such piecemeal efforts did not create the kind of city that met the aspirations of its more genteel inhabitants. This was the spirit that prompted the Town Council, under the energetic direction of Lord Provost George Drummond, to implement its ambitious New Town plan from 1767. While they were unambiguously committed to transforming Edinburgh aesthetically, councillors were also hoping (erroneously, as it transpired) to reap financial returns on property development under Scotland's uniquely feudal system of land tenure (see **Document 36**). Fuller details about the progress of the plan can be found in Youngson (1966); suffice it to say that it had the effect of considerably enlarging the city boundaries and launching an extensive programme of public works that lasted until the 1830s.

EXERCISE 4
Reflecting on the discussion here, did eighteenth-century town planning relate in any way to contemporary enlightened ideas?

If we discount the profit motive, ideas of improvement, civic pride, good order, etc were important. Better town planning certainly reflected economic progress generally, while the health issue fed into medical science.

For all that the idea had been promoted much earlier in the century, Edinburgh's New Town did not make a visual impact until the 1780s, when the laborious groundwork had been laid for building construction. It was the spirit rather than the substance of the venture that initially caught the public imagination, with many contemporaries conceiving the New Town as more than just the practical application of a state-of-the-art building plan. In keeping with the period, there was a patriotic dimension, which had been expressed as far back as 1752 with the suggestion that multifarious benefits would inevitably accrue to both 'SCOTLAND, and by consequence to UNITED BRITAIN'. The New Town was also deemed important because it restored a sense of control over the urban environment. As Nenadic (1988, 121) has explained, 'New town design, symmetrical and grid-like, articulated the desire for a new sort of orderliness to replace existing patterns of incoherent urban growth'. However, this quest for order was not quite the novelty that the grandiose Edinburgh plan would suggest. Glasgow, for instance, was cleared of much of its medieval town centre by major conflagrations during the late seventeenth century. By force of rather dramatic circumstances, a 'new' city emerged which immediately struck visitors with its regularity and attractiveness. Daniel Defoe's effusive remarks about the 'large stately and well-built city' of 1707 revealed the favourable impression that pre-industrial Glasgow could make (Smout 1969, 380).

This harmonious effect was achieved largely because the Town Council had strictly monitored the reconstruction programme to allow for unity of design (Markus *et al* 1995, 113). While the scale was modest compared with Edinburgh's New Town, the later project was also noted for the careful development control

No. 17. View from Glasgow Green, overlooking the River Clyde south to Carlton Place, *c.*1820, from Swan's *Views of Glasgow*. This was an early middle-class residential development, started in 1802. The architect was Peter Nicholson. Note the washing being done on the Green, the grazing sheep, and the shallowness of the river at the time. *By courtesy of the Mitchell Library, Glasgow City Libraries and Archives.*

exercised by the civic authority. The burghal legacy thus allowed for mechanisms to co-ordinate urban improvement, and in the case of Edinburgh underpinned much of the substantial costs, although eventually to the detriment of the common good. Moreover, 'improvement' involved a range of activities intended to ease the flow of trade and commerce in the burghs, as well as enhance the urban fabric. Harbour construction and road and bridge building were increasingly part of this agenda. Macinnes (1996, 32) has shown how bridge and building design were closely tied together in Aberdeen's prestigious city-centre development from the 1790s, using ideas imported from France, where the centralised state imposed 'an incredible uniformity of high architectural and engineering achievement'. He also, incidentally, shows how the eighteenth-century Scottish 'culture of renewal' was exported overseas; for instance, the architect Charles Cameron was particularly influential in Russia at the time of Catherine the Great.

From the late eighteenth century, as the example of Edinburgh clearly demonstrates, moves were being made to build beyond the burgh boundaries, in an effort to ease urban congestion and provide suitably impressive dwellings for the professional and business élite. In Glasgow this territorial expansion was set in motion from the 1770s, reflecting a boom in property speculation as land was subdivided and resold for residential purposes. Accordingly, the Blythswood estate immediately adjacent to the city was transformed by the Campbell family, its elegant terraced housing and gridded street formation based on the fashionable examples of both Edinburgh and London (Walker 1982, 184–5). However, suburbanisation was a phenomenon more generally associated with the nineteenth century, when improved transport facilities opened out the urban hinterland. It must also be stressed that the stark residential division of Edinburgh between the Old and New Towns was by no means complete by 1800, and elsewhere much still remained unchanged. Dundee, for example, was noted for its conspicuous lack of development, despite growing industrial prosperity, with one writer in the 1790s making the telling comment that structurally and socially the city still resembled old Edinburgh.

EXERCISE 5

Read the two extracts from the *Statistical Accounts* (Documents 37 and 38). What differing perceptions of Dundee do these extracts convey?

In the earlier account there is considerable emphasis on the advantages of the city's location for communications, markets, agricultural produce and manufactures. However, much of the development (up to that point) had evidently had little impact on the street layout or buildings of the old town, with consequent high-density tenement housing and considerable overcrowding. The suburbs followed no particular plan either. The later account begins by noting the growth of industry and the greater attention to planning and street improvement. Other public works referred to later in the extract had brought a new water supply and the opening of a new burial ground – both health-related. The statist then reflects on the rapid rise of population (and the linen trade and shipping). The downside was the increase in the poor and the related problem of crime – evidenced by the erection of a new jail! You might add that there is an awareness of the problems rising urban population brought, with substantial efforts to provide remedies, but counteracted by the sheer scale of expansion by the 1840s. If you did not spot all these points, look back at the documents again.

3. THE CHANGING URBAN ENVIRONMENT

Why did towns and cities grow so fast from the mid-eighteenth century? The opening up of market opportunities, especially in the agricultural sector, intensified the role of urban areas as centres for exchange. However, this factor did not solely create the extraordinarily propitious conditions for urbanisation. As Scottish trade and industry expanded, especially in the Clyde basin, there was a need for concentrated pools of labour to service the increasingly complex economy. Technological innovation further accelerated the process, with a sustained period of road, harbour and canal construction opening out access to communities. Settlements emerged in locations of strategic convenience; for instance, Alloa in Clackmannanshire developed because of its position on the Forth estuary, and careful investment in the local infrastructure considerably boosted its potential as a port (Adams 1978, 55). New and distinctively industrial settlements were also established; New Lanark, Catrine in Ayrshire and Stanley in Perthshire (see Chapter 7) are well-known examples of textile communities which employed substantial numbers of operatives. Although unequivocally revolving around the routine of the factory, the dependence of the spinning mills on water power meant that they were initially built away from the larger urban centres, to take advantage of fast-flowing rivers. Only after 1800, with the advent of steam power, was there a clustering of textile factories, especially in Glasgow and its environs.

The tendency towards industrial concentration gathered momentum during the first half of the nineteenth century. It was not confined to the western region, as Dundee's linen sector took off around 1818, after a few false starts in harnessing the new steam technology. A further economic stimulus was provided by vastly improved harbour facilities, so that between 1821 and 1841 the city's population more than doubled from 30,000 to almost 63,000. These figures reflected high levels of migration to the city, both from the surrounding countryside and from Ireland. The latter incomers came predominantly from south Ulster, where the indigenous linen industry provided an obvious point of contact with Dundee. Many of the immigrants were young, unmarried women, and Dundee became unusual among the Scottish cities for the very high percentage of women in its labour force, especially to service the linen and jute industries (Whatley *et al* 1993, 104). As with other urban communities throughout the United Kingdom, Irish immigration accelerated markedly during the 1840s because of the traumatic conditions generated by the potato famine, so that by 1851 almost a fifth of Dundee's population was Irish-born. Glasgow broadly paralleled this figure with 18.2%, and Edinburgh – which did not have a predominantly industrial base – had a much smaller yet significant presence of 6.2%.

Migration from Ireland (see Chapter 6) was by no means new. What was different about the early nineteenth century was the scale of immigration, stimulated by growing employment opportunities and the availability of cheap passenger transport from the 1820s. By mid-century, the concentration of the Irish-born in Scotland was proportionately greater than south of the Border, and not just in the major cities (Devine 1988, 43). Other centres where the Irish presence was important included the textile town of Paisley, the mining community of Coatbridge and the port of Greenock. In these areas there was a particular demand for unskilled labour at low wage rates, although even among the more lowly occupational sectors there could still be competitive friction between Scots and Irish. Moreover, while a substantial percentage of Irish incomers were Protestant, the majority were Roman Catholic; a factor that helped to alienate them even further from the host community. This was the kind of climate that fostered sectarianism, which was sometimes overt, as with the manifestation of Orangeism from the 1820s, but more often subtly exclusive.

The inflow of Irish was only one aspect of migration during the first half of the nineteenth century. Movement was more usual from communities close to the centre, although there were also significant Highland enclaves in the larger Scottish towns. The extent of migration is revealed by the 1851 Census figures, with incomers constituting 53% of the inhabitants of Scotland's ten most populous communities (Devine 1988, 41–2). Such a high level of mobility had the effect of jolting the strong sense of local identity in Scotland; in the words of McCaffrey (1981, 41), 'As the towns became populated by new men with no roots in their place of settlement, so too did the ingredients for distrust and uncertainty grow'. The following contemporary comments about Greenock in 1840 clearly convey this sense of unease, and place the town directly in the general context of urban Scotland at the time:

> . . . it is no more than justice to the inhabitants of Greenock to remark, that where the population is dense, intemperance and licentiousness are too frequently the vices of persons of all ranks; and sea-port towns are more than others exposed to that moral contagion. To this we may add that association for other purposes, by bringing together men of very different and opposite principles, have exerted a most injurious influence on the working classes; and the immigration from other quarters, of families unaccustomed in their infancy to the habits of a well-educated Scottish population, has tended not a bit to lower the standard by which they are wont to regulate their conduct.
>
> (*New Statistical Account* 1845, 429)

The anxieties of Patrick McFarlan, the Church of Scotland minister who wrote these words for the *New Statistical Account*, echoed previous concern about the fragility of community identity in urban Scotland. During the 1820s the Presbyterian theologian, Thomas Chalmers, gave a celebrated critique of the fragmenting nature of city life in his *Christian and Civic Economy of Large Towns*, and went on to

propose an ambitious programme of evangelical outreach to restore the balance (see
Document 23b). He warned of dire consequences if such action was not taken, and
made a particular appeal to the existing agencies of control, whether Church or local
government, to provide stronger leadership. Chalmers repeatedly stressed the virtues
of pre-industrial Scotland, where communities were believed to have been contain-
able and where there was seemingly little social alienation. This vision of the past
was overburnished and imbued with nostalgia; however, it inspired a missionary
commitment from his influential coterie of followers, who perceived urban life as a
matter of moral redemption as much as material improvement, in the quest for social
reintegration (Fraser and Maver 1996a, 396–401).

EXERCISE 6
Look at **Document 23b**. What does Chalmers suggest as possible solutions to the
urban problem as he perceived it?

Chalmers suggested that in order to counteract moral and religious degeneracy
towns should be divided into smaller, more manageable districts, roughly the size of
a country parish. A team of individuals (or missionaries) under the minister would
maintain contact with local communities, spreading Christian values and dealing
with the poor and charitable relief.

Chalmers had first drawn public attention to Scotland's deteriorating urban
fabric during a period of particular social strain, in the immediate aftermath of the
Napoleonic Wars. By that time towns and cities were beginning to materially reflect
the impact of sustained population increase, not least in the incidence of fever and
disease, which hit the major centres especially hard between 1817 and 1819. It has
already been shown in this chapter that many communities were expanding
territorially to provide accommodation for wealthier residents, anxious to distance
themselves from the less salubrious urban heartlands. However, the provision of
working-class housing was much more problematic, especially as speculators were
not willing to invest capital in projects likely to yield minimum returns. As a result,
existing properties were subdivided or 'made-down', while poor-quality tenements
were constructed in garden spaces to the rear of buildings. In Glasgow this created a
warren of inner-city 'backlands', notorious for their lack of basic amenities, like
water, light or ventilation. To compound the growing housing problem, the Scottish
system of land tenure was particularly conducive to the multi-occupancy of
residential dwellings (Saunders 1950, 164–8). Commenting on the impact of
Glasgow's fever epidemic in 1818 (predominantly typhus), the physician Robert
Graham was forthright about overcrowding as a major contributory factor, and
stressed the urgent need to build 'houses for the poor on an appropriate plan, and in
a good situation' (see **Document 39**).

The pronouncements of medical men like Graham became more forceful during
the first half of the nineteenth century, as urban problems intensified with the
inexorable rise in population. The increasingly corrosive environment inevitably
affected health standards. A stark illustration can be shown by the drop in life

expectancy; for instance, in 1821 Glaswegian men and women could anticipate a life-span of forty-two and forty-five years respectively, but by 1841 this had fallen to thirty-seven and forty years (Fraser and Maver 1995b, 352). Infant mortality took a disproportionate toll in towns and cities, with children especially vulnerable to diseases like scarlet fever, smallpox and measles. Moreover, as Robert Cowan, another eminent medical authority in Glasgow pointed out, the virulence of disease was closely associated with economic depression and the resulting social dislocation (Devine 1995, 404). Outbreaks of typhus, especially, reflected the impoverished state of the urban slum-dwellers whose immunity to infection had been all but eroded. Perhaps most searing on the public consciousness were the cholera outbreaks that struck Scotland during 1832 and over the winter of 1848/49. The causes of this waterborne disease were barely understood until the second half of the nineteenth century, so there was much irrational speculation about its seemingly insidious nature and random choice of victims. The second visitation was responsible for 478 deaths in Edinburgh and 3,777 in Glasgow, and perhaps more than any other single factor persuaded the authorities of the need for concerted action on public health.

EXERCISE 7
Why do you think public health was such a preoccupation in Scottish towns and cities, and Glasgow especially?

Essentially it was due to the middle-class fear of contagion and, in Glasgow, the sheer scale of the problem due to rapid immigration, overcrowding and insanitary conditions generally.

4. LOCAL GOVERNMENT

In his 1856 Memoirs, Henry Cockburn – the eminent Whig lawyer – damningly described Scottish town councils prior to the 1833 Burgh Reform Acts as 'sinks of municipal and political iniquity', with his own city of Edinburgh representing the 'Pandemonium' of civic corruption (1910 edition, 87–91; see also Smout 1969, 373). This was a theatrical evocation and intended to be so; the luminosity of mid-Victorian progressivism was being contrasted with the murkiness of reaction, as Cockburn perceived it as having existed under the old regime. He was also demonstrating his strong faith in the legislative changes that had opened out Scotland's municipal institutions to electoral reform, allowing them to become directly accountable to the community.

Such views necessarily gave little credence to efforts to improve the urban environment between 1707 and 1833; whatever the reality, this was not politically expedient. With its forward-looking focus, the influence of reform rhetoric proved to be pervasive, even a century afterwards – Smout (1969, 161–2) wrote that the Scottish municipalities had been 'notorious for their graft' and 'dismally self-interested'. Yet he also recognised that there might be more to this single-dimensional image; that for all their supposed oligarchical omnipotence, Edinburgh's city fathers 'contributed much to the well-being of the town', especially with public works (1969, 373). Recent research has tended to endorse this more generous approach, showing that – as Smout detected – pre-reform local government was by no means as incompetent as the critics have suggested (Maver 1995, 239–41). Accordingly, it was not necessarily inertia or lack of will on the part of burgh authorities that restricted their horizons; rather, they were caught in the dilemma of having to operate under a system that was proving to be increasingly anachronistic. As Saunders (1950) has explained, there was an intricate and seemingly immutable political connection between the royal burghs and Parliamentary representation that accounted for the exceptionally narrow basis of civic power prior to 1833 (see **Article 13**).

The speed and scale of urban concentration from the 1780s helps explain why there was such a profound reappraisal of local government institutions during the 1830s. The more populous the community, the more complex the administrative requirements, yet the existing structures were often ill-equipped to cope. Thus, while the burghs were constitutionally bound to protect the fabric of their defined territory, the financial wherewithal to practically implement all this could be problematic. Conventional methods of raising revenue, such as market duties, generally yielded limited returns. Nor were the assets of the common good inexhaustible. Local taxation, though theoretically more fruitful, was not a realistic option, given the conspicuous lack of public accountability within the town councils. The burgh reform movement, which made tentative headway in Edinburgh during the 1780s, placed particular emphasis on the need for more stringent municipal bookkeeping; a concern that became urgent as the city began to slide into insolvency (Youngson 1966, 257–65). The Scottish municipal authorities were consequently very much aware of their precarious position in relation to finance and freedom of action, during a period of mounting social strain in urban centres. Yet the identification of burgh reform with wholesale political reform prevented successive Governments from taking meaningful action to tighten civic procedures, until the pressures became intolerable.

Instead, alternative mechanisms were adopted in an effort to harness the momentum of urbanisation. Police Boards, with powers of enforcement in areas like watching, street-lighting, paving and cleansing, made an appearance in Scottish towns and cities, beginning with Edinburgh in 1771. Jurisdiction was still ultimately the preserve of the burgh authority, but the increasing incidence of local Police Acts prior to 1833 revealed the extent to which environmental control procedures were becoming formalised in Scotland's urban areas. In an article relating specifically to Aberdeen from the 1790s, Tyzack (1996, 150–67) has shown the commitment of the city's Police Commissioners to tackling problems of public order and lack of amenity resources, even though their task could prove daunting. Crucially, because the Police Board had an elective structure, the constitutional constraints on civic government were effectively bypassed, and the principle of rating and representation established as an important precedent for municipal reform. The Aberdeen experience is important for revealing the strong strand of continuity linking the old regime with the new, and that the break with the past was by no means conclusive in 1833. Indeed, despite the removal of obstacles to outright municipal control, Aberdeen's Police Board continued to co-exist with the town council until 1871, when it was finally merged with the civic authority.

The emphasis on continuity before and after 1833 does not mean to imply, however, that the impact of burgh reform was illusory. The municipal power-base was opened out in the royal burghs and newly-created parliamentary burghs (such as Falkirk, Kilmarnock and Paisley), where the vote was conferred on male householders with property to the value of £10 per annum (Adams 1978, 131). Compared with England and Wales this was not a particularly generous criterion, due to lower overall property values north of the Border, and as a result the personnel returned to the new town councils still tended to represent the wealthiest in the community. The more exclusive nature of the Scottish electoral system can be illustrated by the example of smaller royal burghs, such as Culross, Dornoch and West Anstruther, where there were not even enough £10 householders to supply the requisite number of councillors under the 1833 legislation, so that the old system

No. 18. Dundee from the west, 1803. The city was, at this point, on the verge of industrialisation. Despite the rapid pace of urbanisation in Scotland from the 1780s, this was still a transition process, and older, rural influences still lingered on the city landscape. *Photograph courtesy of St Andrews University Library.*

prevailed until sufficient people acquired the necessary property qualifications. On the other hand, municipal government was now directly accountable to the community, and was not so financially circumscribed in the policies it could pursue. It could also accommodate a much broader range of political opinion than hitherto, although this generally did not bring about overt partisanship on Scottish town councils. Much more than south of the Border, the tradition of the 'common good' overrode party allegiances until well into the twentieth century.

As for smaller communities, the 1833 legislation had the effect of regularising police powers within defined areas, which thereafter were designated police burghs (Adams 1978, 131; Morris 1990, 86–91). This generally eased the mechanisms for implementing environmental control, which previously had to be acquired through expensive and often complex Parliamentary procedures. However, only royal burghs and baronial burghs initially could take advantage of the new measure, thus excluding numerous developing communities, such as the coal and iron towns of Coatbridge and Motherwell. Nor were existing communities particularly quick to avail themselves of the opportunities afforded under the legislation, as there could be a grudging response from residents to the imposition of rating. Further amending legislation in 1847 and 1850 attempted to smooth out some of the irregularities arising from 1833, clarifying precisely who could opt for police board status by setting a threshold of 1,200 inhabitants in broadly-defined 'populous places'. The resulting plethora of police burghs in Scotland was an important concession to local autonomy, and helped give cohesion to hitherto disparate communities; however, their significance began to erode as the nineteenth century progressed, because of the growing need to administer public services on a much larger and cost-effective scale.

Already by the 1830s there was a recognition that the functions of local government were focusing increasingly on the awesome public health problems of many towns and cities. The urgency of the situation was graphically underlined by the revelations of sanitary reformers about the deteriorating quality of urban life. The Scottish section of Edwin Chadwick's 1842 *Report of the Sanitary Condition of the Labouring Population of Great Britain* made particularly uneasy reading, revealing the extent of deprivation not just in the larger urban centres, but in relatively small communities like Tain, Easter Ross. The reports were pervaded throughout with queasy references to the conspicuous lack of sanitary facilities, not least Greenock's monster dunghills, which had earned the town the nickname of 'Old Dirty'. Dirt was perceived as the prime culprit in the spread of disease, and there was an obsession with putrefaction and the belief that decayed matter could release noxious effluvia into the atmosphere. Reformers identified centralised control as a practical solution to the hitherto piecemeal response to the problem, especially for the provision of drainage schemes and water-supply systems, although efforts south of the Border to administer a London-based Central Health Board from 1848 proved controversial. The Scots more doggedly adhered to their tradition of localism, although the co-ordinating influence of organisations like the Health of Towns Association was important. From 1847 a Glasgow branch began to exert pressure for environmental improvement in the city, in tandem with leading civic activists (Maver and Fraser 1996a, 402–3). Attitudes were, therefore, in the process of changing towards the need for interventionism, but the extent of cholera fatalities sharply jolted public confidence, especially as elaborate preventative measures had been taken to stave off its worst effects. Accordingly, solutions on a large scale, and at considerable public expense, began to be seriously contemplated, with the prestigious Loch Katrine water supply finally authorised by Parliament in 1855. In Scotland generally from the 1850s powers became increasingly concentrated in the civic and police authorities, and a much more professional approach began to be adopted towards regulation.

EXERCISE 8
How would you categorise the two main spheres of improvement in public health before 1850?

Essentially these were either environmental (i.e. housing, drainage, water supply, etc) or medical (hospitals, greater understanding of disease, vaccination, etc). Progress, though slow, was being made in both related spheres.

5. THE NINETEENTH CENTURY

Despite the undoubtedly deleterious impact of rapid industrial growth during the first half of the nineteenth century, it would be misleading to dwell exclusively on the disturbing imagery of the sanitary reformers. Indeed, while the entries in the 1842 *Sanitary Reports* tended to focus on conditions in the most blighted and unsavoury areas, observations were also made about, for instance, Greenock's 'numerous body of respectable operatives, who live in comfort, and who feed and clothe their families well' (see **Document 40**). There was also passing reference to 'the more wealthy part of the inhabitants', whose prosperity was due to Greenock's wide-ranging shipping, commercial and manufacturing activities. Scottish towns and cities were broadly similar in accommodating this varied class profile, although the economic orientation of a community could give it more precise emphasis. Smout (1969, 366–90) has drawn the classic contrast between 'professional' Edinburgh and 'business' Glasgow in discussing the urban middle classes; a difference that was to become something of a standing joke as the nineteenth century progressed, especially with Glasgow's assertive attempts to upstage Scotland's capital as the self-proclaimed 'Second City of the Empire'.

Stereotypes notwithstanding, Rodgers' analysis of occupational structure in the four Scottish cities, based on 1841 Census returns, reveals that Edinburgh maintained its unusually high percentage of the professional classes, with almost three times the Glasgow figure (1985, 29). As Scotland's primary administrative centre, this was inevitable, especially in the pivotal sectors of law and finance. However, Edinburgh had the advantage in the diversity of its economy, which was not skewed in the direction of one dominating industry. In the three other cities, textiles employed between a third and a half of the industrial workforce. As in the eighteenth century, Edinburgh was also a more consumer-orientated city; its residents had greater purchasing power and there was more choice of specialised goods. Princes Street had been initially conceived of as a residential thoroughfare, but its changing profile after 1800 illustrated the extent of growing consumer demand, with an assortment of hotels and coach and shipping offices (this was the immediate pre-railway era), plus '. . . several toy shops, tailors, furriers, booksellers, bootmakers, grocers, hairdressers, corset makers, stay-makers, one bird stuffer, one cigar shop, and the Tax Office for Scotland' (Youngson 1966, 231). The number of women employed as domestic servants in Edinburgh was second only to London, suggesting much about the pretensions of the Scottish city and the consolidation of New Town culture by the 1840s.

Yet construction of the New Town had run out of steam by this time, partly because of the bankruptcy of the Town Council in 1833, and partly because middle-class fashions were changing. There was an increasing tendency to move beyond the city limits, to semi-bucolic outlying districts where detached villas could be set in their own spacious grounds (Glendinning et al 1996, 232–3). These residences offered the twin benefits of privacy and purer air; for some the New Town was not far enough from Edinburgh's tainted heartland. Newington and Morningside, to the south of the city, began to develop in this way, although their greatest expansion occurred during the boom building decades of the 1850s and 1860s. There was a similar story in Glasgow, where building development remained remarkably brisk even during the years of recession. Glasgow's villa terrain lay to the south of the city, with the road to Govan (then a village) a particularly favoured location. To the west, a cluster of pastoral estates was being transformed, helped by substantial investment in road construction. Here the terraced style still predominated, although more fluid and eclectic than before. Kelvinside was developed from 1840 according to the meticulous plan of the Fleming family, who favoured both the villa and the terrace, and built impressive examples of both. Like Edinburgh, the process of suburbanisation accelerated markedly in Glasgow during the second half of the nineteenth century, but even by 1850 the outflow of the middle classes was gathering momentum.

The separation of residential spheres was by no means new in Scottish towns and cities, although the pace of later developments fuelled public concern about the polarisation of communities. In Glasgow there was an increasing social divide between the middle-class West End and proletarian East End, which seemed all the more insurmountable because of the immovable inner-city slums. This does not mean that the urban centres languished at the expense of the outlying areas; the development of Edinburgh's Mound area from the 1840s was intended to stem the atrophy of the Old Town, and open up new access routes to the city centre (Glendinning et al 1996, 209). Indeed, for all the moral and sanitary considerations behind the need for urban regeneration, the easing of traffic congestion and the creation of a more efficient communications network were also to the forefront of contemporary thinking. The coming of the railways was therefore crucially important for reshaping urban centres, and opening out Scotland generally. The

Edinburgh and Glasgow line was inaugurated for passenger transport in 1842, and speedily proved its success, not least in profits for the railway company. As the railways increasingly penetrated cities, their level of demand had profound influence on land use, especially in Glasgow, where access to the industrial hinterland was deemed of vital importance by developers (Adams 1978, 113). This was part of the complex rationale behind calls for slum clearance in the city, although it was not until the 1860s that projects could be practically implemented.

Improved transport systems helped to determine more remote residential choices for the middle classes, although towns and cities still had manifold social and cultural attractions. Church life and philanthropic activity were extremely important, while at the secular level there were numerous fine art, musical, literary and scientific societies. Edinburgh's Theatre Royal was the focal point for Scottish drama, and there was an established theatre circuit, which presented a variety of performances from Shakespeare to adaptations of popular novels, especially Walter Scott. Scotland also had a lively newspaper and periodical press throughout the nineteenth century, which had been given a stimulus during the 1820s by the debate over Parliamentary reform. The larger urban centres were able to produce at least one local newspaper, often of fiercely partisan political opinion. The Edinburgh publishing business of Robert and William Chambers was a noted example of an industry that consolidated its world-wide success because of popular reading habits. There was a voracious appetite for literature, not just of the home-grown variety, but from England. In 1841 Charles Dickens could scarcely believe the enthusiastic reception given to him on his arrival in Edinburgh, where he attended the first public dinner ever to be held in his honour. And, of course, Aberdeen, Edinburgh and Glasgow all had prestigious universities, which inevitably contributed to the quality of intellectual life in these cities.

Yet by the 1840s a disturbing netherside to urban culture had also been identified, one that would have been familiar to Dickens, in the seemingly uncontrolled manifestation of drunkenness and anti-social behaviour on the part of the poor. The convivial image of eighteenth-century tavern life, which Robert Chambers had made such a feature in his *Traditions of Edinburgh*, had given way to something altogether more sinister. The growth of the temperance movement was one of many responses to the problem, with its Scottish origins in Glasgow and Greenock during the 1820s. The beneficent influence of teetotalism on the Greenock population was glowingly referred to in the 1842 *Sanitary Reports*: 'it has brought comfort and independence to many a fire-side which formerly knew only misery and degradation' (see **Document 40**). Temperance was not necessarily a middle-class movement intent on social control; it had a politically radical dimension which looked towards self-reliance rather than philanthropy to improve working-class conditions (Fraser 1996, 316–7). On the other hand, the redemptive element of the temperance crusade struck a chord with middle-class evangelicals, who were to become the movement's financial mainstay. Reflecting the Chalmersian ethos, they remained wholly positive in the conviction that moral leadership could render even the most unsavoury cities wholesome and healthy. Such an assertive approach was considered essential for success, given the continuing insecurities about the direction urban life was taking by the mid-nineteenth century.

> EXERCISE 9
>
> Look at **Document 40**. What relationship does the author see between morality, temperance and urban conditions? What problem is specific to Greenock?

Laurie sees a direct link between work, respectability, morality, temperance and standards of living, contrasting the conditions of the artisan class and the pauper population. Notice the strong emphasis on self-help and the relationship drawn between poverty and crime – a great middle-class fear. Greenock's specific problem was large-scale immigration from the Highlands and Ireland, which greatly increased the burden of poor relief locally.

As this chapter has shown, there had long been anxiety about the negative impact of urbanisation in Scotland. The reports cited by Smout (1969, 367) about the squalid conditions prevailing in Edinburgh at the opening of the eighteenth century bear this out. The nostalgic evocation of pre-industrial Scotland, made so much of by the evangelicals from the 1820s, was a useful polemical device; however, its basis in reality was highly questionable. While the evangelicals and others articulated contemporary fears much more forcefully than previously, their mission to reverse the vitiated state of the environment was also in keeping with eighteenth-century attempts to physically impose order on the urban landscape, and with similar stress on moral legitimacy. Underlying this was a tradition of civic consciousness in Scotland which, for all the glaring inadequacies of pre-reform municipal government, still had considerable relevance when it came to regulation and control. Yet although the continuities persisted, and the pace of urban change was by no means uniform throughout Scotland, the unprecedented population expansion by the mid-nineteenth century had come to present a bewildering array of social problems that could not be tackled in a piecemeal or leisurely way. These were the concerns that confronted urban Scots at the beginning of the 1850s and, as we will see, continued to tax the efforts of the authorities into the succeeding century.

REFERENCES TO BOOKS AND ARTICLES MENTIONED IN THE TEXT

*Adams, IH 1978 *The Making of Urban Scotland*. London.

*Devine, TM 1988 'Urbanisation', *in* Devine, TM and Mitchison, R (eds), *People and Society in Scotland. Volume I 1760–1830*, Edinburgh, 27–52.

*Devine, TM 1995 'The urban crisis', *in* Devine, TM and Jackson, G (eds), *Glasgow, Volume I: Beginnings to 1830*, Manchester, 402–16.

*Devine, TM and Jackson, G (eds) 1995 *Glasgow, Volume I: Beginnings to 1830*. Manchester.

Fraser, WH 1996 'The working class', *in* Fraser, WH and Maver, I (eds), *Glasgow, Volume II: 1830 to 1912*, Manchester, 300–51.

Fraser, WH and Maver, I 1996a 'Tackling the problems', *in* Fraser, WH and Maver, I (eds), *Glasgow, Volume II: 1830 to 1912*, Manchester, 394–441.

Fraser, WH and Maver, I 1996b 'The social problems of the city', *in* Fraser, WH and Maver, I (eds), *Glasgow, Volume II: 1830 to 1912*, Manchester, 352–93.

*Glendinning, M, Macinnes, R and Mackechnie, A 1996 *A History of Scottish Architecture*. Edinburgh.

Houston, RA 1994 *Social Change in the Age of the Enlightenment: Edinburgh, 1660–1760*. Oxford.

McCaffrey, JF 1981 'Thomas Chalmers and social change', *Scottish Historical Review* 60, 32–60.

Macinnes, R 1996 'Union Street and the 'Great Street' in Scottish town planning', *in* Brotherstone, T and Withrington, DJ (eds), *The City and Its Worlds: Aspects of Aberdeen's History since 1794*, Glasgow, 25–39.

Markus, TA, Robinson, P and Walker, FA 1995 'The shape of the city in space and stone', *in* Devine, TM and Jackson, G (eds), *Glasgow, Volume I: Beginnings to 1830*, Manchester, 106–38.

Maver, I 1995 'The guardianship of the community: civic authority before 1833', *in* Devine, TM and Jackson, G (eds), *Glasgow, Volume I: Beginnings to 1830*, Manchester, 239–78.

*Morris, RJ 1990 'Urbanisation and Scotland', *in* Fraser, WH and Morris, RJ (eds), *People and Society in Scotland. Volume II: 1830 to 1914*, Edinburgh, 73–102.

*Nenadic, S 1988 'The rise of the urban middle-classes', *in* Devine, TM and Mitchison, R (eds), *People and Society in Scotland. Volume I: 1760–1830*, Edinburgh, 109–26.

Rodgers, R 1985 'Employment, wages and poverty in Scottish cities, 1841–1914', *in* Gordon, G (ed), *Perspectives of the Scottish City*, Aberdeen, 25–63.

Saunders, LJ 1950 *Scottish Democracy, 1815–1840: the Social and Intellectual Background*. London.

*Smout, TC 1969 *A History of the Scottish People, 1560–1830*. London.

Tyzack, R 1996 'No Mean City? The growth of civic consciousness in Aberdeen, with particular reference to the work of the Police Commissioners', *in* Brotherstone, T and Withrington, DJ (eds), *The City and Its Worlds: Aspects of Aberdeen's History since 1794*, Glasgow, 150–67.

Walker, FA 1982 'The Glasgow grid', *in* Markus, T (ed), *Order in Space and Society: Architectural Form and its Content in the Scottish Enlightenment*, Edinburgh, 155–200.

Whatley, C, Swinfen, DB and Smith, AM 1993 *The Life and Times of Dundee*. Edinburgh.

*Whyte, I 1995 *Scotland before the Industrial Revolution: An Economic and Social History, c. 1050–1750*. London.

*Youngson, AJ 1966 *The Making of Classical Edinburgh, 1750–1840*. Edinburgh.

FURTHER READING

Those references marked * in the above list are recommended further reading, along with the following:

Brotherstone, T and Withrington, DJ (eds) 1996 *The City and Its Worlds: Aspects of Aberdeen's History since 1794*. Glasgow.

Devine, TM and Mitchison, R (eds) 1988 *People and Society in Scotland. Volume I: 1760–1830*. Edinburgh.

Gibb, A 1983 *Glasgow: the Making of a City*. London.

Gordon, G (ed) 1985 *Perspectives of the Scottish City*. Aberdeen.

Gordon, G and Dicks, B (eds) 1983 *Scottish Urban History*. Aberdeen.

Fraser, WH and Maver, I (eds) 1996 *Glasgow, Volume II: 1830 to 1912*. Manchester.

Fraser, WH and Morris, RJ (eds) 1990 *People and Society in Scotland. Volume II: 1830 to 1914*. Edinburgh.

Smout, TC 1986 *A Century of the Scottish People, 1830–1950*. London.

PRIMARY SOURCES MENTIONED IN THE TEXT

E Chadwick 1842 *Report of the Sanitary Condition of the Labouring Population of Great Britain*.

Robert Chambers, *Traditions of Edinburgh*, numerous editions, but first published in 1825.

Henry Cockburn, *Memorials of his Time, 1779–1830*, Edinburgh 1910 edition used here, but first published in 1856.

John Galt, *The Provost*, numerous editions, but first published in 1822.

Patrick McFarlan 1845 'Greenock', in the *New Statistical Account of Scotland, Volume VII: Renfrew-Argyll*, London, 405–94.

Highland Society in the Era of 'Improvement'

Allan I Macinnes

INTRODUCTION

This chapter reviews the complex and often controversial history of the Highlands before 1850. Like Jacobitism, with which the area is closely identified, the Highlands can be studied from many viewpoints, from which we have selected:

- The demise of clanship
- Debatable sources
- Pre-Clearance commercialism
- Interventionist agencies
- The process of clearance
- Reactive estate management
- Alternative lifestyles
- Crisis in crofting
- The Highlands *c.* 1850

Although this interpretive chapter sheds much new light on Highland history, and, drawing on recent scholarship, challenges older views, you will find it useful to read Smout (1969), Chapter 14. This will provide you with a backcloth which you should be prepared to adapt as you work your way through this chapter. When you have completed it you should have a good grasp of the main developments shaping social and economic change in the Highlands down to 1850, and be aware too of some of the key controversies in Highland history.

The land issue – its ownership, management and use – was central to the transition from clanship to a commercialised society. This process of change, which was instigated by the chiefs and gentry who traditionally formed the clan élite, has been depicted as the Highland Clearances. Ironically, it was often the clan élite as well as their erstwhile clansmen who figured prominently among the victims of Clearance as estate management throughout the Highlands subordinated the balanced use of landed resources and manpower to prevailing market demands within the context of British imperial expansion. However, two immediate caveats must be observed:

Clearance, as the removal and relocation of people, was not a uniquely Highland, far less an exclusively Scottish, phenomenon. Clearance was an integral aspect of the transition from a traditionalist to a capitalist environment that accompanied industrialisation and the commercialisation of agriculture: a process which accelerated in the British Isles during the eighteenth century, spread to the rest of Europe and North America in the nineteenth century and continues in the wake of colonialism to shape economic development in the Third World to the present day.

This transition in the Highlands was presaged by a series of convulsions which requires the setting aside of perceptions that clanship, as an amalgam of feudal landholding, kinship and local association, was monolithic, static and undeveloped prior to the 'Forty-Five. The presumption of mobility which had underwritten Gaelic society since the Middle Ages was harnessed, from the seventeenth century, to commercial developments that wholly transformed estate management, settlement patterns and economic horizons.

I. THE DEMISE OF CLANSHIP

The legislative and military offensive on the western seaboard after the Union of the Crowns in 1603 had led to the redundancy of the mercenary *buannachan* (or redshanks) as a military caste and expedited the assimilation of the clan élite into the Scottish landed classes. Civil wars in the 1640s had brought about widespread social dislocation, the despoiling of estates and the accelerated accumulation of debts among the clan élite. The work of reconstruction in the Restoration era, facilitated by the profitability of the droving trade in black cattle to England, had instigated tenurial reorganisation that led to the piecemeal phasing out of the tacksmen as managers of traditional townships (multiple-tenant, communal farms) as well as the expansion of landownership among clan gentry. Moreover, absentee landlordism, the racking up of rents and the upward spiral of debts encumbering estates occasioned social tensions between the clan élite and their clansmen. Such tensions were masked by, but were nonetheless critical to, political alignments during the further episodic upheaval occasioned by Jacobite risings between 1689 and 1746 (see Chapter 2).

Indiscriminate repression by the victorious forces of the Whig government in the aftermath of Culloden ushered in a final convulsion in which the accelerated pace of change effected a dramatic social revolution. Clanship was abandoned and abjured through Clearance. The essential significance of the Jacobite defeat at Culloden lay not so much in the repressive reprisals exacted by central government prepared to flirt with Clearance by ethnic cleansing. Nor can the demise of clanship be ascribed to hostile legislation that proscribed the wearing of tartan and scrapped anachronistic heritable jurisdictions and military services. More pertinently, the clan élite that viewed the Jacobite defeat at Culloden as their escape from traditional trusteeship abrogated the personal obligations of clanship.

Ultimately, the land issue was rooted in cultural perceptions about heritage. The traditionalist perception, *dùthchas* ('heritable trusteeship'), had obliged the clan élite to promote security of possession throughout the territories settled by their kinsmen and local associates. The legalistic concept of *oighreachd* (heritable title) allowed the clan élite to reorientate the management of their estates to suit their own commercial interests as landlords rather than as patrons and protectors of their clansmen. The first phase of Clearance, which actually commenced prior to the 'Forty-Five, marked the triumph of the legalistic concept of heritage. By the 1820s the traditional township, the *baile*, was virtually eliminated as the basic unit of land settlement and management in the Highlands (Macinnes 1988, 70–2).

This triumph of the legalist concept was fortified by land law which worked to the benefit of the propertied classes and was further rationalised by the political economy emanating from the Scottish Enlightenment. Accordingly, the removal and relocation of people was publicised as proactive management which integrated the Highlands into the British Empire. There is more than a hint of this thinking in **Document 41**, an extract from Thomas Telford's survey of the Highlands in 1802.

Yet, erstwhile clansmen adhered tenaciously to the traditionalist concept of heritage long after clanship had been abrogated by the conduct of the clan élite. Repeated invocations of *dùthchas* as a customary right were testimony more to cultural disorientation than to outright cultural alienation. Contemporaneous Irish Gaels were able to direct polemical attacks against the alien English forces of government, the landowning classes and the established church.

EXERCISE 1

Read **Document 42**, Duncan Ban Macintyre's poem, and ask how far it seems to 'fit' this description of contemporary Irish writers.

This is clearly different. No individual or class is attacked. Rather, Scottish Gaels remained prisoners of their own culture, thoroughly perplexed and disorientated by the association of commercial landlordism with anglicisation as the clan élite sought assimilation not only into the Anglo-Scottish landed classes but into the imperial exploiting classes as planters, slave traders, colonial officials, military commanders and merchant adventurers.

The criticisms of the vernacular poets, such as Duncan Ban Macintyre, as the main shapers of public opinion within Scottish Gaeldom, were usually expressed deferentially through misplaced strictures against factors, legal agents, outgoing tacksmen, incoming tenant-farmers and even sheep. On the rare occasions when landowners were indicted as instigators of Clearance, citations were usually depersonalised though naming did occur with increasing frequency as settlements established during the first phase of Clearance were dismantled during the second phase which commenced in the 1820s and reached its nadir with the Great Famine of 1845–50 (see Meek 1995).

EXERCISE 2

Reflect on the above discussion, and read **Document 43**. What do you think were the major factors contributing to the demise of the clans?

Briefly, these included legal constraints, military defeat and social dislocation, changes in land tenure, rent increases and, above all, commercial landlordism.

Clearly this is a major and controversial topic which you would do well to explore in greater detail by seeing some of the 'further reading' listed at the end of this chapter.

2. DEBATABLE SOURCES

Because of the cultural connotations of the land issue in the Highlands, the ongoing debate on removal and relocation has often been highly charged. Indeed, a prevailing tendency to condemn or condone the conduct of the clan élite has arguably worked against clarification of why and how Clearance was implemented during the eighteenth century and throughout the first half of the nineteenth. Moreover, much of this partisan and partial analysis has been grounded in an imperfect use of the plethora of original and published sources for the history of the Highlands.

Critics of the clan élite, though laudably redressing the historical imbalance that has favoured the proponents of improvement, tend to take their lead from the vernacular poets in being long on heroic rhetoric but short on critical appraisal (Prebble 1963; Grimble, 1979). The picture of a contented society broken up by alien forces wholly underestimates the cultural tensions within clanship prior to the 'Forty-Five which were provoked by the commercialising of customary relations. Migration to the West Indies, to the American Colonies, as to Lowland cities, was underway in advance of piecemeal tenurial changes. Though undoubtedly augmented by the break-up of the townships, out-migration can be attributed primarily to population growth, itself a product of economic advance and greater social stability. Jacobitism notwithstanding, the Highlands were marked by a decline in militarism, growing pacification and commercial reconstruction from the later seventeenth century. Seasonal migration to the Lowlands in search of gainful employment was already an accepted facet of life in the southern Highlands by the 1740s (see Devine 1995, Chapter 10).

Those who condemn the clan élite tend also to discount the depressing effect of the Highland climate on enterprise. This was not just a matter of incessant rainfall, high winds and snap frosts delaying sowing and prolonging harvests. The relative failure of erstwhile clansmen to respond positively to commercial opportunities was testimony to a mentality shaped by an ingrained sense of defeatism after the 'Forty-Five. Such defeatism was compounded by evangelical missionary endeavours on behalf of Presbyterianism in the later eighteenth and early nineteenth centuries which, by propagating the message that life was a 'glen of tears' to anchor cultural disorientation, placed emphasis on individual salvation rather than collective action to resist Clearance. Too often criticisms of the clan élite have been based on the decontextualising of parliamentary papers, especially commissions of inquiry incidental to land use, and on the sympathetic misreading of evangelical attacks upon the moderates within the Church of Scotland as no more than lackeys of the landlords in the Highlands (Macinnes1983, 74–5).

Certainly, the clan élite were coming under deserved polemical attacks for their abnegation of clanship in favour of Clearance by the 1770s. However, uncritical acceptance of the views of polemicists opposed to commercial landlordism has led to commentary that is both impressionistic and anecdotal. Most reprehensibly, such commentary has wilfully disregarded the detailed records of estate management, including maps and surveys as well as rentals, leases, ledgers and directives, which are by no means apologetic of the conduct of the clan élite. Despite having brought the crofters into the mainstream of Highland history, this commendation must be set against the profound reluctance of the critics of the clan élite to admit that the creation of the crofting community, no less than the cattle ranch or sheep walk during the first phase of Clearance, underwrote the imbalanced use of land and made further Clearance inevitable in response to changing market demands.

Conversely, the condoners of the clan élite stress that the removal and relocation of people consequent on the break-up on the traditional townships was essentially the product of objective geographic, demographic and economic factors, notably the presence of too many people on marginal land distant from the main markets in urban Britain (Turnock 1970; Richards 1982; 1985). Thus, the role of landlords as the principal instruments of economic change was so constricted that native entrepreneurship failed to flourish. Because there were few available or ancillary reserves to sustain a capitalist environment within the Highlands, the clan élite, however regrettable their conduct in abrogating trustee-ship and however remiss their failure to provide adequate incentives and security for their erstwhile clansmen to carry through improvements, had little alternative but to promote Clearance.

Yet both removal and relocation on the break-up of traditional townships into single-tenant farms, planned villages or crofting communities were recognised as subjective acts of estate management by the more perceptive commentators on parochial conditions in both the *Statistical Account* (1790s) and the *New Statistical Account* (1840s); as, indeed, by the compilers of the various county reports on agriculture. These invaluable commentaries also provide indispensable evidence on the incidence and extent of demographic change that fleshes out the figures in the census abstracts.

The marked rise of population within the Highlands was of the order of 54% between 1755 and 1831. This addition of 100,000 people to a population base of around 250,000, which discounts the thousands who migrated to the cities or overseas, was largely brought about by improved dietary prospects following the introduction of the potato from the 1740s. Survival rates were subsequently boosted by widespread inoculation against smallpox from the 1780s. At the same time, this growth was by no means spread uniformly throughout the region, far less within the shire and parish as enumeration districts. Contrast must be drawn between the creation of labour-retentive crofting communities in the islands and along the north-western seaboard, where population growth was as much as 75% in the fifty years prior to 1811, and the selective implementation of labour-shedding cattle ranches and, more especially, sheep walks in mainland districts, where around a third of the parishes had experienced a net loss of population by the 1790s. With the wholesale switch in favour of sheep walks and deer forests at the expense of crofting communities from the 1820s, population decline became the most pronounced demographic trend in the majority of Highland parishes by the 1840s.

Deterministic exponents of Clearance, though usually well versed in the polemics on both sides of the land issue, prefer to draw more on travellers' tales than on vernacular poetry. They also have an uncritical tendency to believe the improving propaganda which sets the worst of traditionalist farming against the best of commercialised agriculture. Particularly overplayed has been the recurrence of harvest failure which, apart from the mortality crisis generated by endemic dearth in the late 1690s, the early 1740s and in 1782–3, was essentially localised and occasional. Conversely, the pastoral emphasis of farming allied to the purchasing power afforded by the relative buoyancy of the droving trade, made Highland townships less vulnerable than their Lowland counterparts to fluctuations in grain supplies. At the same time, improved practices proved a mixed blessing. Apparently first introduced on South Uist in 1743, the potato was established as a staple article of diet by the 1780s throughout the Highlands. Not only did the potato offer yields three-fold greater than oats and up to eight-fold greater than barley, but it was easily grown in small plots and often on hitherto uncultivated ground. As well as its significant contribution to population growth, the potato facilitated the creation of the crofting community based on small individual plots and limited common

No. 19. Poltalloch House, view from the south-east, c.1950. *Photograph courtesy of St Andrews University Library (Valentine Collection, 1937).*

pasture. But these communities, which were created to pursue agriculture as an ancillary pursuit, became overdependent on the potato for subsistence. Localised failures of the crop during the 1820s and more widespread famine in 1836–7 made manifest a fragile economy whose vulnerability was exposed by the Great Famine of 1845–50.

Magisterial work on this famine has brought to fruition another approach to the land issue that primarily seeks to contextualise, to explain and to differentiate rather than to condemn or condone (Devine 1988). This more rigorous methodology, which is grounded in estate as well as public papers, makes systematic and selective use of court records and police reports, newspapers and local government minute books to explode blanket condemnations of Highland landlords and impose a discriminatory view of estate management. The conduct of landlords, both indigenous and incomers during the Great Famine, is by no means whitewashed. Crofting communities which tended to face evictions during the second phase of Clearance were those of kelpers whose labours as seaweed burners were deemed redundant, not those of fishermen still able to engage in the inshore herring fishery. Crofting problems notwithstanding, the continuing viability of commercial pastoralism ensured not only the desirability of Highland estates but an expanded landmarket from the 1820s. Accordingly, the combination of geographic, demographic and economic factors which had generated the moment for a social revolution in the Highlands during the first phase of Clearance had constricted but not determined the managerial options of Highland landlords as members of the Anglo-Scottish establishment during the second phase.

There is a continuing need to build up a reliable corpus of case-studies for diverse districts to provide thorough scrutiny of the relationship between land use and enterprise during the Clearances. Despite the common espousal of improvement on the part of landlords, the principal features of estate management would appear to be the persistent underdevelopment of landed resources and a marked failure to industrialise beyond the level of the extractive industries. Whereas the Lowlands were embarking upon a second phase of industrialisation associated with the heavy industries from the 1830s, the Highlands underwent a second phase of Clearance in favour of sheep-walks and deer forests.

Differing patterns of development give superficial credence to the view of the Lowlands as a beneficiary of the British Empire and the Highlands as another internal colony on the Celtic fringe. Certainly, the financing of the clan élite's social aspirations commenced from a weaker economic base than the rest of Britain. Nonetheless, indebtedness was an accepted characteristic of the Anglo-Scottish landed classes, likewise the tendency to use profits accruing from marketable commodities to sustain conspicuous expenditure. Albeit commercial activity throughout eighteenth-century Scotland was heavily dependent on advances of credit, the economy of the Highlands undoubtedly lacked the depth and diversity manifest in the Lowlands. Yet this contrast is more subtle than stark in terms of entrepreneurial endeavour, as evident from a case-study of commercial landlordism in Argyllshire based primarily on estate papers supplemented by the cadastral records of ownership, bankruptcy and legal sequestration; fiscal, administrative and judicial minutes and procedures of local government; and newspaper reports, particularly adverts for migration, hiring labour, letting farms and selling estates. Within such a construct, the Clearances appear not as the inevitable product of a lack of development. Rather, the Highlands were constricted by underdevelopment and the notable failure to sustain the proactive management detectable in the commercial endeavours of the clan élite prior to the 'Forty-Five.

EXERCISE 3

What are the key points of historical debate surrounding the land issue? What kinds of sources are mentioned and which do you think have the greatest potential for the historian?

You should, for example, be able to identify the problems surrounding the role of the landlords, the economics of traditional agriculture, the extent of commercialism and the demography of the Highlands. A wide range of sources are cited including vernacular poetry, travellers' diaries, estate and legal records, parliamentary papers and the *Statistical Accounts*, among others. All have their uses although clearly some – travellers' accounts for instance – tend to be impressionistic. The need is for systematic use of a comprehensive range of sources, applying quantitative methods where appropriate as in the work of Professor Devine.

3. PRE-CLEARANCE COMMERCIALISM

In marked contrast to the Western Isles where the chiefs and clan gentry were traditionally content to exact landing and storage dues from Lowland or Ulster fishing enterprises, the clan élite of Argyllshire, particularly those around the Clyde coast, were actively involved in the development of inshore fishing. In the process, smuggling of contraband goods, not only luxury goods like brandy, wines and tobacco through the Isle of Man, but also salt for curing fish from Ireland, became a communal commercial activity in coastal districts. The clan gentry of Argyll were also to the fore in promoting improved farming. The prospect of wholesale tenurial reform stimulated the formation of the Argyll Company of Farmers as a co-partnery in October 1735, with a capital stock of £3000; albeit the Company was more significant for espousing than accomplishing exemplary improvements. Undaunted, the Whig interest in the county sought to promote a linen manufactory at Inveraray in the aftermath of the 'Forty-Five. Spinning schools supplied with looms were to be established throughout the county and premiums paid for the growing of flax, the spinning of yarn and the weaving of coarse cloth. Although the consequent fiscal commitment stalled manufacturing during 1753, this initiative did serve to occasion an eleven-fold increase in linen production which temporarily elevated Argyllshire to the forefront of Highland counties producing linen stamped for sale between the 1750s and the 1760s.

The commercial advantage enjoyed by Argyllshire, where younger sons of clan élites who had no immediate prospect of acquiring land were actively encouraged to accumulate capital through trade as well as the law and military service, was undoubtedly enhanced by the exemplary influence of the ducal house of Argyll. The chiefs of Clan Campbell were commended and sought public approval for their patriotic benevolence as innovative estate managers in eradicating tacksmen, founding planned villages, instituting textile works, sponsoring fishing communities, developing quarries and encouraging plantations; activities which they regarded as integral, not colonial aspects of British economic and social integration. No less significant was the county's relative proximity to Glasgow, Scotland's imperial entrepot; a connection formalised by the establishment of a Highland Society in the city in 1727, thirteen Argyllshire landowners being among its seventy-eight founder members. Operating formally as a charitable body intent on promoting apprenticeships and educational services, the Society brought together aspiring and assured entrepreneurs among the landed, commercial and professional classes.

Probably the most sophisticated commercial enterprise, arising initially from mercantile contacts in Glasgow and the Clyde ports, was the marketing portfolio of the Campbells of Ardchattan. Commencing in 1688 as agents for recovering debts owed to Clyde merchants, the Inveresregan Trading Company, launched in 1706, presaged a series of co-partneries engaged in droving, timber dealings, grain shipping, tobacco importing and even coal mining. From their base in the Lorne district of Argyll, their merchandising operations extended from Caithness through the Perthshire Highlands to Dublin. Albeit three of their seven companies did not last a decade and only two lasted beyond two generations, they promoted direct trade links with the West Indies and the American South and they encouraged tobacco spinning as a cottage industry in Argyllshire. Their commercial networking also straddled the political divide prior to the 'Forty-Five, when their trading partners included the Camerons of Lochiel, who were more intent on developing Fort William as a commercial centre than as a garrison town. The various commercial activities of these Jacobite entrepreneurs in Lochaber ranged from dealing in black cattle, timber, grain and tobacco through the smuggling of contraband wines from France to legitimate trading with the West Indies, Philadelphia, New York and Boston.

From the 1730s, access to the colonies was as significant as proximity to the industrialising centres of Lowland Scotland for the promotion of Highland entrepreneurship. In Georgia, the transplanting of communities from the central and northern Highlands, led by younger sons of the clan élite with limited landed prospects, was primarily intended as frontier protection in the face of repeated Spanish attempts to reassert sovereignty in the American South. In North Carolina, the Argyll Colony projected in 1739 was based on small plantations around the Cape Fear River which exploited tar, turpentine and tobacco as well as the more familiar cattle, flax and timber. Although sustained by tacksmen and tenants who lost out in tenurial reforms, this colony was principally an entrepreneurial undertaking of landlords. In Jamaica, where the original 'Argyll Colony' was established at least a decade before that in North Carolina, large plantations concentrated on sugar and rum production. Some Argyllshire landowners adventured in both colonies, others maintained a connection through the slave-trade. A few families who had first moved in from 1713 had settled permanently on the island by the 1750s. But most Argyllshire families, in common with other Scottish commercial networks, endured tropical conditions to build up their capital reserves before returning to Britain.

4. INTERVENTIONIST AGENCIES

As the debate within government circles switched from punitive severity to remedial leniency in the aftermath of the 'Forty-Five, the policy of civilising the Highlands became identified not only with enforced pacification but with the promotion of commerce as a patriotic British endeavour. An example is to be seen in **Document 44**. State-sponsored terrorism gave way to state-sponsored improvement. In response to a plethora of civilising schemes from unctuous ideologues and unplaced opportunists, the Whig government had decided that thirteen forfeited estates of Jacobite chiefs and gentry were to be annexed inalienably to the Crown in 1752, as corridors of improvement that were to be models of planning and management for the Highlands.

Another eight years were to elapse before the Board entrusted with the management of the Annexed Estates became operational. In addition to promoting loyalty to the Hanoverian dynasty, the Board was charged to diversify the Highland economy and promote Presbyterianism. The task of linking vocational education, basic English literacy and rigorous moral instructions to uphold the British establishment was carried out in conjunction with the Society in Scotland for the Propagation of Christian Knowledge (SSPCK). Previously supported by covert subventions from the British State in order to contain Jacobitism, the SSPCK gradually became a more sympathetic force in Gaeldom, publishing the New Testament in Gaelic in 1767 – the first authentic Scottish Gaelic translation since the Reformation (another thirty-four years were to elapse before the whole Bible became available in Gaelic). Assisting the SSPCK was but one more burden for the overstretched factors on the Annexed Estates whose pay was index-linked to a 5% fluctuation in grain prices but not to increased productivity.

Deficient financing and administrative indifference ensured that the Commissioners' impressive blueprints for commercial transformation never got off the drawing board. The financing of the Annexed Estates was dependent on the cash surplus from the capital raised from the sale of forfeited estates in the Lowlands, not on an annual grant from the government. At the same time, the rents on the Annexed Estates, after initial survey and valuation, were frozen by the Commissioners. In essence, this was deficit financing. The constant erosion of the capital sum raised from sales was an impediment to long-term projects. Moreover, inherited debts were not cleared but continued. This burden was often a multiple of the yearly rent and in some instances a considerable multiple from six to fifteen years. Accordingly, on some estates meaningful improvements were largely confined to replacing property destroyed by the military in the aftermath of the 'Forty-Five. Although the accession of George III in 1760 was marked by noted Lowland improvers being added to the Commission in Edinburgh, its expenditure remained under the rigid control of the London Treasury (Smith 1982). Bureaucracy flourished through lack of targeted accountability and energetic management in Scotland. No Commissioner would appear to have personally visited any Annexed Estate, although the Commission did send Rev John Walker on a tour of investigation in 1764 (see **Document 45**) and appointed a Riding Officer as their substitute.

Following the end of the Seven Years' War in 1763, the Annexed Estates primarily became an agency for the relocation of demobilised soldiers and sailors, a task not infrequently achieved by the removal of erstwhile clansmen. The cost of resettlement for sailors alone amounted to £6000 as against an average annual surplus from the rents of £4500. The Commission's fourteen-year period of effective planning virtually ended in 1774 with the abandonment of all industrial ventures. When the government decided on disannexation in 1784, there was a general recognition that the estates were distinguished because of their comparatively bad condition, especially their manifest neglect of improved agriculture. The burden of inherited debts on many estates had become chronic, varying from the equivalent of thirteen to thirty-five years' rents, the latter figure being tantamount to bankruptcy. Although the Commission was not a major force in directly transforming the Highlands, the Annexed Estates did have a significant exemplary role in accelerating the break-up of traditional townships through the creation of single-tenant farms, planned villages and crofting communities.

Shaping the public agenda for improvement within an imperial context was continued from 1784 by the Highlands and Agricultural Society, which brought together the Scottish Whig establishment to enhance commercial assimilation with the Lowlands. The Society also provided a political lobby that complemented the cultural remit of the Highland Society of London, established in 1778, to promote the rehabilitation of the Gael through respect for cultural traditions and end the proscription on the wearing of tartan. This latter task was accomplished by 1782. However, the rehabilitation of the Gael owed less to cultural considerations than to military service.

Highland regiments were raised from 1757, primarily for their usefulness as a highly mobile and hardy light infantry in North America during the Seven Years' War. This deployment of Highland troops regardless of previous Jacobite affiliations offered a militarist channel for the resumption of the cultural trappings of clanship – wearing tartan and playing bagpipes. More importantly, the raising of regiments offered an imperial avenue for the political rehabilitation of the Jacobite clan élite. In addition to the two Highland Regiments raised by the 'Forty-Five, the six regiments of the line and the two fencible regiments for domestic defence mobilised during the Seven Years' War, another ten regiments of the line and three fencibles were raised during the American War of Independence (see Clyde 1995). The Napoleonic Wars from 1793 to 1815 raised this total to 23 regiments of the line and 26 fencibles – recruitment in excess of 48,300 men, a fighting force

THE
PRESENT CONDUCT
OF THE
CHIEFTAINS
AND
PROPRIETORS OF LANDS
IN THE
Highlands of SCOTLAND.

Towards their Clans and People, confidered
impartially.

By a HIGHLANDER.

*He that getteth Riches, and not by Right, fhall leave
them in the midft of his Days, and at his End fhall
become a Fool.* Jeremiah.

*Be thou a Stream of many Tides againft the Foes of
thy People, but as the Gale that moves the Grafs
to thofe that afk thine Aid.* Fingal.

The Second Edition.

Printed in the Year 1773.

No. 20. Frontispiece of pamphlet 'The present conduct of the chieftains and
proprietors of lands in the Highlands of Scotland. Towards their Clans and People,
considered impartially. By a Highlander (1773). *Reproduced by kind permission of
the National Library of Scotland.*

equivalent to twice the assessed fighting potential of all the clans during the Jacobite risings. Highland Regiments did exhibit a propensity to mutiny when threatened with regrouping among Lowland regiments, when denied bounties and arrears of pay or when their final military destination was concealed. Nonetheless, their sterling service in North America, the West Indies and India as well as on the continent provided the ostensible excuse for the British State to wind up the direct management of former Jacobite estates and restore the disinherited.

Imperial advantage in having a ready reservoir of skilled sailors in the Highlands reinforced the commercial potential of expanding from inshore to deep-sea operations involving whaling as well as pelagic and white fish. Accordingly, the winding up of the Annexed Estates resulted in a direct financial subvention to the British Fisheries Society which operated in the four decades after 1786 as an interventionist agency under the direction of the Scottish Whig establishment rather than the Treasury. However, the actual management of the British Fisheries was attended by familiar problems of attenuated decision-making and financial control from London. Investment was concentrated on a few villages, such as Ullapool and Lochbay (Skye) which were not necessarily the best locations for fishing or even in areas where fishing was an accustomed lifestyle. Money tended to be tied up in fixed assets such as buildings rather than advanced as working capital for boats and tackle. The prohibitive Salt Laws and bounties for catching and curing herring, which were only gradually overhauled during the 1790s, were scaled to suit large commercial operations established elsewhere in Scotland. Such eclectic fishing policies were not geared to secure extensive co-operation either from landowners or erstwhile farmers in the Highlands.

Despite the rather patchy records of interventionist agencies, both culturally and commercially, planning was accepted as an integral feature of estate management within the Highlands. The employment of professional surveyors was recognised as indispensable from the 1760s. The improving objectives for landlords commissioning surveys were aesthetic as well as commercial. The main priority was to find the best site for a family seat and assess the landscaping necessary to enhance the setting of the new mansion. Surveying, which was often the prelude to wholesale removal and relocation, highlighted the principal features of the process of Clearance in the new era of commercial landlordism.

EXERCISE 4

List the key interventionist agencies mentioned and, after reading **Article 14** by Smith, suggest which was most successful and why. There are references to the SSPCK in Smout (1969).

Your list should include the Board of Commissioners for the Annexed Estates, the SSPCK, the Highlands and Agricultural Society and the British Fisheries Society. The second part is more difficult from what you have to go on here, although, of the formal bodies, the Annexed Estates and the British Fisheries Society seem to have achieved most, albeit that the impact of the BFS was often different to what had been anticipated. But imperial military service clearly had the greatest economic and social effect.

5. THE PROCESS OF CLEARANCE

Piecemeal tenurial tinkering had usually occurred on most estates to a greater or lesser degree in all Highland districts prior to the 'Forty-Five. The introduction of competitive bidding, however, which can be traced to Kintyre at the outset of the eighteenth century, was not systematically applied until 1737, when the tenurial reforms instigated by the house of Argyll set the pattern for ending the *baile* as the basic unit of management as well as cultivation. The virtual elimination of the traditional township was effected to sustain the political and social standing of John, second Duke of Argyll, as a Whig grandee. A temporary recession in droving was considered sufficient grounds for eliminating the tacksmen in order to monopolise all rents levied in Morvern, Mull and Tiree. Tenurial reform through competitive bidding, ideologically justified by the Whig belief that material and cultural progress necessitated the replacement of customary relationships, entailed the commercial exploitation of *duthchas*. Tacksmen were set against clansmen to secure the lease for each township. If the tacksman offered the higher bid, he was obliged to farm as the single tenant, retaining a few clansmen as cottars or servants. If the clansmen outbid him, they continued to farm their multiple tenancy, but were deprived of the tacksman's managerial and marketing expertise (see Cregeen 1969). Although subsequent bidding was modified in the interests of commercial patronage, the upswing in droving encouraged over-bidding. But the rival desires of tacksmen and tenantry to retain their heritage impaired their livelihood and opened the way for enterprising gentry from other clans as well as Lowland farmers, particularly when commercial farming of cattle was challenged by that of sheep with the introduction of such breeds as the Border blackface from the 1760s and subsequently the Cheviots from the 1790s. These breeds, though less hardy than the native Highland, were of greater carcass weight to feed the expanding urban masses and yielded greater quantity of wool for the burgeoning textile industry. Because the stocking of sheep was capital-intensive – the business tended to be dominated by graziers with flocks of at least 600 – and because the new breeds' needs for diversity of pasture and winter grazing were deemed incompatible both with the retention of black cattle and multiple tenancy, single-tenant farms tended to expand.

At the same time, landlords were determined to retain a large labour pool, not least on account of the prestige associated with their provision of recruits for the British army and navy. In turn, rising population levels led to congestion within surviving multiple tenancies where the high yields from marginal land afforded by the potato led to the abandonment of customary strip farming in rigs in favour of individual smallholdings consolidated as crofting communities. In interior districts, erstwhile clansmen became increasingly dependent on supplementary income from illicit distilling and seasonal migration unless they found employment in such extractive industries as timber cutting or charcoal burning, quarrying for lime and slate or even mining for lead and coal. In all such instances, agriculture was relegated to an ancillary pursuit (Devine 1994). The bulk of erstwhile clansmen removed from interior glens and straths were relocated in congested coastal districts, some to exploit inshore fishing, others to supply the chemical market for soap and potash with ash from ferns and bracken. The majority of the displaced were engaged in burning seaweed to manufacture kelp for glass works and bleaching textiles. The manufacture of kelp, a commodity particularly noted for its volatile prices from the 1730s, continued to expand on the western seaboard when the American Wars of Independence restricted alternative supplies of wood-ash and the Napoleonic Wars deprived the chemical industry of barilla. In the Western Isles, where single-tenant farms had evolved to exploit the cattle trade without necessarily switching to sheep-walks, kelping not agriculture was confirmed as the main economic pursuit by the 1790s. The limited summer season for collecting and converting seaweed into kelp led to the retention of enormous labour pools not just of crofters but of cottars and squatters. Because earnings from kelp were usually offset against rising rents and purchases of meal to supplement a potato diet, conditions within the crofting community were progressively driven below subsistence by rampant subdivision.

> EXERCISE 5
> Review the sub-section here and construct a 'model for clearance'. If you have access to it, you will find Devine (1995), Chapter 9, helpful.
> Utilising **Document 46**, consider the factors which have led historians to conclude that the new economic system was vulnerable to collapse.

I won't provide a response to the first of these questions, but if you have any doubts, read over this section again. The two books by Devine (1988; 1994) are particularly helpful if you have access to them. The extent to which the crofting communities were dependent on the success of by-employments generated by external demand is clear. Seasonal migration on a large scale also played an increasingly important role in sustaining the new economic and social order (Devine 1995, Chapter 10).

6. REACTIVE ESTATE MANAGEMENT

Whereas the dual impact of debt and enterprise had led to the expansion of the land market in the seventeenth century, a measure of consolidation was the most pronounced feature in the eighteenth century. That the upsurge in landownership was not sustained can partially be attributed to the passage of the Montgomery or Entail Act of 1770, which allowed landowners to apportion up to two-thirds of costs incurred by estate improvements to succeeding generations. The downward spiral in numbers can readily be associated with a lack of continuity in landownership, a trend accelerated after, but not instigated by, the 'Forty-Five.

Notwithstanding periodic liability to forfeiture, Jacobitism made no impact of lasting significance on the land market. By way of contrast, the Clearances led to a further phase of fragmentation of estates. The perceptible increase in number of landowners, though less expansive than in the seventeenth century, owed more to the determination of Highland entrepreneurs to exploit commercial pastoralism than to incoming industrialists who wished to indulge in recreational capitalism.

Distinction must be drawn, however, between the rhetoric and reality of commercial landlordism in an expansive and buoyant market. Despite the manifest but not uncritical desire for improvement among the landed and professional classes in the Highlands, the latter half of the eighteenth century witnessed a shift from proactive to reactive estate management. Proactive management, signposted by the introduction of competitive bidding, by diversified land-use and proto-industrialisation, and by commercial expansion within an imperial framework, was, arguably by the 1790s and certainly by the end of the Napoleonic Wars, giving way to reactive management characterised by over-reliance on hill-farming, by largely unsustained planning, and by growing dependence on external sources of income accumulated from marriages, imperial service and stocks and shares. Landowners establishing villages for quarrying, kelping and, more generally, for fishing too often condoned reliance on crofting and unplanned growth rather than sustained investment despite the growing industrial markets, particularly for slates, bleaching agents and herring from the Highlands.

Indeed, the initial phase of Clearance is littered with well-intentioned projects never brought to fruition. Thus, the transformation of the fishing industry in the Sound of Harris, initiated by Alexander MacLeod after he purchased the island from his chief in 1778 with monies accrued from a profitable career with the East India Company, was not sustained after his death in 1790. His son, Alexander, preferred to retain a lucrative civil post in India. The much discussed Sutherland Clearances, which went against the grain of relocating and removing gradually over several generations, should not be regarded as typical in terms of timescale. Clearances effected between 1807 and 1820 by Elizabeth Gordon, Countess of Sutherland, were capitalised by monies generated in the English Midlands on the Bridgewater estates of her husband, George Gower, Marquis of Stafford. Despite accomplishing the profitable introduction of sheep-farming, the creation of a transport infrastructure and the sumptuous erection of Dunrobin Castle, Clearance in Sutherland was of a piece with the rest of the Highlands in not leading to sustained commercial diversification (Richards 1973).

That proactive landlordism was not maintained can be attributed to commercial networking throughout the Empire no less than absenteeism in Lowland cities or London and the Home Counties. Absenteeism was undoubtedly significant in the removal of rental income to support assimilation in Anglo-Scottish landed society. Yet, the shake-out in Highland landownership from the outset of the nineteenth century can be ascribed primarily to unsound investments in commercial ventures at home and abroad, coupled to banking constrictions during successive crises of liquidity in 1772, 1797, 1802–3, 1810 and 1815–6 rather than to any failure to adapt or diversify land use by absentees. Among the principal beneficiaries of these sales were indigenous Highland entrepreneurs who had successfully exploited the imperial dimension, most notably the MacCallums or Malcolms of Poltalloch who were accruing immense profits not only as planters but as storekeepers in Jamaica.

From Lucca in Hanover parish, they expanded their activities to supply primarily Scottish planters throughout the island and extended their trading ventures in the Caribbean, including the selling and leasing of slaves, from Tobago to Honduras. Despite the inherently speculative nature of the trade, profits from rum and sugar led to their accumulation of vast wealth. By the outset of the 1770s, the Malcolms of Poltalloch were repatriating profits in excess of almost £30,000 from a yearly turnover of around £82,000 on five plantations, a turnover which had increased to £134,000 by 1792, rising above £410,000 by 1812, to £720,500 from eight plantations by 1826 before settling in excess of £1,084,000 by 1849. From Jamaica they diversified as merchant adventurers and slave traders between the West Indies, Central and North America. The bulk of their repatriated wealth was used partly to build up their social position in London and Edinburgh, but principally to work and accumulate capital. They invested successfully in London's West Indian docks, in Yorkshire shipbuilding and, above all, as shipping insurers specialising in the lucrative liabilities of the South and China Seas. It was only the outbreak of the Napoleonic Wars in 1793 and the subsequent French economic blockade around the British Isles that led the Malcolms to invest seriously in the Highlands. They used their colonial wealth to force up prices on the land market to such an extent that they moved from small to large landowners in a single generation. Despite the limited featuring of the Highlands in their investment portfolio, the Malcolms of Poltalloch had a basically sound and progressive record as agricultural innovators, estate improvers, commercial planners, transport developers and industrial sponsors between the 1790s and the 1840s when they had expanded their colonial horizons to the development of Southern Australia.

Yet, the Malcolms earned not undeserved notoriety for the riotous clearance of Arichonan on their Argyllshire estates in 1848, at a time when the family was erecting a new mansion at Poltalloch, the fourth either built or refurbished since 1793. As an economy measure for a house built at a cost in excess of £100,000, the mansion, which also served as a business centre, was restricted to two rather than three floors. It may be tempting to equate the insensitivity of clearing Arichonan during the Great Famine with the family's oppressive response to slave protests in Jamaica and disregard for aboriginal rights in Australia. However, the principal grounds for popular dissension on their Highland estate, which necessitated the mobilising of most of the Argyllshire constabulary to effect clearance, was the reversal of the Malcolms' hitherto enlightened paternalism in order to profit from the upsurge in sheep over cattle prices. As evident from a lintel over a surviving doorway in the deserted settlement of Arichonan, the people were protesting against their summary eviction from a township that had been comprehensively rebuilt as recently as 1835.

Notwithstanding the exponential increase in the finances of the Malcolms, the Caribbean connection was high-risk and not invariably profitable. The credit restrictions imposed on planters, particularly those involved directly in the slave

No. 21. 'Tussle for the Keg' by John Pettie. *City of Aberdeen Art Gallery and Museums Collections.*

trade from Africa, were aggravated by discriminatory colonial rates of interest. Despite increasing industrial demand for cotton, the West Indies trade was materially disrupted during the Napoleonic Wars, a situation compounded by anti-slavery legislation which pushed up overheads for labour supply and provisioning. Undoubtedly, service in India, which had already been targeted by the absentee clan élite as the next eligible place for making money after the Caribbean, became the most lucrative and secure imperial prospect from the 1780s. Income accrued from Highland estates at the close of the eighteenth century was often around a tenth of the monies accumulated annually by imperial entrepreneurs from stocks and shares in the East India Company, the Scottish banks and Consolidated Government Funds. Conversely, the sums initially expended in acquiring Highland estates were often no more than a tenth of the total expenditure laid out in stock and interest-bearing loans. While monies from Empire brought the land market in the Highlands into line with the rest of Britain, the evidence that imperial service made a significant contribution to improved and diversified land-use is at best patchy. The most telling feature of commercial landlordism by the outset of the nineteenth century was the growing dependence on external funding, which tied estate management as much to the fluctuations in the financial as in the agricultural markets.

EXERCISE 6

What impact do you think imperialism has had on Highland history?

The evidence on this is inconclusive at this stage, but you might note that the Highlands were generally treated much like overseas possessions, and clearly there is an imperial dimension to Highland history. Success abroad also brought investment in Highland estates, so it was something of a two-way process.

7. ALTERNATIVE LIFESTYLES

The new horizons opened up by entrepreneurship and empire were by no means the preserve of landowners. The historiographical heat engendered by the Clearances has tended to understate the active involvement of tenantry and labourers as well as the landed élite in putting commercialism before clanship. The piecemeal, but systematic, removal of tacksmen which characterised the first phase of Clearance had undoubtedly hampered the capacity of indigenous no less than incoming landlords to sustain community support for changes in land use. Nonetheless, purported resistance to tenurial and commercial change during the Clearances cannot be equated with endemic resistance to enterprise by erstwhile clansmen. The conservatism manifest in the acceptance of rampant subdivision within traditional townships and thereafter in crofting communities must be counterpoised by the commercial experience accrued from regular hiring and livestock fairs, from the spread of consumerism, and from the different labour rhythms experienced in the course of seasonal migration.

Although wage regulation had been abandoned by the 1790s, the persistence of personal services or boon work points to the continuing difficulty of adjusting from customary to commercial relationships; a difficulty that was essentially cultural not environmental. At the same time, the profitability of droving, which had encouraged the clan élite to push up rents whenever leases were renewed, had accustomed the tenantry within traditional townships to offset rent increases, together with their consumer expenditure, against anticipated earnings from the marketing of black cattle on their behalf by drovers. As a result, their lifestyles were generally not geared to the handling of money. Hence, the failure of the drovers to assess the profitability of black cattle, as occurred in 1772, 1776, 1782, 1793, 1803 and 1816, occasioned periodic financial crises in estate management which pushed up the debts of the clan élite and the rent arrears of their erstwhile clansmen.

Even emigration, another topic about which historians' views are far from uniform, can be viewed on one level as a community protest against estate re-orientation, but can be deemed on another level to involve entrepreneurial flair. Although families left the Highlands prior to the expiry of leases because they were unable to meet high rents, and although pronounced upward movement in commodity prices tempted landlords to abrogate leases by legal chicanery, removal and relocation were linked umbilically to competitive bidding for renew-al of leases. Thus, the 'rage for emigration' in the later eighteenth century can more accurately be styled entrepreneurial than voluntary. Relatively affluent tacksmen and tenantry were not prepared to accept downward social mobility and depression of their living standards when freehold land was on offer in North America. Emigration to Savannah in Georgia, Cape Fear in North Carolina, Albany in New York, Glengarry County in Ontario, Prince Edward Island and subsequently Nova Scotia had the character of a community movement led by tacksmen removed from their managerial function by Clearance and supported by former tenants whose concept of *duthchas* was not sustained by their prospective relocation into the ranks of crofters, farm servants and day labourers (see Bumstead 1982). Potential emigrants to the Glenaladale settlement on Prince Edward Island at the outset of the 1770s were required to negotiate both their acquisition of single-tenant farms and conditions for indentured labour. The colonial promoter, John MacDonald of Glenaladale, one of the leading gentry of the Clanranald, incurred the wrath of fellow landowners who had abrogated clanship but wished to retain cheap sources of labour for estate management as well as military recruitment.

The combined efforts of government and landlords to retain a reservoir of manpower during the Napoleonic Wars led to the passage of two significant measures by 1803. The Passenger Vessels Act, which pushed up the costs of overseas passages under the guise of improving medical and dietary provision, served merely as a temporary check to emigration and encouraged tenantry to move to the Lowlands and elsewhere in urban Britain to escape the congestion of the crofting community. By 1827, rapacious shipping interests and irresponsible land-lords had combined to secure a relaxation of medical provisions on transatlantic passages in order to facilitate the transportation of destitute crofters. Whereas Highlanders had removed from traditional townships with some resources, those facing relocation from crofting communities usually required financial assistance. However, government provision of assisted passages, usually to Canada, was designed as much to relieve cyclical industrial depression in the cities as structural poverty in the Highlands. Although medical provision was restored and emigration agents were appointed at British ports from 1832, government was primarily concerned not with assisted passages but with informing migrants about prospects for land and work in the colonies.

The associated promotion of the Commission for Roads, Bridges and Canals in 1803 also offered no substantive check to emigration, despite the exhortations of Thomas Telford that the state should intervene (**Document 41**). Indeed, the construction programme for roads and bridges, which was based on matching funding from government and landlords, soon outstripped in terms of timescale and costs the development potential of the Great Glen as an arterial route for commerce. The showpiece construction of the Caledonian Canal made little attempt to balance expenditure against future income. A seven-year programme costed at £350,000 when it commenced in 1803 was still not completed in 1839 when expenditure exceeded £1,000,000. The failure of gross income to match running costs was compounded when the move from sail to steam underscored the failure of the canal to achieve sufficient depth and width for the passage of large commercial vessels. The Crinan Canal, which had actually opened for trade between Glasgow and the Hebrides in 1801, also had insufficient breadth and depth to cope with large steam vessels. Its leaky embankments were a burdensome and embarrassing expense to the house of Argyll and other prominent, landed subscribers, who invested almost £100,000 in stocks and secured loans without any meaningful returns before the Treasury assumed financial oversight in 1814. Nonetheless, the Crinan Canal did help secure the dominance of Argyllshire quarries as the leading slate producers in Scotland and was more successful than the Caledonian in enhancing tourism by steam packet. But the attention given to roads, bridges and canals detracted significantly from private endeavours to build quays and harbours to further the development of market towns. Moreover, the fluctuating labour demands of the localised construction programme offered no more than temporary outdoor relief for the underemployed Gael.

EXERCISE 7
How would you explain the 'rage for emigration' in the later eighteenth century? What steps were taken to check it? If you can, see Devine (1994), Chapter 12.

Emigration could be a communal activity sometimes organised by tacksmen or landlords, sometimes by colonial agencies. Among the steps taken to prevent it were the Passenger Vessels Act and investment in Highland transport to encourage local economic development.

8. CRISIS IN CROFTING

Economic recession in the aftermath of the Napoleonic Wars exposed the fragility and vulnerability of the Highlands in general and the crofting community in particular to market forces. Not only did cattle prices fall markedly, but the main props of crofting collapsed during the 1820s. Inshore fishing was undermined by the contrary nature of the herring shoals (Gray 1957). The combined impact of cheaper organic imports and the mass production of inorganic substitutes occasioned the terminal decline of kelping and the commercial burning of fern and bracken. Crofters' supplementary earnings were critically impaired by central government tightening up its policing of illicit distilling while scaling down its construction programme. Seasonal migrants to the Lowlands faced competition from Irish labour taking advantage of cheap steamer fares between Belfast Lough and the Clyde, although such temporary migration persisted and had become more diverse in an industrial context by 1850 (Devine 1995, Chapter 10). Thrown back on their dependence on the potato, the crofting community became prone to localised famines of increasing frequency as well as to outbreaks of contagious diseases like cholera.

> EXERCISE 8
> Much out-migration, however, was permanent. Read **Documents 47 and 48** and note the difference in the official attitude to emigration by 1826. What distinction can be drawn between the out-migration of the later 1700s and the 1820s and 1830s?

Clearly there was a greater element of compulsion, both in terms of official attitudes and economic necessity. The evidence here is not optimistic about the conditions of those who left the Highlands, either for the Lowlands, or abroad.

The growing view in official, as in landed, circles that the crofting community housed a redundant population that required further clearance was flagged up by the famine of 1836–7 and consolidated by the Great Famine of 1845–50 (Devine 1988, 12–32).

> EXERCISE 9
> Do you agree with this assessment of the situation? Use Smout (1969, 351-60).

What is clear is that parts of the Western Highlands and Islands of Scotland were faced with acute difficulties in the three decades which followed the Napoleonic Wars.

Mobilisation of destitution committees in Glasgow, Edinburgh and London raised £70,000 for oatmeal and potatoes to prevent widespread deaths from starvation after two years of harvest failure by 1837. However, as the scale of destitution outstripped the customary mechanisms for poor relief, a keen debate emerged within the destitution committees to prevent recurrence. Rev Norman

MacLeod, the principal Presbyterian minister to the Gaelic community in Glasgow, who has been eulogised as *Caraid nan Gàidheal* (Friend of the Gael), advocated wholesale removal of people to Canada and even went so far as to contract favourable terms with a shipping agent. The view that prevailed, however, was that of CR Baird, a medical officer of health concerned about the propensity of the Gael to disease within Glasgow and other urban environments (see **Document 48**). In order to prevent wholesale urban immigration of the destitute, education was seen as the panacea in staggering the eventual migration of a workforce with adaptable skills for industry. However, the call to remove up to 80,000 crofters and their dependents was implemented wilfully by landowners on the recurrence of famine, which coincided with the amendment to the poor law that threatened compulsory local assessments.

As Devine's monumental study has shown, the fact that the potato blight, which spread from Ireland in 1845 and lasted for at least five years throughout the crofting community, did not lead to a demographic catastrophe can be attributed to the combined efforts of landowners, government and relief agencies (Devine 1988; see too Devine 1995, Chapters 9 and 11).

> EXERCISE 10
>
> Read **Documents 49 and 50**. What opinions do you form about the role and attitudes of landowners to the crisis of the second half of the 1840s?

Although limited, the evidence examined here presents a more complex picture than you might have assumed would emerge. Both indigenous and incoming landowners can be indicted for exploitive and heartless behaviour towards the crofting community. In like manner, both made genuine and concerned endeavours to exercise purposeful and productive paternalism to offset economic distress. The majority of landowners accepted their responsibilities to their tenantry albeit some had to be cajoled and admonished by government agents, the most notable of whom, the unfortunately named Sir Edward Pine-Coffin, was despatched from the south-west of Ireland. Although the delays and vacillations which had contributed to the Irish tragedy were not repeated, the government's ideological commitment to the free market ensured that its direct contribution to famine relief was limited. Inconvenient depots were established at Tobermory in Mull and Portree in Skye for the sale of meal slightly below the prevailing rates in a market inflated by European grain shortages. The Drainage Act was extended from Ireland to fund the employment of destitute crofters as ditchers. Loans compensating landlords for the abolition of the Corn Laws in 1846 were applied selectively to restructure crofting communities towards fishing rather than agriculture. However, the principal means of combating destitution was again left to the relief agencies stimulated by the commendable endeavours of the newly established Free Church of Scotland to distribute aid to the worst-afflicted islands on a markedly non-denominational basis. From 1847 until its funds ran out in 1850, a central board of management organised loosely in two sections from Glasgow and Edinburgh took on the prime responsibility for warding off famine. The Lowland landowners, lawyers and businessmen who dictated policy from the cities knew little about crofting and they subjected the crofters to rigorous means testing before providing sufficient rations to prevent starvation. At the same time, the central board was not always sympathetic to Highland landlords, particularly those who abandoned their own work projects in order to get subsidised labour for a network of destitution roads. Above all, the central board, though neither inclined nor empowered to interfere in estate management, made no sustained attempt to build up an alternative coastal infrastructure to support fishing.

Two incidental criticisms remain about the generally accepted view on the avoidance of a demographic catastrophe during the Great Famine. In the same way that nowadays doctors remain reluctant to specify AIDS on death certificates, starvation was unlikely to have been assigned as the immediate or primary cause of death in the 1840s. There appears to be little or no supporting evidence that Highland landlords sought to ship off the starving as happened during the famine of 1836–7. But can we be absolutely sure that there was no piecemeal repetition of this practice until further research is undertaken on Clyde port records and on the appeals for relief in kirk session registers of Highland congregations in the towns and cities of Lowland Scotland?

9. THE HIGHLANDS *c.* 1850

The Great Famine had ended reliance on the potato as the dietary insurance policy for the crofting region. There was no possibility of a return to the status quo for crofters who had hitherto relied on kelping or illicit distilling, but some prospects of viability for those prepared to engage in fishing and diversify their pursuit of seasonal migration. Government and landlords, however, saw the promotion of further, if selective, migration as the only structural solution to crofting congestion. Because a community threatened with starvation was hardly capable of producing worthwhile rents and because the continuation of crofting at the margins of destitution threatened the bankruptcy of estates, landowners intensified their drive towards commercial viability through sheep-farming and deer forests. Despite the limited incidents of violent resistance to evictions, the mixed conduct of Highland landlords during the great famine had placed them firmly on the defensive not only nationally, but internationally. Aggressive promotion of commercial over customary relationships prior to the 'Forty-Five had given way to the defensive maintenance of economic individualism in the wake of the Great Famine. The absolute decline in Highland population detectable in census returns after this demographic catastrophe also served to galvanise concern among the middle class in the Lowlands as well as exiled urban Gaels about the purported superiority of unfettered economic individualism.

BOOKS AND ARTICLES REFERRED TO IN THE TEXT

Bumsted, J M 1982 *The People's Clearance, 1770–1815*. Edinburgh.
*Clyde, R 1995 *From Rebel to Hero: The Image of the Highlander, 1745–1830*. East Linton.
Cregeen, ER 1969 'The Tacksmen and Their Successors', *Scottish Studies* 13, 93–144.
*Devine, TM 1988 *The Great Highland Famine*. Edinburgh.
*Devine, TM 1994 *Clanship to Crofters' War: The social transformation of the Scottish Highlands*. Manchester.
*Devine, TM 1995 *Exploring the Scottish Past: Themes in the History of Scottish Society*. East Linton.
*Gray, M 1957 *The Highland Economy, 1750–1850*. Edinburgh (reprinted 1976).
Grimble, I 1979 *The World of Rob Donn*. Edinburgh.
*Macinnes, AI 1988 'Scottish Gaeldom: The First Phase of Clearance', *in* Devine, TM and Mitchison, R (eds), *People and Society in Scotland. Volume I: 1760–1830*, Edinburgh, 70–90.
Meek, DE 1995 *Tuath is tighearna; Tenants and landlords: an anthology of Gaelic poetry of social and political protest from the Clearances to the Land Agitation (1800–1890)*. Edinburgh.
Prebble, J 1963 *The Highland Clearances*. London.
Richards, E 1973 *The Leviathan of Wealth*. London.
*Richards, E 1982 and 1985 *A History of the Highland Clearances*, 2 vols. London.
Smith, A 1982 *Jacobite Estates of the 'Forty-Five*. Edinburgh.
Statistical Account of Scotland 1791–99. 21 volumes. Edinburgh.
Turnock, D 1970 *Patterns of Highland Development*. London.

SUGGESTED FURTHER READING

Those references marked * in the above list are recommended further reading, along with the following:

Gaskell, P 1980 *Morvern Transformed*. London.
Hechter, M 1975 *Internal Colonialism: the Celtic Fringe in British National Development*. London.
Hunter, J 1976 *The Making of the Crofting Community*. Edinburgh.
Macinnes, AI 1994 'Landownership, Land Use and Elite Enterprise in Scottish Gaeldom: From Clanship to Clearance in Argyllshire, 1688–1858' *in* Devine, TM (ed), *Scottish Elites*, Edinburgh, 1–42.
Macinnes, AI 1996 *Clanship, Commerce and the House of Stuart, 1603–1788*. East Linton.
Mitchison, R 1981 'The Highland Clearances', *Scottish Economic and Social History* 1, 137–49.
Youngson, AJ 1973 *After the Forty-Five*. Edinburgh.

SOME PUBLISHED PRIMARY SOURCES

Published texts
Cregeen, ER (ed) 1964 *Argyll Estate Instructions, 1771–1805*. Edinburgh (Scottish History Society).

Campbell, J 1774 *A Political Survey of Britain: Being a Series of Reflections on the Situation, Lands, Inhabitants, Revenues, Colonies and Commerce of this Island*, 2 vols. London.

Adam RJ (ed) 1960 *John Home's Survey of Assynt*. Edinburgh (Scottish History Society).

Knox, J *A Tour through the Highlands of Scotland and the Hebrides Isles in 1786*. Edinburgh.

Adams, IH (ed) 1979 *Papers on Peter May Land Surveyor, 1749–1793*. Edinburgh (Scottish History Society).

Robson, J 1794 *General View of the Agriculture in the County of Argyll and Western Part of Inverness-shire*. London.

McArthur MM (ed) 1936 *Survey of Lochtayside 1769*. Edinburgh (Scottish History Society).

MacKay, MM (ed) 1980 *The Rev. Dr. John Walker's Report on the Hebrides of 1764 and 1771*. Edinburgh.

MacLeod, A (ed) 1978 *The Songs of Duncan Ban Macintyre*. Edinburgh (Scottish Gaelic Texts Society).

Matheson, W (ed) 1938 *The Songs of John MacCodrum*. Edinburgh (Scottish Gaelic Texts Society).

Pamphlets

A Highlander *The Present Conduct of the Chieftains and Proprietors of Lands in the Highlands of Scotland towards their clans and people, considered impartially* (London, 1773)

Murray, Sir Alexander of Stanhope 1740 *Letter and Remonstrance*. London.

[Thom, W.] 1776 *A Candid Enquiry into the Causes of the Late & Intended Migrations from Scotland in a letter to J – R – esq. Lanarkshire*. Glasgow.

Campbell, George, 8th Duke of Argyll 1886 'On the Economic Condition of the Highlands of Scotland', *Journal of the Statistical Society of London* (December 1886), 503–34.

Social Class

———————————————— *W Hamish Fraser*

INTRODUCTION

This chapter examines aspects of class in Scotland during a period of considerable
social change. It looks at definitions of class and the close relationship between class
and politics during the period 1700–1850. The topic is approached under the
following headings:

- The debate on class formation
- Approaches to class in the eighteenth century
- A ruling class?
- The emergence of a middle class
- Middle-class politics
- The making of a working class
- Politics and class
- Owenite Socialism and Chartism
- Conclusion

By the time you have worked your way through the chapter you should be able
to appreciate some of the ways in which class has been defined and to
understand the debates surrounding the concept of class. You should also have
gained an insight into changing class and power relationships in Scotland before
1850.

I. THE DEBATE ON CLASS FORMATION

It is probably true to say that no issues of social theory and social science have
produced as much controversial debate as the analysis of social class. Class was
central to the interpretations of British social history put forward by the many
Marxist-influenced historians whose writings shaped social history from the 1940s
until the 1980s. But even non-Marxists incorporated much of this thinking into their
own analysis of social change. While many of what were widely held ideas are now
under sustained intellectual attack, nonetheless there is a great deal of life remaining
in the debate and we will focus here on some of the issues which have been raised. A
useful introduction can be found in the material of the OU Social Science second
level course D.207 *An Introduction to Sociology*, Block 2, Study Section 16, *Class
and Politics in Marxist Theory* (OU 1981). The challenge to the Marxist position
can best be followed in Joyce's *Class* (1995).

At one level, there is the question of *class structure*. If human society is to be grouped in some way, what is the best way of doing it? How many social groups are required for a useful understanding of how society operates? Was society becoming more fragmented or more homogeneous as a result of the economic and social changes taking place? Some of that debate can be found in Neale's *History and Class. Essential Readings in Theory and Interpretation* (1983). In your reading you will come across terms such as 'the propertied classes', 'the merchant class', the 'professional class', the 'skilled working class', all of which imply that something other than a three-fold division of classes is necessary. But arguments about structure have become entwined with debates on *class formation*. To Marxists, the relationship which people have to the means of production decides which class they are in, but also shapes how they will act in certain circumstances. This, in capitalist societies, will ultimately lead to a two-fold division between those who control the means of production and those who do not; between property-holders and the propertyless; between employers of labour and the sellers of labour power. Increasingly, the latter will be an industrial proletariat exploited by the capitalists.

But this experience will in turn produce a struggle between the exploiters and the exploited which will create a sense of class, a consciousness of being in a class that is in conflict with another class: what Marx called a class-*for*-itself as opposed to a class-*in*-itself. The consciousness of being a class-*for*-itself meant being aware of the historical role which a class would play in transforming society, because Marx believed that it was the antagonism inherent in relationships between classes which brought change in society. A capitalist society emerged when the bourgeoisie became conscious of their historic mission to challenge feudal structures. But, in turn, the class consciousness created among workers by the struggles within capitalism would become a revolutionary consciousness which would lead to the overthrow of capitalism.

The timescale of these developments was always vague in Marxist writings since there would inevitably be resistance by the class in power, by means of political manipulation, through ideological propaganda and, if necessary, by physical force. Not all members of a class would immediately recognise their real interests. But, in Marxist thinking, the process could not be permanently halted: there *had* to be progression towards a socialist society and a great deal of historical writing over the past half-century and more has lain in tracking that process. Much social history has been about looking for the first signs of, and then tracing the development of, class consciousness, explaining the barriers to its growth and analysing why the proletarian revolution failed to occur.

By far the most influential historian examining the social development of an industrial society has been EP Thompson. In his path-breaking *Making of the English Working Class* (1963), from which, by the way, he specifically excluded Scotland: 'It is possible, at least until the 1820s, to regard English and Scottish experiences as distinct.' (*ibid*, 13), Thompson argued that between roughly 1780 and 1830 there emerged a working class, conscious of itself as a class. It was partly shaped by the process of industrialisation, as the skilled craft workers, the weavers, tailors, shoemakers, the pre-mechanisation artisans, were increasingly proletarianised. But the very experience of this process and the battles to resist it helped create a sense of being a class. 'Class formations', he wrote, 'arise at the intersection of determination and self activity: the working class "made itself as much as it was made"' (Thompson 1978a). And elsewhere:

> To put it bluntly: classes do not exist as separate entities, look around, find a class entity and then start to struggle. On the contrary, people find themselves in a society structured in a determined way (crucially, but not exclusively, in productive relations), they experience exploitation (or the need to maintain power over those whom they exploit), they identify points of antagonistic interest, they commence to struggle around those issues and in the process of struggling they discover themselves as classes, they come to know this discovery as class consciousness.
>
> (Thompson 1978b)

Thompson did not see class just emerging in the workplace, important as relationships at the point of production were. He added a cultural dimension to economic factors, showing how working people, in trying to cope with social change and resist its devastating effects on their lives, drew on the traditions and values of their own communities. Finally, there was the impact of political action which could pull together and give coherence to the experience of work and community.

To Thompson and others, the evidence of the emergence of a working class was in the protest movements which appeared in the early nineteenth century, which used the language of class, which organised on a class basis and which were prepared to consider revolutionary tactics. It was most clearly apparent, it was argued, in the Owenite-inspired trade unionism and, even more so, in the Chartism of the 1830s and 1840s.

The difficulty was then to explain why this revolutionary fervour did not persist and why a socialist revolution failed to occur. Various arguments have been deployed. Some emphasise divisions within the working class between artisan and factory-based worker, between skilled and unskilled. Yet others, influenced by the writings of Gramsci, have focused upon how difficult it was for workers to escape from an all-pervasive middle-class cultural hegemony which intensified divisions among the workers, undermined traditional community values and made it difficult for the proletariat to perceive their true situation and to think in terms of class. It created a 'false consciousness' which delayed or misdirected the class struggle. Labour did not recognise where its 'real' interests lay and, without relative homogeneity, a working-class consciousness could not emerge (Foster 1974; Gray 1976).

There were, of course, many historians who did not accept the teleological assumptions of Marxist theory. Yet others rejected what Thompson, Foster and others saw as evidence of class consciousness and potential revolution. In a famous review of Thompson's book, Geoffrey Best asked, 'Where was the flag-saluting, foreigner-hating, drunken, wife-beating working man?' Yet others rejected any notion that economic position would determine political attitudes and emphasised the consistently limited economic concerns of workers' organisations. However, few did not succumb to the temptation of using the terms 'working class' and 'middle class', generally undefined and often fudged by using 'working *classes*' and 'middle *classes*'.

But the idea of some kind of linear development of class has been powerfully challenged in recent years from a number of different directions. Economic historians have pointed to the unevenness of economic development and, therefore, of the actual experience of industrialisation for different groups of workers. There was no sudden creation of a factory-based proletariat; old forms of production persisted well into the nineteenth century. Social historians have identified the persistent strength of divisions created by race, religion and gender. The most exciting recent work has taken a fresh look at the language of protest and called into question even further both the Marxist use of class terms and the casual use of them by non-Marxists. Such work – and it now proliferates in writings on class in England, although not, unfortunately in Scotland – sees class not as some objective reality but as a socio-linguistic construct, changing over time and depending on who is using the term. It argues for a much more subtle awareness of the contemporary meaning of the language used and of the changed meaning which terms such as 'class' had at different points in time. Stedman Jones (1983, 90–178), looking at the protest movements of the 1830s and 1840s, argued that language was the means by which the experience of individuals was ordered and understood, but, he noted, 'it is important to stress that more than one language is capable of articulating the same set of experiences'.

Finally, the challenge to Marxism has also encouraged more historians to turn their attention away from the working class to the middle class. Again there is a debate on the timing of the emergence of this class. Harold Perkin (1969) believed that it emerged very quickly in the period after the end of the Napoleonic Wars. Others concentrate on the new political awareness of the 1830s and 1840s. But a great deal of recent work, particularly that concerned with the growth of consumerism, has pushed aspects of middle-class formation back into the eighteenth century (Thompson 1996). In this area too some of the most important work has stressed the importance of noting the changing meaning of language. Wahrman (1995) shows how the term 'middle class' increasingly came into common parlance, but how the meaning of that term changed radically under different political circumstances.

EXERCISE I

What different terms does Smout use in *A History of the Scottish People* (Chapters 12, 13, 15 and 19) to describe social structure?

What major economic changes taking place in eighteenth-century Scotland were affecting class structure?

How many classes do *you* consider necessary to describe the social structure at the beginning of the nineteenth century?

I have been able to identify at least twelve different uses of the term 'class' or 'classes' and many other terms describing the social position of groups.

The major economic changes included agricultural improvement, industrialisation, and major transport and commercial developments, all of which had a significant effect on social relationships. Consider whether a three-fold division into landed class, middle class and working class seems adequate or whether it would be more meaningful to talk in terms of a five-fold division with an upper and lower middle class and a skilled and unskilled working class. Perhaps you think that even further sub-division is necessary.

2. APPROACHES TO CLASS IN THE EIGHTEENTH CENTURY

Surprisingly little work has been published on social class in Scotland compared with the huge literature available for England. One says 'surprisingly', because the structure of society was one of the central concerns of the writers of the Scottish Enlightenment and many of the ideas about the development of classes which found their ways into modern thinking had their roots in the writings of Adam Ferguson, David Hume, John Millar and Adam Smith among others in eighteenth-century Scotland. All of them were trying to explain the processes of change in human society in a way which played down the role of divine intervention. They believed in the possibility of economic, social and intellectual progress and were trying to understand the levers which made such progress possible.

These eighteenth-century writers paid much attention to the social divisions in society. Both Ferguson and John Millar wrote of the alienating effect of industrial change, turning 'the labouring people, who form the great body of the nation . . . into the mere instrument of labour . . . like machines, actuated by a regular weight, and performing certain movements with great celerity and exactness, but of small compass and unfitted for any other use' (quoted in Camic 1983, 79). Millar's first major work was *The Origin of the Distinction of Ranks: or, An Inquiry into the Circumstances which Give rise to the Influence and Authority in the Different Members of Society* (1779). Millar and his compatriots rarely used the term 'class'. They spoke of rank and station, 'the middling ranks', 'the labouring poor', the 'superior ranks', 'people of middling fortune', or of 'interests', the 'landed interest', 'the manufacturing interest', but one can detect the beginnings of a class analysis. David Hume, who wrote an essay 'Of the Middle Station in Life', identified 'the middling rank of men' as the products of the expansion of commerce and industry, which brought 'authority and consideration to that middling rank of men, who are the best and firmest basis of public liberty' (Wahrman 1995, 63). In other words, implicit in such a statement was the view that social groups were a product of economic circumstances and would act in a particular way because of that. John Millar's biographer notes:

> Ranks and classes are, of course, even for Millar not completely interchangeable terms. They both clearly have status implications, but "classes" and class distinction begin to have, for Millar already, some what of an oppositional, and exploited-exploiting, an invidious character not always inherent in "ranks" as such.
>
> (Lehman 1960, 139)

Millar's writings increasingly pointed towards a division of society into three, landlords, capitalists and labourers, and tending towards two, owners and wage earners. He noted a rising business class, 'the superior orders of mercantile people . . . quick sighted in discerning their common interests, and, at all times, indefatigable in pursuing it' (quoted in Lehman 1960, 339). Adam Smith too, as has increasingly been recognised, was not some crude, free-market ideologue and, as **Document 51** indicates, he had grave reservations as to the direction of social change.

EXERCISE 2
Read **Document 51**. What does Smith have to say about social class as he saw it?

Briefly, he emphasises the social inequalities which must inevitably arise in a commercial society and the impact that was likely to have on social relationships generally.

Although aware of the implications of economic change, none of these Scottish writers was an advocate of great social change. They were deeply suspicious of the corrupting dangers of a commercial society and their ideal society was still firmly based on a traditional rural order. They were also operating in a society where a powerful Calvinist outlook still prevailed, which regarded ranks as sanctioned by the decrees of divine Providence.

3. A RULING CLASS?

Nenadic (1988, 118) has declared that 'In 1760 there was no tangible sense of class in Scotland. As in England, society was hierarchical and layered, the layers linked by economic interests and regional loyalties and the pervasive system of paternalism and patronage'. Historians have had some difficulty in agreeing how best to describe social relationships before the period of most rapid industrialisation. Was it 'classless' despite the great differences in wealth and status, because people did not think in class terms? Conflicts within society were between country and town, between tradesman and merchant, between interests not between classes, vertical antagonisms not horizontal ones. Yet others have talked of a 'one class society', arguing that only the aristocracy had the awareness and ideology to exercise class power. (For a discussion of these interpretations, see Morris 1979, 12–20). With both of these interpretations one has the problem of explaining the social conflicts which do appear in the eighteenth century. Were these examples of 'latent' class conflict? Thompson, in tackling this issue, has argued that it is possible to have class struggles even if classes in a nineteenth-century sense do not exist. He and others have used the term 'plebeian' to cover a whole range of the 'lower orders' from casual labourers through to small craftsmen, shopkeepers and publicans, alongside a ruling class of gentry and wealthy bourgeoisie. He writes of gentry and plebeians or gentry and crowd bound together in a reciprocal relationship. In return for deference and order, in a society with limited means of maintaining order, the gentry had to engage in a considerable degree of paternalism. Failure to do this could result in crowd actions not intended to be revolutionary, but definitely intended to remind the gentry of their obligations. It is the increasing abandonment of this sense of a reciprocal relationship on the part of the ruling gentry that begins to transform social relationships more sharply into class ones.

In looking at eighteenth-century Scotland it is difficult not to be aware of a powerful sense of identity existing within the ranks of the Scottish gentry. This Scottish landed class, below the level of the great aristocrats who, after 1707, largely directed their activities to London, showed many of the attributes of a class, conscious of itself as a class. They devised a political system to protect their political power and their economic interests. Providing something like 85% of the advocates and all the judges, the Scottish landowning class used the legal system to extend the privileges and rights of their class against the great nobility and against outsiders (Mitchison 1978, 83–5; Stein 1970, 148–66). The Scottish gentry had a clear aim 'to maintain its traditional dominance of Scottish society and to control the direction of change within that society' (Dwyer and Murdoch 1982, 211–20). To achieve that goal they were quite prepared to tap into the commercial opportunities provided in the expanding economy, with new capitalist approaches to estate management in both Highlands and Lowlands replacing traditional ties of kinship and patronage. As Smout (1966, 218–34) has shown, landowners were a driving force behind Scottish industrialisation. They were also quite prepared to assimilate the occasional wealthy newcomer into their ranks. At least some new mercantile wealth generally found its way into landed estates. Devine (1995, 29–32) has documented the transformation of tobacco and sugar money into land in the West of Scotland: by the 1780s the Glasgow merchant, Alexander Spiers, was the largest landowner in Renfrewshire. But, at the same time, there was a concern to keep most of the middle ranks at a little distance, and the laws of entail, another effective protection measure by the landed class, ensured that there were only a few estates coming on the market and that the new money increasingly stayed in the towns. It is there that a middle class began, ever so slowly, to be identified and not one necessarily driven by a desire to emulate the higher ranks. Smout (1969, 234) noted:

> The eighteenth century landowners strove side by side with the middle classes to develop a new kind of dynamic economy, as they believed to their mutual

advantage – and when they succeeded, it became a Frankenstein to rend off their limbs of privilege and leadership.

The concern with class among the writers of the Scottish Enlightenment reflected the concern with challenges to the landed class with which the *literati* generally saw themselves as being associated. By the 1780s their literary skills were being used to ridicule as 'mushrooms' the new monied interests which were threatening to challenge the hegemony of the old order (Dwyer and Murdoch 1982, 226–39).

EXERCISE 3
How do you think the gentry in Scotland maintained their dominance in the eighteenth century?

In no particular order of importance you might cite: their role as heritors; their control of the legal system; their powers of patronage; and their recognition of the importance of new economic opportunities.

No. 22. Watercolour by Walter Severn (1869) of the dining room at Newhailes, Musselburgh. The dining room for entertaining guests became a focus of middle-class culture in the late eighteenth and early nineteenth centuries. *Crown copyright: RCAHMS/Private collection.*

4. THE EMERGENCE OF A MIDDLE CLASS

The difficulty in defining the parameters of the middle class is well recognised. As Smout (1969, 362) noted, 'A lawyer like Duncan Forbes or Lord Milton, who moved easily in the circles of dukes, had nothing in common with a master tailor in Dundee, whose apprentice lived in his own household: neither of them had much in common with a dancing master in Montrose, trying to polish the manners and steps of provincial youth. Perhaps it was this variety that inhibited the emergence of any commonly accepted expression to denote what we now mean by the middle class'. However, more recent work on both Edinburgh and Glasgow has begun to focus on ways in which those in the middle ranks were beginning, by the middle decades of the eighteenth century, to develop a culture which was separate from that of the landed élite. The work of Nenadic (1988, 109–26; 1994, 122–56; 1995, 278–311) and Houston (1994, 147–233) has convincingly argued that certain styles of life and patterns of consumption were gradually differentiating a middle class from those above and below and steadily helping create a class identity.

The clearest evidence of a new consumerism and of sharper social divisions was in the development (from the last decade of the century) of new housing patterns, most conspicuously in the Edinburgh New Town, but Glasgow, Aberdeen and elsewhere all had their pale imitations of Craig's Edinburgh masterpiece. Residential segregation strengthened a sense of class identity. Youngson (1966) argued that the new town destroyed a previous 'unity of social feeling' in Edinburgh, but Houston's argument is that it merely 'marked the physical recognition of social differences which already existed' and which had begun 'quarter of a century or more before its first stones were laid' (Houston 1994, 12, 75). Within the new houses, new patterns of consumption developed which were not necessarily based on emulation of the higher ranks, but reflected new, distinctively middle-rank patterns. Nenadic (1994, 122–56) has written of the significance of domestic hospitality helping create 'group cohesion' among the new business wealth of Glasgow and Edinburgh by the end of the eighteenth century.

The growing numbers in the ranks of the bourgeoisie in all the growing Scottish towns gave confidence, and a flourishing of clubs and societies further helped meld a cultural identity. This identity had powerful local aspects, but it is possible to argue that the well-known concern in the late eighteenth century with anglicising speech among the middle ranks reflected concerns that went beyond the local. Morris (1983, 104, 110) points out that the spread of voluntary societies from the end of the eighteenth century played a crucial role in enabling 'the middle classes to move towards the creation of a consciousness and cohesion amongst themselves and become a middle class'. They created 'networks of people of similar social positions and outlooks in different towns, breaking down community loyalties and politics and replacing them with national, class ones'.

Just as a sense of identity among the gentry was created by the perceived challenge from the 'mushrooms' below, so the middle ranks became concerned to distinguish themselves from the less well-off and became ever more anxious about the threat from the poorest. These anxieties are reflected in a variety of ways. There are signs of sharpening divisions between masters and men in the workplace. Social segregation was increasingly the norm in the public houses and the masonic lodges and there was growing concern about how to 'control' the 'labouring poor'. In the ever more crowded and increasingly 'threatening' cities, street demonstration and even riot – once something which could include a wide range of ranks and a familiar mechanism for warning those in power – seemed too much a potential threat to property (see below for more on this). When the threat of disorder from below seemed greater than the threat of tyranny from above is not entirely agreed. According to Houston (1994, 329–30; 382), by the 1740s riot in Edinburgh had 'become an expression of social divisions rather than a sign of general consensus within urban life'. Others would push the process rather later in the century (Fraser 1988, 272–80; Logue 1979, 128–54). Certainly by the 1780s, in Glasgow, popular street disturbances were leading to demands from the propertied for effective policing, but they came up only with Sunday schools (Brown 1987, 131) and it took another decade and more before a police force came about (Maver 1995, 249–51). Increasingly groups of the middle ranks saw themselves as the rational products of an enlightened age and consciously structured their world in a different way from in the past. No longer was public mingling with the urban crowd so acceptable and middle-class political action, like middle-class life, became preoccupied with 'order', 'rationality' and 'discipline'. Protest became orderly and rational, through selective meeting, formal association and the printed page (Nenadic 1990, 65–82). It was a process which speeded up in the nineteenth century. Middle-class behaviour was being carefully differentiated from both the landed élite and the less well-off. It was the middle class, for example, which carefully separated the public and the private sphere, with women kept firmly in the latter, and there was a growing tendency to contrast the 'self-denial' of the middle-class man with the 'sensual indulgence' of the working class (Clark 1995, 221).

> EXERCISE 4
> Read the extract from Nenadic's writings (**Article 15**) and comment on the evidence she uses to support the case for an emerging middle-class identity by the early nineteenth century.

The main points of evidence would include patterns of dining and entertaining; style and position of housing.

5. MIDDLE-CLASS POLITICS

Crucial in Marxist theoretical concepts of class is the argument that economic interests and cultural developments (the relative weightings of the two remain controversial) will lead to political action. There are plenty of examples of protests from middle-rank groups when their economic interests were threatened by the landed-dominated legislature, against corn laws, against the window tax, against church patronage, but as Wahrman (1995) has shown, the idea of the middle class having a political role appeared only slowly and was regularly redefined in changing circumstances. What is often taken as the first sign of an awakening political awareness in Scotland came in 1782 with the Letters from 'Zeno' in Edinburgh's *Caledonian Mercury* calling for an end to the election of burgh MPs by unelected town councils. Written by a wealthy merchant, Thomas McGrugar, these were moderate enough in their tone, but not lacking a class perspective:

> To admit the dregs of the populace to a share in government would be both imprudent and improper. They are disqualified by a natural ignorance and hebetude, which render them unfit to be their *own* directors and, therefore, they must be directed by *others*. In all governments, these must be subjugated by laws enacted for them by others, because they are incapable of giving consent. But men in the middle ranks of life, who generally constitute the majority of every free community, cannot be excluded from a voice in the appointment of their representatives, because this would deny them the right to self-government, for which they are qualified by their knowledge and extent of property, which must give them a weight in every free state, and a title to share in the legislation. To withhold from these, therefore, the exercise of this right, must be a deviation from the principle of the British constitution.
>
> (*Caledonian Mercury*, 28 December 1782)

Note that the claim was not just based on property, but on middle-rank 'knowledge' compared with that of the ignorant.

An even more confident view that 'the middle rank' was where 'almost all the sense and virtue of society reside' (to quote Sir James Mackintosh's *Vindiciae Gallicae* of 1791, penned in response to Burke's attack on the French Revolution) came out in many of the political writings of the early 1790s. But, as Wahrman (1995, 31–73) shows, there was often an ambivalence between the idea of the middle class as creators of the revolution as a step towards a more rational and orderly world, and the middle class as *in the middle* offering stability and order between the extremes of aristocratic rule and mob rule.

Contrary to what is often suggested (for example by Young 1979), the Whigs in Edinburgh through their journal, *The Edinburgh Review*, launched in 1802, did not see themselves as spokesmen for the new middle class. They were certainly calling for reform of the political system, but that traditional Edinburgh link between gentry and the Edinburgh legal profession remained strong and, through until the 1820s, they operated as a relatively unified élite. The debates were about political power and influence and about the most effective ways of maintaining the existing structures – by repressive measures against any who challenged them or by minor concessions to remove the discontents. There was never any question of overturning the social order. The Whig intellectuals saw themselves as doing little more than correcting the excesses of the natural élite by some minor modification of the system.

No more than their predecessors among the Edinburgh *literati*, they were not about transferring power from one class to another.

It was not until after the bitter social unrest of the post-war years, and particularly after Peterloo in 1819 and the Radical uprising of 1820, that the Whig reviewers seriously began to pin their hopes on the middle classes as the vehicle for social progress, but also as the necessary ally of the gentry against disorder. To the landed élite the middle classes seemed safe and their anti-radical stance showed a commitment to political stability. Mackintosh, in 1818, saw a middle-class franchise as an alternative to universal suffrage. Never had the 'middling classes' been 'so respectable and improving' (Chitnis 1986, 113). At the meeting at Edinburgh's Pantheon calling for the dismissal of Liverpool's Government and the summoning of Parliament, Francis Jeffrey, editor of the *Edinburgh Review*, talked of a cleavage between the upper and middle ranks as 'the great radical evil' of the time: 'It is to fill up this chasm, to occupy the middle ground, and to show how a large proportion of the people are attracted to the constitution, while they lament its abuses, that such meetings as this should be assembled'. His associate, Henry Brougham, in 1822 was telling readers of the *Review*, 'The time is approaching, if it has not arrived, when a considerable number of the middle classes must be admitted within the walls of the Legislature' (Wahrman 1995, 255).

By the time the Reform Act of 1832 was passed few had doubts about the existence of a middle class, but it is a measure of the relative weakness of its political presence that in the discussion on the Scottish Reform Bill, dominated, of course, by the Edinburgh Whigs, unlike in the debates on English reform, there was little said about the merits of the middle class, and TB Macaulay was very much speaking from an Edinburgh Whig perspective when he declared, 'Reform so that you may preserve'. The Scottish Act did not open the door to middle-class political power: it affirmed gentry control of Scottish politics. The middle class still had some way to go before it had fully matured politically.

Part of the difficulty was that the middle class continued to be far from homogeneous and there were many 'fractions' within it. Many of the larger towns had long been run by a wealthy élite in collaboration with the gentry of the county (Donnelly 1981, 30). But there were signs by the early nineteenth century of an urban middle class, dependent on business and with few rural links, beginning to challenge the dominance of the old merchant/landed élite, and of a growing dichotomy between the urban and the rural. In a number of towns after 1815 there were renewed demands from business and professional people for the opening up of local government to popular election. Often these criticisms of the old élites might come initially from within the élite group, but, as **Document 52** shows, in using popular pressure and the argument of public opinion, those pushing for reform succeeded in generating a wider political awareness. There were also growing economic grievances against aristocratic government, arising from levels of taxation and which became focused upon the Corn Laws. The agitation for repeal of these laws, gathering pace in the 1830s, increasingly adopted the language of class: an effete and idle aristocracy using political power to protect themselves, defending their privileges at the expense

of the industrious sections of society. It is, however, perhaps further evidence of the
relative weakness of middle-class identity within Scotland that, although the anti-
Corn Law campaign was launched there, it could not be sustained in the 1830s and
the initiative passed to Manchester (Cameron 1979, 70–91).

These divisions *within* the middle class also powerfully revealed themselves in
the struggles within Presbyterianism. The Church had long been a focal point of
social tensions, and some of the schisms of the eighteenth century clearly had social
aspects to them. There was resentment at gentry patronage or at assertions of social
distinction within church buildings. Many of the upwardly mobile of the middling
ranks identified with the dissenting Secession and Relief Churches, rather than with
the Established, ending up eventually in the United Presbyterians. Or they identified
with the evangelical rather than moderate congregations of the Church of Scotland
(Brown 1987, 30–38). Grievances against assessments to maintain Established
churches and continuing irritation over patronage further heightened political
awareness. Significantly, it was in 1833, the year after the Reform Act, that, for
the first time, the evangelicals achieved a majority in the General Assembly.
MacLaren's important studies of the Disruption years in Aberdeen (MacLaren
1974; 1983) show the process coming to fruition ten years later with the newer
urban middle class rebelling against the domination of the old landed/merchant
establishment and forming their own Free Church.

MacLaren is also one of the few historians of Scotland to consider the changes in
the professions. According to him, ministers, lawyers and doctors in the early
nineteenth century shook free from the constraints of patronage and developed a
professional identity which embedded them within the developing middle class
(MacLaren, 1989). As many historians have argued, it was this professional
grouping who contributed much to the distinctive voice of the middle classes as
the nineteenth century progressed.

The picture emerges of a politically divided middle class in the towns, but, none
the less, one that was gradually developing a distinct cultural identity. There was
limited space on the Scottish scene for political manoeuvring by the middle ranks
before 1832, but after that time economic grievances pushed them into political
activity, and in local government and in church government they ousted the old
order.

EXERCISE 5
Reflecting on the foregoing discussion, what institutions do you think helped
create a middle-class identity in towns during the early nineteenth century? As
well as the church, you should consider voluntary societies, patterns of residence
and political concerns.

Read **Article 16** by MacLaren. Why did religion became a focus for social
tensions?

MacLaren makes clear the immense power which kirk sessions had over poor relief,
education and over the lives of individuals. Influence on such bodies was important

since the secular and the religious roles of an elder were closely interwined. The newer 'fraction' of the middle class used the forum of kirk sessions among other things to challenge the older élite.

6. THE MAKING OF A WORKING CLASS

Smout (1969, 448) concludes that the industrial labour force was not really a 'working class' in our modern sense of the term, nor were the 'labouring classes' united in a 'class war' against their employers. But in contrast, Young (1979, 81) boldly asserts of the same period: 'Far from the peaceful, law abiding, docile working class portrayed by most historians, the Scottish working class was already the most militant, class conscious and politically aware working class in Europe'. In other words, looking at the same period and at much the same evidence, two dramatically conflicting conclusions are possible.

Eighteenth-century Scotland was certainly not lacking in incidents of social disorder. Indeed, the evidence of these incidents steadily increases. Richards (1973, 35–50) challenged the view that the Highlanders docilely accepted clearances and documented many different kinds of protest in resistance to the commercialisation of Highland estates. Whatley (1992, 170–88) has added considerably to Logue's earlier accounts of popular disturbances in the Lowlands, making use of the concept of a plebeian culture ritually challenging the dominant position of the ruling class. Such studies suggest parallels with Thompson's eighteenth-century England of class struggle before class. A sense of injustice, a sense that past rights were being removed and customary patterns were being altered, could produce explosions of protest from a broad plebeian grouping against all kinds of figures of authority, landowners, excisemen, the military, the press gang, intended to provide forceful reminders of paternalist responsibilities. Many such protests were sporadic and rarely co-ordinated between communities. Nevertheless, in the language of the protesters it is possible to catch a sense of a world view which was increasingly at odds with that of improvers and could, in the Highlands, for example, take a religious form (Hunter 1974; Bruce 1983, 554–72). Meal mobs also fundamentally challenged the assumptions of capitalist farming about the nature of the grain market (Lythe 1967, 26–36). Thompson (1991, 185–258) wrote of a persisting belief in a 'moral economy' as opposed to a market economy. But Houston (1994, 329–31) detects changes in the patterns of Edinburgh crowd behaviour from the mid eighteenth century which point to a more sectional pursuit of interests by specific social groups.

Similar tensions were apparent in the workplace, between worker and employer or master and servant as the social relationship was almost always defined. There is no doubt about the extent of the changes affecting both tradesmen and the 'labouring poor'. Massive and multifaceted changes took place in the organisation of production, conditions of work and community structures at a rate very much faster than anything experienced in England. Changes which had taken a century or more in England were squeezed into a few decades in Scotland. Dickson and Spiers'

No. 23. Portrait of Francis Jeffrey, by Colvin Smith. Jeffrey's *Edinburgh Review* pressed for the middle classes to be admitted to the franchise. © *Scottish National Portrait Gallery*.

1980 article illustrates the impact of some of the developments. It would have been astonishing if they had not involved fundamental changes in how workers viewed the world, in the institutions that developed to cope with the changes and in the language used to comprehend them.

There was nothing new in industrial disputes over attempts to alter working conditions and even to push up earnings (Fraser 1988) but there was little evidence in the early decades of the century of struggling against the system. Apprentices and journeymen saw themselves as part of a customary hierarchy which could reasonably be expected to lead them in time to being independent masters. Disputes were generally over particular masters breaking from customary patterns and there was a common concern by masters and journeymen to protect the craft from outsiders. This craft exclusiveness, organised round the trade incorporations, was seen by others as something which needed to be controlled and regulated for the protection of the wider community.

The transformation from craft identity to employer/worker identity is one that speeded up in the late eighteenth century. In the *Statistical Account of Edinburgh* the bookseller, William Creech, outlining some of the many changes he had seen in a twenty-year period, noted that in 1783, compared with twenty years before, few masters now took apprentices into their own home or interested themselves in the personal life of the apprentice; 'If they attended hours of business, masters took no further charge' and the training of them was left to the journeymen. Older patterns of masters providing daily food and drink, and even shoes and clothing, on a regular basis gave way to a relationship based only on cash payments. While there were many small working employers, some were consciously trying to distance themselves from their workers. Edinburgh journeymen tailors were complaining in the 1760s that 'Master Taylors sett up to live like gentlemen and to prey upon poor journeymen and enhance their own profits'. Masons complained of wage rates being fixed by masters with no consultation, and 'the journeymen masons are resolved one and all, to show the world that they are free men and not bond slaves' (Fraser 1988, 50).

Industrial conflict does not, any more than meal riots or the stoning of excisemen, in itself indicate the emergence of a working class. Many of the strikes were against individual employers and confined to particular crafts. Also trade unions are always problematic in discussions of class formation since much of their activity is devoted to controlling the labour supply, to protecting one group of workers, usually skilled craftsmen, against those outside the craft, against 'incomers' from country into town and increasingly in this period against women workers, and emphasising the separation of trades. A more fundamental shift was required. To quote one study of working-class formation in Europe, what changed in the early nineteenth century was that 'Working people, for the first time, altered their vocabularies and world views to speak and think of themselves as workers, rather than just as members of this or that trade' (Katznelson and Zolberg 1986, 23). From at least the 1790s there are signs of a tendency to look beyond both the immediate community and the immediate trade. Edinburgh shoemakers in 1798 gave cash aid to striking shoemakers in Hull and in Glasgow. But they also got help from journeymen in other crafts, curriers, hatters, combmakers and tailors. The following year, weavers in Glasgow discussed with colliers the implications of possible state wage regulation (Whatley, 1995; Fraser 1988, 71). By 1811 the prospect of anti-union legislation was bringing about meetings of delegates of different trades to resist a measure which 'would rivet the chains of slavery on the necks of all who earn their bread, under the employment of another; thus dividing the population of the country into two classes, the one tyrants and the other slaves'. By the late 1820s such committees in both Glasgow and Edinburgh had a near-permanent existence (Fraser 1988, 89, 128–9). As elsewhere in Europe, 'The vertical linkage of master and workers weakened and the horizontal ties joining workers together regardless of trade strengthened' (Katznelson and Zolberg 1986, 25). According to this argument trade unions helped transform a 'latent' class identity into class institutions, overcoming sectionalism.

The post-1815 economic difficulties both in town and country intensified this process. Alexander Richmond, the notorious police informer, noted in his *Narrative of the Condition of the Manufacturing Population* (1824):

> Rank, and everything previously held sacred and venerable, was laughed at to scorn; the minds of the people were completely inflamed; a line of demarcation was drawn between the different ranks of society, and rooted antipathy and a ferocious spirit of retaliation was engendered in the minds of the labouring classes.

EXERCISE 6

Rev Thomas Chalmers was called to the Tron Kirk in Glasgow in 1817 from the relative social tranquillity of rural Fife. He was immediately shocked by what he saw and the dangers inherent in the city. Read **Document 23b** and comment on his explanation of the differences between Edinburgh and Glasgow. What does James Hogg in **Document 53** have to say about the position in the countryside?

Briefly, in the former, workers supplied the immediate needs of the better-off, while, in manufacturing towns, the relationship is that of capitalist and labourer and mutually hostile. Hogg gives a strong endorsement to the view that agricultural changes were exacerbating social divisions.

The term 'working classes' was coming into use (Donnelly 1976, 29); by the end of the 1820s it was well-established. The Glasgow trade societies issued their own newspapers aimed at the working class and with shares 'to be held by the working classes particularly'. Edinburgh trade societies soon followed with a *Trades Monthly Journal*, which, it was claimed, reviled 'the masters and the higher classes' (note the linking of the two) 'as oppressors and tyrants'. On the industrial side, there would appear to be support for Young's assertion that a class-conscious working class was in existence (see also Clarke and Dickson 1988). In 1837–8 the state had to intervene to break the power of the cotton spinners, organised in the most powerful trade union (Fraser 1988, 151–70).

7. POLITICS AND CLASS

So far no account has been taken of political movements and of the development of political consciousness among the working class. There is a tendency in some writing to elide words like 'radical', 'popular', 'plebeian', 'democratic' too readily into 'working class' and similarly to assume that 'ruling class' and 'employers' are one. There is also a temptation to assume that the handfuls who got involved in underground political activity were somehow representative of a wider, but silent, majority. There may, however, be some support for such a view. The father of Edinburgh's future Lord Provost and MP, Adam Black, a stonemason, in the 1790s was, according to his biographer, 'entirely in sympathy with the Friends of the People; but, with characteristic Scottish caution, he did not join any of their associations, having no desire to be set down as a "dangerous" or "auspicious" person by "the watch" of the city'. But an organisation like 'The Friends of the People in Scotland' was in no sense a working-class movement. It was 'to give security to *property* against fraudulent pretences of those whom caprice, interest, or ambition might instigate to swindle it from them'. It was 'to *reform* and not to *subvert* the order of society'. Some of the less well-off were undoubtedly roused by the developments. There were warnings from across the country of stirrings among 'the lower class of people', 'enemies to subordination', 'hoping to bring about a division of landed property'. But such statements tended to come from fearful country gentlemen who regarded anyone who disturbed social tranquillity as a potential revolutionary.

The difficulty is in deciding when, or, indeed, whether, political protest movements can in fact be identified as class movements. They were rarely, if ever, confined to workers. They tended, like most revolutionary movements, to be led by social misfits. Their attacks were not on employers or capitalists, but on what was regarded as a corrupt government. References to 'the people' did not refer to workers, but to all those who were not corrupted by government. Thomas Muir, an advocate, or Thomas Fyshe Palmer, an Etonian, Unitarian clergyman, can scarcely be regarded as typical representatives of any class, least of all the working class. The authorities had some truth on their side when they saw 'emissaries of sedition' as playing a part in stirring unrest. But, as McFarland (1994, 162) argues, ideas become dangerous when they become 'practically adequate' and 'both credible and coherent with the actual experience of the intended audience'. She and others would argue that there were moments in the 1790s and again post-war when the calls for change chimed with workers' economic grievances. John Brims writes of 'a new-found confidence' among those he calls the *menu peuple* – the small masters, shopkeepers, less than prosperous professional men, skilled tradesmen - in their demands for parliamentary reform in 1792 linked with a 'levelling spirit' which terrified the better-off, and which tore apart the wider alliance in favour of reform (Brims 1990, 41). Some contemporary observers certainly saw the events of these years as creating new class divisions. George Home of Wedderburn, writing in 1792, talked of the 'middle class' becoming aware 'that any Convulsion must produce unavoidable ruin to them, and are now doing everything in their power to restrain that Spirit of Sedition they have raised' (quoted in Brims 1990, 40). It may be that the extent of the social danger in movements like the United Scotsmen has been underplayed, and McFarland has certainly broadened our understanding of this movement. But many more flocked to the volunteers than to revolutionary movements and, as Dickinson (1989, 104) has shown, there was 'a very popular and pervasive belief that British liberties and British prosperity were the product of parliamentary monarchy, the rule of law and the prevailing social order'. Thomis and Holt (1977) were not convinced that the economic concerns of workers coincided with the political concerns of radical reformers.

Yet others, however, have been concerned to explain why there was so little protest given the extent of the social transformation which was taking place. It is too easy merely to put it down to the repression of the legal system and the intimidatory tactics of Lord Braxfield, although one should not underestimate how repressive Scottish society was in these years. But Devine (1990) has rightly emphasised the very different economic and social context of Scotland at the end of the eighteenth century from that of England and the lack of real challenge to the dominance of the gentry. Despite rising prices and occasional food shortages, standards of living were probably rising for most in Scotland. But, also, far from having firmly committed themselves to unrestrained capitalism, the dominant groups in Scotland quite consciously retained some of the paternalistic attitudes of an older society. The courts continued to intervene to regulate wages, the system of poor relief was used flexibly, the relationship between tenant and farmer, even in the Lothians, still involved the more personal payments in kind. It was when these 'older' attitudes began to disappear that social tensions mounted.

The most powerful moment was probably in the years between 1815 and 1820, when economic distress and rural and industrial dislocation coincided with, and helped strengthen, tensions. Much of the old paternalism had finally broken down: wage regulation had been swept away, the poor law began to be interpreted with a new harshness, the pace of commercialisation of farming was speeded up, apprenticeship was deprived of legal sanction (Fraser 1988, 100–13). Radical political language began to make sense in the context of economic discontent. The ruling order was also vulnerable because, as discussed above, this was precisely at the time when a new sense of 'middle class' was emerging. How widespread the support for the radical movements of 1816 to 1820 was is still not clear. Thomis and Holt (1977, 76) dismiss the so-called Radical War of April 1820 as 'the futile gestures of tiny minorities'; Young, and also Berresford Ellis and Mac A'Ghobhain in their book, *The Scottish Insurrection of 1820* (1970), see class, economic distress, revolutionary ideas and an anti-English nationalism, which had persisted within popular culture since 1707, coming together in the movement.

The activities around 1820 were class movements to the extent that they were largely peopled by workers, many of them displaced handloom weavers, a few also from the new cotton mills, spinners and millwrights. Thomas Chalmers, in a letter to William Wilberforce (**Document 54**), indeed believed that the most active were 'the

well-paid workmen of cotton-mills and other manufactures'. On the other hand, the
extent to which the participants were conscious of themselves as spokesmen for a
working class is more questionable if one looks at the political language which they
used. They still tapped into the discourse of eighteenth-century radicalism, present-
ing their demands as those of the 'people' demanding an end to 'old corruption', the
corruption of a basically sound constitution by a small group. If this group could be
ousted, then change could come about. Whether the work of *agents provocateurs* or
not, the language of the Proclamation of the 1820 rising is that of eighteenth-century
radicalism, where 'the interests of all Classes are the same' to resist 'Despotism', to
redress grievances, to return the constitution to its ancient purity.

> EXERCISE 7
> Read the Address of April 1820 (**Document 55**). What did the radicals see as the
> causes and cure of their grievances?
> Is there any evidence of this being a 'nationalist' document?

The main cause of grievance was identified as 'corruption' and the cure was the
restoration of the consitution. You might regard this as a nationalist statement
because of the references to country and 'native soil', but the ancient constitution
which it seeks to restore is a British one.

The direction that most recent writing on radicalism has taken us, influenced by
what has been called the 'linguistic turn', is not to see radicalism as a product of the
economic and social experience of workers, as evidence of a working-class
consciousness, but to see how the politically active used language to construct an
identity which sometimes was 'the people' and at other times was 'the working
classes'. Radicalism had to create as broad a constituency as possible and had to
form alliances between workers who had very different experiences of industrialisation, and petty bourgeois figures and even middle-class intellectuals. To do this they
used unifying imagery which had its roots in earlier protests, such as covenanting or
jacobitism or anti-unionism (Brims 1989, 50–59).

8. OWENITE SOCIALISM AND CHARTISM

Most of the political reform movement of 1831–32 was not so very different in tone
from early radical movements, although there was a conscious effort to eschew
violence. It is significant that it was during 1831 that there was a concerted effort to
blame the events of April 1820 on *agents provocateurs*. But there had been changes
in the intervening years. Industrial relations had become more bitter as further
changes in industrial organisation were pushed through, and as more experienced
the harshness of factory life. The process of residential division of social classes was
gaining pace, as those who could afford it were moving away from city centres to
avoid the smoke, smells and noise, but also to escape the poor. Trade unionism
revived and spread; collaboration between unions increased. But there were also
alternative ways of viewing and describing the position of the working class

available to the more able leaders. The ideas of Robert Owen, William Thompson and John Gray among others were beginning to gain an audience. Their focus was different from that of early radicalism. For them, the exploitation of workers lay not in the corruption of a fundamentally good system, but was implicit in the capitalist system – or the competitive system – as it was more commonly described, and until that was changed there could be no real change. The leading Scottish Owenite, a Glasgow joiner called Alexander Campbell, whose views can be read in **Documents 56 and 57**, had no doubt that in a capitalist system conflict between capital and labour was inevitable (Fraser 1996).

By no means everyone went along with such an interpretation. Sections of the trade unions firmly believed in collaboration with middle-class reformers. The Glasgow trades' newspaper, *The Herald to the Trades Advocate*, made clear that 'We prefer a gradual remodelling of the constitution to a violent and otherwise inevitable revolution'. The middle-class parliamentary reformers succeeded in identifying the 'enemy' as the 'aristocracy' or as merely a corrupt Tory clique. Despite people like Campbell who called for a Scottish Workers' Parliament 'to take the whole management of their affairs into their own hands', most politically active workers were prepared to follow the lead of the middle-class reformers. There was as yet no single industrial proletariat; old artisanal traditions still survived and, as Duncan (1981, 67) argues, many of the small tradesmen who were involved in the Chartist movement 'could not believe in the necessity or the desirability of a fundamental change in the ownership and distribution of property and veered to the defence of existing property relationships whenever a threat appeared to them from below'.

Most of the activists in the meeting of April 1838, which is usually taken as marking the beginning of the Scottish Chartist movement, were plebeian members of the earlier 1831 political union. Their critique was still very much one which identified the aristocratic Whigs as the barrier to reform. Although there were occasional utterances from Scottish Chartists which were critical of the middle class, the language of the editor of the *Scots Times* (10 July 1840) was much more typical:

> So long as oppressive laws and iniquitous monopolies were maintained by the
> Aristocracy, which equally affected the employer and the employed, it was
> evident that the competitive system would compel masters to do what in other
> circumstances they would not think of, and so long were the workmen not only
> justified, but bound to protect themselves in the best manner possible.

Such statements and the female perspective articulated in **Document 58** would appear to give powerful support to Gareth Stedman Jones's argument that Chartism needs to be understood as a *political* movement, to which a number of different social groups were attracted, rather than a predominantly *social* movement emanating from the economic concerns of the sections of the working classes (Stedman Jones, 1983, 90–175). But **Document 57** shows how social concerns were not far beneath the surface.

TO THE ELECTORS

AND

NON-ELECTORS

OF THE COUNTY OF

ROXBURGH.

GENTLEMEN,

I have been invited by a great many Reformers of your County, to present myself as a Candidate at your coming Election. Most cheerfully do I comply with your request. In doing so, I shall fearlessly advocate the rights of the people against those who from ignorance, prejudice, and pride oppose them. I shall assert the high claims of principle in opposition to expediency. I shall denounce the injustice, partiality, and tyranny of those who, whilst raising their voice against certain monopolies, are resolved to perpetuate the worst and blackest of them all--a monopoly of freedom and of power, in defiance of the just claims of all men to equal civil and political privileges. The following are some of the great objects I shall support :

I. ADULT MALE SUFFRAGE.

2. ANNUAL PARLIAMENTS, EQUAL REPRESENTATION, and the PAYMENT of MEMBERS.

3. A vast reduction in the expenditure of Government.

4. Direct Taxation only, exacted from Property by a graduated scale.

5. Free Trade in all things throughout the world.

6. Freedom to speak and write on all subjects, Civil, Political, and Religious.

7. Freedom of Religion to all Sects and Parties, giving state supremacy to none.

8. The Education of the whole people under the control of Parish Boards chosen by the Electors.

These, Gentlemen, are my principles, and they are those of a great many of yourselves. Need I say, then, that I shall rejoice to see you give them triumphant support in the face of their foes at the approaching ELECTION.

I am, Gentlemen, your obedient servant,

JOHN FRASER.

Edinburgh, July 2, 1841.

No. 24. Chartist election poster from Roxburgh. *Reproduced by kind permission of Scottish Borders Archive and Local History Centre, Selkirk.*

The striking feature of Chartism in Scotland is its relative weakness. As a mass movement it has very little life after 1842 and it markedly failed to develop a class critique. The inadequacies of the Scottish Reform Act, the absence of the Poor Law Amendment Act and the continuing focus on the church deprived the Scots of some of the key features which allowed Chartism to tap into class hostility in England. All the older works lay emphasis on the moderation of the Scottish movement (Wright 1953; Wilson 1970). The need to be aware of local variations to these generalisations is brought out in Clarke (1990, 106–21), but the picture of moderation has not been fundamentally challenged. There was a debate among Chartist activists about the rhetoric that was necessary to maximise support. Studies of Chartism in Aberdeen show this very clearly. There was, however, no fundamental division between 'physical force' and 'moral force' protagonists; the debate was over tactics. Similarly, groups who favoured collaboration with middle-class reformers existed side by side with groups who were ready to disrupt Anti-Corn Law League meetings (Duncan 1989, 78–91; a more strongly Marxist interpretation of the same movement is to be found in McCalman 1970, 5–24). The political analysis of Chartism made it very difficult to separate working-class from middle-class aspirations. On the other hand, there were many other aspects associated with the Chartist movement, which bear further study – the Chartist Churches, co-operation – which did reveal the deep cultural differences which already existed between working class and middle class.

EXERCISE 8

Read **Article 17** How does McCalman explain the moderation of Aberdeen Chartism?

Note how McCalman argues that political attitudes stem from experience of work and that this meant that the working class was divided. He also points out the dominance of middle-class ideology among the Chartist leaders with its focus on aristocracy and privilege as the cause of working-class distress.

9. CONCLUSION

Most of what has been said lends support to those who argue that there already existed a middle-class hegemony in the 1830s and 1840s from which it was increasingly difficult for the working class to escape. The pressure of education, church, press and publicity had succeeded in creating a cultural perception that there could be no real alternative to capitalism, that free trade would bring in its wake prosperity for all and that to resist it was wholly anachronistic. Trade unions who tried to control entry to the trade were denounced as a threat to that prosperity. This cultural hegemony made it difficult for those who argued an alternative scenario, such as Owenite Socialists and their successors, to be heard. If there were problems – and clearly in the 1840s there were – then the fault must lie, not with the system, but with those who were corrupting it. Hence the aristocracy continued to be blamed for the maintenance of the corn laws, which created food shortages. Or the Irish, flocking into Scotland in the 1840s to escape the famine, were to blame for unemployment, and, as Catholics, were lacking, it was implied, the self-help spirit of the native Presbyterian. When Presbyterian virtue failed to provide prosperity, then the fault lay in individual moral character, in sexual self-indulgence and probably in drink. A powerful temperance movement, middle-class led, working-class manned, succeeded in blaming much of society's ills on the curse of drink. As a result, for many workers, the divisions of society were not between classes but between 'the idle and non-idle classes, between the rough and the respectable, and between the religious and non religious' (Clark 1995, 118). Few were able to escape this perception and, as a result, Scotland became the heartland of mid-nineteenth-century Liberalism, rallying to the cry that land reform would solve most of the urban problems, keeping attention firmly focused on the plight of ever-shrinking numbers of highland peasants and carefully ignoring the plight of the Scottish urban masses. Even the late nineteenth-century labour movement found it difficult to escape from this hegemonic view. It was a measure of the success of middle-class ideology that by the 1850s hardly any working-class organisations met in the more democratic atmosphere of the public house. It is a further indication that the bourgeois perception of separate spheres for men and women had become thoroughly ingrained in Scottish male working-class attitudes (Clark 1995; Gordon 1991).

There are many other aspects of class which can be discussed. The debate on What and When and Why and How remains as fierce as ever. There is agreement that explanations of class based on a simple economic reductionism are no longer tenable and that historians have to be aware of the complexity of social interaction. There were many things which were fracturing broad social groupings – levels of income, sources of income, levels of education, religion, political perceptions, race. At the same time, there were powerful forces pushing people into thinking of themselves in class terms. There is no doubt that the language of class was in widespread use by the middle of the nineteenth century. The middle classes while reasonably successful in challenging gentry dominance, felt deeply threatened by evidence that the workers were apparently rejecting many aspects of the middle-class vision of how society should operate (see, for example, Smout (1976) on sexual attitudes). At the same time, the middle classes were physically and psychologically separating themselves from the working class (Gauldie 1976). They were left with the dilemma about how to maintain social control. On the other side there were undoubtedly deep divisions among workers, but alongside these were cultural pressures which were encouraging class perceptions. There were working-class streets and working-class shops and working-class leisure pursuits and working-class institutions from which the middle class were excluded. Powerful as middle-class hegemony was, it was not swallowed unthinkingly by workers, and antagonism to the imposition of middle-class control grew increasingly powerful. Class may be difficult to pin down, but it cannot be ignored, either here or in the later period you will study in Volume 2.

REFERENCES TO BOOKS AND ARTICLES MENTIONED IN THE TEXT

Berresford Ellis, P and Mac A'Ghobhain, S 1970 *The Scottish Insurrection of 1820*. London.

Brims, J 1989 'The Covenanting Tradition and Scottish Radicalism in the 1790s', *in* Brotherstone, T (ed), *Covenant, Charter and Party. Traditions of Revolt and Protest in Modern Scottish History*, Aberdeen, 50–9.

Brims, J 1990 'From Reformers to "Jacobins": The Scottish Association of Friends of the People', *in* Devine, TM (ed), *Conflict and Stability in Scottish Society, 1700–1850*, Edinburgh, 31–50.

Brown, C 1987 *The Social History of Religion in Scotland since 1730*. London.

Bruce, S 1983 'Social Change and Collective Behaviour: the revival in eighteenth-century Ross-shire', *British Journal of Sociology* 34, 554–72.

Cameron, KJ 1979 'William Weir and the origins of the "Manchester League" in Scotland, 1838–39', *Scottish Historical Review* 58, 70–91.

Camic, C 1983 *Experience and Enlightenment. Socialisation for Cultural Change in Eighteenth Century Scotland*. Edinburgh.

Chitnis, AC 1986 *The Scottish Enlightenment and Early Victorian English Society*. London.

*Clark, A 1995 *The Struggle for Breeches. Gender and the Making of the British Working Class*. London.

Clarke, T 1990 'Early Chartism in Scotland: A "Moral Force" Movement?', *in* Devine, TM (ed), *Conflict and Stability in Scottish Society 1700–1850*, Edinburgh, 106–21.

*Clarke, T and Dickinson, T 1988 'The Birth of Class', *in* Devine, TM and Mitchison, R (eds), *People and Society in Scotland. Volume I: 1760–1830*, Edinburgh, 292–309.

Devine, TM 1990 'The Failure of Radical Reform in Scotland in the late eighteenth century', *in* Devine, TM (ed), *Conflict and Stability in Scottish Society*, Edinburgh, 51–64.

Devine, TM 1995 *Exploring the Scottish Past: Themes in the History of Scottish Society*. East Linton.

Dickinson, HT 1989 *Britain and the French Revolution*. London.

*Dickson, A and Speirs, W 1980 'Changes in class structure in Paisley, 1750–1845', *Scottish Historical Review* 59, 54–72.

Donnelly, FK 1976 'The Scottish Rising of 1820: A reinterpretation', *Scottish Tradition* 6, 27–37.

Donnelly, T 1981 'The economic activities of the members of the Aberdeen Merchant Guild, 1750–1799', *Scottish Economic and Social History* I, 25–41.

Duncan, RE 1981 'Artisans and proletarians: Chartism and working-class allegiance in Aberdeen', *Northern Scotland* 4, 51–67.

Duncan, RE 1989 'Chartism in Aberdeen', *in* Brotherstone, T (ed), *Covenant, Charter and Party: traditions of revolt and protest in modern Scottish history*, Aberdeen, 78–91.

Dwyer, J and Murdoch, A 1982 'Paradigms and Politics: Manners, Morals and the Rise of Henry Dundas, 1770–1784', *in* Dwyer, J, Mason, RA and Murdoch, A (eds), *New Perspectives on the Politics and Culture of Early Modern Scotland*, Edinburgh, 210–48.

Foster, J 1974 *Class Struggle and the Industrial Revolution: Early Industrial Capitalism in Three English Cities*. London.

*Fraser, WH 1988a 'Patterns of Protest', *in* Devine, TM and Mitchison, R (eds), *People and Society in Scotland. Volume I: 1760–1830*, Edinburgh, 268–91.

Fraser, WH 1988b *Conflict and Class: Scottish Workers, 1700–1838*. Edinburgh.

Fraser, WH 1996 'The Owenite Movement in Scotland', *Scottish Economic and Social History* 16, 60–91.

Gauldie, E 1976 'The middle class and working class housing in the nineteenth century', *in* MacLaren, AA (ed), *Social Class in Scotland, Past and Present,* Edinburgh, 12–35.

Gordon, E 1991 *Women and the Labour Movement in Scotland, 1850–1914.* Oxford.

Gray, R 1976 *The Labour Aristocracy in Victorian Edinburgh.* Oxford.

Houston, RA 1994 *Social Change in the Age of Enlightenment: Edinburgh, 1660–1760.* Oxford.

Hunter, J 1974 'The emergence of the crofting community: the religious contribution, 1798–1843', *Scottish Studies* 18, 95–116.

Katznelson, I and Zolberg, AR 1986 *Working-Class Formation: Nineteenth Century Patterns in Western Europe and the United States.* Princeton.

Lehman, W 1960 *John Millar of Glasgow, 1735–1801.* Cambridge.

*Logue, KJ 1979 *Popular Disturbances in Scotland, 1780–1815.* Edinburgh.

Lythe, SGE 1967 'The Tayside Meal Mobs, 1772–73', *Scottish Historical Review* 46, 26–36.

McCalman, S 1970 'Chartism in Aberdeen', *Journal of the Scottish Labour History Society* 2, 5–24.

McFarland, EW 1994 *Ireland and Scotland in the Age of Revolution.* Edinburgh.

*MacLaren, AA 1974 *Religion and Social Class. The Disruption Years in Aberdeen.* London.

MacLaren, AA 1983 'Class Formation and Class Fractions. The Aberdeen bourgeoisie, 1830–1850', *in* Gordon, G and Dicks, B (eds), *Scottish Urban History,* Aberdeen, 112–29.

MacLaren, AA 1989 'Patronage and professionalism: The "Forgotten Middle Class", 1760–1860', *in* McCrone, D, Kendrick, S and Straw, P (eds), *The Making of Scotland: Nation, Culture and Social Change,* Edinburgh, 123–42.

Maver, I 1995 'The Guardianship of the Community', *in* Devine, TM and Jackson, G (eds), *Glasgow, Volume I: The Beginnings to 1830.* Manchester, 239–77.

Mitchison, R 1978 'Patriotism and national identity in eighteenth century Scotland', *in* Moody, TW (ed), *Nationalism and the Pursuit of National Independence,* Belfast, 73–95.

*Morris, RJ 1979 *Class and Class Consciousness in the Industrial Revolution, 1780–1850.* London.

Morris, RJ 1983 'Voluntary Societies and British Urban Elites, 1780–1843', *Historical Journal* 26 (1), 95–118.

Neale, RS 1983 *History and Class. Essential Readings in Theory and Interpretation.* Oxford.

Nenadic, S 1988 'The Rise of the Urban Middle Class', *in* Devine, TM and Mitchison, R (eds), *People and Society in Scotland. Volume I: 1760–1830,* Edinburgh, 109–126.

Nenadic, S 1990 'Political Reform and the "ordering" of Middle-Class Protest', *in* Devine, TM (ed), *Conflict and Stability in Scottish Society, 1700–1850,* Edinburgh, 65–82.

Nenadic, S 1994 'Middle-Rank Consumers and Domestic Culture in Edinburgh and Glasgow 1720–1840', *Past and Present* 145, 122–56.

Nenadic, S 1995 'The Middle Ranks and modernisation', *in* Devine, TM and Jackson, G (eds), *Glasgow, Volume I: The Beginnings to 1830,* Manchester, 278–311.

Perkin, H 1969 *The Origin of Modern English Society.* London.

Richards, E 1973 'How tame were the Highlanders during the Clearances?', *Scottish Studies* 17, 35–50.

Smout, TC 1966 'Scottish landowners and economic growth, 1650–1850', *Scottish Journal of Political Economy* 2, 218–34.

Smout, TC 1969 *A History of the Scottish People, 1560–1830.* London.

Smout, TC 1976 'Aspects of Sexual Behaviour in 19th-Century Scotland', *in* MacLaren, AA (ed), *Social Class in Scotland: Past and Present,* Edinburgh, 55–85.

Statistical Account of Scotland 1791–99. 21 volumes. Edinburgh.

Stedman Jones, G 1983 *Languages of Class: Studies in English Working Class History, 1832–1982.* Cambridge.

Stein, P 1970 'Law and Society in Eighteenth Century Scottish Thought', *in* Phillipson, NT and Mitchison, R (eds), *Essays in Scottish History in the Eighteenth Century*, Edinburgh, 148–66.

*Thomis, MI and Holt, P 1977 *Threats of Revolution in Britain, 1789–1848.* London.

Thompson, EP 1963 *The Making of the English Working Class.* London.

Thompson, EP 1978a *The Poverty of Theory.* London.

Thompson, EP 1978b 'Eighteenth century English society: class struggle without class?', *Social History* 3, 133–65.

Thompson, J 1996 'After the Fall: Class and Political Language in Britain, 1780–1900', *Historical Journal* 39, 785–806.

*Wahrman, D 1995 *Imagining the Middle Class. The Political Representation of Class in Britain, c.1780–1840.* Cambridge.

Whatley, CA 1992 'Royal Day, People's Day: The Monarch's Birthday in Scotland, c.1660–1860', *in* Mason, R and MacDougall, N (eds), *People and Power in Scotland. Essays in Honour of T.C. Smout*, Edinburgh, 170–88.

Whatley, CA 1995 'Scottish "Collier serfs" in the 17th and 18th centuries: a new perspective', *in* Westerman, E (ed), *Vom Bergau-zum Industrierevier*, Stuttgart, 239–54.

Wilson, A 1970 *The Chartist Movement in Scotland.* Manchester.

Wright, LC 1953 *Scottish Chartism.* Edinburgh.

Young, JD 1979 *The Rousing of the Scottish Working Class.* London.

Youngson, AJ 1966 *The Making of Classical Edinburgh, 1750–1840.* Edinburgh.

FURTHER READING

Those references marked * in the above list are particularly recommended for further reading, along with the following:

Fraser, WH 1989 'The Scottish Context of Chartism', *in* Brotherstone, T (ed), *Covenant, Charter and Party: traditions of revolt and protest in modern Scottish history*, Aberdeen, 61–75.

MacLaren, AA 1976 *Social Class in Scotland, Past and Present.* Edinburgh.

Smout, TC 1986 *A Century of the Scottish People, 1830–1950.* London.

Thompson, EP 1993 *Customs in Common.* London.

Whatley, CA 1990 'How Tame were the Scottish Lowlanders during the Eighteenth Century?', *in* Devine, TM (ed), *Conflict and Stability in Scottish Society, 1700–1850*, Edinburgh, 1–30.

Environment

———————————————— *T C Smout*

INTRODUCTION

Environmental history is a new discipline, especially in its application to British history. It deals with the relationship between human society and the natural world, seeking to discover not only what impact we had upon nature, but also how nature's constraints impacted upon us. Therefore it is the history of air and soil, of vegetation, of mobile living things from mammals to micro-organisms, and of ourselves. Because we have used nature, it is about landscape change and the fruitful exploitation of natural resources; because we have misused nature, it is also about pollution, disease and the destruction of biodiversity. The best writing on environmental history deals with America (eg Cronan 1985), India (eg Guha 1990), or more generally with the impact of Europeans on other continents (eg Crosby 1986; Grove 1995; MacKenzie 1990). For the British Isles, Oliver Rackham has written inspiringly on the history of the English countryside (Rackham 1986) and there have been studies of pollution (Brimblecombe 1987; see also Clapp 1994), but much of what is usually described as the environmental history of Britain is in fact the provenance of geographers dealing in prehistoric time, often with great methodological sophistication (eg Simmonds and Tooley 1981; Chambers 1993). In Scotland the environmental history of recent centuries is not even in its infancy, though it is a developing foetus kicking lustily in the womb (Smout 1993). For this reason it is hardly possible to refer readers to the same range of articles in the accompanying volume as for most other chapters in this book.

The century and a half covered by this volume laid the foundations both of our modern exploitation of resources and the modern troubles that spring from the mistaken belief that nature can be conquered. The following aspects will be addressed here:

- Changing attitudes
- An environmental crisis in the eighteenth century?
- The new Lowland farming
- The Highland environment
- The origins of modern pollution
- People and micro-organisms

Much of the commentary is speculative, either because even relatively straightforward research has never been done, or because the answers to the questions posed may be impossible to obtain without much more scientific methodologies than most historians trained in the humanities can handle. Yet one of the most exciting things about environmental history is its potential to unite the arts and sciences in a common quest to explore the past. By the time you have worked your way through this chapter I hope you will share my enthusiasm for this new inter-disciplinary approach to the past and will have an understanding of the questions it raises about how resources were used before the mid-nineteenth century.

I. CHANGING ATTITUDES

There is a sense in which the biggest change of all in the years 1707 to 1850 was a transformation in attitudes towards the environment. In the sixteenth and seventeenth centuries, and for most people for much of the eighteenth century, the natural world was accepted more or less as an unalterable fact of life. The first task was to describe it, and the accurate description of Scotland became a major intellectual undertaking in the seventeenth century, partially succeeding when Blaeu in Amsterdam in 1654 published maps of Scotland based on the earlier work of Timothy Pont, partially failing when Robert Sibbald in the 1690s omitted to publish the topographical collections made by Sir Robert Gordon of Straloch and by himself. The task that Gordon had set himself in the middle of the seventeenth century was ably fulfilled by Sir John Sinclair when he published the *Statistical Accounts* of all the parishes in Scotland in the 1790s. Gordon had told his collaborators that, in providing local descriptions of their areas, they were 'not to have anything in their writings too extravagant or beyond the truth, nor make an elephant of a fly, a failure that most of us in relating our affairs are subject to. The faithful and full description of our districts remains untouched' (Mitchell 1906, II, 288). Such a faithful and full description was what the ministers who wrote the parish accounts for Sinclair ultimately provided.

The tones, however, of the collections made in the seventeenth century and those of the *Statistical Account* are often rather different. Whereas the latter are full of reports of landuse change, of commendation for good farming practice and condemnation for bad, and of observations as to how the parish could be improved by new drains or new roads, the seventeenth-century accounts only seldom identify either change or the potential for change. For them, Providence had set a backcloth, often a very pleasant backcloth, for human life. Thus from the Borders:

St. Mary Loch is in circuit at least six miles, surrounded with pleasant green Hills and Meadows; the hills overspread with flocks of sheep and Cattel, the Rocks with herds of Goats, and the Valleys and Meadows with excellent corn and Hay. It is fed with several little Springs and Brooks but chiefly with the Water of Meggit which with a clear stream runs gently down a long Plain and discharges itself prettily in its very bosom.

And, from the opposite end of Scotland:

In the inland localities this district [Sutherland] swells into numerous mountains, which open into many pastures and fruitful valleys, whence the clearest streams and rivers descend. These valleys are plenished with convenient and pleasant dwellings, and maintain countless varieties of all sorts of cattle, while of game also, and of wild and domestic birds, there is a ready supply. But where it touches either the sea or the above-mentioned firth, it is wonderful how rich it is in crops, and these the best and soonest ripe, and there is no scarcity of other commodities desirable for living comfortably and cheerfully.

(Mitchell 1906: see also **Document 59**)

Descriptions of this sort hardly distinguish between the economic and the aesthetic, but in the course of the eighteenth century a strong tendency emerged to set the two into separate compartments. This is evident in the parish descriptions in the *Statistical Accounts* of the 1790s, where sections that deal with agriculture tend to be apart from those that deal with local antiquities and beauties, but at least both are usually mentioned because Sir John Sinclair asked for each to be covered. By then, however, in the later eighteenth century, there was a phenomenon unknown in Sir Robert Gordon's day – on the one hand, specialist writers on agricultural improvement like Adam Dickson, Lord Kames and Sir John Sinclair himself, and on the other hand specialist writers on the romantic beauty of the countryside, like William Gilpin and the Wordsworths. Both improvers and romantics were highly critical about what they saw. For the improver, there was always something that could be done better, some opportunity neglected, some resource untouched (**Document 60**). For the romantics there was always some foreground insufficiently picturesque, or some loch intrinsically inferior to the English lakes because of the arrangement of islands, trees and mountains (**Document 61**).

By and large, however, the improvers disapproved of untamed nature as a missed opportunity or a useless waste, and the romantics praised it as uplifting to the human spirit. Occasionally their views coincided, but differed from those of the seventeenth century. Peat bogs provide a good example. In the seventeenth century they were regarded primarily as a useful local resource: by the early nineteenth century they had come to be viewed as dreary wastelands, but potentially capable of being drained and improved. It was not until the late twentieth century that they came to be seen as reservoirs of biodiversity and carbon sinks helping to slow global warming (see **Article 18**).

Most importantly, however, the very division between the improvers and the romantics sacrificed the holistic attitudes of the seventeenth century and paved the way for modern dichotomies. From the improvers we have inherited a view that nature can be conquered, the immense hubris of modern man:

The leitmotiv of Western history known as 'our increasing control over nature' is actually an absurd, barefaced oxymoron. Nature has always been in total control, both in the basic, merely logical sense that the characteristics of Nature which make it inhabitable for us can no wise be taken for granted, and in the more disturbing, factual sense that Nature has already considerably reduced our domain.

(Duncan 1991)

From the romantics, on the other hand, we have inherited the view that wild nature is to be admired, that it is necessary for the good of our spiritual health, and that to damage it is to be guilty of vandalism. In the long run, though hardly before the end of the nineteenth century and especially during the twentieth century, there emerged from a junction of the romantics and the new biological sciences a conservation movement fundamentally opposed to the unchained modern equivalent of improvement, but with limited practical ability to impede economic growth (Sheail 1976; Smout 1991). The recent emphasis on 'sustainability' is an effort to square the circle, but in order to make it work we have perhaps to recover some of the delight and acceptance of the world as we find it that characterised the seventeenth-century topographers.

> EXERCISE 1
>
> Read **Document 59** through carefully. What do you think were the main points the writer was trying to convey to his reader in his account of Durness? Would you expect to find modern accounts of Durness written like this, and if not, how and why would they differ?

He is describing, in vivid and colourful language, the wealth of the natural resources, both of the sea and the land. While Nature has endowed Durness with a valuable sea-fishery, fine harbours, rivers, lochs and forests (in the Scottish sense of hunting grounds), the hand of people is evident in the farms and fertile pastures well stocked with black cattle and sheep. Although he might have been exaggerating to flatter local pride, he conveys a sense of pleasure in living in a richly-endowed environment. Modern accounts would usually be written differently for different audiences. Some would probably emphasise scenic beauty for the tourists, some discuss 'development opportunities' for superquarries, deep-sea anchorages, holiday homes and golf-courses, and some dwell on the 'poverty' of natural resources, on clan feuds, clearances and depopulation. It is unlikely that many would show the same delight in things just as they are.

An improving ideology was not, of course, a Scottish monopoly. It stemmed from international intellectual movements rooted in Baconian empirical philosophy and the late seventeenth-century scientific movement of the Royal Society of London, in Descartes and the eighteenth-century French *agronomistes*, and more generally in the European Enlightenment (for surveys of the changing attitudes to the natural world see in particular Thomas 1983; Oelschlaeger 1991; Worster 1977). Nor was the advent of the Scottish improvers a consequence of the Act of Union. Even Sir Robert Gordon of Straloch was essentially Baconian when he condemned the late medieval topographer Hector Boece who 'turned aside to marvels, in most of which, as the truth has been thrown overboard, there is nothing marvellous'

(Mitchell 1906, II, 288). The first Scottish tracts explicitly about improving Scottish farming methods were published in Edinburgh by James Donaldson in 1697 and 1698, and by Lord Belhaven in 1699: the latter was vehemently opposed to Union with England. On the other hand the Union obviously facilitated growing familiarity with more advanced farming techniques in England, and two of the earliest and most influential practical improvers in Scotland were MPs in the Westminster Parliament, John Cockburn of Ormiston working in East Lothian, and Archibald Grant of Monymusk in Aberdeenshire (Handley 1953).

The extraordinary Scottish zeal for agrarian improvement is discussed in Smout (1969, 291–301). Something like it can be found in the eighteenth century elsewhere in the United Kingdom, in France, in the German states and in Scandinavia, yet in Scotland the improvers were peculiarly intense, driven by a heady mixture of patriotic zeal and fashion towards the national objective of catching up with England in material wealth. As it was assumed that the true basis for most wealth lay in agricultural production, as was undoubtedly true for individual landowners, the patriotic and the personal coincided to drive forward change. By the 1790s few parishes lacked at least one landowner who by the force of his example and power was proud of his reputation as an agricultural improver. The view of such men was that they were the repositories of all agrarian wisdom, that most of their tenants were stupid and needed to be taught; if they would not learn, they must be replaced. The most notable productions of the end of the century, the *Statistical Accounts* and the two series of *General Views* on regional agriculture also overseen by Sir John Sinclair, which overlapped into the first two decades of the nineteenth century, were full of praise for innovation and heaped contempt on the practices of the past.

Historians at first were inclined to take the landowning improvers at their own valuation of themselves (Handley 1953; 1963; Symon 1959), but then became deeply sceptical about their true importance, arguing on the one hand that it was the clever tenant who deserved most of the credit as landowners were too amateurish to make a real impact (Campbell 1977) and on the other that agricultural change was so long-drawn-out, with its roots in the seventeenth century, that the concept of an 'Agricultural Revolution' created by improvers was inappropriate (Whittington 1975; see also Whyte 1995, 132–69). The latest study in depth (Devine 1994) has rehabilitated the concept of an agricultural revolution in Scotland after 1760 by demonstrating the scale of productivity gains, and acknowledged the critical nature of the landowners' leadership – or at least that of their professional landstewards and factors. Even if it is true that success was primarily dependent on the skill and adaptability of practical farming tenants, and on a favourable price structure in the late eighteenth century as population growth and urbanisation created new demands for food on the marketplace, such a change could hardly have come about without the enthusiasm and support of the landed classes, and that was undoubtedly forthcoming. But what did the changes that they initiated or supported do to the environment itself?

2. AN ENVIRONMENTAL CRISIS IN THE EIGHTEENTH CENTURY?

In 1994, Thorkild Kjærgaard published an arresting book on Danish environmental history in which he claimed that Denmark was facing a severe crisis of environmental degradation by the middle of the eighteenth century, from which it was saved by a combination of agrarian change at home and industrialisation abroad (Kjærgaard 1994). His argument concerning the causes of the crisis points to over-exploitation of natural resources stimulated by excessive tax demands and calls on raw materials, especially wood, from a warlike crown: it is a picture of deforestation, subsequent loss of fertile land by sand-blow and flooding as hydrological systems were disturbed, and of declining fertility of farm land, as peasants, faced by chronic fuel shortages, burned straw and animal dung to keep themselves warm instead of returning it to the ground as manure, and as the natural fertility of the ground wore out. The cure, says Kjærgaard, came about when farmers, led by their great landowners, began to restore fertility by a programme of tree planting to stabilise sand, by the drainage of swamps; and, above all, by use of red clover to fix

No. 25. Thinly wooded Highland countryside in Glen Affric, photographed by RJ Adam (on pony) in 1930. This scene is typical of ground relatively lightly grazed by domestic stock and deer, as much of the Central Highlands must have been at the beginning of the eighteenth century. *Photograph courtesy of St Andrews University Library.*

nitrogen in the soil; and when the industrial revolution in Great Britain helped to cure the fuel crisis by providing cheap coal abroad, and helped the efficiency of agricultural tools by similarly providing cheap iron and steel. By 1830, the crisis was over.

Kjærgaard's picture of the crisis does not totally convince, partly because reduction of tree cover, c.1550–1750, was from 20–25% of the land-surface to 8–10%, which seems rather small to create the chaos alleged, and the effect of sand-drift, which he calls 'the weakest link in the Danish ecosystem', turns out only to have been upon 5% of the land surface. Nevertheless he marshals much evidence of a serious imbalance between population and resources in eighteenth-century Denmark, and it is worth considering whether a comparable environmental crisis could have faced Scotland at the same time, and been cured by similar solutions.

Certainly the question of fuel shortage, which Kjærgaard regards as a looming 'entropic nightmare' for the entire European community in the eighteenth century, was not at all prominent in Scotland. Abundant supplies of peat and coal generally obviated scenes like those in Denmark where shivering peasants went to bed with their coats, hats and boots on. Yet there were a few parishes, for example in Aberdeenshire and Perthshire, where fuel was scarce and population fell as migration to more habitable places occurred, and elsewhere it was quite common to use turf in place of peat as a fuel, considerably damaging the pasture. As for deforestation, Roy's map of the 1750s, and a further survey of 1812, suggest that by then only about 4% or 5% of the land surface was covered with trees – far less than in Denmark – and the proportion in the Lowlands might have been as low as 2% or 3%. On the other hand this phenomenon was not new: certainly by the fifteenth century there had been complaints of wood shortage and descriptions of central Scotland as largely devoid of trees. Perhaps the hydrological disturbances associated with loss of forest cover would take a time to develop, but in Scotland sand-blow was important only in two or three circumscribed localities in the seventeenth and eighteenth centuries – at Culbin on the Moray Firth, at Strathbeg in Buchan and on the Outer Hebridean machairs. Bad drainage and extensive swamp and bogland had been an observed feature of Scotland since Roman times, but there was no contemporary evidence in the sixteenth and seventeenth centuries that swampland was expanding, only that it was extremely common.

Nevertheless, we cannot dismiss the case for an environmental crisis in eighteenth-century Scotland out of hand. Firstly, population stood at c.1,250,000 in 1755, compared to perhaps 1,000,000 in 1700 and 500,000 in 1500 (the earliest figure in particular is very speculative). But over two and a half centuries the population had been subject to an exceptionally high emigration rate (especially in the seventeenth century), to repeated famine before 1700 (leading to a possible population drop of 20% in the 1690s), to changes in diet that involved consuming less animal-based produce and more meal (which most would consider a drop in the standard of living) and to falling real wages, 1550–1650 which (unlike in England) did not recover in the following century (Gibson and Smout 1995). A case could be made that Scotland was failing to support her enhanced population properly, and as the overwhelming majority lived directly on the land, perhaps the land itself was failing to cope with the strain of extra numbers.

The fertility of the soil depends on a number of factors. One of the most critical is the pH level. If the soil becomes too acid, through waterlogging or excessive rainfall washing out the natural lime, it will gradually inhibit the growth of nearly all agricultural plants and stop the growth of wild clover and other leguminous plants that fix nitrogen. The removal of tree cover will greatly increase the direct impact of rain upon soil, and as the Scottish forest resource had been on the retreat for five thousand years, it is probable that for much of that time the pH level of the soil had been falling steadily, but perhaps at an accelerated rate in the Lowlands after the late Middle Ages. Even more important for soil fertility is a supply of soluble nitrogen that plants can absorb. It can be obtained from forest humus, but that source dissipates relatively quickly. It can also be obtained from certain pasture plants, notably legumes like clover, from manures (dung, seaweed, turf) and from the atmosphere itself. The problem was that it washed away so rapidly, and in practice the only way to avoid a steady reduction in fertility was to intensify manuring.

From the thirteenth century onwards an answer had been sought in the manufacture of so-called plaggen soils, identifiable in the Netherlands, Germany and Ireland as well as in Scotland, made by transporting volumes of turf from the hill to the 'inbye land' where the crops were grown and many animals pastured close to the farm settlement. This process inevitably impoverished the hill by reducing its capability to graze stock, but enriched the cropping grounds with what was termed 'midden faill' (**Document 62**). This was an enormously labour-intensive task which, after eight hundred years, provided a topsoil of 80 cm depth at Papa Sour in Shetland (Davidson and Simpson 1994). Such labours provided phosphorous-rich soils, but the nitrogen bonus was short-lived and depended on constant replenishment from new turf. In the long run the sustainability of this kind of peasant response is questionable. If the cornucopia of nature had a slow leak, and people were unable to plug it, it is possible that Scotland, along with much of northern Europe, indeed came to face an environmental crisis by the earlier eighteenth century.

EXERCISE 2

From the foregoing, and considering **Documents 60** and **62**, what is your own opinion on the likelihood of an environmental crisis in early eighteenth-century Scotland? What evidence, archaeological, historical or scientific, would be necessary to provide a convincing case either way? Is it realistic to suppose we can ever find it?

It seems possible that an environmental crisis like that postulated for Denmark occurred in Scotland. Sand-drift was more limited, but in Scotland there was even less forest left, water-level conditions were even more inhibiting for good farming, and some practices like turf-stripping suggest it would have been hard to maintain the level of soil fertility indefinitely. The problem lies in distinguishing between a situation that was *bad*, and one that was *becoming worse*, and proof of the latter is very hard to come by. Archaeologists might be able to investigate and date deserted settlements in the uplands. Palynologists, who research the pollen record embedded over millennia in wetlands, might be able to tell us more about the changing appearance of the landscape, for example where the woods decayed and what crops were grown at different times. Geomorphologists and soil scientists might be able to show changes in erosion and sedimentary deposition rates in lochs and rivers. Historians might do more to work out yield ratios in agriculture. We might find some of the answers, but Scottish documentary sources are already relatively well worked, and the scientific techniques are in many cases still in their infancy in respect to precise or recent dating.

3. THE NEW LOWLAND FARMING

If there was a crisis, was it overcome within the eighteenth century? Even by 1790 there is every sign of a rapid increase in agricultural productivity in the Lowlands, and there also the first sustained improvement in living standards for centuries as real wages rose and diet came again to include a modicum of meat and cheese (Smout 1969, 302–31; Devine 1994). Was the change achieved by the same methods as in Denmark, and do the improvers deserve any credit for it? If the root of the problem in traditional agriculture was acid soil and deficiency in nitrogen, they should have concentrated first on promoting liming and the introduction of nitrogen-fixing crops, of which the most effective was red clover.

To a considerable extent, this is what they did. In the Scottish context, clover was introduced as part of new rotations on enclosed fields (replacing the old, open rigs), where 'sown grasses' were alternated with grain, or 'green crops' with 'white'. By 'sown grasses' was understood a mixture of clover and ryegrass, as advocated in the influential treatise of the Earl of Haddington in 1735 – not the first to practise it in Scotland, but the first to give it publicity and prestige. By the 1790s, 46% of the parishes in Lanarkshire, 62% of those in Fife and 71% in Angus were using sown grass rotations. They were no less keen on liming, either digging marl from calcareous deposits or burning limestone in kilns to make powdered lime. Here again they had no priority of discovery, as lime was already being described in the seventeenth century as the 'usual way of gooding the land' in the Lothians: but the improvers universalised its use across the Lowlands. The most remarkable under-taking was perhaps the limeworks of the Earl of Elgin in Fife, who in 1777 and 1778 invested £14,000 in building nine large draw-kilns, a harbour, waggon-ways and a village for 200 employees. The concern used 80,000–90,000 tons of limestone and 12,000 tons of coal a year, loading 1,300 separate cargoes with a total annual value of over £10,000. The lime was distributed throughout the Forth and Tay area, and even up to the Moray Firth.

Apart from promoting the transforming power of clover and lime, the improvers also did much to help introduce two critical root crops, turnips and potatoes. The first transformed the keeping of animals over winter – more animals alive meant heavier stocking on the pastures in summer, and the production of more manure without the same need to skin the land for turf, thus restoring fertility to the hill. The main impact of turnips came in the first half of the nineteenth century and depended in the first place on a buoyant market in the towns for mutton and beef. Potatoes were so quickly adopted from the middle of the eighteenth century that it is easy to overlook the role that landowners had initially in introducing them. They were an extremely important addition to the basic foodstuffs of a population that hitherto had relied so much upon oatmeal. Lastly, and late in the day, there came great breakthroughs in draining land, associated with the work of Smith of Deanston in the 1820s and 1830s, and the invention of the subsoil plough. The old swampy fields and morasses of so much of the Lowlands could only after that be brought under cultivation.

In other ways the efforts of the improvers to promote better agriculture were less fruitful, much more conservative and related to the old ideas of manufacturing soil with muck and turf. Not all was futile – a new emphasis on using human dung on the fields within about five miles of Edinburgh not only cleaned up the city but enabled parishes like Duddingston and Colinton to produce vastly more wheat, and similar efforts were made round other towns. Other improvers tried to improve the soil by composting a wide variety of wastes, like dogfish after their livers had been extracted (round Aberdeen), or soap waste, whale blubber, soot and rags (Davidson and Smout 1996). There was a great deal of contemporary discussion on the virtues or otherwise of paring and burning turf and peat moss as a way of reclaiming land: most commentators were against it, at least by the end of the Napoleonic Wars – as was said in Ayrshire, 'you may raise one great and one moderate crop, but the moss will never produce another of much value'. Little is heard of this by the middle of the nineteenth century.

It must not be forgotten that improvers, properly so called, were all sorts of people, from the great landlords of the eighteenth century to the skilled land-stewards and large tenant farmers who had largely replaced the landowners as effective innovators even before the early nineteenth. They were a literate body of men, swapping ideas through journals, books and the many reports edited by Sir John Sinclair, but they were empiricists, not scientists. The materials they had to hand were almost entirely local (only lime was moved any distance, and that mainly by sea); and they were almost exclusively organic. Whether it is fair to describe what happened between 1750 and 1850 as overcoming an environmental crisis, or merely the gearing-up of farming from a position of stagnation to one of growth, the transformation of Lowland agriculture in that century was undoubtedly a triumph of environmentally friendly farming. This should not, however, be attributed either to unusual virtue or vision on the part of landowners or farmers. There is no reason to suppose that had they had access to pesticides, chemical fertilisers and heavy machinery they would not have made full use of them.

EXERCISE 3
Reflect on my discussion here in conjunction with Ian Whyte's account of social change in Chapter 5. What were the overall costs and benefits of the agricultural

transformation? Were there environmental costs, too? How do you think they compare with the costs and benefits of agricultural change in this century?

The most obvious overall costs could be seen as the creation of a class of landless labourers, and the easing off the land of many who were regarded as inefficient or undesirable farmers, to emigrate overseas or swell the population of the developing towns. The benefits included the greatly improved production of food, better diet for many and higher standards of living in other ways for some. The land became more productive as its natural fertility was unlocked or enhanced, and agricultural change was generally environmentally benign since it was based on organic methods. The most serious cost was perhaps in attitudes, as the improvers assumed they could manipulate nature at will without serious side effects. In this century, the increase in agricultural productivity has far exceeded the modest advances of earlier times, and the input of modern methods has had a huge adverse impact on countryside biodiversity: many are now questioning if farming based on lavish chemical inputs

No. 26. Mr Mackinnon about to lead his peats, Barra, 1925. For centuries the bogs were the main resource of the country people for fuel. Fraser Darling calculated in 1945 that 15,000 peats were used in a year by a household of four, and that winning and leading peats took almost a month's work for the crofter and his family. Do you spend more or less than one-twelfth of your income on fuel bills? *Photograph courtesy of St Andrews University Library.*

is itself ultimately sustainable. The attitude, however, that we can manipulate nature at will, without a cost, is still eighteenth-century.

4. THE HIGHLAND ENVIRONMENT

In the Highlands, the human impact on the environment, 1707–1850, was no less radical than in the Lowlands, but it does not have the same image of success. (For a full account of Highland history, see Chapter 9.) Controversy in environmental history focuses on three aspects – deforestation, the sustainability of traditional farming, and damage to the upland ecosystems by the massive introduction of Lowland sheep. The noted ecologist Frank Fraser Darling articulated an influential theory which united all these aspects: the Highlands, he believed, had become a 'wet desert', due to massive deforestation caused by English timber extractors and iron masters in the seventeenth and eighteenth centuries, to the ending of traditional farming practices that had emphasised cattle above sheep before the clearances, and to the devastating impact of muirburn and heavy, close grazing that followed the introduction of the Cheviot and removed the soil nutrients from the hill, leaving it a kind of northern Sahara (Darling 1947, 1955). Consequently, the ecology of the Highlands had been shattered by outsiders in pursuit of profit:

> Man does not seem to extirpate a feature of his environment as long as that natural resource is concerned only with man's everyday life: but as soon as he looks upon it as having some value for export – that he can live by selling it to some distant populations – there is real danger.

It turns out, however, that nothing was quite so simple. To take deforestation, for instance. There is little evidence from the earliest maps – Pont (c.1590), Avery (1720s-1730s) and Roy (1750s) – for dense woodland cover throughout the Highlands. Roy's survey suggests that about 6% of the Highland land-surface was then forested with native woods, which is nothing like the original 60–80% cover proposed from pollen studies at the woodland climax five thousand years ago. Huge declines had already occurred before the Romans, probably mainly because of climatic change – the notion that a trackless 'Caledonian Forest' was encountered by the invaders was largely a function of misreading early sources (Breeze 1992; Smout 1994). Furthermore, it is difficult to find evidence that outside timber speculators did much damage, except (as in the case of an Irish partnership in Glen Orchy in the 1720s) sometimes on a local scale: a more usual pattern (as at Abernethy, Rothiemurchus, Strathglass and Loch Arkaig in the 1730s and 1740s) was of greedy and deluded English speculators signing ambitious contracts with equally greedy but more cynical Highland landowners, and failing to cut more than a few hundred trees apiece before finding the wood either to be inferior or to be incapable of being profitably extracted (Smout 1997). While there were later episodes of extravagant woodcutting in the old pine resource, they mainly took place in forests like Glenmore and Rothiemurchus that subsequently regenerated.

As for the iron masters, some of the early ones operated on a cut-and-run basis much like some forestry companies do in the third-world rain forests at the present day. After 1750, however, they were an important spur to better woodland management. The dukes of Argyll, for example, only became seriously interested in caring for their oakwoods after the Lorn Furnace Company bid for them, and the company provided advice on sustainable management drawn from their Lake District experience. The Lorn Furnace Company after a century of operation in the West Highlands left the local woods in as good, or better, condition than they found them, although at the peak of operations they were needing to use, on rotation, up to 10,000 acres of oak coppice (Lindsay 1975).

Ironworks were in any case few and far between in the Highlands (inconsiderable in number compared to the Weald or the Forest of Dean), and much more broadleaf woodland was cut by tanners seeking, especially, oak bark for its tannin content. Again the intervention of outside market forces seems to have led in the long run to better management. While the early, mainly Irish, exploiters in the first part of the eighteenth century had few ideas about woodland management, by 1800 careful coppicing and cutting on standard rotations of around twenty to twenty-five years was commonplace in the most heavily exploited areas in Argyll, Perthshire and Dumbartonshire (Document 63).

In many respects the heyday of sustainable management in the Scottish woods appears to have been between 1780 and 1830, when external market forces were at their peak. It fell off disastrously, and left the woods neglected to the mercies of deer and sheep after the 1830s, because cheap iron came to be made from coal fuel (no longer needing a woodland location), chemicals began to replace natural tannin and foreign softwood was again very cheaply imported. The main value of woods over most of Scotland by 1850 seems to have been as rough grazing, or as part of a sporting estate, harbouring red deer, roebuck, black grouse and reintroduced capercaillie: that fate did them no good at all. In some places birch was still exploited for making bobbins, or burned to produce pyroligneous acid, and oak coppicing often went on until the end of the century, producing by-products of steadily diminishing value.

To what, then, are we to attribute the gradual decay of the woods, if it is not to the opportunistic exploitation of outsiders? Eighteenth-century improving writers were in little doubt that they were decaying – that is to say that many were not regenerating, and in some places that they were disappearing. Climatic change cannot be ruled out as part of the explanation: the failure of western pinewoods to regenerate after heavy felling (for example, in Glen Orchy and Glen Coe) contrasts with the experience in the East, and may be due to heavier rainfall covering the ground with moss and peat in ways that made it difficult for pine seedlings to push through. On the other hand most contemporaries suspected that the fault lay with peasant misuse, not least the general use of the woods for grazing and shelter and the presence of innumerable feral goats. They tried to put a stop to both, but usually without attempting to compensate the peasants for their loss of subsistence: consequently, when the profitability of good woodland management was lost again after 1830, the farmer's animals (though now sheep rather than goats) returned in force. But in parts of Sutherland the damage that had already been inflicted on the woods before 1800 was such that they were disappearing of their own accord, so that the peasants' cattle could not be sheltered in them anyway and their ability to keep stock at former densities was basically undermined: to some, this was an argument for going over to sheep (Document 64).

There are other signs that traditional Highland practices were perhaps not as sustainable as might be supposed, at least in the face of the rapid increase in population that took place in the north and west between the start of the eighteenth century and 1840. Dodgshon (1994; see Article 19) has suggested that many townships were finding it impossible to maintain the necessary levels of fertility in their grain lands without calling on more and more labour to cut turf and carry seaweed as manure inputs, and that this in turn necessitated more mouths to feed but (unless there was access to boundless seaweed) a declining turf base on which to run the essential dung-producing animals. The advent of potatoes, and their immediate adoption by a supposedly conservative peasantry, got Highland society off this vicious downward spiral by providing another and independent way to maintain a tolerable subsistence for the population.

EXERCISE 4

Do the above considerations change your view of the origin of the Clearances in any way? Why do you think that environmental factors of this sort have been hitherto neglected by historians?

It might shift the argument towards considering the sustainability of earlier tenant practices in Highland farming, both before and after the introduction of the potato. It is not enough to consider population growth in isolation: it has to be weighed against the techniques the population used to support itself. Nor is it enough to consider the landowner's unreasonable pursuit of profit: if he was faced with an environmental crisis, what would 'acting responsibly' imply? Probably environmental factors have been neglected because historians found them hard to assess or thought them unimportant. They are certainly at present hard to assess with precision.

By 1850 over most of the Highlands, however, the peasant societies that had struggled with maintaining fertility in the old townships had been transformed into coastal crofting communities or even eradicated by their own landlords, and their position on the land had been largely taken over by a small number of sheep farmers running an enormous number of sheep. The impact on the upland landscape was dramatic, as inbye lands were grassed over, townships pulled down and the hill shielings allowed to decay and their lands merged into the general hill pastures. Was this also an ecological disaster as Fraser Darling and others alleged? There is a good deal of late nineteenth-century evidence showing that contemporaries believed that the productivity of the hill pastures had declined severely since the introduction of Lowland sheep (Hunter 1977). On the other hand, although ecologists frequently identify overgrazing as a problem causing a decline in biodiversity in the uplands, modern agricultural science has not conclusively confirmed that sheep farming is damaging to the actual fertility of the hill in the way that Fraser Darling asserted: he argued that nutrients were removed in smoke and flame by muirburn, and in the bone, wood and flesh of the animals driven to market, but experiments seemed to indicate that more came down in the form of atmospheric deposition than was ever removed by sheep farming. The most recent study (Mather 1993) is ambivalent, seeming to show some decline in lambing ratios over large parts of the Highlands, 1880–1980, but not putting the cause absolutely beyond doubt. In any case, Mather's study cannot answer whether or not there was a large drop in upland fertility in the century before 1870.

If there had been such an early drop, what would have been the cause? It can hardly have been a consequence of the straightforward destruction of mature forests in the hills and straths as Fraser Darling believed, but it might have been the effect of sheep bringing about a massive decline in montane scrub, such as dwarf birch, juniper and alpine willow, and their replacement by heather and, in particular, coarse grasses with much less nutritional input and ability to produce nitrogen-rich humus. If this has been the case, then the vegetation cover by 1880 might have looked very much as it does today, and scientists might well be unable to prove that further deterioration has been very grave. But this is speculation. In the absence of better detailed evidence on the character of upland vegetation around 1780 when the sheep began to be brought in, it will be hard to take discussion further. Eighteenth-century travellers very occasionally give us an insight, but it is seldom of the extensive, clear and conclusive nature that environmental historians would like.

EXERCISE 5
Look at **Document 65**. What does it actually tell us about land cover in the Cairngorms? Are there any ambiguities or contradictions in the account? If there was more varied or shrubby vegetation on the hills than at present, does the document suggest a reason?

It tells us about many species of tree and herb found in the area described, and a modern ecologist could check to see if conditions are still the same. It is a little disconcerting, though, to read in one place that in Glen Avon 'the hills on each side' are covered with trees or scrub and in another that it is 'hemmed in by mountains . . . covered with moss and heath': presumably he is talking about cover at different altitudes, but it is ambiguous. Robertson points out that the inhabitants, for whom he has more pity than condemnation, are unable to keep as many animals as the hill pastures could support because of the absence of winter fodder. The implication is that the ground would be much more lightly grazed than today when sheep, and indeed deer, get large quantities of supplementary feed.

5. THE ORIGINS OF MODERN POLLUTION

Early modern Scots had a cavalier attitude towards dirt and pollution. The visitor to seventeenth-century Edinburgh needed a strong stomach (**Document 66**), and it was not much better when James Boswell described Dr Johnson's visit to the city in 1773:

> A zealous Scotsman could have wished Mr. Johnson to be without one of his five senses upon this occasion. As we marched slowly along, he grumbled in my ear 'I smell you in the dark!' But he acknowledged that the breadth of the street, and the loftiness of the buildings on each side, made a noble appearance.

The normal rural way to dispose of human ordure was to put it directly on the ground, or to throw the contents of a chamber pot on the midden outside the door to compost along with animal dung, straw, old thatch, dead animals and any other organic rubbish. A midden was an important manure resource – it was said in the nineteenth century that farmers in the North-East would doff their hats to a well-made midden. Trouble arose when exactly the same habits were transferred to the towns and cities where getting rid of sewage and refuse was much more difficult. Thus early travellers complained of the risk in Edinburgh of being hit by the contents of the pots as they walked down the streets, or having to lodge in houses where the sewage tubs had not been emptied for days ('the scent thereof annoyeth and offendeth the whole house'); and officials complained of the filth of the butchers who left the vennels so full of the guts of animals and other slaughterhouse waste that 'there can no passage be had through the same'.

Eighteenth-century magistrates in the capital made a more determined attempt than their predecessors to control such abuses. As Boswell explained, they had stopped people throwing 'foul water' from their windows, 'but from the structure of the houses in the old town, which consist of many stories, in each of which a different family lives, and there being no covered sewers, the odour still continues'. Nor was it easy to stop people hoarding filth to make a penny or two. Stale human urine was used in textile manufacture, and in the seventeenth century bleaching techniques were never quite good enough to get rid of the smell in linen sheets. It was still used two hundred years later by the Victorians in fashionable tweed manufacture: the weavers of Hawick during an industrial dispute withheld their chamber pots from their employer in order to bring pressure to bear. Horse-droppings were kept by some of the poor under their beds in the nineteenth-century cities to sell on to street collectors who came round to pick them up. 'Where there's muck there's brass' need not have been only a Yorkshire proverb.

Many of these practices mattered little when towns were small, but came to pose serious problems with large-scale urbanisation in the first half of the nineteenth century. In the early stages, too, the refuse was almost entirely organic, but by 1800 the disposal of mineral and chemical wastes was also beginning to pose large problems.

In the absence of any network of underground sewers, waste of all sorts was dumped into streams and rivers (for a general account, see Smout 1986, Chapters 1 and 2). The Cowgate Burn in Edinburgh discharged onto the flat marshy land near

Holyrood Palace, which was subsequently found to be uninhabitable for the visit of Queen Victoria and Prince Albert in 1842: the value of these 'water-meadows' for the proprietor as a source of rich fodder for the animals of the city was such that it proved difficult even for the royal family to exert pressure to regain control. Similarly the dukes of Buccleuch, with long-standing riparian rights on the River Esk, spent a generation in legal actions with local paper-makers before they gained even partial redress for the pollution of the stream.

In the early days of the Industrial Revolution there was a greater dependence on water-power than steam-power, but after the Napoleonic Wars the balance shifted decisively toward steam. With the rising output of coal came new forms of pollution; Edinburgh, always a coal-burning town, became 'Auld Reekie', the first signs of acid rain had appeared in Galloway lochs by mid-century (Battarbee et al 1988), and manufacturers dumped vast quantities of industrial ash and cinders into already overloaded rivers. This, combined with the effluent of chemical works and iron furnaces, had sterilised large parts of the freshwater Clyde and even of its saline estuary by 1850, though things have improved since: thirty-two species of fish swim now in parts of the estuary where no fish at all survived in the mid-nineteenth century.

No. 27. Detail of John Slezer's 'Prospect of Edinburgh', c.1695. The city, of about 40,000 inhabitants at the time of the Act of Union, then disposed of much of its sewage by dribbling it into the north Loch (centre right) where Princes Street Gardens are now. A countryside of unhedged and rigged fields began immediately beyond: the New Town was built there in the later eighteenth century. *Photograph courtesy of St Andrews University Library.*

The problem of pollution did not begin to be seriously tackled until in 1863 the Alkali Act appointed inspectors to enforce a rule that alkali manufacturers condense at least 95% of their hydrochloric acid gas instead of releasing it into the atmosphere (Clapp 1994). This had come about because of the noxious conditions around St Helens in Lancashire, but they were replicated on a smaller scale by the alkali works in Glasgow. The principle of an inspectorate, itself borrowed from the Factory Acts, gradually spread to other areas of environmental regulation, but in a period beyond the scope of this chapter.

EXERCISE 6
Read the above in conjunction with Irene Maver's chapter on urbanisation (Chapter 8). Why do you think environmental pollution was tolerated for so long?

In the first place it was tolerated because in town and countryside alike attitudes towards pollution were rooted in the long-standing social customs of all classes. Refuse of all sorts was dumped as a matter of course in the nearest convenient place, with no particular consideration of what it might do to your own or your neighbour's well-being. Furthermore, in the growing cities of the Industrial Revolution the deteriorating environment affected mainly the workers in overcrowded tenements, and the middle and upper classes had little incentive to seek remedies until it began seriously to impinge on their own well-being. The same was true of public health and water supply.

6. PEOPLE AND MICRO-ORGANISMS

Few aspects of the relationship between people and the environment are more important for human history than the power of micro-organisms. Generally this means the diseases which affect our own species, but not always. Highland history, and to a still greater degree Irish history, was altered almost overnight when the fungus *Phytophora infestans* attacked the potato crop. It had not been known in Europe before 1830, when it, or something like it, struck in Germany and again in parts of the Western Highlands in the same decade. These were relatively small-scale outbreaks, but in 1845–6 the blight swept through northern Europe and left the potatoes of Ireland and Scotland a stinking, suppurating mess in the soil. The impact in Scotland has been well chronicled (Devine 1988). It is sufficient here to emphasise that the fungus came as a bolt from the blue: its arrival could not have been foretold, and contemporary science had no remedy for it. It swept aside the staff of life from many tens of thousands of Highlanders, reducing them to utter destitution and leading to exacerbated clearance, depopulation and emigration. With hindsight it is tempting to say that some such disaster was inevitable for those societies foolish enough to rely so heavily on one crop, yet in earlier centuries the Scots as a whole had relied just as heavily on another crop (oats) for their daily subsistence, without ever paying the same penalty. It is fairer to say that they were the victim of an unforeseeable natural disaster.

EXERCISE 7

If the arrival of *Phytophora infestans* was an unforeseeable freak of nature, what happens to the arguments that Highlanders (and Irishmen) were irresponsible to allow their populations to grow so rapidly between 1750 and 1840 - or that clearances before 1845 were justifiable on the grounds of over-population?

If the potato cultivation of the period before the famine was truly 'sustainable', i.e. if it could have supported the contemporary levels of population indefinitely, then the Highlands and Ireland were not, in their own terms, over-populated: to call them so is to abuse the historian's privilege of hindsight because we know that after the blight struck, those lands could not support the same numbers. On the other hand, many contemporaries considered even before 1845 that in areas like Donegal and Skye the misery of the population and its level of voluntary out-migration were increasing, suggesting that the potato had after all failed to deliver a new equilibrium between population and resources. Some investigation for this period similar to Dodgshon's research on the pre-potato economy of the Western Highlands is needed.

The history of human diseases has produced many surprises comparable in their impact on people to the potato blight's effect on crops, most famously the arrival in Europe of bubonic plague from the Far East in the mid-fourteenth century. In our period, the coming of Asiatic cholera caused some 24,000 deaths in Scotland during its four visitations between 1832 and 1866 – an inconsiderable number compared to the deaths from tuberculosis and other more traditional infectious diseases, but disproportionately culling the economically active and the middle-aged (see **Article 20**). Its main importance was as the 'Great Sanitary Reformer', its terrifying and unfamiliar character spurring the authorities to begin to clean up the urban environment of the great cities along the lines advocated by Edwin Chadwick, though its side-effect in this respect was much less in rural areas and smaller municipalities such as those in Fife (Patterson 1992).

There was, moreover, nothing surprising about the rising toll taken by many familiar infectious diseases as urbanisation increased. Typhus (carried by lice) and typhoid (carried in infected water) were indistinguishable to contemporaries – along with a number of other diseases just called 'fever'. By the mid-nineteenth century, in the big cities, such fevers were helping to cause mortality crises of a kind that had not been seen in Scotland since the seventeenth century, especially in years when unemployment lowered incomes and consequently also resistance to disease (Flinn 1977).

Smallpox, having risen in incidence since before the start of the eighteenth century, was tackled partly by inoculation from the mid-eighteenth century, but much more effectively by vaccination by the early nineteenth century – the first of the great killers to be curbed by medical science. Nevertheless it remained a serious killer until the compulsory Vaccination Act of 1863, and many of the children's lives saved by vaccination in the early part of the century were lost to an increasing incidence of measles, whooping cough and scarlet fever, to none of which nineteenth-century medicine could provide a cure (see Table 1). The same was of course true of tuberculosis, the greatest killer of all, which, like so many other infections, flourished and spread most readily in the foul and overcrowded towns (see Table 2).

TABLE 1: CHILD MORTALITY IN GLASGOW, 1783–1812

(Annual average deaths from specified causes as percentage of all deaths under age ten)

CAUSE OF DEATH	1783–88	1789–94	1795–1800	1801–06	1807–12
Smallpox	19.5	18.2	18.7	8.9	3.9
Measles	0.9	1.2	2.1	3.9	10.8
Whooping Cough	4.5	5.1	5.4	6.1	5.6

TABLE 2: DEATH FROM INFECTIOUS DISEASE IN GLASGOW, 1800–1865

(Deaths from specified diseases as percentages of all deaths in Glasgow)

CAUSE OF DEATH	1800–10	1836–42	1855–65
'Fever'	9.8	16.1	9.5
Whooping cough	6.8	5.3	5.6
Tuberculosis and bronchitis	22.8	16.8	29.6
Smallpox	6.6	5.0	1.9
Measles	7.5	6.6	3.1
Bowel diseases	8.9	12.1	11.4
Total	62.4	61.9	61.1

Source: Flinn 1977, 389, 391.

One rural disease, however, disappeared of its own accord largely before 1800: malaria, the 'ague' of contemporary accounts, simply ceased to bother the country areas where it had once been the bane of existence. The usual explanation is the drainage of marshes, but many were not drained at all. Another reason recently given for its disappearance in eighteenth-century Denmark may also be applicable to Scotland: it hinges on the preference of the local malaria-carrying *Anopheles* mosquito, *A. atroparvus*, for cattle and other domestic animals rather than for human beings. In earlier centuries, runs the argument, animals had been in short supply round the townships at certain times of year and the mosquitoes turned to humans for blood, but with the agrarian changes of the eighteenth century, particularly when summer stall feeding was introduced but also simply if animals were kept in pasture near the house, the mosquitoes were able to feed on preferred animal blood, in which the malaria parasite is unable to survive (see **Article 21**). The interconnectedness of nature means that environmental history is full of unexpected links and consequences of this sort.

EXERCISE 8

Before the twentieth century, medical science, except in the case of smallpox, conspicuously failed to cure infectious diseases. Micro-organisms, however, will fail as species if they kill off too many of their hosts: it can be argued that they therefore endanger individuals but not societies. How far do these facts help to explain fatalistic attitudes in popular culture and religion, and sluggish progress towards public health reform? What else was at work to delay more vigorous action to prevent infectious disease? Consider this in the light of Chapter 8.

I will leave you to think of your own response to this complex question, but ask you to consider carefully who constitutes and leads 'societies' and how popular attitudes in culture and religion are formed. The theory of the 'selfish gene' suggests that individuals capable of reproduction would not (biologically speaking) be much concerned about the death of parents, or about the deaths of children providing they could still procreate others with similar biological prospects: they would certainly not be concerned about the death of individuals to whom they were not genetically linked, unless that death threatened to bring about their own through an infection that they could not escape. Marxist theory proposes that the ruling classes in any epoch seek their collective self-interest at the expense of the rest of the population. Such self-interest would not rule out, ultimately, better public health for the labouring masses as the value of their labour increased. I need hardly remind you (a) that these are only theories, not proven universal truths or explanations (b) there are other theories and (c) no theory encapsulates the total truth.

SUMMARY

By 1850, the Scottish environment was beginning to change rapidly in its relationship to human society. In the first place, people had begun to consider the possibilities of manipulating nature to a degree unimaginable before. Secondly, the earth had been made to yield up a far greater quantity of food and resources with, as yet, few obviously adverse ecological effects. Nevertheless, thirdly, adverse effects were not totally lacking – it could be argued that a long-term decline in fragile areas like the Highlands was exacerbated, and signs that an urbanised society was a seriously polluting society were already evident, particularly in the rivers and in the pall of smoke over the cities. Lastly, humans still had little control over micro-organisms – the great achievements of the first phase of modern agrarian and industrial change took place in the absence of any very effective agricultural or medical science. The triumphs and troubles of the century after 1850 stemmed from this situation, but have both developed in proportion to the growth of science and technology.

REFERENCES TO BOOKS AND ARTICLES MENTIONED IN THE TEXT

Battarbee, RW 1988 *Lake Acidification in the United Kingdom 1800–1986: Evidence from Analysis of Lake Sediments*. London.

Breeze, DJ 1992 'The Great Myth of Caledon', *Scottish Forestry* 46, 331–5.

*Brimblecombe, P 1987 *The Big Smoke: a History of Air Pollution in London Since Medieval Times*. London.

Campbell, RD 1977 'The Scottish Improvers and the Course of Agrarian Change in the Eighteenth Century', *in* Cullen, LM and Smout, TC (eds), *Comparative Aspects of Scottish and Irish Economic and Social History, 1600–1900*, Edinburgh, 205–15.

Chambers, FM (ed) 1993 *Climate Change and Human Impact on the Landscape*. London.

*Clapp, BW 1994 *An Environmental History of Britain Since the Industrial Revolution*. London and New York.

*Cronan, W 1985 *Changes on the Land: Indians, Colonists and the Ecology of New England*. New York.

*Crosby, AW 1986 *Ecological Imperialism: the Biological Expansion of Europe, 900–1900*. Cambridge.

Darling, FF 1947 *Natural History in the Highlands and Islands*. London.

Darling, FF 1955 *West Highland Survey*. Oxford.

Davidson, DA and Simpson, IA 1994 'Soils and Landscape History: Case Studies from the Northern Isles of Scotland', *in* Foster, S and Smout, TC (eds), *The History of Soils and Field Systems*, Aberdeen, 66–74.

Davidson, DA and Smout TC 1996 'Soil Change in Scotland: the Legacy of Past Land Improvement Processes', *in* Taylor, AG, Gordon, JE and Usher, MB *Soils, Sustainability and the Natural Heritage*, Edinburgh, 44–54.

Devine, TM 1988 *The Great Highland Famine*. Edinburgh.

Devine, TM 1994 *The Transformation of Rural Scotland: Social Change and the Agrarian Economy, 1660–1815*. Edinburgh.

Dodgshon, RA 1994 'Budgeting for Survival: Nutrient Flow and Traditional Highland Farming' *in* Foster, S and Smout, TC (eds), *The History of Soils and Field Systems*, Aberdeen, 83–93.

Duncan, CAM 1991 'On Identifying a Sound Environmental Ethic in History', *Environmental History Review* 15, 1–8.

Flinn, MW (ed) 1977 *Scottish Population History from the Seventeenth Century to the 1930s*. Cambridge.

Gibson, AJS and Smout TC 1995 *Prices, Food and Wages in Scotland, 1550–1780*. Cambridge.

*Grove, RH 1995 *Green Imperialism: Colonial Expansion, Tropical Island Edens and the Origins of Environmentalism, 1600–1860*. Cambridge.

Guha, R 1990 *The Unquiet Woods: Ecological Change and Peasant Resistance in the Himalaya*. Berkeley, California.

Handley, JE 1953 *Scottish Farming in the Eighteenth Century*. London.

Handley, JE 1963 *The Agricultural Revolution in Scotland*. Glasgow.

Hunter, J 1973 'Sheep and deer: Highland sheep farming, 1850–1900', *Northern Scotland* 1, 199–222.

*Kjærgaard, T 1994 *The Danish Revolution: an Ecohistorical Interpretation*. Cambridge.

Lindsay, JM 1975 'Charcoal iron smelting and its fuel supply: the example of Lorn furnace, Argyllshire, 1753–1876', *Journal of Historical Geography* 1, 283–298.

Mackenzie, JM 1900 *Imperialism and the Natural World*. Manchester.

Mather, A 1993 'The environmental impact of sheep in the Scottish Highlands', *in* Smout, TC (ed), *Scotland Since Prehistory: Natural Change and Human Impact*, Aberdeen, 79–88.

Mitchell, A (ed) 1906 *Geographical Collections Relating to Scotland made by Walter Macfarlane* (3 vols). Edinburgh.

Oelschlaeger, M 1991 *The Idea of Wilderness from Prehistory to the Age of Ecology*. New Haven and London.

Patterson, S 1992 'Cholera in Fife: The Great Sanitary Reformer', *Proceedings of the Royal College of Physicians of Edinburgh* 22, 238–53.

*Rackham, O 1986 *The History of the Countryside*. London.

Sheail, J 1976 *Nature in Trust: the History of Nature Conservation in Britain*. Glasgow.

Simmonds, I and Tooley, M (eds) 1981 *The Environment in British Pre-history*. Ithaca: Cornell University.

Smout, TC 1969 *A History of the Scottish People, 1560–1830*. London.

Smout, TC 1986 *A Century of the Scottish People, 1830–1950*. London.

Smout, TC 1991 'The Highlands and the Roots of Green Consciousness, 1750–1850', *Proceedings of the British Academy* 76, 237–64. Reprinted as *Scottish Natural Heritage Occasional Paper No. 1*. Perth.

*Smout, TC (ed) 1993 *Scotland Since Prehistory: Natural Change and Human Impact*. Aberdeen.

Smout, TC 1994 'Trees as Historic Landscapes: Wallace's Oak to Reforesting Scotland', *Scottish Forestry* 48, 244–52.

*Smout, TC (ed) 1997 *Essays in Scottish Woodland History*. Aberdeen.

Statistical Account of Scotland 1791–99. 21 volumes. Edinburgh.

Symon, JA 1959 *Scottish Farming Past and Present*. Edinburgh.

*Thomas, K 1983 *Man and the Natural World; a History of Modern Sensibility*. London.

Whittington, G 1975 'Was there a Scottish Agricultural Revolution?' *Area* 7, 204–6.

Whyte, ID 1995 *Scotland Before the Industrial Revolution: an Economic and Social History, c.1050–c.1750*. London and New York.

*Worster, D 1977 *Nature's Economy: a History of Ecological Ideas*. Cambridge.

* The asterisked items are interesting examples of environmental history, but not, for the most part, focused on Scotland.

Culture

Gerard Carruthers

INTRODUCTION

Scottish cultural history in the period 1707–1850 was greatly influenced by the large-scale shifts in Scottish identity during this time. A heightening of nationalist sentiment in Scotland was one response to the loss of the Scottish parliament in 1707, while other contemporary strands of Scottish thought sought, in the wake of parliamentary union with England, to emphasise British and cosmopolitan identities to the nation. Commentators have often perceived particularly sharp tensions between these different aspirations of identity making for a Scottish culture in conflict until the middle of the nineteenth century. By this time, in the wake of radically changed commercial, industrial and political patterns in Scotland, Britain and the wider world, much of the cultural distinctiveness of Scotland seemed to have vanished for good and the ideal of any kind of real Scottish autonomy of identity probably seemed to most Britons to be both impractical and undesirable. Scottish culture from 1707 to 1850, then, can be read as a kind of battleground where a beleaguered defence of distinctive Scottish values was attempted and gradually overcome by the priorities of the new British superstate and by the encroachments of the modern world.

One of the most amenable sites for exploring issues of Scottish cultural identity can be found in the nation's literature but this area also seems to throw up something of a puzzle as the vibrancy of Scottish literature in much of this period seems to sit rather uneasily with the notion of Scottish culture's gradual eclipse. This strange disjunction is what Daiches (1964) has famously identified as the 'paradox' of Scottish culture in the eighteenth century. In this depiction, Daiches essentially argues that the fervent Scottish literary activity during this time (especially from around 1760 to the 1820s) demonstrated a national culture's noisy death rattle. Scottish cultural 'health' is the major issue which we have to consider in the forthcoming chapter as we focus on the literary culture of the period.

This chapter is divided into a number of sections. These sections are designed to highlight some of the most important cultural and literary impulses at work in Scotland during the period. Sometimes major questions will be raised in the chapter without the provision of any definitive answer since the issues surrounding such ideal concepts as a national culture or a literary tradition are many and vexed. It is hoped that you might explore and develop answers for yourself as you become aware of the debates surrounding Scottish literature in the period. The main divisions of the chapter are:

- Cultural Nationalism: The Scots poetry revival
- Cosmopolitanism: The Scottish Enlightenment
- Robert Burns
- The Age of Scott
- Towards Victorian Britain
- Conclusion

1. CULTURAL NATIONALISM: THE SCOTS POETRY REVIVAL

The events surrounding the Union of 1707 led to loud Scottish lamentation. Political writings by the likes of Andrew Fletcher of Saltoun (1653–1716) and George Lockhart of Carnwath (1681–1731) spoke of the betrayal of the nation and of its impending ruin (in both cultural and economic terms); on the dissolution of the Scottish parliament its chancellor Lord Seafield famously spoke of 'the end of an auld sang'. In this climate there was an accentuation of interest in the Scottish past and attempts were made to clarify and retrieve something of this past. One outcome of this mood was the widening of Scottish identification with the exiled royal line of Stuart (which of course had been born in Scotland). This had an influence well beyond that minority of Scots who took part in the various Jacobite rebellions as the political and cultural nostalgia associated with Jacobitism fostered and dovetailed with various antiquarian historical and literary activities to produce a very virile strain of what today we might call cultural nationalism. This cultural nationalism, or the assertion of a nation's peculiarly proper outlook and means of expression, is seen most clearly in the long eighteenth-century revival of poetry in Scots which toward the end of the century produced Scotland's national poet Robert Burns.

The beginning of the Scots poetry revival is to be found in the editorial work of the Jacobites James Watson (d. 1722) and Thomas Ruddiman (1674–1757). The work of these two men initiated a strong tradition of revivalist literary production which, as is so often the case with 'revivals', also led to a number of new emphases in Scottish literature. This is especially the case with Watson. Watson's anthology of Scottish poetry, his *Choice Collection of Comic and Serious Scots Poems* (1706–1711) is largely a collection of sixteenth-century Scottish court poetry (and is patchy in its presentation of Scotland's greater medieval poetic heritage) but it features also two verse-forms which were to become synonymous with eighteenth-century literary nationalism in Scotland. 'Christ's Kirk on the Green', ascribed to King James I (1394–1437), and 'The Life and Death of the Piper of Kilbarchan' by Robert Sempill of Beltrees (?1595–?1665) provide the 'Christ's Kirk' and 'Habbie Simpson' stanzas respectively, which, especially in the case of the latter, were to become a kind of cultural signature for poets writing in Scots. These two stanzas were of long European lineage but over the course of the eighteenth century came to be seen as being particularly Scottish. In the two poems mentioned, their rhythmically jaunty stanzas complement festive or carnivalesque subject-matter, and these features of form and focus are frequently appropriated by eighteenth-century Scots poets in their keynote mode of social and national satire.

1.1. *Allan Ramsay (1684–1758)*

The first great translator of Scotland's literary past into its creative present in the eighteenth century was Allan Ramsay, a wigmaker in Edinburgh and a cultural entrepreneur *par excellence*. A founding member of the Easy Club, one of the earliest secular debating societies in eighteenth-century Scotland, Ramsay also opened a bookshop (which incorporated what was effectively the first circulating library in Britain), attempted to establish a theatre (much to the disapproval of the puritanical Edinburgh city fathers) and wrote and edited poetry in Scots.

Following in James Watson's footsteps, Ramsay produced two highly influential poetry anthologies, *The Ever Green* (1724) and *The Tea-Table Miscellany* (1724–1737). The first of these collections (where Ramsay had access to the pioneering medieval literary scholarship of Ruddiman) reiterated more forcefully the point being made by Watson's work, that Scotland had a strong literary heritage in Scots, and both Ramsay's anthologies placed some emphasis on the folk and ballad culture of Scotland. Even more important in setting in place the key features for much of the poetry in Scots in the subsequent century, Ramsay's usage of folk-elements and elements of an often rude or grotesque Scottish medieval poetry is to be found in his own original poetry written from the second decade of the eighteenth century. The conjunction of these modes is particularly amenable to eighteenth-century Scots poets as it provides a bulwark of attitudinal and linguistic features which can be opposed to both the Puritanism of Scottish Calvinism and the ruining alien refinement in Scottish society and culture which these poets often perceived.

EXERCISE 1

Read **Document 67** which is an excerpt from Ramsay's preface to *The Ever Green* where he describes the virtues of past Scottish poets. What are the key features of Ramsay's attitudes to the notion of a national literature? Might there be any dangerous cultural narrowness lurking in his pronouncements?

It might be fair to say that in his preface Ramsay indulges in a kind of idealised overstatement since he feels the sense of a distinctive Scottish culture and literature to be under threat. The rhetoric of cultural purity wielded by Ramsay and those Scots poets who follow him is far from being adhered to in their poetic practice. It might be argued that much traditional Scottish criticism has tended to take Ramsay and others too much at their word and emphasises rather narrowly their Scottish qualities while, at the same time, over-zealously lamenting their usage of 'alien' (especially English) elements in their poetry. In his most purely Scottish mode, Ramsay adopts the 'habbie' stanza, writes in an energetic colloquial Scots, speaks from a position of solidarity with the more demotic side of Edinburgh life awash with drink and lowlife festival, and often cocks a snook at authority.

EXERCISE 2

Read **Document 68**: 'Lucky Spence's Last Advice' (1718). Notice the use of the 'habbie simpson' stanza already alluded to. How does this form contribute to the overall effects and tone Ramsay is after? Clearly, the poem is a piece of extended inversion as it collides the dignified forum of the last words of a dying person with undignified subject-matter. What sort of view of society emerges from this subversion?

One way of contextualising Ramsay's poetic essay on lowlife subject matter is to say that it speaks of an Edinburgh, a Scottish and a British culture generally viewed as lacking a healthy centre. This, of course, is in keeping with Ramsay's views on the new constitution of the British state following 1707, but it speaks not simply of the alienated attitude of an anti-Unionist. The grotesque fantasy in 'Lucky Spence' points also to a wider eighteenth-century British Tory mentality diagnosing a society being damaged by increasingly dominant market forces. The 'habbie simpson' stanza-form and the practical, businesslike guide to prostitution in the poem contribute to a riotously bitter critique of contemporary society. Ramsay the Tory moral satirist is very evident in one of his finest pieces, 'Wealth, or the Woody' (1720) ('woody' = the gallows). The poem highlights Ramsay the confident Scottish Augustan as in Scots-English, and with a closely observed metaphorical and epigrammatical wit which owes something to the influence of Alexander Pope and his contemporaries in mainstream English literary culture, it satirises the notorious financial scandal of the South Sea Company's stock-speculation scheme of 1719–20. We again see Ramsay in a different mode to that of the mere ghettoised cultural nationalist in his 'Epistles to William Somerville' which show him ostentatiously adopting the mantle of a 'Briton'. In these verse-epistles Ramsay writes to an English poet who has admired his writing in Scots and demonstrates also his knowledge of the English poetic tradition. Sometimes taken as showing signs of national schizophrenia, these poems can be read instead as Ramsay demonstrating his bicultural facility and implying that he is the man of broader heritage and possibility than the Englishman.

EXERCISE 3

Read David Daiches' classic identification of Ramsay's cultural 'crisis of identity' (**Article 22A**) which is of a kind many commentators have found in numerous Scottish writers from the eighteenth century onwards. Is Daiches completely fair as he points toward the implications of Ramsay's cultural 'dualism', or, in the manner I have begun to suggest, might Daiches' description indicate a cultural facility in Ramsay which, far from being entirely culpable, is necessary and in some sense perhaps even healthy? Read also **Article 22B** which is a very recent appraisal of the multifarious ideological elements influencing Scottish culture at the beginning of the eighteenth century.

1.2. Robert Fergusson (1750–1774)

Of a number of poets following in the footsteps of Allan Ramsay before Burns, the most talented was Robert Fergusson. The known facts of his life (and death), however, are fairly scanty. His parents were emigrants from the North-East to Edinburgh where Fergusson was born. (As a result, the Scots of his poetry mixes Buchan dialect with Edinburgh street parlance and other Scots usage.) He was a talented scholar and attended the University of St Andrews, after which he became a legal clerk in the capital. Fergusson first published his work in the *Weekly Magazine* run by Walter (nephew of Thomas) Ruddiman (1719–81) and died aged 24 in the Edinburgh madhouse. The cause of his death is variously attributed to a constitution infirm from childhood, an excessive lifestyle (for which the subject-matter of his poetry is turned to for evidence), or religious melancholia. The latter two explanations are often used by commentators who wish to make the case for Fergusson's death being attributable to his reaction to the unamenable culture of Scotland. A complaint frequently voiced (the first so to hint at this was Fergusson's great admirer Burns who petitioned for the erection of a tombstone at the pauper's grave of his predecessor) is that Fergusson, writing at the height of the Scottish Enlightenment's attempts to trumpet the culture and civilisation of Scotland, was ignored by the

No. 28. Princes Street with the Royal Institution building under construction, 1825. Painting by Alexander Nasmyth. © *National Gallery of Scotland.*

Edinburgh *literati* who were, therefore, virtual accessories in his death and the attendant loss to Scottish literature.

Fergusson makes a series of complaints about Scotland which are typical of cultural nationalism in Scots poetry. In 'Elegy on the Death of Scots Music' (1772) Fergusson complains about the modish Italian cultural influence now infecting Scottish folk-music; 'The Ghaists' (1773) laments central government's fiscal exploitation of the vulnerable post-Union state of Scotland; 'The Farmer's Ingle' (1773) celebrates the primitive but virtuous culture of the Scots peasantry as a last repository of historic Scottish values; and a series of carnivalesque poems (with Jacobite overtones) respond to the 'misrule' of the pro-Hanoverian Scots or 'Whigs' (in the specialist Scottish usage).

> EXERCISE 4
> Read **Document 69**, Fergusson's carnivalesque 'The King's Birth-Day in Edinburgh' (1772). In what light do those in authority and the common people emerge from the poem? Notice the status of the holiday and the depiction of a city militia formed out of the Highland diaspora in the wake of the upheavals of Jacobitism, among other elements in a fairly comprehensive picture of cultural atrophy. (For a very detailed examination of the socio-cultural context of this and many other poems, see Freeman (1984)).

'The King's Birth-Day in Edinburgh' represents a high-holiday public occasion and a society shot through with undignified behaviour and values. The essential point is that any proper cultural or political authority has been demitted and so (rather as in 'Lucky Spence') anarchic tendencies take over. Again, then, we have a piece in which carnival enjoyment and disgust intermingle.

Taking much of his cue from Ramsay, Fergusson is, however, a much more profound Scots poet than Ramsay. His versatile work also includes the fantasy, 'Mutual Complaint of Plainstanes and Causey' (1773), which draws on the 'flyting' mode or the combative verbal energy of Medieval Scots poetry as the pavement and the road debate, in very contemporary eighteenth-century fashion, the differing and equally vexing social traffic they carry; 'Auld Reikie' (1773), which is a long affectionate look at the Old Town of Edinburgh combining a documentary portrait of the social bustle, sights and smells of the capital in different phases of the day with a witty, political and philosophical overview; and the contemplative 'Ode to the Gowdspink' (1773), which places the Scots language in the setting of late-Augustan lyricism and looks toward the expression of melancholia and alienation found in Romanticism. With Fergusson, then, even though he died so young, we see the Scots poetic tradition expanding in range and taking on a new and confident sophistication.

2. COSMOPOLITANISM: THE SCOTTISH ENLIGHTENMENT

That set of activities and movement in ideas which commentators refer to as the Scottish Enlightenment is part of the wider eighteenth-century *milieu* of European

Enlightenment. As such, the Scottish Enlightenment is concerned with the universal application of reason for the improvement of the mental and material condition of humankind. In Scotland, however, the peculiar circumstances surrounding national identity and existing cultural patterns have led many commentators to read the impact of the Enlightenment as highly problematic. The Scottish Enlightenment has often been viewed as being much more conservative than, say, the French Enlightenment and this is attributed to the reliance of the Scottish version on activists largely drawn from the moderate wing of the Scottish Presbyterian church and professional men (lawyers most prominently) who found cause for optimism over the material future of Scotland in the new politically united Britain. This presence in the Enlightenment mindset in Scotland, it can be argued, led to a cultural strain which was both reactionary and artificial. On the other hand, however, some of the impulses the Scottish Enlightenment released can be said to have allowed the renourishing and broadening of Scottish culture.

2.1. *Scotland: Civilised and primitive*

Scottish Enlightenment activists, primed to some extent by a sense of national vacuum and by a sense of opportunity in post-Union Scotland, played a great part in redrawing the cultural profile of their country. The man often credited as the 'father' of the Scottish Enlightenment, Francis Hutcheson (1694–1746), an Ulster Scot who took up the chair of Moral Philosophy at Glasgow University in 1729, was instrumental in the rise of a new secular intellect in Scotland as he argued the notion of a 'moral sense' possessed by all humans (Christianised or not) and championed the study of aesthetics. The interests of Hutcheson, a presbyterian minister, speak of a new moderate sensibility in Scotland which began to challenge Scottish Calvinism's tendencies toward theocracy and puritanism. If the traditionalists of the Scottish church were hostile to Hutcheson, they found a positive *bête noire* in David Hume (1711–76) the philosopher who avowed scepticism and whose *A Treatise of Human Nature* (1739–40) is heretically mechanistic in its empirical analyses of the workings of human nature across many mental and social aspects. The urbane generosity in the outlook of Hutcheson and the intellectual rigour of Hume set the scene for an increasingly cosmopolitan or outward-looking mindset in Scottish culture.

Of all Scottish thinkers, Hume was keenest to quicken the cultural pulse of Scotland so that England, its new constitutional partner, should not think the country backward. His writing in its wide range of interests and powers of reasoned analysis is eloquent testimony to the breadth and modernity of outlook the eighteenth-century Scot might be seen to possess. In particular, Hume's shorter showpiece essays, published from 1741 (and hugely popular in their own day), represent a stylistic and intellectual achievement which might lead us to expect a place for them in the canon of Scottish literature. This place, however, has never been granted by Scottish critics. (You might wish to speculate on why this is the case.)

EXERCISE 5

Read the extract from Hume's essay 'Of the Delicacy of Taste and Passion' (**Document 70**). Attempt to sum up the man of taste or culture as prescribed by Hume.

For Hume, people of culture involve themselves in highly refined processes of behaviour and thinking. The cultured person ought to safeguard against losing himself in emotional extremes but is also expected to exercise an emotional and intellectual sensitivity in appraising situations (in the extract these situations are all matters of aesthetic reception and include 'polite' conversation, poetry and abstract reasoning). Thus properly engaged, the cultured mental state leads to a kind of situation of moral superiority where the individual is raised above the merely material appetites.

Although not too dissimilar to many other statements of 'cultural theory' being made across Europe at this time, Hume's rigorous prescription can be read as symptomatic of an overbearing anxiety to promote standards of civilised culture in a culturally insecure Scottish nation. His essays can also be read as a symptom of anglicisation since they are part of an attempt to foster a 'polite' culture in his native land based, to a large extent, on the neo-classical regulation of manners, morals and art as promulgated by English Augustanism and found most centrally in its great periodical, *The Spectator*. Among other evidence frequently cited for the imposition of an alien, synthetic strain of culture on Scotland from the early decades of the eighteenth century are the various compilations of 'Scotticisms' (Scots usage to be avoided when writing 'correct' English) compiled by Hume and several other Scottish men of letters, a plethora of literary and aesthetic criticism by Scots which tends toward values of moral conservatism and neo-classical prescription, the construction of 'New Town' Edinburgh from the 1760s as the socially sanitised 'Athens of the North', and a series of literary productions which can be seen as narrowly tailored to the cultural predilections of the Scottish Enlightenment *literati* (a term favoured by those so described at the time but often derogatory when used by twentieth-century commentators). Much of the socio-cultural programme associated with the Scottish Enlightenment, then, it might be argued, represents an 'alienation from things native' (Craig 1961, 63), and so contrasts starkly with the more unforced and uninhibited imaginative energies of the Scots poetry movement.

EXERCISE 6

Read **Articles 22C and 22D** by Nairn and Simpson, two of the most incisive commentators upon the cultural agenda of the Scottish Enlightenment. Make notes on the historical context suggested by these commentators and use these to weigh up the following discussion.

Let us turn our attention to some of the most important exemplars of literary creativity encouraged and engineered by the Scottish Enlightenment *literati*. Some of these are perhaps justly forgotten today. Into this category would fall *The Epigoniad*

(1757) by William Wilkie (1721–72) which was hailed by David Hume as a great breakthrough for the Scots in the writing of epic poetry. Centred on ancient Greek history, it stretches across six thousand sonorous Miltonic lines and demonstrates the rather anachronistic tendency in the *literati's* blueprint for providing Scotland with a 'high' literature they felt it lacked. (An irony here is that Wilkie was also friend and teacher to Robert Fergusson at St Andrews university and could himself compose energetically humorous Scots verse on occasion). Another dull literary manifestation is to be found in the blind Thomas Blacklock (1721–91) who was celebrated as a lyric poet for a time in the 1760s. He was a protégé of Hume and other Scottish thinkers who were fascinated by Blacklock's seemingly instinctive capacity for description in spite of his handicap. In fact this was very little to do with instinct and more to do with his immersion in Augustan verse of the day which he blandly mimicked, marking his own contribution by adding a large dash of prudish and pietistic morality. With Wilkie and Blacklock, then, we find the Scottish Enlightenment's involvement with a rather frigid imagination regulated by conservative formulaic and moral considerations.

Some of the other literary productions associated with the Scottish Enlightenment should be dismissed less lightly. The drama *Douglas* (1756), written by the clergyman John Home (1722–1808), was circulated among Hume and others in the salon society of Edinburgh (see Sher 1985). Suggestions for revision and practical support in staging the play from this quarter brought it triumphantly to the stage in a city and in a country which had puritanically eschewed the theatre. Given this vacuum in Scotland, it is perhaps no surprise that the play should rather rigorously observe the properties of the dramatic unities, spout a rather stiff heroic diction and rely on strong Shakespearean overtones of plot and character. At the same time, however, it does draw on native Scottish culture as it bases its plot partly on the old ballad 'Gil Morice' and deals with the ancient Scottish wars with the Norsemen. These aspects lead to the articulation of the notion of the wild, romantic Scottish landscape as an appropriate context for melancholy and passionate events, and as a result *Douglas* represents one of the first steps towards the modern interest in Scotland as a place of alternative imaginative vision. (The European Romantic movement a little later draws great inspiration from this notion of a primitive, mystical cultural outlook as found in Scotland).

Another production which has to be seen in the context of the Enlightenment quest for Scottish literature is the poetry of 'Ossian' which was famously loved by Napoleon Buonaparte. In the early 1760s, James Macpherson (1736–96) published poetry which he claimed to be translated from the Gaelic of several third- and fourth-century oral bards, the most prominent among whom was Ossian. Macpherson's claims and his trips into the Highlands to recover an increasing amount of this material were heavily supported by a number of fellow Scots (Hume is yet again prominent) and loudly denounced as forgery by the great Scotophobe Samuel Johnson. Modern scholarship broadly concludes that Macpherson did indeed collect and translate a quantity of old oral material but that he supplemented and arranged this for better narrative coherence.

The Scots were particularly keen on Macpherson's work as it provided an ancient buttress to a seemingly scant Scottish literary heritage and perhaps even more importantly because it appeared to vindicate anthropological and critical ideas of the Scottish Enlightenment. Macpherson's productions featured prominently acts of heroic virtue which seemed to corroborate the primitivism of moral philosophers like Hutcheson and Thomas Reid (1710–96) who emphasised an instinctive or feeling capacity in man for appraising the world through a moral lens. The poetic manner in which they were written also exemplified for critics such as Hugh Blair (1718–1800) the 'sublime' or emotively delineated natural scenes unencumbered by the more precise metaphorical techniques of later ages. The Ossianic poetry, then, reflects a side of Scottish Enlightenment taste not so exclusively taken up with dry neo-classical formulaicism. Having said this, the primitive 'feeling' in Ossian (which like Home's *Douglas* points the way to Romanticism's collision of naked emotion and nature), might be argued to be present in too unremittingly isolated or rarefied form. Again, then, we have a rather one-dimensional text conforming to the *a priori* and rather synthetic Scottish Enlightenment notions of what ancient man and ancient poetry should look like. Two other points ought to be made about the Enlightenment enthusiasm for the Ossian poetry. As the *literati* rejoiced in discovering this ancient culture of the Gaidhealtachd, they ignored a very vital resurgence in eighteenth-century Gaelic poetry, seen in the work of Alexander Macdonald

No. 29. The only meeting of Burns and Scott (in Sciennes House, Edinburgh). From the painting by Hardie. *Abbotsford House.*

(*c. 1695–c.* 1770) and Rob Donn (*c.* 1715–78). On the more positive side, the intense Enlightenment activity in examining Ossian strengthened the long-standing Scottish interest in aesthetics and literary criticism, and although works resulting from this such as *Blair's Lectures on Rhetoric and Belles Lettres* (1783) are typically too prescriptive, in world terms they also pioneer the development of reflective reading skills.

Another literary text which is usually seen to sit at the cutting edge of Scottish Enlightenment cultural engineering is the novel *The Man of Feeling* (1771) by the Edinburgh lawyer and man of letters Henry MacKenzie (1745–1831). Spectacularly popular in its day in Britain, the novel is frequently cited as the nadir of the sentimental literary mode. It features Harley, a young man of the most refined sensibility who witnesses a catalogue of the most pathetic human circumstances and whose response is invariably to weep. The extreme mawkishness of the novel is often traced to the influence of the moral philosophy of the Scottish Enlightenment and particularly to the doctrine of 'sympathy' most centrally associated with Adam Smith (1723–90). In *The Man of Feeling*, Harley's extreme instinctive sensitivity to a catalogue of evil misfortune involving deflowered virgins, orphaned children and bereaved parents leads to his eventual breakdown and death, and this is sometimes read as being emblematic of the intellectual and social mannerism and impracticality inherent in the sympathetic sensibility. This reading, however, misses both the irony of the novel and the fact that Smith's doctrine demands (and here we can see parallels with what we have seen in Hume) sympathy in feeling and restraint in behaviour. What is also sometimes overlooked is that in spite of the silly mannerism of Harley's behaviour, he represents an individual who is so alienated that he can no longer cope with a world whose logic is brutally selfish and commercial. Smith's doctrine and the novel both protest against a world inadequately concerned to uphold the values of community and humanity.

If James Macpherson had presented a somewhat customised exploration of ancient Scottish culture, there were many more straightforward attempts to celebrate and convey the 'lost' or hidden heritage of Scotland. Around the middle of the century, the drawing-rooms of polite Scottish society saw an intense interest in Scottish song and ballad often channelled through women such as Jean Elliot of Minto (1727–1805) who refashioned and popularised the enduring stalwart of Scottish folk-music, 'The Flowers of the Forest'. Interest in the distinctive situation of contemporary Scottish life was also evident as Scottish writers attempted to communicate the complex reality of a country both civilised and primitive at the same time. The most stunning examples in this regard are the epistolary novel, *The Expedition of Humphry Clinker* (1771) by Tobias Smollett (1721–71) and the *Journal of a Tour to the Hebrides* (1786), a factual account by James Boswell (1740–95) of an expedition with his friend Samuel Johnson. Both of these texts have in common profound sociological and psychological investigations (and again these aspects can be traced to the interests of the Scottish Enlightenment) in their attempts to educate the reader in the cultural location of Scotland. Boswell, although seeming to write in straightforward, documentary form, was very much a stage-manager as he selected the incidents he recorded to highlight to the maximum the collision of Samuel Johnson, the great arbiter of British culture, with the experience of Scotland. In Smollett's novel a touring Welsh family (whose males are, however, Oxford-educated and to all intents and purposes represent 'middle England') are startled to find a 'hot-bed of genius', as Smollett calls the Scottish Enlightenment at its height, co-existing with an exotic provincial culture steeped in the historic traditions of Scotland.

> EXERCISE 7
> Read the two extracts from Smollett (**Document 71**) and Boswell (**Document 72**). In the first extract, what is the logical absurdity in Tabitha's belief that there are only the heads of sheep to eat? Amid the comedic overtones there is a very measured diagnosis of British cultural tension. What are the terms of this and why do you think reference is made to 'South Britons'? In the second extract, might Boswell be attempting to make any serious cultural point (perhaps with regard to both Scottish and English manners)?

As Smollett is wryly highlighting, if there are sheep's heads in Scotland there must also be sheep's bodies. Clearly, Smollett is pointing to wild, popular prejudice against his country. He then goes on to table a kind of claim for mutuality in perspective as he labels England (and Wales) as 'South Britain' (and so implicitly tags Scotland as 'North Britain' – a favourite Scottish Enlightenment term of identity). This is very subtle as it implies that each of the British nations has to define itself respectfully in relation to the others.

Boswell is doing something similar to Smollett in spotlighting, in his very minor incident, a lack of communication. Again the point is that different cultures are going to have to attempt to understand one another if Britain is to work (though there is also, perhaps, a sly, superior note in the implication that the lowlander Boswell is the one with the comprehensive outlook amid the clash of the Highlands and England).

3. ROBERT BURNS

Robert Burns (1759–1796) represents the culminating achievement of the eight-eenth-century Scots poetry revival. He built on the work of Ramsay and Fergusson and added new dimensions to the poetic use of Scots as he drew widely on folk-materials and the most current intellectual resources and problems of his day. Born into a pious peasant family, Burns was instantly in touch with a presbyterian tradition with a high regard for education and literacy, a background of intellectual religious puritanism, country folk-traditions and the rigours of a farming life which was becoming increasingly uncertain in the wake of the Agrarian Revolution. Adding to the cultural minestrone which Burns imbibed was the influence of the

Scottish Enlightenment and other ideological currents transforming the direction not only of Scotland but of the western world in general.

From Kincardineshire in the North-East, Burns' father settled in Ayrshire as a gardener and a farmer and was frequently in financial difficulty. Nonetheless, he insisted on an education for Robert and his brother under a private schoolmaster (the services and cost of whom were shared with like-minded neighbours) as well as some further schooling. The myth, then, of the uneducated rustic, 'the heaven-taught ploughman', as Henry Mackenzie christened Burns in a famous review, is clearly untrue. Mackenzie and the Edinburgh *literati* who lionised Burns in the capital in 1787 failed to recognise the intellectual, and very urban, tradition of Scots poetry from which Burns sprang, intent as they were on 'discovering' yet another manifestation of primitive Scottish poetic vision. Irony resides not only in the failure of the Scottish Enlightenment to recognise the eighteenth-century Scots literary tradition in which Burns operated but also in its failure to identify the very cosmopolitan energies in Burns which had been fostered by his exposure to the satellite Ayrshire Enlightenment.

Burns' *Poems, Chiefly in the Scottish Dialect* (the 'Kilmarnock edition'), published in 1786, came about because of Burns' local popularity. To some extent, his work was known in manuscript form by a wide range of country folk in his district (though the precise extent of this is shrouded by the prodigious biographical mythology surrounding Burns), but more important in bringing about Burns' publication was the fact that his work was loved in Ayrshire intellectual circles comprising young lawyers, businessmen and farmers who met in masonic lodges and Enlightenment-inspired societies such as the one Burns had famously helped found in 1780, the Tarbolton Bachelors' Club. It was in this context of the Ayrshire Enlightenment that not only were the infamous libertine energies of Burns encouraged, but his more meaningful intellectual awareness was inculcated through debate and discussion of the issues and literature of the day. The various aspects of this awareness are apparent in the 'Kilmarnock edition'. The volume includes 'The Twa Dogs', which represents the fantastic tradition of Scots poetry as two dogs debate the artifice of human society. The piece features a collision of Ayrshire dialect and class critique with a wide awareness of British cultural mores resulting in a searing satire. Class difference is again registered but in both more bitterly personal and near-apocalyptic terms in 'To a Mouse' where Burns points to a dangerous state of affairs where landowners blindly control the destiny of the peasantry according to their own priorities. This poem indicates a radical political voice in Burns which had been born out of his family's peasant-hardship, was influenced by notions of liberty trumpeted by the American Declaration of Independence and was to be further sharpened by the French Revolution. Coming directly from the influence of the Scottish Enlightenment, as it sought to temper the theocratic fanaticism of some sections of Scottish Calvinism, is the first of Burns' great religious satires, 'The Holy Fair', where Fergusson's carnivalesque territory is occupied so as to counterpoint the mass-Calvinist field-meetings of the eighteenth century with the reality that these allow many of their participants to indulge in a more natural communion of sexual and alcoholic enjoyment. Omitted from the volume, though written in 1785 (and excised by the editor from the first collected Burns in 1800), is 'Holy Willie's Prayer' in which the eponymous Willie believes that he is one of those predestined for salvation. This brilliant comic monologue is informed by savage psychological insight (which again owes something to the Scottish Enlightenment enquiries into moral philosophy and anthropology) where Willie's religion is seen to be a spur to an egotism leading to megalomania in which he sins profusely against Christian moral values. The following stanza indicates the masterfully oxymoronic language where Willie speaks in an orthodox religious fashion but is really boasting of his sexual prowess:

> Yet I am here a chosen sample,
> To show thy grace is great an' ample;
> I'm here a pillar in thy temple,
>   Strong as a rock,
> A guide, a buckler, an' example
>   To a' thy flock.

Another element to be found in the 'Kilmarnock edition' is Burns' treatment of the supernatural traditions of the peasantry in the likes of 'Address to the Deil' and 'Halloween'. Burns' attitude to this across his *oeuvre* is one of enjoyment coupled with respect and this is very much the case in perhaps his greatest piece, 'Tam O' Shanter' (1790). The poem draws on a wide battery of British poetic resonances to set up a mock-heroic clash between a drunken Scottish peasant and the forces of Hell. As well as being a comedy, however, the poem celebrates its little-man protagonist whose battle against overwhelming supernatural odds represents a stoic resilience in life as meaningful as the response of more intellectual or cultured individuals. The poem marks that point in eighteenth-century Scottish cultural history where the Scots poetry movement is at once most local and most cosmopolitan as it suggests a relativism in all human perception.

EXERCISE 8

Read **Document 73**, one of the most famous poems from the 'Kilmarnock' collection, 'To A Louse', which is, clearly, about that traditional literary concern, vanity. In the poem there is, however, a rather morbid blurring of the distinction between the categories of humanity and nature and, bound up with this, a depth of psychological reflectiveness which speaks of a sensibility largely unknown only slightly earlier in the poetry of eighteenth-century Europe. Examine these aspects which point to Burns' position in the vanguard of the emerging Romantic movement as the poem deconstructs the way in which our notions of self are largely the result of social construction.

Read also **Article 22E** where Carol McGuirk sums up something of Burns' multifarious artistic profile, suggesting the way in which he makes imaginative capital from Scotland's complex cultural history.

'To a Louse' features a 'flyting' voice of mock outrage at the presumption of the louse in daring to attach itself to the fine young country girl. Gradually, we become aware that the girl herself, and all humanity in fact, are presumptuous in the airs and graces with which they attempt to mould social distinction and differentiation. At the same time, however, there is an element of sympathy for humanity in the way in which it manipulates appearances so as to raise itself above the animal kingdom. In the end it is left somewhat open as to whether or not seeing ourselves naturally or 'as ithers see us' would be altogether a desirable thing.

4. THE AGE OF SCOTT

The early nineteenth-century period in Scottish culture, often referred to as the 'age of Scott', is marked by similar tendencies to those we have observed already. In the Scottish literary climate of this time we find more of the retrospective reconstruction associated with cultural nationalism in the eighteenth century and a continuation of the cosmopolitan spirit associated with the Scottish Enlightenment. Both of these tendencies coalesce (perhaps properly for the first time) in the rise of a Scottish novel which represents a wide gamut of Scottish cultural history and attempts to expose this to highly sensitive analysis. Most prominently, this novel is interested in

No. 30. Photograph of Burns' chair and writing desk from Ellisland Farm (now in Burns' House, Dumfries). *Mick Sharp*.

exploring the mentalities generated by Scottish religion, the highland experience and lowlands experience, especially as each of these areas comes into contact with a rapidly modernising world.

4.1. Walter Scott

It is an intriguing fact that Scotland's two most celebrated writers, Burns and Walter Scott (1771–1832), should have lived within such a short time of one another. Scott, even more explicitly than Burns, was very concerned with representing distinctive Scottish cultural patterns which he felt to be under threat of disappearing and, along with Burns, is the man most responsible for successfully communicating notions of Scottish identity to the modern world. This is perhaps the true paradox of Scottish literary history – that out of seeming threat to an indigenous cultural identity should emerge a celebration and broadcasting of that identity in a way which had never previously happened. Not only this, but the process was accompanied by literary innovation. If this is the case in relation to Burns' new combination of literary and folk materials (seen most strikingly in 'Tam O'Shanter'), it is also the case in Scott who is often credited with the invention of the historical novel.

> EXERCISE 9
> No Scottish literary figure arouses wider critical controversy than Scott. Read three views of Scott by Noble, Muir and Gifford (**Articles 22F, 22G and 22H**) and pick out the main points in their placement of Scott in relation to Scotland.

Scott's literary career began in classic Scottish fashion as a reconstructor. Influenced by the folk elements in Burns (whom Scott claimed to be his favourite writer) and in German Romantic writers of the period, and perhaps above all by his own family background in the remote Borders of Scotland, Scott produced for his first major publication *The Minstrelsy of the Scottish Border* (1802–3). This collection of ballads features legendary and historical matter, and this powerfully mythic terrain is that which occupied Scott in his own original writing. For over a decade Scott utilised the psychologically gripping scenarios of romance and war, which he found in the ballads, in his own long narrative poems which became huge bestsellers in Britain, Europe and America. Poems such as 'The Lay of the Last Minstrel' (1805) and 'Marmion' (1808) were at the forefront of the Romantic movement's medieval revivalism. There is in Scott, then, a great interest in culture and society, in Scotland and elsewhere, prior to the great watershed of the Reformation, and this can be read as part of the Romantic movement's reaction against a world that had seemed, over the previous two hundred and fifty years, to become increasingly rationalistic and materialistic and perhaps less imaginative.

Apparently as a result of being eclipsed in the popular reading stakes by the altogether racier poetic productions of Byron, Scott turned to publishing novels. He did this anonymously. (No-one knows for sure why he protected his identity. The explanations range from the fact that the novel-form was perhaps especially disreputable in Calvinist Scotland and that Scott was eager to safeguard his successful legal career, to the possibility that he was adding to the mystique of his material.) With his first novel, *Waverley* (1814), Scott is often credited – or blamed – with inserting the Highlands into the European imagination. The novel features the Jacobite rebellion of 1745 in which Scott's fictional protagonist, a young Englishman, Edward Waverley, becomes involved. On the way to join his government regiment in Scotland just as the rebellion is brewing, Waverley is falsely accused of treason, becomes a fugitive and is briefly but intensely loyal to the Jacobite cause. He redeems himself at the last minute, however, by gallantly rescuing a Hanoverian officer in the midst of battle.

> EXERCISE 10
>
> Read the extract from the postscript to *Waverley* (**Document 74**) and consider how the changing face of Scottish history seems to be viewed. Does it seem to support any of the readings of the critics you have considered in the last exercise?

Scott's postscript is an attempt to sum up the changing face of Scotland in a very even-handed manner. First of all, he is acknowledging the sheer rapidity of change from the eighteenth century which, as his river metaphor shows, he feels anyone would find difficulty in controlling or comprehending. At the same time, he tabulates gain and loss; he seems to see his nation as less divided than before but lacking in a certain amount of its former cultural colour and even, perhaps, its human values.

   Waverley itself can be read in various ways so as to cast light on Scott's relationship to Scotland. We can match its main plotline with the three critical perspectives we have considered already. For Edwin Muir (1936), Scott was essentially trapped by the fact that any distinctive Scottish culture was finally lost with the overwhelming victory of the British state in 1746. Scott, then, was left with a neutered subject-matter around which he could weave only colourful but meaningless adventure stories. Andrew Noble (1985), one of Scott's harshest critics, goes even further, seeing not simply empty romance in Scott's work but cultural fabrication. For Noble, Scott emerges as a propagandist and prophet of Hanoverian commercial and imperial progress, as he ignored the most contemporary issues affecting the Scotland of his day (such as industrialisation), and peddled escapist pageantry as a kind of sop to Scotland's many grievances. Gifford (1988) offers a more sympathetic, view. He observes, as others before have (most notably the Marxist critic Georg Lukacs), that Scott invented the historical novel. For Gifford, this new novel-form involves engagement with the psychological relationship of the individual to large-scale historical events and the way in which environmental circumstances play their part in contributing to particular cultural mindcasts (thus, Scott's Highland landscape symbolism accords with the wild, romantic culture of the Highland clans which the outsider Waverley begins to have sympathy for as he enters into it). What Gifford is pointing to in Scott's development of the historical novel is the way in which this acknowledges a sense of the mythic power of cultures which stand in tense and tragic relationship to the 'progress' of history. Gifford's reading allows Scott unusually full credit as a Romantic writer who was in many ways rather pessimistic about the course of civilisation.

Scott's political life has often been considered as supporting evidence in the assessment of this relationship to the culture of Scotland. There was a politically reactionary side to Scott (his friend James Hogg was being half-serious when he said that the Reform Bill of 1832 had killed Scott) and there was one bizarre real-life experiment in cultural engineering which is also frequently adduced as evidence of Scott's faulty instincts. In 1822, Scott stage-managed the ceremonies to welcome King George IV to Scotland. Scott contrived that the king be publicly paraded dressed in the most garish tartan outfit. The Hanoverian king, then, was being reinvented as 'Bonnie Prince Charlie'. What does this incident say about Scott? Was he culturally confused, a cultural iconoclast, or someone desperately attempting to highlight and educate in aspects of Scottish identity which were fading in the light of the modern world? If you wish to explore Scott's treatment of Scotland, his two other great Scottish historical novels are *The Tale of Old Mortality* (1816) and *The Heart of Mid-Lothian* (1818). A useful shortcut, however, is the short story 'The Two Drovers' (1827).

4.2. Scott's contemporaries

Scott was part of a very vigorous fictional and journalistic culture in early nineteenth-century Scotland. This came to be centred on *Blackwood's Magazine* (founded in 1817), a periodical which was traditionally Tory in its politics and was set up to counter another great Scottish periodical, *The Edinburgh Review*, which had been established in 1802 as a Whig publication but which was seen by many by the second decade of the nineteenth century to be altogether too culturally iconoclastic. Where the *Edinburgh*, with its roots in those parts of the Scottish Enlightenment which attempted to be most urbane and scientific, was sceptical of the new wave of Romantic writers (including Scott), *Blackwood's* attempted to foster many of the new Romantic values. Its output of Romantic criticism under the stewardship of John Wilson (1785–1854) and John Gibson Lockhart (1794–1854) was, in fact, rather shallow (sidestepping, as it tended to do, the more radical political agenda of many Romantic writers), but as a forum for featuring some of the most exciting new fiction of the day and as an encourager of the new genre of the short story – a fact which is still inadequately appreciated today – it is seminally important.

Blackwood's provided an outlet for fiction of the historical and folkloristic kind which featured often profound social and psychological observation. Associated with the magazine was John Galt (1779–1839) who, like Scott, wrote historical fiction but of a kind which was more explicit about the specifics of the changing political and commercial scene. One of his most telling novels in this respect is *Annals of the Parish* (1821) which charts the collision of a rapidly changing Scotland, Europe and world on the mindset of an Ayrshire minister, Micah Balwhidder.

EXERCISE 11

Read the extract from *Annals of the Parish* (**Document 75**) where Balwhidder chronicles the year 1793. What are the main elements indicating a Scotland in transition and upheaval? Are the tensions in the clash of mindsets particularly Scottish or more universal?

Scott shows the eclipse of one Scottish mindcast – that of the Jacobite – and Galt in *Annals* shows another – that of the older Presbyterian mindset with its belief in portents and providence. Balwhidder believes his dream to be divinely ordained and to be revealing to him the evil nature of revolutionary France. In the cold light of the real day, however, in his encounter with the weavers, he realises that these French-inspired radicals are more sincere Christians than Mr Cayenne, a crass, factory-owning magistrate. Through such skilful writing of ironic juxtaposition, then, we glimpse an increasingly complex Scotland – and indeed Britain and Europe – where issues of religion, class and politics are not easily to be distinguished.

Another writer associated with *Blackwood's*, James Hogg (1770–1835), was as clever a social and psychological analyst as John Galt. His *Memoirs and Confession of A Justified Sinner* (1824) portrays the psyche of the extreme Calvinist explored by Burns in 'Holy Willie's Prayer'. Robert Wringhim believes himself one of 'the elect' promised salvation by God and so able to commit rape and murder with impunity. The novel features a two-part narrative: that of an Enlightenment editor who has come into possession of Robert's memoirs, and the sinner's own chilling account. This novel and, indeed, the life of Hogg, is often taken as a telling exemplar of the cultural tensions of Scotland. Descended from old Covenanting stock and inheriting a knowledge of folklore from a mother who was a Borders 'tradition-bearer', Hogg, the most successful poet in Scots following Burns, dealt in his poetry with the historical and supernatural legends of the Scottish country and earned the romantic epithet the 'Ettrick Shepherd'. At times in his literary output a celebrator of the Covenanters of Scotland (the harsh, heroic Presbyterians who were persecuted in the seventeenth century for their refusal to allow state interference in their religion), at times a 'sentimental Jacobite', and at other points showing a great awareness of sociological and historical change as analysed by the Scottish Enlightenment, he is seen as typically confused in his allegiances. Many commentators, however, have been perhaps too alarmed by the absence of a unitary or consistent stance in Scottish writers and in Scottish literature in general. It might be argued that a nation's culture is often multiplicitous or even multicultural. Hogg's *Confessions*, with its dual narrative structure, might be taken as a fruitful case in point here. It refuses to accord finality of veracity to either the traditional, supernatural or the enlightened explanation of events in the novel. In this way it stands as one of the greatest Scottish exemplars of Romanticism as it absorbs old and modern outlooks and sharply contrasted attitudes in the one nation, and declines to circumscribe the truth absolutely.

It is a traditional argument in Scottish literary criticism that Scotland did not really partake fully of Romanticism because of its confused and Enlightenment-led (and so politically conservative) culture. It is perhaps true that Scotland did not produce any very great poetry of radical political vision in the early nineteenth century (in the way that England has a Shelley or a Byron). However, in the novels of Scott, Galt and Hogg, and one other writer whom we might have mentioned, Susan Ferrier (1782–1854), a great observer of the claustrophobic status of women in society, Scotland registers the turmoil of the age, and brings a particularly sharp focus to bear upon the violence being inflicted on older patterns of cultural psychology. Such subject matter, it might be argued, represents the Scottish contribution to the anguish, uncertainty and tense creativity of Romanticism.

EXERCISE 12
Read FR Hart's account of the rise of a climate of Scottish fiction in the nineteenth century (**Article 22I**). Which factors identified by Hart in this rise seem most credible?

5. TOWARDS VICTORIAN BRITAIN

Scottish literature is traditionally held to have gone into eclipse sometime in the 1830s when Scott, Galt and Hogg had disappeared from the scene. There seems to be a dearth of significant fiction until the 1860s when the Scottish rural novel made its appearance and poetry in Scots after Hogg plummeted to the level of the 'Whistle-Binkie' collections (published from 1832 onwards), featuring a sentimental, socially disengaged use of the Doric (arguably, the use of Scots poetry for serious purposes was only properly revived in the 1920s). The career of Thomas Carlyle (1795–1881), the last great Scottish man of letters to emerge from the Enlightenment *milieu*, is often taken as exemplifying the watershed in Scottish culture and literature. Carlyle moved to London in 1834, having found Scotland, it is sometimes alleged, no longer able to provide a suitable audience for his large-scale philosophical and historical work. According to one view, Scotland was too conservative and provincial to support his Germano-Romantic vision of the need for radical intellectual action in a society that was becoming too mechanistic (under capitalism), and only in the wider context of Britain as it headed toward the Victorian age could Carlyle find an audience that could respond to his visionary ideas. (Carlyle's essay, 'Signs of the Times' (1829), gives a brief flavour of his ideas.) The emigration of Scottish intellectuals to take advantage of the new British superstate as this emerged in the commercial and imperial realities of London-centred Victorian society is often seen as the final nail in the coffin of a culture which had flourished in a rebellious distinctiveness in the wake of 1707 but which had always been under threat (often internally) and which had finally run out of cultural dynamism and any real institutional support.

6. CONCLUSION

This chapter has been geared toward surveying Scottish literature in relation to the vexed areas of national and social change in the period 1707–1850. As you are by now no doubt aware, the critical, cultural and historical arguments surrounding all this are extremely diffuse and not easily digested at once. At the same time, however, you may have become aware of a number of larger problematic areas in relation to the way in which much of the traditional debate over Scottish literature is conducted (and has been conducted in this chapter). A major question you may wish to consider for yourself is: to what extent does 'healthy' creative literature rely upon a 'healthy' and coherent sense of nationhood? (And correlatively, even if there is such a thing as 'healthy' nationhood, might it be that tensions in national identity are actually conducive to the most fruitful literary creativity?) We might also question the notion of culture (especially 'national' culture) as dealt with in this chapter as rather too monolithic: where, for example, you might ask, does the traditional debate over Scottish literature allow cognisance of, say, Scottish women's writing or the writing of the working-class? (In respect of these rather neglected areas of Scottish literature in the period, if you are interested in them, good starting points are, respectively, the Aberdeen literary histories and the Leonard anthology listed in the bibliography.) Scottish literary history, like any other kind of history, must be constantly open to reinterpretation and its particular canon and texts to reinvestigation.

REFERENCES TO BOOKS AND ARTICLES MENTIONED IN THE TEXT

*Craig, D 1961 *Scottish Literature and the Scottish People*. London.
*Daiches, D 1964 *The Paradox of Scottish Culture*. Oxford.
Freeman, FW 1984 *Robert Fergusson and the Scots Humanist Compromise*. Edinburgh.
*Gifford, D 1988 'Myth, Parody and Dissociation: Scottish Fiction 1814–1914', *in* Gifford, D (ed), *The History of Scottish Literature* Volume 3, Aberdeen, 217–59.
*Hart, FR 1978 *The Scottish Novel: From Smollett to Spark*. Cambridge, Mass.
*McGuirk, C 1987 'Scottish Hero, Scottish Victim: Myths of Robert Burns', *in* Hook, A (ed), *The History of Scottish Literature* Volume 2, Aberdeen, 219–38.
Muir, E 1936 (1982 edn) *Scott and Scotland*. Edinburgh.
Nairn, T 1981 *The Break-up of Britain*. London.
*Noble, A 1985 'Urbane Silence: Scottish writing and the nineteenth century city', *in* Gordon, G (ed), *Perspectives of the Scottish City*, Aberdeen, 64–90.
*Ouston, H 1987 'Cultural life from the Restoration to the Union', *in* Hook, A (ed), *The History of Scottish Literature* Volume 2, Aberdeen, 11–31.
*Sher, R 1985 *Church and University in the Scottish Enlightenment: the Moderate Literati of Edinburgh*. Edinburgh.
*Simpson, K 1988 *The Protean Scot*. Aberdeen.

FURTHER READING

Those references marked * in the above list are recommended further reading, along with the following:

Crawford, R 1992 *Devolving English Literature*. Oxford.
Crawford, T 1979 *Society and the Lyric*. Edinburgh.

Gifford, D (ed) 1988 *The History of Scottish Literature* Volume 3. Aberdeen.

Hook, A (ed) 1987 *The History of Scottish Literature* Volume 2. Aberdeen.

Leonard, T (ed) 1990 *Radical Renfrew*. Edinburgh.

MacQueen, J 1982 *Progress and Poetry*. Edinburgh.

MacQueen, J 1989 *The Rise of the Historical Novel*. Edinburgh.

Noble, A 1982 'Versions of Scottish Pastoral: the *literati* and the tradition, 1780–1830', *in* Markus T (ed), *Order and Space in Society*. Edinburgh.

Watson, R 1984 *The Literature of Scotland*. London.

Education
————————————————— *Donald J Withrington*

INTRODUCTION

In this chapter we look at developments in education, a sphere vital to many aspects of Scottish social, political, economic and cultural history. This is an area of historical study riven by controversy arising from its centrality in the debate about greater availability of education, the supposed prevalence of more democratic ideals, and higher levels of literacy and work-related skills than in England and elsewhere. Another series of powerful myths, you may say, but we shall see. The topic is approached under the following sub-heads:

- The pre-Union inheritance
- A new age? Schooling in the market place
- The academy movement
- The state of schooling, and the schooling of the state
- Why should government intervene?
- Strains in the system before the 1830s: the towns and the Highlands
- The 1830s and 1840s
- The Scottish universities

By the time you have completed this chapter and worked through the associated documents and articles you should have a clear idea of the major trends, several specific developments and the key areas of debate in the history of education to 1850. Before proceeding you might like to note that Smout (1969, Chapter 18) devotes a considerable amount of space to this topic.

I. THE PRE-UNION INHERITANCE

Until the 1960s it was widely believed that the provision of schooling in Scotland before the parliamentary Union had hardly begun to match the protestant reformers' ideal at the Reformation, of at least one school in every parish, and grammar schooling (schools teaching the classical languages) in towns and populous parishes. That view has been largely overturned. It is now clear that schooling was not nurtured in periods of presbyterian ascendancy in the seventeenth-century Church, only to decline in times of episcopacy; indeed, in the long period of episcopacy, from 1660 to 1690, there was both consolidation and extension in the numbers of schools (Beale 1983, 13, 97–99). By the early 1690s, at least in the eastern Lowlands and the southern and eastern Highlands, some 90% of all parishes had schools supported by their landowners and tenants (Withrington 1965, 121–42; 1985, 66–68). The evidence for other regions is more scattered, yet, in general, where there are records we find schools, sometimes of long standing.

Thus the pre-Union inheritance in schooling was certainly not meagre. It had found support in the Church, nationally and locally; it had been backed by government; and it was sustained by the localities which had to finance the enterprise. Yet in 1696 government repeated and extended the regulations laid down in an earlier act in 1646 (which had been rescinded at the Restoration), which leaves something of a puzzle. If there was already a wide provision of schools, why was the new act needed? Was this move, as has been suggested (Anderson 1995, 3), 'part of the political and religious settlement following the 1688 revolution'? If so, why wait until 1696? The answer may lie in the prolonged period of dearth and famine which struck Scotland in the 1690s. The so-called 'Ill Years' of King William's reign brought widespread impoverishment. Children were not being sent to school; school fees were not being paid to the teachers; and the teachers' salaries (in effect, retainers provided from an agreed 'stent' or local taxation on land) were not being paid on time. Schoolmasters and their families were sometimes left with no option but to leave their parishes; occasionally, if they remained, they might even be supported by payments from the parish poor-box.

Government was thus prompted to do something about the plight of those in severe difficulties and passed the Act for Settling Schools (**Document 76**) to maintain and reinvigorate the existing plan of schools, to be paid for by a local tax on all (owners and occupiers) for the benefit of all. Parishioners were reminded of their educational obligations to the local children and their duty to care for their teachers. The act renewed the regulation which laid down the payment of a stipend, a minimum of £5.11s. and double that as a maximum, and demanded that proper accommodation be provided for a schoolroom. There was no need to remind the national Church to maintain its oversight of the system, but the act gave presbyteries the backing of the commissioners of supply (the body of major landholders in each county) in any dealings with recalcitrant heritors. Evidence for large tracts of the Lowlands shows that even the poorest localities strove to fulfil these requirements (Bain 1965, 99–108; Beale 1983, 127–38; Withrington 1963, 108–11).

EXERCISE 1
Was the 1696 act, as it has sometimes been described, the 'magna carta' of Scottish education?

What would you regard as the main similarities and differences in **Document 76** (an extract from the Act for Settling Schools) and **Document 77**, a contract for a new schoolmaster made before the act, in November 1695?

The 1696 act reiterated earlier aspirations and tightened up on administration and funding. Levels of minimum provision seem to have been reached in many parts of the Lowlands and in some parts of the Southern Highlands (Withrington 1986, 60–

69). **Document 77** shows the problems of provision that could exist, for example, in scattered rural parishes like Minnigaff in Kirkcudbright.

We are fortunate that a group of documents from 1700 has survived which allows us a glimpse of the condition of schooling in the south-west of Scotland. (The main Church records are sometimes limited to notes of the appointment of school-masters, fee payments for poor scholars, etc.) In 1700 the synod of Glasgow and Ayr invited its presbyteries to report on the state of schooling in their bounds and to suggest improvements. The replies showed no concern about either the number or the availability of schools in their districts. Instead, the presbyteries concentrated on the content of what was taught and how it was taught, launching an attack on the limitations of the usual curriculum in the parochial schools – reading, writing, arithmetic, Latin, perhaps a smattering of mathematics – and on the dullness of the current teaching methods (Withrington 1970, 170–74).

Since, it was argued, only a small proportion of (male) pupils required Latin to go on to university, why should the generality of scholars be forced into learning the classical languages? – 'a meer loosing of so much time', commented the Glasgow reply, 'and that of their best time for learning of things that may be more usefull for . . . those designed for trades and occupations in the world'. However, studies in the classics and mathematics were still seen as socially and intellectually useful and a significant proviso was made in the proposals for change. Latin was to be retained in the curriculum for the benefit of the sons of poorer families who depended on access to university to make their way in the world. The better-off, with parents who were established in business or who had family connections which would assure them of an easy career path after school, did not *need* Latin and the security of access to the universities.

What was to be offered in place of Latin? Here there was a large measure of agreement among the presbyteries: subjects such as geography and history (especially with a view to their commercial applications), also geometry with 'the use of the Quadrant, compass and the rule of proportion' (in preparation for occupations at sea and in land mensuration), with 'a compend of all Trades and Sciences'. Generally, the non-traditional subjects were recommended for all: they were seen as so enlivening and valuable that all pupils should attend them, taking up perhaps the first five years of their schooling, before deciding whether to study Latin and mathematics, and the elements of Greek and Hebrew if they were on offer.

EXERCISE 2

Can you suggest why the reform of Scottish schooling was being demanded?
Why might the dating of the presbyteries' comments seem surprising?

Demand for the reform of Scottish schooling could be regarded as a reflection of the need to modernise the curriculum for vocational objectives and certainly to introduce 'useful arts', subjects likely to be needed in a more commercially and scientifically minded society (sound familiar?). You might say that it is notable that these plans came so soon after the 'Ill Years' and the Darien disaster and also in advance of the Union of 1707.

2. A NEW AGE? SCHOOLING IN THE MARKET PLACE

Even before the Union, some councils had sponsored teachers of 'new' subjects in their burghs (Withrington 1970, 169–70). By the 1720s an important change had occurred: instead of hiring or licensing private teachers, councils began to arrange for subjects additional to the old curriculum *within* the towns' own schools. The emergence in Ayr of separate teaching of 'the mathematical sciences' in 1721, and in Dumfries of a public 'writing or commercial' department or school-within-a-school in 1723, were early signals of what was to come. In 1746, in a much more rigorous reconstruction, the Ayr burgh school was divided into three departments: classical; English; and mathematical (Strawhorn 1983, 19–28; Withrington 1970, 176–77). The main beneficiaries were to be those 'whose parents cannot well afford to maintain them at Universities'. Elsewhere, other councils were also ready to add the 'more useful parts of learning' to the basic curriculum in their schools. On 31 May 1748, the *Aberdeen Journal* carried an advertisement for the master of Elgin Grammar School, announcing that, in addition to English, Latin and writing, 'he directs the studies of such young Lads as incline to Trades, Merchandize, etc . . . to such Branches of Education as are most adapted to the way of life they choose'. Nor were these developments to be found only in the Scottish burghs. By 1750, for example, in the North-East, the parochial schoolmaster of Old Deer was listing 'Book-keeping after the Italian method, Geography and Algebra, all taught at reasonable rates' as additions to the 'usual' curriculum of parochial schools (*Aberdeen Journal,* 3 April 1750).

The extension of the curriculum in local, publicly financed schools no doubt owed something to notions of what was fashionable in learning, but the 1740s in Scotland provided their own stimulus to parochial schoolmasters to adapt their teaching to a rising demand for the new subjects. Most of these teachers had stipends near the minimum laid down in 1696, which had suffered badly from a severe recent inflation, and the later years of the 1740s saw the first attempt by parochial schoolmasters in Scotland to form an association to promote their professional interests, including improvement of their standard of living. They met to petition parliament to increase their stipends and to persuade heritors and sessions to allow them to charge higher fees, but the appearance of petitions from parish ministers, using the same arguments about inflation for an augmentation of *their* stipends, effectively killed off the chance of parliamentary support for either group (Withrington 1988a, 163). Nonetheless, some help was given to hard-pressed teachers by allowing them to raise, even if marginally, fees for the standard curriculum – the 3Rs and Latin. The opportunity was widely taken, however, to permit a higher scale of fees for any 'modern' subject. While the 3Rs might be taught for, say, 2s a quarter and the 3Rs with Latin for 3s, rates of 10s or more per quarter were allowed for each of practical mathematics or bookkeeping or French or navigation. Financial salvation for the master and his family was thus often achieved by responding to the demands of local parents for such additional subjects. Yet everywhere the principle which the West of Scotland presbyteries had made clear in 1700 was quite specifically maintained: parochial schoolteachers were instructed not to neglect the 3Rs and Latin. Whereas in eighteenth-century England the classics became the undoubted preserve of the middle and upper classes in the endowed grammar and 'public' boarding schools, in Scotland classical learning was kept alive deliberately to support the aspirations (and social mobility) of the lower orders.

In the major towns, with populations large enough to support a master and, perhaps, an assistant (doctor or usher) in its grammar school, there was no rush by burgh councils to reorganise their existing schools and the new subjects were often privately taught in rooms close by. In smaller burghs and in some rural parishes, however, it was the public teachers who incorporated the new subjects into their curricula, for otherwise they might lose out to private teachers. Towns like Dumfries, Ayr and Elgin were soon joined by many others: existing schools were reconstructed, and their courses so arranged that children would go through English subjects (including writing and 'flourishing') and mathematical and scientific studies before their parents needed to decide if they could afford to keep them at school for instruction in the classics. The spread of these developments soon sparked off warnings about a likely decline in the numbers learning Latin at school and hence in the amount and quality of Latin teaching, and produced no little anxiety in the Scottish universities. In 1760 the Principal of University and King's College in Old Aberdeen warned his colleagues that:

> now that Education is put upon a more rational and useful footing, there are many students who know nothing of either Latin and Greek. Their plans and schemes for Life do not depend on the knowledge of these Languages, and yet by attending other classes they may learn a great deal of useful Knowledge. And therefore . . . it is highly inexpedient, as well as unreasonable, to think of fixing down one uniform and determined scheme of education, so as to oblige every individual Student to learn the same things . . .
>
> (Withrington 1970, 190)

In themselves, the modest changes taking place had provided little direct threat to the universities, so long as the professors kept up their student numbers by offering the study of non-classical subjects to any 'occasional' attenders who had no interest in fulfilling the requirements for graduation. Yet, in 1760–61, the town council of Perth was about to launch an explicit attack on the existing forms and character of higher education in Scotland (*ibid*, 180–81; and **Document 78**).

EXERCISE 3

Why was customer demand so effective in prompting changes in schooling in the first half of the eighteenth century?

I'll leave you to work this one out for yourself. Look back over this section and also at **Document 78.**

3. THE ACADEMY MOVEMENT

The plans announced for the founding of the Perth Academy, in addition to the town's thriving and well-regarded grammar school, offered parents a concentrated two-year course as an *alternative* to the four years of university study for the MA degree. The Perth scheme of 1760 intentionally went beyond what was increasingly available elsewhere, the addition of a scattering of modern subjects to the old curriculum. What was proposed in the Academy was a strictly structured, coherent and intensive study of 'the arts and the sciences'. Encompassing the non-linguistic parts of the university undergraduate curriculum, the Perth course also took in a comprehensive range of practical and useful subjects, all to be taught to a high level. The advantages were, the promoters claimed, that a first-class, modern, higher education would be available locally, at much less expense than education in the university towns in Scotland; and the entire course would be completed in a much shorter period, with the 'young men' under greater parental supervision and at less moral risk than in a great city. The sciences at Perth were to include arithmetic, accounting and bookkeeping; mathematics, navigation and astronomy; and natural philosophy. The arts teaching comprised the history of philosophy and the rise and progress of arts and sciences; natural history; poetry, rhetoric, logic and moral philosophy; chronology and civil history. A separate writing-master was to be engaged for an hour and a half each day, and an hour was set aside for those with some classical training to have further instruction in the 'superior Greek and Latin classics' – added as some kind of assurance for those parents who were still not convinced of the inefficacy of the old learning or who wished to leave open the option of university study.

The naming of the new school as an 'academy', to distinguish it from the 'mixed' schools of Elgin and elsewhere, and to make it plain that it was very different from any university, was deliberate and followed the example of the dissenting academies in England which had made the sciences central in their curricula. What is both curious and significant about the story of the Perth Academy is that its attempt to undermine the Scottish universities in this way should have survived for only some forty years, and also that its example was not followed by other *public* agencies although private enterprise was quick to respond, for example in Glasgow **(Document 79).**

There is little doubt that this happened because the universities proved more resilient and flexible than might have been predicted in 1760 (see below). It also reflected the fact that in Scotland the universities were regarded as both public and *national* institutions, as the recognisable 'top' to a long-revered educational structure which benefited the whole nation. Parents across the social classes, the poorer aided by the availability of bursaries, could expect to send their sons to them. Perhaps the new alternative may just have seemed too radical.

The Perth enterprise, however, was instrumental in spreading the new designation of 'academy' throughout Scotland. Ayr would follow its lead in 1794. Indeed when, from the 1780s onward, grammar schools extended their curricula to include the new classes, they were frequently named 'academies'. Yet despite the example given in Perth, the public academy generally took on a 'mixed' form, adding the 'new' utilitarian subjects to the classics and the elements of mathematics, but still seeing one of its main functions as preparing pupils for university entrance. And so, when in 1807 Perth Town Council decided to amalgamate the academy and its grammar school into one multi-department building (keeping the title of Perth Academy for the whole), the attempt to construct a public substitute for a university education ended. Thus in 1807 a new Kilmarnock Academy was developed as 'merely an extension of the parochial system . . . well adapted for large towns', with three teachers appointed 'in the parochial school, that is, the academy, one for the classics, one for English, and one for the commercial department' (*New Statistical Account* v 558) – a long way from the radical spirit of Perth in 1760 and Ayr before that. The name 'academy' was being widely attached to schools which added modern subjects to their classical training, without necessarily giving those subjects a special status or prominence. In 1820, 'in place of what was originally the parochial school', the new Arbroath Academy had a rector and three masters who taught a classical and mathematical department, a commercial department, an English department, and 'general schools' for the 3Rs (*New Statistical Account* xi, 103–4). But not all schools which were divided in this way bothered to rename themselves: in Kirriemuir in Angus, for example, in 1833 the parochial school – still so called – had three masters teaching its separate classical, commercial and English departments (*ibid*, 186–87). Even when private schools took the name 'academy', it did not imply that they shunned the teaching of the classics. In 1824, indeed, the new Edinburgh Academy was founded as 'a great classical school', one intended to outshine the burgh's unreformed grammar school. The 'academy movement' in Scotland had drifted significantly from the guidelines of the Perth experiment of 1760.

EXERCISE 4
Read **Document 78** and write an assessment of the reasons for Perth's decision to found its academy.

You might well sum this up as enlightened improvement, combined with commercial expediency. There was also a strong element of civic pride and a recognition of the spin-offs – social, economic and cultural – which would arise from the academy. There would be the additional advantages, you might note, of civilising the Highlands (which were on Perth's doorstep) and of preventing the corruption of youth elsewhere (a backhanded swipe at Edinburgh?).

4. THE STATE OF SCHOOLING, AND THE SCHOOLING OF THE STATE

There has been much recent debate about the effectiveness of the provision of schooling in Scotland in the eighteenth century. In particular, questions have been raised over its 'democratic' character and about whether it succeeded in promoting the universal literacy planned for by the religious reformers in 1560. Some confusions have arisen because of a lack of clarity in the definitions employed. It has not been always clear whether reading-literacy or writing-literacy (sign-literacy) was the focus of discussion; nor have commentators who wanted to test the strength of the 'Scottish tradition in education' always been in agreement about how that should be defined. Before the 1790s, the historical sources do not provide data by which we can easily assess general capabilities in reading. Some scholars have therefore concentrated on data for writing-literacy, considering that this alone can be assessed from more-than-anecdotal evidence, mainly from the signatures on documents (especially legal documents) by persons from a wide range of social classes (Houston 1985, *passim*). But, generally, these signatures represent a meagre proportion (and a limited geographic and social spread) of the whole population;

No. 31. 'Interior of an Infant School', from David Stow's *The Training System* (1836). *Photograph courtesy of Glasgow University Library, Department of Special Collections.*

moreover, since writing was often not learned at the same time as reading, and since many more girls than boys did not learn to write at all or had no occasion to practise a barely-learned writing skill, attempts to construe general judgements about the effectiveness of schooling on literacy from signature data in later life are fraught with problems. Smout (1982, 115–27; **Article 4**) highlighted some of these in his study of the Cambuslang religious revival of 1742. It seems safer to judge levels of ability in reading or in writing from evidence about the extent of provision of schools, along with available anecdotal comments. Yet we must be cautious not to underestimate the numbers instructed in reading, by counting only those known to have been at school or regular attenders at school. Some women in Cambuslang had learned to read at home, and others had notably improved their literacy skills after school-age. Such out-of-school teaching remained an important means of instruction, particularly for girls. In 1834 the minister of Dunnet in Caithness recorded a long-term practice, reported also in many parishes in Orkney: 'It is impossible to ascertain correctly the number of children under five years of age who have been taught to read because . . . a great proportion of the children of that age are taught at home by their parents or other members of the family: many of the females receive no further education than they get in that way' (*Education Enquiry* 1834, 185).

EXERCISE 5
What difficulties confront historians who wish to determine levels of literacy in eighteenth-century Scotland?

To summarise, historians are confronted with problems in defining what constitutes literacy; and with inconsistencies in, and limited coverage of, the data.

Fortunately, for some forty years from the 1790s, there is an extraordinary sequence of nationwide surveys conducted by parish ministers and parochial schoolmasters which allowed contemporary governments to make reasonable assessments of the extent of educational provision in Scotland. Sir John Sinclair's *Statistical Account of Scotland* was the first, constructed from returns from every parish taken in the years 1791–99. Sinclair was late in adding questions about schooling in his circulars and there are some gaps in the responses, but it is a valuable source nonetheless. Generally, save in the cases of very large parishes divided by rivers and lochs and hills, predominantly in the Highlands, there is relatively little complaint about the sheer amount of available schooling. In all regions, however, it was made clear that one school (established within the requirements of the 1696 Act) was sufficient only exceptionally to house all school-age children: in any sizeable parish, and wherever the population was scattered, a single school maintained under the legal requirements could not serve parochial needs. Hence the parish heritors often provided buildings and small stipends to additional schools and teachers in the more remote corners, thus extending the community provision required in law. Some parishes had endowments for schooling, left in wills of local people, which were used to pay the fees of poor scholars or to provide small retainers for extra teachers. Often, groups of parents who lived at a distance from the parish

school combined to give board and lodging to 'a young man' who for part of the year
held a school for their children in their houses, and was paid a stipend or fees. Also,
where the numbers of children were sufficient, there were 'adventurers' (those who
offered their services as teachers without any security of contract) who set up schools
for whatever income the market could generate (**Document 80**).

The weight of the commentaries in the *Statistical Account* leads to three
conclusions. Firstly, ability to read was widespread in Scotland in the 1790s:
generally, families were keen to avoid the social stigma earned by those whose
children were so little schooled that they were unable to read. Secondly, ability to
write (especially among girls) was often much more limited: lack of proficiency in
this skill, however, carried less of a stigma, at least among the lowest orders. Thirdly,
there were many complaints that the legal, parochial schools were often in decline,
mainly because well-qualified masters could no longer be attracted to serve in them
(Anderson 1995, 11–13, 15–17; Withrington 1988a, 171–74).

One essential factor in this decline was the impact of the inflation of the 1780s
on the incomes of many parochial schoolteachers. As the Holywood, Dumfriesshire,
minister remarked:

> Considering the importance and labour of the office of a schoolmaster, and the
> greatly increased and increasing expense of living, the parochial school salaries in
> Scotland are exceedingly low. For the good of the country, the encouragement of
> learning, and the decent support of so useful a body of men as the parochial
> schoolmasters, they ought to be considerably augmented . . .
>
> (*Statistical Account* iv, 226)

Some ministers complained that schoolteachers in poorer rural parishes were hardly
able to earn more than field-labourers, and that their social and economic standing in
the local communities had been very badly affected; little wonder that at vacancies
only poorly qualified candidates would offer themselves. Consequently, fewer
country schoolmasters were able to provide Latin teaching or, sometimes, anything
beyond the merest rudiments, to the detriment of the local poor and better-off alike.
Parents who could afford to were sending their children, both girls and boys, to private
schools (often out of the parish) or formed local subscription schools with high fees
which could serve only part of the community. There was also an insistent refrain in
many of the returns, especially from the Highlands, that good teaching at affordable
fees within a national system was what was needed (Withrington 1988a, 171, 180).

EXERCISE 6
'The Scottish educational tradition had broken down by the 1790s.' Outline the
case that could be made for this statement. Is there a good case to be made
against it?

Read the three entries in **Document 80**. Use these to make an assessment of the
value of the evidence for schooling in the *Statistical Account*.

Again I'll leave you to work out these questions for yourself. If you have any doubts, look back over my discussion in the preceding section. The extracts in **Document 80** provide a valuable insight into the variety of provision and problems that existed in three very different communities. Despite the inconsistencies of approach the qualitative statements and quantitative data provide the basis for some interesting comparative analysis.

5. WHY SHOULD GOVERNMENT INTERVENE?

Sinclair was convinced that the publication of the returns to his *Account* was instrumental in persuading government (and, this time, the *British* parliament) to consider intervention. But another factor was that the parochial schoolmasters had recently proved themselves to be invaluable local agents for government. In the 1790s they had made up the parish lists for raising local militia (to serve as a home guard in wartime), and their local knowledge had also proved to be of essential value in compiling the parish returns for another government enterprise, the first official population census of 1800–1801. In 1802 the General Assembly reminded government of the parish teachers' vital role 'in combating subversion and contributing to the improvement, the good order and the success of the people of Scotland' in recent revolutionary times (Anderson 1995, 32). The various pressures paid off when in 1803 parliament passed an education act to amend and extend that of 1696. That set government on a new course, one which entailed more direct oversight of Scottish schooling (*ibid*, 32, 311; and see **Article 23**).

The new act greatly increased the levels of stipend, permitted parishes to provide additional schools (side schools) out of a substantially increased local taxation, insisted that modest schoolhouses should be provided for the schoolmaster and his family (or some equivalent allowance paid), and transferred some controls (for example over aspects of curriculum, appointments, stipend and conditions of service) from the Church to the civil authorities (heritors and JPs). Better stipends brought in better teachers who attracted larger numbers of pupils who then paid a good deal more in fees. By the 1820s the incomes of parochial schoolteachers had often at least doubled since before 1803 (*Parochial Education, 1826*: for example, returns for Assynt, Sutherland; Ardrossan, Ayrshire; Larbert, Stirlingshire). The numbers of masters able to teach Latin, Greek and mathematics had also risen and that helped to produce an increasing number of students in the five Scottish universities. The spread of 'new' subjects was also maintained or enhanced, even in remote localities – with book-keeping, French, land mensuration and geography, for example, being very widely taught.

When governments mounted parliamentary enquiries in the 1820s and 1830s into the state of schooling – prompted by worries over social breakdown – the results demonstrated that school attendance rates in Scotland and reading-literacy rates were generally very high (Withrington 1988a, 174–85). The 1818 returns had shown, however, that even an extended and improved system of public education, as provided in the parochial and side schools, was not supplying all the required school places: in most parishes, subscription and charity and private schools could be found. Over the country as a whole, if we define as 'publicly provided' all those schools which were supported in any way out of heritors', tenants', magistrates' or endowed funding, half of all pupils were still to be found in non-public schools: in the industrialising Lowlands, and in the Highlands and Islands, voluntary and charity enterprise was the major provider (Anderson 1983a, 526; Withrington 1988a, 177–78). For many in Scotland that raised the question of whether the state was meeting its obligations to the people. With so much schooling outside the 'established' system, was the education of youth in sufficiently secure public control?

> EXERCISE 7
> Read **Article 23**. Why was state intervention in Scottish education so generally welcomed?

Again I will leave you to come to your own conclusions about this, but basically social order, public utility and cost were important factors.

6. STRAINS IN THE SYSTEM BEFORE THE 1830s: THE TOWNS AND THE HIGHLANDS

6.1 *Town developments*

The largest towns, as we have seen, normally retained their grammar schools, since demand for classical teaching was sufficient to provide good livings for the rector and his fellow-masters. There, from the eighteenth-century onward, the general teaching of the 3Rs, prior to pupils entering the grammar curriculum, was left either to supplementary 'English schools' under town support and control, or to adventure schoolteachers who occasionally had modest retainers from the council. A town's own English schools might be permitted to charge such high fees that they were not available to the majority of the inhabitants, leaving the majority of townspeople to seek out what instruction they could afford in the often numerous charitable or private schools (Law 1965, 31–57, 144–56). The better-off were increasingly pressed to support free or cheap schooling for their poorer fellow-citizens, just as they were prompted to provide subscriptions for coals or clothing. Often the response was good, especially when some churchman or magistrate argued that the moral and religious training which was provided would save society from the ravages of increasing criminality or from increasing demands for poor relief. New methodologies in schooling, especially those which offered a highly successful means of teaching very large numbers of children simultaneously, were much discussed and warmly supported. Hence the public approval for Dr Andrew Bell and Joseph Lancaster when they toured Scotland in the 1810s to demonstrate their 'monitorial' systems which employed older children as supplementary instructors, under the strict regulation of the master (adapted by Robert Owen at New Lanark – see Chapter 7). The responses from the large towns in the *New Statistical Account* acclaimed monitorial methods as being remarkably effective in passing on basic elements of education; they were admirably fitted, it seemed, for pupils with limited prospects and with little or nothing to pay.

The political and social upheavals at the close of the Napoleonic Wars, associated in the minds of Church leaders such as Thomas Chalmers with the evils of non-churchgoing, deism, and a rising tide of immorality in the towns, gave a particular stimulus to calls for the wider provision of urban schools in which religious and moral teaching would be central. 'Society', it was contended, would be saved only through a return to common schooling under the auspices and close supervision of the Church. Chalmers saw the answer in the traditional community schooling of rural Scotland. Translate that to the largest towns, by providing instruction in 'parochial' schools which was so good that the better-off would be glad to have it and so cheap that the poor could afford it, and social cohesion could be preserved and the lapsing brought back into contact with the Church (Anderson 1995, 39–43; Withrington 1988b, 47–49). In 1820 Chalmers included these comments in his speech at the opening of two new schools funded by the congregation of St John's, Glasgow (Hanna 1849–52, ii 240–46):

> . . . so far from wishing the children of the various ranks in the parish not to mingle at these schools, I want them to mix as extensively as they may. A far blander and better state of society will eventually come out of such an arrangement. The ties of kindliness will be multiplied between the wealthy and the labouring classes of our city . . . And what then is the object it may be asked? It is not to turn an operative into a capitalist: it is to turn an ignorant operative into a learned operative . . . to transform him into a reflective and accomplished individual – not to hoist, as it were, the great ponderous mass of society into the air where it would have no foundation to support it, but . . . to diffuse through it the light of common and Christian intelligence.

But there were limits to the numbers of school places which Chalmers and his Evangelical supporters could provide from congregational and other Church resources. Indeed, they argued for so comprehensive an enlargement of the existing public system (more parochial schools under close Church supervision) that all the non-public schools would be made redundant. They turned to government for the necessary funds by which to extend national schooling, and for the building of new churches for the national Establishment. The Liberal governments after 1832 declined to provide the money for either, and gave little and grudgingly afterwards. The educational surveys that had been made had convinced them – in particular their educational *guru*, Henry Brougham – that the 'mixed' system of publicly funded and voluntary schools worked well, and that the nationalising of the school structure would be stupendously costly: moreover, they were very cautious about any proposal which, in a country which now had many religious sects, would give an unfair advantage to one, the national Church of Scotland. (The Liberals depended on the votes of the dissenters for their political survival and did not dare to be seen to favour the Established Church.) Educational as well as ecclesiastical factors were to underpin the Church-state conflict which engulfed Scotland in the next ten years.

6.2. Educational deprivation? The Highlands and Islands

It has long, and wrongly, been thought that the Highlands and the Northern and Western Isles were all but destitute of public schooling in the eighteenth century, on the assumption that there was the most meagre provision of parochial schools under the 1696 Act, and that education was largely in the hands of charitable societies, predominantly the SSPCK (Society in Scotland for Propagating Christian Knowledge) (Durkacz 1983, 45–72). Yet the evidence from the Society's own agents, from visitors to the Highlands, and from Sinclair's *Account* indicates otherwise (Withrington 1988a, 164–71). Some of the earliest data, for as many as 105 parishes in the Gaelic-speaking North and West, come from an enquiry made by the SSPCK in the 1750s: of these parishes over 80% had schools provided by the heritors and tenants, some supporting up to six schools on public funds, teaching at least the rudiments but often more. The constant problem facing Highland communities was the extent of their parishes and the scattered nature of the population. A single parochial school could not provide universal schooling in the parish, and localities strained to provide, from their meagre resources, some acceptable spread of schooling. The division of one larger-than-legal salary to support multiple winter-only schools in remote glens was one practical response: the public provision of the means for universal instruction in the rudiments was deemed more important than maintaining one centrally placed Latin school which could serve only the few (see **Article 24**).

The returns for Highland parishes to Sinclair in the 1790s confirm the variety in local attempts to meet educational need. In Moulin in Perthshire, the parochial school taught Latin, bookkeeping and mathematics as well as the elementary subjects to some fifty pupils; five other schools, in different parts of the parish, with a total enrolment of about 180, were 'taught by persons who have undertaken that employment of their own accord, where children learn to read English and Gaelic' (*Statistical Account* xii, 764). In the united parishes of Lismore and Appin in Argyll, there was one parochial school on the island of Lismore and two more in Appin, an SSPCK school 'at the Slate Quarry in Glenco', and 'sometimes one or more smaller schools kept up at the expense of the inhabitants in the more remote parts of the parishes' (*Statistical Account* xx, 355–56). Time and again, the ministers in the Highlands and Islands called on government to bring a more equitable treatment in school provision to the vast and scattered parishes. And yet the government surveys of schooling in 1818, 1826 and 1834 confirm that, in all but the least favoured districts of the Highlands and Islands, such had been the resilience of the local communities that schooling was widely available (Withrington 1988a, 178, 181–84). A few so-called parliamentary schools, set up in 1838 in the largest and most needy parishes, were all that government directly contributed (Read **Document 81**: not all sources can be taken at face value!).

EXERCISE 8
Why did the legal structure of parochial schooling prove to be so inadequate in
the industrialising Lowlands and in the Highlands?

Read the entries in **Document 81**, for one large Argyllshire parish in the 1820s-
1830s: which of the entries do you find most helpful, which least, and why?

Your response might include the following points: the scale of the problem caused by
larger numbers and costs, and in the Highlands the sheer extent of parishes, the
scattered population and the unresolved problem of Gaelic/bilingualism (a situation,
incidentally, that might be contrasted with that in Wales at the same time). As to the
extracts, all give their own insights into education in the parish. Extract (a) is least
informative; (b) and (c) were the combined efforts of the parochial schoolmasters
and a lively and concerned parish minister.

7. THE 1830s AND 1840s

The 1834 survey may have been generally reassuring about the levels of school
provision and attendance, but it also gave a platform for some anxious comments by
ministers and teachers. It confirmed, for instance, that the public provision of
schools was still losing ground to that of unendowed and private teachers, especially
in the major cities and in central Scotland. (The two parochial schoolmasters in
Falkirk had complained in 1826 that their schools and incomes had been grievously
hurt from 1816 onwards by 'the great influx of schoolmasters into the parish', then
25 in number, all private adventurers: by 1834 there were 33.) Such occurrences
were especially worrying to the Church of Scotland, whose General Assembly was
now under the domination of Chalmers and the Evangelicals. They believed that the
morality of the nation was under threat from developments which had put
impressionable youth into the hands of teachers outside the influence of the
Establishment, who might have all kinds of dubious religious affiliations or none
at all. Reeling from attacks on the principle of a national religious establishment by
Scottish presbyterian dissenters and congregationalists, they became even more
committed to the ideal of an extended national system of publicly funded schools,
nurtured by the national Church. In their arguments they were dismissive of all
educational provision outside the state structure, as lacking any security in its moral
character and professional quality, a view exemplified in a pamphlet entitled
Scotland a half educated nation, published in 1834. This highly partisan publication did not seek to make a balanced analysis, but was a passionate attack on what it
called the 'let alone principle' in school provision – a principle which allowed the
market place to rule, and one which often meant that parents were left to the
sometimes costly and usually dubious instructions of a self-appointed private master
or mistress when reliable and cheap public schooling was not available for all
children in the local community. The far-fetched assumption made in the pamphlet
was that Scotland was half-educated because only half of its children could be

No. 32. High School of Edinburgh: the early school buildings in Blackfriars' Garden, 1578–1777 (top) and the buildings in High School Yards, 1777 to 1820s (bottom). *From WCA Ross 1934* The Royal High School *(Oliver and Boyd) Edinburgh, opposite pages 1 and 20.*

accommodated in the publicly funded and publicly managed schools. In general, however, neither the efficiency nor the standards of the private or unendowed schools merited the blanket condemnation they received from its author, George Lewis (Withrington 1983, *passim*).

Let us turn to the 1834 survey, which for the first time includes data on the numbers of children under the age of 15 who were able to, or were actively learning to, read and write. It was believed in many European countries that a ratio of 1 in 8 at school in the whole population was very acceptable, and a ratio of 1 in 6 was a matter for much self-congratulation. The regional results of the Scottish survey in 1834 were:

	ATTENDANCE	READING	WRITING
Highlands, Islands	1 IN 8.7	1 IN 6.1	1 IN 13.3
North-East	8.3	4.8	9.0
Fife, Lothians	7.9	6.2	12.7
Central, West	10.7	5.7	14.3
Borders	9.8	5.0	9.9
Scotland	9.0	5.6	12.2

(Source: Withrington 1988a, 183–85)

The returns made clear that the 'means of instruction' were readily available, but many were anxious that they were not being used as they should have been, especially in the largest towns. Yet, in terms of the proportion of the population reported as being reading-literate, the results were very impressive. No doubt, definitions of 'ability to write' may well have varied in the returns, yet the figures undoubtedly indicate the possession of a skill in writing more substantial than the mere ability to sign one's name. Scotland, surely, was no half-educated nation in 1834 (**Document 82**).

> EXERCISE 9
> Why might figures of school attendances be doubtful indicators of literacy (or other learning)?
>
> **Document 82** contains educational data from the 1834 survey for three very different urban/industrial parishes: how valuable are these for assessing the effectiveness of schooling in industrial parishes in Scotland?

Attendance at any one time of the year is itself no measure of literacy, as shown in the total numbers of those reading or learning to read. The 1834 data show that there is no exact correlation, and this is largely substantiated by the evidence in

Document 82. The extracts there give a valuable (and variable) insight into the character of education in these communities.

Nonetheless, there were complaints in 1834 that some parents in the towns were not waiting until their children could read with ease before sending them to work in mills and factories; and young working men were no longer attending evening classes in their former numbers to extend a school learning which, in many instances, had been much interrupted. Similar warnings came from parishes in the Highlands and Islands. Continuing hardship and intermittent dearths, the drain of the emigration of the younger and abler in local populations, and crises in relieving the adult destitute, were putting a high premium on child labour; and there was little money for school fees. The tale was of broken attendances at school and too little chance for teachers to build on previous instruction. In the Highlands and the towns the same predictions were voiced: unless measures were taken to forbid children under a certain age from taking up full-time employment, the next generation of the lower orders in Scotland would grow up ignorant and ill-lettered (see Document 82). In the West of Scotland particularly, there was also the problem of immigrant Irish children: their parents were often poorly educated and (in their early years in Scotland) unconcerned about educating their offspring. Worse still, it was complained that their alien ways were weakening the traditional resolve of the Scottish urban poor to scrimp and save to send their children to school. The greater influx of impoverished and unlettered Irish after the famine of the mid-1840s only increased these apprehensions. The response in the 1840s was to leave the problem to the do-gooders and their industrial feeding schools; but the problem proved intractable, and the question hung fire, for a later age to grapple with.

In 1843 the Disruption in the Church of Scotland added to the existing problems in the nation's schooling. The new Free Church, determined to match its rival, the remnant Establishment, set up its own Educational Scheme, initially as a means of providing work for the eighty or so parochial schoolteachers who left their posts or were forced out of them, but in time incorporating as many as seven hundred schools, in effect congregational schools, across the country. These were not all new schools, many being existing private schools whose teachers transferred into the scheme, but for all that it was a remarkable achievement. By 1845, however, it was proving to be extremely costly, at a time when the Free Church had run into deep financial crisis. A few of the older leaders in the new church believed that the solution was to hand over their schools to government, which could then be persuaded to legislate for a new national system of schooling that included them along with the parochial schools, under local management committees which would not be dominated by either religious grouping. The old dream of an inclusive national system was thus revived, only to be dashed by the younger Free Kirk leaders and by a new Privy Council policy which for the first time extended state aid to schools erected by the non-Established sects. There were, however, drawbacks to the Free Church's acceptance of the Privy Council aid: firstly, it undermined its claim to be the 'real' national church of Scotland, waiting in the wings to be recognised as such by government; secondly, it put the Free Church on a par with all other dissenting sects in the land, most grievously on a par with Roman Catholicism – the very fount, as they saw it, of religious error and of detestable, bigoted popery. But the Young Turks in the Free Church won: they took the state's money, brought a new sectarianism into Scottish schooling, and would delay for two decades the chance of introducing an inclusive national educational system (Withrington 1993, 79–97).

> EXERCISE 10
> Why did religion, and the churches, energise but also inhibit attempts to re-found the national system of schooling in Scotland in the earlier nineteenth century?

Put at its simplest, the presence of the non-established churches helped extend provision but, at the same time, brought considerable diversification and inhibited cooperation in framing a standard system.

8. THE SCOTTISH UNIVERSITIES

Just as schooling had been seen since the Reformation as an important national enterprise, to be secured by the Church and state working together, so too the five Scottish universities were judged to be national institutions – a top tier of the national educational structure. Unlike the colleges of Oxford and Cambridge, those in Scotland were poorly endowed. From the Reformation onwards, the Scottish universities were largely dependent on government support for the founding of new teaching posts and for maintaining old buildings and erecting new ones. Government had no compunction in the 1690s, or in the era of Jacobite rebellion after the union, in purging the Scottish universities of religious and political opponents, and in the 1690s it interfered directly in the internal affairs of the colleges, by setting in train discussions which were intended to impose a standard (national) curriculum and teaching in them all.

Thereafter, apart from a few 'regius' professorships paid from royal revenues and (until the extraordinary public expenditure vested in resiting and rebuilding Edinburgh in the late eighteenth century) a very modest fund for buildings, mainly in short-term repairs, the Scottish universities were left to fend for themselves. Consequently, in general, these institutions and their teachers could survive only by maintaining or increasing student numbers and thus income from student fees.

Yet in the middle decades of the eighteenth century this was the very income which was under direct threat. As we have seen, the appearance of 'new' subjects in burgh and parochial schools, particularly the emergence of an alternative advanced education in Ayr and Perth and other 'academies', was to prove a constant anxiety, most of all for the three smaller universities which had relatively few students – St Andrews, King's in Old Aberdeen and Marischal in New Aberdeen. The last-named led the way in counter-attack. Its Senatus significantly recast the old Aristotelian curriculum because the 'present order of teaching Philosophy' had become 'very improper' for changing times, since it forced very youthful students to struggle with

abstractions about evidence and reasoning before they had sufficient factual
knowledge with which to reason, and required so much time to be spent on logic
and metaphysics early in the course that it excluded 'some very useful parts of
knowledge'. The descriptive and experimental sciences (mathematics, chemistry,
natural history, physics) were brought forward into the second and third years of the
course, and not until the final year were students to wrestle with the 'sciences of
mind', moral philosophy, logic and metaphysics. This novel and radical curriculum
was soon adopted by King's College, and in part and less enthusiastically by St
Andrews. Neither Edinburgh nor Glasgow was to change its stated curriculum for
another hundred years: they did not need to do so as the greater regional populations
which these colleges served, and the numerous English and Irish dissenters they
attracted, sheltered them from the worst impact of the rise of academies.

Edinburgh and Glasgow were, however, as active as their counterparts in
striving to increase student numbers, especially fee-paying attenders, since students
with bursaries (who usually took the four-year course) generally added little to the
teachers' incomes. University study was therefore made deliberately attractive to
those who did not need it for their career prospects and who had no interest in
completing the course of study in the Arts, by relaxing a host of older regulations
relating to admission and attendance. The order in which subjects had to be taken
was soon virtually disregarded; the length of the university year was reduced to five
or six months; a would-be student's lack of extended school instruction in the
classical languages was made less of a barrier to admission to college classes in, say,
physics or moral philosophy; and the costs and also the discomforts of college
'discipline' were soon removed, so that by the turn of the century it was no longer
insisted that students should be resident or should take meals at the college table. In
the two small Aberdeen universities the holders of bursaries remained a substantial
proportion of the student body, and they followed the revised and modernised
curriculum which had been introduced there, but in Glasgow and Edinburgh the
bursars were a very small group faced with an unreformed course of study, within a
large body of attenders who were welcomed to whichever classes they wished to pay
for, in whatever order they wished to take them (Anderson 1983b, 27–32; Withrington 1992, 133–5).

By the early decades of the nineteenth century there was mounting public
concern about the state of the Scottish universities. In journals, newspapers and
pamphlets there were anxious comments about the effects of low standards of entry
and low standards of performance; about the shortened university year; and about
the quality of appointments to professorships (mostly in the patronage of the
existing professors); increasingly, too, there was criticism of professorial misman-
agement of the financial affairs of the colleges, and widespread suggestions that such
public and national institutions should be under more effective public scrutiny. In
the early 1820s it also became known that holders of Scottish medical qualifications
and degrees might no longer be licensed to practise in England and Wales.

Heightening demand for a government enquiry was answered by Robert Peel,
Home Secretary; a royal commission was appointed to investigate and report on the

organisation and functioning of the universities. This commission was not the 'surprise' attack on Scottish higher education which has been claimed (Davie 1961, 24 *et seq*) and it was not dominated by high-born anglicisers but by Scottish lawyers who had mostly been schooled and trained in Scotland. The commission's appearance was widely welcomed, even in Tory newspapers; and its report in 1830 was also warmly received, save by a few Tory diehards, to become a blueprint for modest yet effective reform by which to revive and regenerate the Scottish universities.

The core arguments of the commissioners were relatively few, and were carefully set out (see **Document 83**). They agreed that the universities had been weakened by developments since the mid-eighteenth century. The dominance of market forces had got out of hand, so that the flooding of university classes (in Edinburgh and Glasgow especially) by 'occasional' students, picking and mixing their classes, had tended to divert professors' attention away from their prime duty of care and support for those students who needed to follow the regular curriculum. There were social as well as intellectual arguments for impressing on the professors the value of encouraging a more systematic training and ensuring that those who took it were properly taught and nurtured in their learning. The commissioners aimed to reform the curriculum in Arts so that it was more in tune with society's demands in a 'new age' (in effect, to be more like that already in place in the Aberdeen colleges), to improve standards by introducing a modest entrance examination (already in operation in Marischal College), and to ensure a more exacting oversight of student performance throughout four years of regular study. The national character of the universities was emphasised in proposals to impose a standard curriculum in all the colleges and also a new and shared administrative structure: while the professors would retain their control of teaching and of discipline as it related to study, the oversight of financial affairs, regulations for awarding degrees and student appeals were to be given to a rectorial court mainly composed of men of substance and prominence in each university town. Yet in most universities these proposals were to be applied only to a minority: it was vitally important to safeguard professorial incomes from the fees of those who had no intention to qualify themselves for graduation. While arguing the case for the reformed curriculum, the commission was careful to comment:

> Attendance at a University, to a greater or lesser extent, is considered as part of the ordinary education of the inhabitants of Scotland; it is anxiously desired by many, whose views are not directed either to the future prosecution of literary studies or to any of the learned professions, and by many who are intended for the ordinary occupations of the middle ranks of society. Students of this description constitute no inconsiderable proportion of those who attend the Universities. They attend only for the number of years which suits their convenience; they select the classes which are best adapted to their particular views, and often begin with those which are the last in any regular Curriculum. It is evident that if students of this description were to be subjected to restraint in their course of study, and if no one could attend the Moral or Natural

Philosophy classes, for example, who had not gone through the previous classes of a regular Curriculum, they would be virtually excluded from the Universities; they would seek and they would find elsewhere instruction in the branches of knowledge which they required, and a numerous class of Students, whom on every account it is highly desirable to educate in the Universities, would be withdrawn. For these reasons, we are of the opinion that the Curriculum of Arts should be imperative only on those who may be candidates for Degrees, or who may require certificates of a regular university education.

(*Report* 1830, 25)

The Reform Acts, changes in ministry, and the emergent Church-state conflict in Scotland (the Church evangelicals led by Thomas Chalmers locking horns with the Melbourne government) all had their influence in delaying parliamentary adoption of the 1830 Report. The impact of the Disruption also made governments of all political hues very hesitant to address directly the question of university reform in Scotland (Anderson 1983b, 51–4). Yet, individual colleges quietly introduced some of the recommendations made in 1830. But progress was too slow for the most determined of the younger reformers within the universities (*ibid*, 54–7, 66–9; Carter and Withrington 1992, 46–54). By the mid-1840s a concerted movement for reform, led by John Stuart Blackie, professor of Humanity (Latin) in Marischal College in New Aberdeen, gathered public support. In 1846, in an address to the nation, Blackie set out a programme which was aimed at improving standards: better and more advanced schooling was needed to prepare pupils for language studies at university, a strict entrance examination ought to be introduced in all colleges (both would attract better men into university teaching), radical reconstruction of the curriculum was badly needed, and there ought to be continuous and effective government supervision of the universities (Blackie 1846, 10–12: see **Document 84**). In all his writings, Blackie acknowledged the value of the guidelines for reform which had been laid out in the Report and in the printed volumes of evidence collected by the Commissioners of 1826–30. Almost all their recommendations, and Blackie's, were adopted once government acted – but that had to wait until 1858.

In conclusion, then: consider whether (and on what grounds) the Scottish universities could be considered as national institutions, and think more generally about the implications which the levels of educational provision, at school and university, and the curricula which were taught, had on the main areas of social, economic and cultural life in Scotland before 1850.

REFERENCES TO BOOKS AND ARTICLES MENTIONED IN THE TEXT

**A *Digest of Parochial Returns made to the Select Committee appointed to inquire into the Education of the Poor, Session 1818,* volume 3, PP 1819, ix.

Anderson, RD 1983a 'Education and the state in nineteenth-century Scotland', *Economic History Review* 36, 518–34.

*Anderson, RD 1983b *Education and Opportunity in Victorian Scotland: schools and universities*. Oxford (reprinted 1989, Edinburgh).

*Anderson, RD 1995 *Education and the Scottish People, 1750–1918*. Oxford.

Bain, A 1965 *Education in Stirlingshire from the Reformation to the Act of 1872*. London.

*Beale, JM 1983 *A History of the Burgh and Parochial Schools of Fife*. Edinburgh.

Blackie, JS 1846 *Education in Scotland. An Appeal to the Scottish People on the Improvement of their Scholastic and Academical Institutions*. Aberdeen and Edinburgh.

Carter, JJ and Withrington, DJ (eds) 1992 *Scottish Universities: distinctiveness and diversity*. Edinburgh.

*Davie, GE 1961 *The Democratic Intellect: Scotland and her Universities in the Nineteenth Century*. Edinburgh.

Durkacz, VE 1983 *The Decline of the Celtic Languages*. Edinburgh.

**Education Enquiry. Abstract of Answers and Returns made pursuant to an Address of the House of Commons, 1834*. PP 1837, xlvii.

Hanna, W 1849–52 *Memoirs of the Life and Writings of Thomas Chalmers*. 4 vols. Edinburgh.

*Houston, RA 1985 *Scottish Literacy and the Scottish Identity: illiteracy and society in Scotland and Northern England, 1600–1800*. Cambridge.

*Law, A 1965 *Education in Edinburgh in the Eighteenth Century*. London.

**New Statistical Account of Scotland* 1845. 15 volumes. Edinburgh.

**Parochial Education, Scotland. Returns to an Address of the honourable House of Commons, 1825*. PP 1826, xviii.

Smout, TC 1982 'Born again at Cambuslang: new evidence on popular religion and literacy in eighteenth-century Scotland', *Past and Present* 97, 114–27.

**Statistical Account of Scotland, 1791–1799*. New edition: Withrington DJ and Grant IR (gen eds). 20 volumes. Wakefield.

Strawhorn, J 1983 *750 Years of a Scottish School: Ayr Academy, 1233–1983*. Ayr.

Withrington, DJ 1963 'Schools in the Presbytery of Haddington in the 17th century', *Transactions of the East Lothian Antiquarian and Field Naturalists' Society* 10, 90–111.

Withrington, DJ 1965 'Lists of schoolmasters teaching Latin, 1690', *Miscellany of the Scottish History Society* 10.

*Withrington, DJ 1970 'Education and society', *in* Phillipson, NT and Mitchison, R (eds), *Scotland in the Age of Improvement: essays in Scottish history in the eighteenth century*, Edinburgh, 169–99.

Withrington, DJ 1983 ' "Scotland a half educated nation" in 1834? Reliable critique or persuasive polemic?', *in* Humes, WM and Paterson, HM (eds), *Scottish Culture and Scottish Education*, Edinburgh, 55–74.

Withrington, DJ 1986 'Education', *in* Maclean, L (ed), *The Seventeenth Century in the Highlands*, Inverness, 60–9.

*Withrington, DJ 1988a 'Schooling, literacy and society', *in* Devine, TM and Mitchison, R (eds), *People and Society in Scotland. Volume 1: 1760–1830*, Edinburgh, 163–87.

Withrington, DJ 1988b ' "A ferment of change?" Aspirations, ideas and ideals in nineteenth-century Scotland', *in* Gifford, D (ed), *The History of Scottish Literature, volume 3, Nineteenth Century*, Aberdeen, 43–63.

Withrington, DJ 1992 'The Scottish Universities: living traditions? old problems renewed?', *The Scottish Government Yearbook 1992*, Edinburgh, 131–41.

Withrington DJ 1993 'Adrift among the reefs of conflicting ideals? Education and the Free

Church, 1843–55', *in* Brown, SJ and Fry, M (eds), *Scotland in the Age of the Disruption*, Edinburgh, 79–97.

FURTHER READING

Those references marked * in the above list are recommended further reading, along with the following:

Anderson, RA 1997 *Scottish Education since the Reformation. Studies in Scottish Economic and Social History 5.*
Hamilton, D 1989 *Towards a Theory of Schooling.* London.
Houston, RA 1982 'The literacy myth? Illiteracy in Scotland, 1630–1760', *Past and Present* 96, 81–102.
Houston, RA 1983 'Literacy and society in the west, 1500–1850', *Social History* 8, 269–93.
Houston, RA 1989 'Scottish education and literacy, 1600–1800: an international perspective', *in* Devine, TM (ed) *Improvement and Enlightenment*, Edinburgh, 43–61.
O'Day, R 1982 *Education and Society, 1500–1800: the social foundations of education in early modern Britain.* London.
Saunders, LJ 1950 *Scottish Democracy, 1815–40: the social and intellectual background.* Edinburgh.
Smout, TC 1969 *A History of the Scottish People, 1568–1830.* London.
Smout, TC 1986 *A Century of the Scottish People, 1830–1950.* London.

SOME PUBLISHED PRIMARY SOURCES

Those references marked ** in the list of references referred to in the text are published primary sources which may be of interest, particularly in carrying forward local studies of schooling.

Index

Act Anent Peace and War 11
Act of Security for the Church of Scotland
  (1706) 2, 9, 11, 19, 20, 46
Act for Settling Schools (1696) 276, 288
Act of Union (1707) 1, 2, 46–7, 48, 137–8
Agricultural improvement 94, 95–6,
  101, 105, 119, 139, 233–4, 238–40
Agricultural Revolution 86, 126, 234
Aliens Bill (1705) 11, 13
Alkali Act (1863) 247
Annexed Estates 186–7, 189
Argathelian party 52, 53, 54
Argyll Colony 185–6
Argyll Company of Farmers 184
Argyll, Duke of (John Campbell) 16, 35,
  51–3, 56, 190
Argyll dynasty (Clan Campbell) 160,
  185, 242
Arichonan Clearance 193
Arkwright 131, 137, 140, 143, 144, 145
Atholl 30, 139, 144, 145
Ayr Bank failure 96, 141

Baird, C.R. 199
Bairds of Gartsherrie 148
Bank of Scotland 141
Baxter 135
Belhaven 234
Bell, Andrew 286
Bell, Henry 140
Black, Adam 220
Blackie, John Stuart 296
Blacklock, Thomas 261
Blackwood's Magazine 270, 271
Blair, Hugh 262
Board of Heritors 66
Board of Manufacturers and
  Fisheries 39–40, 140
Boswell, James 245, 263, 264
'Bothy ballads' 104
Boulton, Matthew 131, 140

British Fisheries Society 189
British Linen Bank 141
Brougham, Henry 214, 287
Buccleuch 246
Burns, Robert 45, 264–7
Bute 54

Cadell, William 136
Caledonian Canal 197
Cambuslang revival 68–9, 283
Cameron, Charles 163
Cameron of Lochiel 35, 185
Cameronians 28
Campbell, Alexander 223
Carlyle, Thomas 272
Carron Company 136, 140, 147, 148
Census returns 108–9, 110, 155, 171,
  200, 285
Central Health Board 170
Chadwick, Edwin 170
Chalmers, Rev Thomas 70, 74–6, 81,
  165–6, 219, 221–2, 287, 289, 296
Chambers, Robert 161, 173
Chambers, William 173
Charles Edward Stewart (Young
  Pretender) 24, 31, 33, 35, 37, 38, 40
Chartist movement 223, 224, 225
Child employment 145, 292
Claim of Rights (1689) 10
Clearance 177–84, 190–1, 192, 216,
  243, 247
Cleland, James 110
Clerk, John 17, 147
Clerks of Penicuik 147
Coal 133, 136, 138, 139, 146–8
Cockburn, Henry 58, 167
Cockburn, John of Ormiston 94, 160, 234
Commission for Roads, Bridges and
  Canals (1803) 197
Common good 159, 170
Convention of Royal Burghs 157–8
Cope, John 35

Corn Laws   214, 215
Cottars displacement   97–8, 99
Cotton industry   133, 139, 140, 142–6
Covenanters   73
Cowan, Robert   167
Cox   135
Craig, David   9
Creech, William   218
Crinan Canal   197
Crofting communities   181, 182–3, 190–
    1, 198–200, 243
Crompton   140, 143
Cromwell, Oliver   4
Culloden   23, 38, 178
Cumberland   27, 36

Dale, David   135, 144, 145
Dalrymple, John   12
Darien scheme   13, 16, 278
Defoe, Daniel   1, 19, 162
Dempster   145
Dickens, Charles   173
Dicks   139
Dickson, Adam   232
Disruption of the Church of Scotland
    (1843)   44, 75–7, 79, 215, 292, 296
Dissenters   73–4
Dixons of Govan   148
Donalson, James   234
Donn, Rob   263
Douglas   261
Drainage Act   199
Drummond, George   161
Dundas Despotism   54–5
Dundas, George of Dundas   94
Dundas, Henry (Viscount Melville)   45,
    49, 54, 55, 57–8
Dundas, Robert (2nd Viscount
    Melville)   58
Dundas, Robert of Arniston   53, 54
Dupplin   20

Edinburgh New Town   161–3, 211, 260
Edinburgh Review   45, 213, 214, 270
Elcho   37
Elgin   139
Elliot, Jean of Minto   263
Emigration   116–17, 119, 120–1, 196–7,
    198, 199, 236
Enclosure   94, 95, 96, 105, 139, 140, 142
Enlightenment   3, 52, 61, 69–70, 141,
    179, 210, 233, 258–64

Entail (Montgomery) Act (1770)   191
Evangelical Party   67, 68–70, 74, 215, 289

Famine   93, 126, 179, 182, 198, 199–
    200, 236, 276
Ferguson, Adam   57, 207
Ferguson, Robert   257–8
Ferrier, Susan   272
'Fettering bonds'   147
Fisher, Edward   68
Fletcher, Andrew of Saltoun   9, 10, 17,
    254
Food output   126–7
Free Church of Scotland   59, 75–6, 77,
    79–80, 199, 215, 292–3

Galt, John   45, 71, 158, 270, 271, 272
Garbett, Samuel   136
Garden, James   26
General Views   234
George I   51
George III   54, 187
Gilpin, William   232
Glasites   73
Glorious Revolution   7, 23
Godolphin   17, 20
Gordon, Robert of Straloch   231, 233
Graham, John (Bonnie Dundee)   23
Graham, Robert   166
Graham, Thomas   142
Grant, Archibald   234
Gray, Robert   223
Great Famine (1845–1850)   179, 183,
    193, 198, 199–200

Halkett, Peter of Pitfirrane   17
Hamilton   15, 16, 28, 139
Hargreaves   143
Harley, Robert   51
Hatchett, Charles   148
Health of Towns Association   170
Hearth tax returns   109, 112
Heritable jurisdictions   2, 53–4, 178–9
Highland Regiments   187, 189
Highland Society of London   187
Highlands and Agricultural Society   187
Hogg, James   271, 272
Home, George of Wedderburn   220–1
Home, John   261
Houldsworths of Coltness   148
Hume, David   52, 207, 259–60, 261
Hutcheson, Francis   52, 259, 262

Ilay (Archibald Campbell) 28
Industrial Revolution 130, 132
Infectious disease 124–5, 166, 167, 170–1, 198, 248–50
Inveresregan Trading Company 185
Irish immigration 80, 82, 83, 116, 164–5, 292
Irish Union (1801) 57–8
Iron 136, 138, 139, 140, 147–8, 242

James VI 4
James VII 7
James Edward Stewart (Old Pretender) 4, 35, 39
Jeffrey, Francis 214, 217
Jenner, Edward 125–6

Kames 232
Kelly, William 140
King's list 52

Lancaster, Joseph 286
'Levellers' Revolt' 95
Lewis, George 291
Linen 134–6, 137, 140, 142, 164, 184
Lockhart, George of Carnwath 15, 16, 17, 30–1, 33, 34, 39, 48, 51, 254
Lockhart, John Gibson 270
Lord Advocate 47, 55
Lorn Furnace Company 242
Louis XIV 4, 7, 9, 34
Louis XV 34
Lovat (Simon Frazer) 25

Macaulay, T.B. 214
MacDonald, Alexander 263
MacDonald, John of Glenaladale 196
McFarlan, Patrick 165
McGrugar, Thomas 213
Macintyre, Duncan Ban 179
Mackenzie, George (Earl of Cromartie) 7, 13
MacKenzie, Henry 263, 265
Mackintosh 214
Mackintosh of Borlum 35
MacLeod, Alexander 192
MacLeod of MacLeod 26
MacLeod, Rev Norman 198–9
Macpherson, James 261–2
Malcolms (MacCallums) of Poltalloch 193

Malt Tax 30, 31, 52
Mar (John Erskine) 8, 16, 19, 24, 25, 32, 34, 35
Migration 110–11, 117, 118–21, 164–5, 180
see also Emigration
Millar, John 207–8
Moderate party 54, 57, 67, 69–70, 71, 215
Montgomery (Entail) Act (1770) 191
Murray, George 27, 36, 37, 38
Murray, Rev Andrew 67
Mushet 148

Neilson 148
New Statistical Account 101, 110, 165, 181, 281, 286
Nutrition 126–7, 181, 236, 238

Old Pretender (James Edward Stewart) 4, 35, 39
Old Scots Independents 73
Oldknow, Samuel 141
Order of the Thistle 7
Ormonde 34
Ossian 261–2, 263
Owen, Robert 145, 146, 223, 286

'Pamphlet war' 3
Passenger Vessels Act (1803) 196
Paterson, William 141
Patronage Act (1714) 71
Peel, Robert 294
Perth Academy 280, 281
Pine-Coffin, Edward 199
Pitt, William the younger 55
Planned settlements 99, 139, 142, 160, 181
Police Boards 168–9, 170, 212
Poll tax lists 87–8, 91, 109, 112
Pont, Timothy 231, 241
Porteus Riot 31, 52, 53
Potato cultivation 181, 182–3, 198, 238, 239, 243
Potato famine 119, 164, 183, 199, 247–8
Presbyterian Church of Scotland 1–2, 8, 64, 74, 215
Prestonpans 35
Privy Council 2, 46
Public health 170–1, 245–6

Queensberry   1, 10, 12, 15, 16

Radical War (1820)   221–2
Ramilles   5
Ramsay, Allan   255–6
Ramsay, John   73
Reform Act (1832)   43, 58–9, 214
Reid, Thomas   262
Relief Church   73, 74, 215
Revivalism   68–9
Richmond, Alexander   219
Robertson, George   99, 100
Robertson, Rev William   54
Roebuck, John   136, 140
'Rough Wooing'   4
Roxburghe   18, 19, 52
Royal Bank of Scotland   39, 141
Ruddiman, Thomas   254
Ruddiman, Walter   257

Sanitary reformers   170–1
Sanitary Reports   170, 173
Scott, Andrew   82
Scott, David   55
Scott of Dunninald   139
Scott, Walter   45, 51–2, 53, 173, 268–70,
   272
Scottish Estates (Scottish Parliament)   1,
   18
Seafield (James Ogilvy)   12, 15, 16, 19,
   30
Secession Church (Seceders)   73, 74, 215
Secretary of State for Scotland   47, 52,
   53, 58
Seton, William of Pitmeddon   9, 10, 12, 14,
   15, 16
Seven Years' War   147, 187
Seymour, Edward   5
Sheep farming   181, 183, 243–4
Sibbald, Robert   231
Sinclair, John   109, 139, 148, 231, 232,
   234, 239, 283, 285
Small, James   95–6
Smallpox vaccination   125–6, 181, 248
Smith, Adam   52, 57, 141, 207, 208, 263
Smith, Adam sn.   47
Smith of Deanston   239
Smollett, Tobias   263, 264
Society in Scotland for the Propagation of
   Christian Knowledge (SSPCK)   28, 186
Solicitor General   47, 55, 58
Spiers, Alexander   209

Squadrone Volante   18, 48, 52, 53
Stansfield, James   137
Statistical Accounts   95, 98, 109, 110,
   163, 181, 218, 231–2, 234, 283, 284,
   285, 288
Sutherland Clearances   192

Technological innovation   131, 140
Telford, Thomas   140, 179, 197
Temperance movement   173, 174, 226
Tenant displacement   96–7
Tennant, Charles   135, 140
Textiles   133, 134–6, 142–6, 164, 184
Theatre Royal   173
Thompson, William   223
'Tobacco Lords'   139
Toleration Act for the Episcopalians
   (1712)   27
Town Councils   158, 159, 162, 167, 169,
   213
Town planning   161–3, 172
Trades Monthly Journal   219
Treason Act (1709)   28, 30
Treaty of Union see Acts of Union
Triennial Act (1694)   17
Tweeddale   18, 53

United Scotsmen   221

Vaccination Act (1863)   248

Walker, Rev John   187
Walpole, Robert   33, 51, 52
War of American Independence   55
War of the Austrian Succession   33
War of Spanish Succession   4, 11, 32
Watson, James   254
Watt, James   131, 140
Webster census   109
Webster, Rev Alexander   109, 115
Weekly Review   257
Wemyss   13
Whitefield, George   68
Wilkie, William   261
William III   4, 7
Willison, John   68
Wilson, John   270
Wine Act   11
Wyndham, William   34

Young Pretender (Charles Edward
   Stewart)   24, 31, 33, 35, 37, 38, 40